Tourism, Hospitality & Event

This book series covers all topics relevant in the tourism, hospitality and event industries. It includes destination management and related aspects of the travel and mobility industries as well as effects from developments in the information and communication technologies. "Tourism, Hospitality & Event Management" embraces books both for professionals and scholars, and explicitly includes undergraduate and advanced texts for students. In this setting the book series reflects the close connection between research, teaching and practice in tourism research and tourism management and the related fields.

More information about this series at http://www.springer.com/series/15444

Anna Scuttari

Cycling and Motorcycling Tourism

An Analysis of Physical, Sensory, Social, and Emotional Features of Journey Experiences

Springer

Anna Scuttari
Eurac Research
Bolzano, Italy

ISSN 2510-4993   ISSN 2510-5000 (electronic)
Tourism, Hospitality & Event Management
ISBN 978-3-030-17699-0   ISBN 978-3-030-17697-6 (eBook)
https://doi.org/10.1007/978-3-030-17697-6

© Springer Nature Switzerland AG 2019
This work is subject to copyright. All rights are reserved by the Publisher, whether the whole or part of the material is concerned, specifically the rights of translation, reprinting, reuse of illustrations, recitation, broadcasting, reproduction on microfilms or in any other physical way, and transmission or information storage and retrieval, electronic adaptation, computer software, or by similar or dissimilar methodology now known or hereafter developed.
The use of general descriptive names, registered names, trademarks, service marks, etc. in this publication does not imply, even in the absence of a specific statement, that such names are exempt from the relevant protective laws and regulations and therefore free for general use.
The publisher, the authors and the editors are safe to assume that the advice and information in this book are believed to be true and accurate at the date of publication. Neither the publisher nor the authors or the editors give a warranty, expressed or implied, with respect to the material contained herein or for any errors or omissions that may have been made. The publisher remains neutral with regard to jurisdictional claims in published maps and institutional affiliations.

This Springer imprint is published by the registered company Springer Nature Switzerland AG
The registered company address is: Gewerbestrasse 11, 6330 Cham, Switzerland

Foreword

Although the experience economy paradigm was hugely inspired by tourism practice, the analysis and design of tourist experiences in destination contexts has only recently been developed in tourism research. The spread of innovative and often, digital methods to analyse, track, monitor and ultimately, design tourists' actions, interactions and emotions in a time–space context has enabled this transition, opening up the new field of design science and new avenues for tourism research. The doctoral thesis of Anna Scuttari represents a valuable attempt to measure the unmeasurable, to address the connection between the physical elements of tourist destinations and the individual sensory and emotional perceptions of tourists. This work sets a milestone in experience analysis, both from a theoretical and a methodological point of view.

Anna Scuttari develops the analysis by assessing particular types of experiences that have been underexplored in the previous research: journey experiences. Thereby, she indirectly addresses the affective value of space as it is constructed and mediated by speed, which is a crucial aspect of the experience journey. The study of journey experiences is framed within a new and interdisciplinary interpretation of the destination space: the mobility space. By developing this framework, Anna Scuttari manages to link four disciplinary fields: mobilities, transport geography, experience economy and affective science. Although sharing common features, these fields were not theoretically and empirically integrated in the previous tourism literature. The mobility space is defined as a perceptual space—as a stage where journey performances are co-created, in a sort of dialogue between the human and non-human elements. Hence, the topographical space is shaped, in a Lefevbrian flavour, by the tourism practices in motion and vice versa; experiences are guided by the 'spatial fix' of the destination. This enlightening framework is not only theorised, but also measured using innovative tools for affect and mobility analysis. Methodological assemblages of different techniques are generated throughout this dissertation, using mobile methods as a starting point to develop mobile sensory methods.

Mobility thereby becomes a frame and a filter for the destination, defining space boundaries and travel affect, but also shaping the potential actions of tourists. This is the core value of this book: it interprets mobility not only as displacement, but also as interactive place-making and experience-making processes.

Ingolstadt, Bavaria, Germany
Prof. Dr. Harald Pechlaner
Catholic University of Eichstätt-Ingolstadt

Acknowledgements

I would like to express my deepest appreciation to all those who have advised and helped me on my long dissertation journey, and particularly to my supervisor, Prof. Harald Pechlaner, who believed in me more than I did at the beginning of the journey, and supported me in making important thematic and methodological choices along the way that helped me to complete my research. Without his guidance, trust and help, this dissertation would not have been possible. I would also like to thank my co-supervisor, Prof. Anita Zehrer for supporting me in the identification of the methodological framework that I needed to choose in order to take the right direction in the analytical phase of the work. Both were crucial in the research design and for the innovativeness of the results. I am also very grateful to Prof. Bernard Lane, who read first drafts of the thesis and supported me with his immense expertise on sustainable tourism during the delicate writing phase of the journey, when the work had to turn into foreign (English) words. Your advice was precious.

Special thanks go to my family for their wise counsel and sympathetic ears. You were and are always there for me and you were the best travel companions I could ever have. Thank you to my father and mother, Marco and Paola, my partner Domenico and his children Gabriel and Asya, and to my cousin Carol and all the other members of my family for their silent and constant support. Thank you also to my wonderful friends: Simona, Mara, Elsa and Arianna.

There were also several (partly unexpected, but enlightening) travel encounters along my dissertation journey. The Eurac Research team in Bolzano and the Ph.D. candidates' team in Eichstätt and Ingolstadt were wonderful travel mates, sharing moments of excitement and discomfort, always in a sense of belonging, more than the competition. Special thanks go to Gerhard Vanzi, Alberto Scotti, Peter Laner, Ingrid Kofler, Marika Gon, Anja Marcher, Michael Volgger and all the other team members for their support along the way. I would also like to thank the individuals and organisations that helped me in finding technical solutions for the data collection phase. I thank the SHORE™ team of the Fraunhofer Institute for Integrated Circuits IIS for the possibility to use the facial recognition software SHORE™ for my research purposes; I am grateful to the Get on Studio team, for suggestions on how to extract raw data from the add-on tool; I would also like to mention Prof. Caroline Scarles of the School of Hospitality and Tourism of the University of Surrey, Dr. Elaine Yang of the Griffith Institute For Tourism and Prof. Mads Bødker of the Copenhagen Business School for their suggestions on video and sensor data analysis and on the creation of personas; and finally, the team at the bike rentals 'Dolomiti adventures' and 'Specialised', as well as the directors of the hotels 'Hotel Melodia del Bosco' in Badia Valley and 'Hotel Mesdì' in Fodom Valley for supporting the recruitment phase.

Last, but not least, I acknowledge the patience and enthusiasm of all the research participants, who were fascinated by the research topic and willing to dedicate to me their travel time. Without their journeys, my journey could not have existed.

Contents

1 Introduction 1
  1.1 Context and Rationale 1
       1.1.1 Theoretical Context 5
  1.2 Research Aims and Research Questions 7
  1.3 Research Design 9
  1.4 Thesis Outline 10
  References 12

2 Tourist Mobility as an Experience Maker:
Understanding the Blank Space 17
  2.1 Introduction 17
  2.2 Tourist Mobility and Transport 18
       2.2.1 On Site: Transport Geography and the Tourist Transport System 20
       2.2.2 On the Move: The New Mobilities Geography 25
  2.3 Tourist Experiences 35
       2.3.1 In a Harmony: The Orchestra Model of Tourist Experience 41
       2.3.2 On the Stage: The Experience Economy and Its Implications for Tourism 42
  2.4 Emotions in Tourism 47
       2.4.1 Inside Out: Affective Science and Its Application to Tourism 48
  2.5 Mobile Journey Experiences: An Interdisciplinary Framework 52
       2.5.1 Mobile Journey Experience 53
       2.5.2 The Mobility Space 55
  2.6 Chapter Summary 58
  References 59

3 Methodology ... 71
3.1 Introduction ... 71
3.2 Research Strategy ... 72
    3.2.1 Theoretical Perspective ... 72
    3.2.2 Methodological Strategy ... 73
    3.2.3 Case Study ... 75
    3.2.4 Research Questions and Associated Methods ... 81
3.3 Documentation and Secondary Data ... 83
    3.3.1 Rationale ... 83
    3.3.2 Documentation and Data Types ... 83
    3.3.3 Analysis ... 84
3.4 Mobile Video Ethnography: Ride-Alongs and Bio-Sensing ... 88
    3.4.1 Rationale ... 88
    3.4.2 Recruitment Strategy ... 95
    3.4.3 Data Collection, Research Design and Administration ... 98
    3.4.4 Data Analysis ... 100
    3.4.5 Reflection on Mobile Video Ethnography, Ride-Alongs and Bio-Sensing ... 103
3.5 Emotion Measurement: Self-reporting Techniques, Video Elicitation, and Facial Action Coding ... 105
    3.5.1 Rationale ... 105
    3.5.2 Recruitment Strategy, Data Collection, Research Design and Administration ... 110
    3.5.3 Data Analysis ... 112
    3.5.4 Reflection on Emotion Measurement ... 112
3.6 Integration of the Quantitative and Qualitative Results: Thick Description and Personas ... 114
    3.6.1 Rationale ... 114
    3.6.2 Data Integration and Administration ... 116
    3.6.3 Reflection on the Integration of Quantitative and Qualitative Data ... 118
3.7 Chapter Summary ... 118
References ... 119

4 Results: Physical, Sensory, Social and Emotional Features of Journey Experiences ... 125
4.1 Introduction ... 125
4.2 Context Description: Features of the Transport System on the Sella Pass ... 126
    4.2.1 The Sellaronda Road Transport System ... 126
    4.2.2 The Sella Pass Road: Technical Features and Travel Demand ... 129
    4.2.3 Key Findings ... 131

	4.3	Journey Experience Description: Space, Time and Speed	132
		4.3.1	Sella Pass Mobility Space and Its Temporal Sections	132
		4.3.2	Journey Duration: Time and Speed	133
		4.3.3	Key Findings	139
	4.4	Journey Experience Description: Physical and Social Features	139
		4.4.1	Physical Features: Primary and Secondary Tasks Besides Driving	140
		4.4.2	Social Features: Overtaking, Velo-Formations, Verbal and Non-verbal Interactions	144
		4.4.3	Key Findings	153
	4.5	Journey Experience Description: Sensory and Emotional Features	154
		4.5.1	Sensory Features: Travel Glance, Sound and Silence	154
		4.5.2	Emotional Features: The Thrill of Speed, the Worry to Stay in Line	162
		4.5.3	Key Findings	171
	4.6	Journey Experience Description: The Overall Picture	172
	4.7	Chapter Summary	175
	References	176
5	**Results: Selected Individual Journey Experiences**	179
	5.1	Introduction	179
	5.2	Motorcyclists Second-by-Second	181
		5.2.1	Juan and the Custom Cruiser	181
		5.2.2	Marco and the Naked Bike	187
		5.2.3	Key Findings	195
	5.3	Cyclists Second-by-Second	195
		5.3.1	Peter and the Guided Tour	196
		5.3.2	Gabriel and the Sport Performance	205
		5.3.3	Carlo and the Same-Day Tour	214
		5.3.4	Key Findings	219
	5.4	Personas Description: An Engaging Perspective on Cyclists and Motorcyclists	222
		5.4.1	Hypotheses for Personas Description	222
		5.4.2	The Motorcycle Tourer: Alberto	225
		5.4.3	The Aggressive Motorcyclist: Pedro	227
		5.4.4	The Mountain Lover: Markus	228
		5.4.5	The Athlete: João	229
		5.4.6	Key Findings	231
	5.5	Chapter Summary	232
	References	233

6 Discussion and Conclusion ... 235
6.1 Introduction ... 235
6.2 Key Findings ... 236
6.2.1 Speed and Its Variation as the Main Mediator for Actions and Perceptions ... 238
6.2.2 Contextual Conditions, Velo-Formations and Encounters as Crucial Experience Aspects ... 239
6.2.3 Individual Attitudes and Behaviours as Ways to (Re-)Construct Space ... 240
6.2.4 Generalisability of Findings ... 241
6.3 Theoretical Contribution ... 242
6.3.1 Journey Experiences: Performances on the Move ... 242
6.3.2 The Mobility Space: A Moving Stage ... 244
6.3.3 Human-Vehicle Hybrids: Mobile Co-creators of the Mobility Space ... 246
6.4 Methodological Contribution ... 247
6.4.1 Mobile Mixed Methods in Real-Life Environmental Setting ... 247
6.4.2 Measuring (Mis)Understandable Experience Worlds: New Insights for Experience Research ... 248
6.4.3 Network Graphs as Tools to Represent Individuals and Journey Features Across Time ... 249
6.4.4 From Customer Experience Analysis to Mobility Space Design: The Use of Personas ... 250
6.5 Managerial Contribution ... 251
6.5.1 Cycling and Motorcycling: Mobile Tourism Products to be Enhanced ... 251
6.5.2 Road Planning Based on Micro-Data: An Opportunity for Road Safety ... 253
6.5.3 Transition Management Towards Sustainable Mobility: Evidence-Based Policies and Niche Marketing ... 253
6.6 Limitations ... 256
6.6.1 Sensor Setting, Data Quality Control, and Synchronisation ... 256
6.6.2 Research Participants, Travel Companions and the Researcher ... 258
6.6.3 Methodological Limitations and Future Challenges in Mobile Video Ethnography ... 259
6.7 Chapter Summary ... 260
References ... 261

7 Outlook... 263
   7.1 Introduction 263
   7.2 Methodological Prospects for Future Research 264
       7.2.1 Mobile and Bio-Sensing Methods to Understand Tourist
             Transport Systems 265
       7.2.2 Visual and Psychophysiological Methods to Investigate
             Tourist Experiences 265
       7.2.3 Ethical Issues Related to Bio-Sensing,
             Psychophysiological and Visual Methods 267
   7.3 Tourism's Transformative Power......................... 269
       7.3.1 Experience Design............................. 270
       7.3.2 Transdisciplinarity 270
   References 271

Appendix... 275

Chapter 1
Introduction

千里之行, 始於足下
[A journey of a thousand miles begins with a single step]
Lao Tze (604 BC-531BC)

Abstract This introduction presents an overview of the content and structure of the book. It presents the context and rationale of the study, linking tourism and mobility research. It illustrates its theoretical background, defining the two key issues of this research: mobility spaces and journey experiences. It focuses on the main research questions and objectives and introduces the research design. Finally, the last section presents the structure of work.

1.1 Context and Rationale

A "symbiotic relationship" connects mobility and tourism both in the literature and in practice (Page 2008, p. 102): without mobility, tourism cannot happen, at least in non-virtual reality. At a technical level, mobility is a facilitating factor for tourism (Kaul 1985). At a social level, mobility is a mediator in the perception of places, spaces and landscapes (Larsen 2001; Larsen and Guiver 2013; Urry and Larsen 2011). However, mobility might also be seen as a valuable part of the tourism activity itself. Based on the acknowledgment of this positive relationship of mobility for tourism, the transport *as* tourism paradigm hypothesises a positive intrinsic value of travelling (Mokhtarian and Salomon 2001; Siddall 1987), arguing that a certain degree of travel affinity might exist among travellers, corresponding to the willingness to travel "just for the fun of it" (the so-called *undirected travel*) (Mokhtarian and Salomon 2001) (Fig. 1.1). Therefore, tourists' activities on the move might represent attractions themselves: the so-called "moving visitor attractions" Lumsdon and Page (2004, p. 6). Transport *as* tourism corresponds, therefore, to the idea of *undirected travel* by Mokhtarian and Salomon where "travel *is* the activity, movement *is* the object and a destination […] is to varying degrees incidental" (2001, p. 697). Experiences on the move are

```
                                                           OPPORTUNITY FOR
                                                           DESTINATION
                                                           COMPETITIVENESS

         ◄── Mobility          Mobility ──►
            for tourism        as tourism
         (Utilitarian travel)  (Undirected travel)

TECHNICAL/                                        SOCIAL/SOCIOLOGICAL
TECHNOLOGICAL LEVEL                               LEVEL
(technology of transportation)   tourist vs. traveller   (Value creation)

Travel = ancillary                                Travel = primary
End point = primary                               End point = ancillary
```

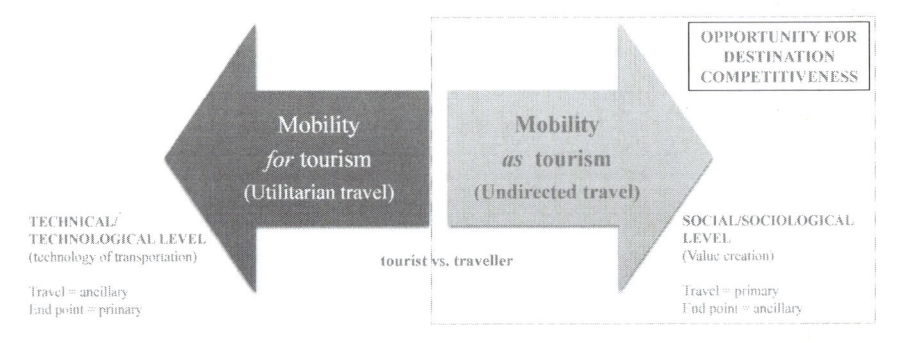

Fig. 1.1 Tourist mobility: technological and sociological perspectives. (Own elaboration based on Lumsdon and Page 2004; Mokhtarian and Salomon 2001; Culler 1981)

influenced by the means of transport chosen (Lumsdon and Page 2004; Page 2008), its slowness/speed (Dickinson and Lumsdon 2010) and the individual and socially embedded attitudes to travelling (Mokhtarian and Salomon 2001; Williams 2013).

Thus, the mode of transport, the quality of transport as well as the end-user are all supposed to have an influence on the intrinsic value of mobility, in a continuum between low-value and high-value mobility options (Moscardo and Pearce 2004). This continuum might also be related to the analogue continuum between tourists and travellers (Culler 1981).

The role of mobility as an experience maker is underexplored in tourism research (Lohmann and Pearce 2012; Larsen 2001). Indeed, most of the literature on tourism mobility still focuses only on the "mobility *for* tourism" paradigm (Lumsdon and Page 2004), i.e. it interprets transport as a derived demand (Banister 2008) and concentrates on technical and economic issues more than on social and experiential issues (Scuttari and Della Lucia 2015). The focus is often on accessibility and on how accessibility potentially influences the creation of new destinations (Bieger and Wittmer 2006; Rey et al. 2011) and makes tourism demand rise significantly (Khadaroo and Seetanah 2007). Mobility is interpreted as an opportunity cost of moving in time-space (Prideaux 2000) and trips are the "necessary evil of tourist travel" (Gunn 1994). The utility of travel is mainly considered as negative (Mokhtarian and Salomon 2001) and it is measured in economic and temporal terms, often using the travel distance decay model (Clawson and Knetsch 1966). The experiential value of mobility ("transport *as* tourism") is only rarely assessed (Moscardo and Pearce 2004), overlooking the fact that mobility is recognised to be, for some tourists, part of the tourism experience (Lumsdon and Page 2004).

A first step towards the analysis of transport as (part of) tourism was done through studies on the impact of transport infrastructures (Khadaroo and Seetanah 2007; Seetanah and Khadaroo 2009; Khadaroo and Seetanah 2010) and of public transport performance (Thompson and Schofield 2007; Kozak and Rimmington 1999) on tourism attractiveness or competitiveness. Although these studies focused on the instrumental

1.1 Context and Rationale

role of mobility in generating customer value and not on its intrinsic value, they were a first milestone in the process of considering mobility as part of the overall tourism experience. A further step was made by Schiefelbusch et al. (2007), by conceptualising *integrated travel chains* as holistic tourism products where both attractions and *mobile attractions*, i.e. activities on the move, combine according to the tourist target groups involved. Finally, and more recently, some academic work has been produced on passenger experiences in different transport fields related to tourism. Some of this evidence suggests that slow mobility provides more intense experiences than fast mobility (Lumsdon and McGrath 2011) and that motorized mobility enables different perceptions of landscapes than non-motorized mobility (Larsen 2001). But deeper insights are lacking, especially in ground transport (Jensen 2010; Dickinson and Robbins 2007). Concerning air transport, studies on airports (Wattanacharoensil et al. 2016, 2017) analyse and highlight the wide range of non-transport experiences offered in these transport hubs and their role in the development of tourist destinations. In the field of water transport, cruise holidays are also interesting platforms to study tourist experiences; they are claimed to be "rich experiential consumptions" (Hosany and Witham 2009, p. 360) on prototypical experiential platforms where the physical environment of the ship offers several tangible and intangible benefits, from transport to entertainment. Aesthetical aspects of the experience prevail on educational, entertainment and escapist aspects, but all of them contribute to the memorability and recollection of the cruise holiday (Hosany and Witham 2009). Notwithstanding the somehow developed field of cruise experience analysis, little attention has been given to the understanding of the experiential value of travelling itself: it is argued by Hosany and Witham (2009), that cruise experiences are increasingly influenced by ship's facilities, rather than by travel routes.

The relatively recent interest of tourism scholars in *affective science* (the scientific study of emotion and affect) (Scuttari and Pechlaner 2017; Volo 2017) has enabled the spread of new approaches to analyse experiences on the move and in real time. Zakrisson and Zillinger (2012) and Kim and Fesenmaier (2015) were pioneers in measuring real-time mobile experiences through GPS tracking technologies and electro-dermal activity (EDA). Kim and Fesenmaier (2015), provided some first insights into the understanding of tourist experiences while exploring in urban environments. Nevertheless, they explicitly focus on the experiential value of visiting attractions, whereas the travel action per se is considered as instrumental and somehow relegated to the background. Zakrisson and Zillinger (2012) put mobility at the very core of their research, focussing on the overall movement patterns of tourists in different seasons and with different travel motivations, clustering visitors according to their degree of mobility. Nevertheless, both contributions do not address undirected travel and its experiential value. Some insights into the experiential value of undirected travel are proposed in literature on tourism "lifestyle" sports, where activities on the move are deemed as specific attractions. For example, using a qualitative phenomenology approach based on in-depth interviews and self-reporting of emotional arousal, Hagen and Boyes (2016) investigate the link between rider affect and different components of experiences on mountain bike trails, revealing that the strongest ride affects were brought about by overcoming multiple track obstacles during the experience.

Understanding experiential and the emotional features of experiences on the move has important managerial and practical implications. Particularly in sensitive Alpine community-type destinations (Holding 2001; Flagestad and Hope 2001), the weighted balance of tourism and transport is relevant to ensure sustainable tourism and transport habits in the medium and long term. Indeed, the discovery of community-type destinations happens on the move, often through base holiday trips (daily visits within the destination setting starting from the accommodation facility), and sometimes through round trips (circular routes from multiple accommodation facilities), or by undertaking linear trips (Campbell 1967; Flognfeldt 2005). These trips are both performed to reach a point of interest, e.g. to visit museums, churches, lakes, mountain peaks etc. (*directed travel*), but also to experience travel journeys, e.g. by the act of cycling, mountain biking, motorcycling, bus tours, hiking etc. (*undirected travel*). Whatever, both directed travel and undirected travel produce traffic flows that sometimes are challenging to manage, both for morphological and political reasons. On the one hand, the contrast between areas of low population density and (possibly crowded) remote attractions (Currie and Falconer 2014; Teal and Becker 2011) can make it difficult to provide public transport based alternatives to private motorised transport. On the other hand, some forms of public transport alternatives, e.g. bus transport, might not be attractive substitutes for tourists "travelling for the fun of it" (Mokhtarian and Salomon 2001, p. 708), e.g. doing a motorcycling/cycling tour on panoramic roads.

Changing tourist modal choices is also a difficult task from a political point of view, because there is a risk of negative economic impacts resulting from traffic management measures—e.g. road closures, tolls, etc.—for the entire destination area, due to a decrease in visits. These difficulties lead to a lock-in of the status quo by regional governments: they acknowledge the traffic impacts of tourism, but are reluctant to act (Scuttari et al. 2013). Therefore, filling knowledge gaps about tourist behaviour is crucial to overcome this lock-in, or so-called tourism-traffic paradox (Scuttari et al. 2019). Only the development of deeper knowledge about the intrinsic value of directed and undirected tourist travel can lead to a more profound understanding of tourist flows, not only in relation to the accessibility of traditional tourist attractions, but also in order to assess and account for the emotional values of the means of transport as *mobile attractions*. This wider knowledge on mobility as an experience maker offers a potential *new leverage* for policies in charge of reducing environmental impacts related to transport (Dickinson and Robbins 2007, 2008; Peeters et al. 2007; Becken et al. 2003). It helps to reflect on the substitutability of means of transport in terms of experiential value—and not only in terms of travel time or comfort—and opens up the possibility of more enlightened policies for modal shift. At the same time, it also offers insights towards promoting low-carbon and more sustainable transport solutions through their positive experiential value, which may be important additions to their instrumental function of reaching destination attractions.

1.1 Context and Rationale

In the light of the above, a number of strategic opportunities stand out as important in exploring the valorisation of different forms of mobility as experience makers in tourism destinations (Holding 2001). Innovative tourism products at the interface between mobility and transport, innovation in transport infrastructure to configure space for the enhancement of tourist experiences, traffic management measures that leverage on the experiential (and not only the utilitarian) value of transport. Not least, all these possible strategies could help increase the sustainability of tourist transport in its wider sense. To achieve this goal and to manage the transition towards more sustainable tourist transport practices, tourism-related knowledge in the field of undirected travel is needed. This is the main challenge that this dissertation is concerned with.

1.1.1 Theoretical Context

To understand tourist mobility as an experience maker, this dissertation brings together and applies to the tourism context four streams of literature, using an interdisciplinary framework: mobilities, transport geography, the experience economy and affective science. The integration of these four perspectives allows the development of a definition of the notion of mobility space as a framework to assess journey experiences.

Geographical approaches to transport offer a possible interpretation of the spatial and temporal dimensions of transport, relying on system theories (Bertalanffy 1968; Luhmann 1984) to conceptualise the transport system (White and Senior 1991; Tolley and Turton 1995; Fincham et al. 2010). The transport system refers mainly to three aspects: infrastructure, operational service, and travel behaviour (Mills and Andrey 2002). Further aspects, such as historical development patterns, technological settings, economic, political and social factors have impacts on shaping the transport system, but are not at the core of geographical approaches to transport (White and Senior 1991). Geographical approaches to transport have been applied to tourism in the framework of the tourist transport system (Duval 2007; Page 2008; Prideaux 2000). The tourist transport system combines "the physical movement of visitors using one or more forms of transport—the logistical component—and the travel experience—the experiential component" (Scuttari et al. 2013, p. 615).

While in transport geography the experiential component is ancillary and the logistical component is primary, in mobilities geography the opposite is true. Indeed, the new mobilities paradigm conceptualized by John Urry introduces a "movement-driven social science in which movement, potential movement and blocked movement are all conceptualized as constitutive of economic, social and political relations" (Urry 2007, p. 43). As argued in the socio-spatial theory by Lefebvre (1991), space and society are mutually constituted within this approach. Physical, mental, and social space are distinct from one another, yet always exist together, as different aspects of "space". The interplay between places and people occurs in relation to a *spatial fix*, i.e. spatial, infrastructural and institutional moorings that configure and enable mobility (Hannam et al. 2006). The mobilities paradigm *enlarges the spatial-temporal perspective to mobile journeys*, adding layers for their analysis, based on the concepts of embodiment, rhythm and its interruption, fluid motion, and materiality.

This dissertation project bridges the new mobilities paradigm and transport geography approaches by introducing the concept of mobility space (Pechlaner et al. 2012). The mobility space is a "space of travel opportunities" (Canzler and Knie 2002), which relies on existing infrastructure and transport services in a given area, connects attractions and is shaped through journey experiences happening in it. In this perspective, mobility is not simply the transport-based link between region of origin and destination (accessibility), or between accommodation facilities and tourist attractions (internal mobility): it represents a driver of territorial knowledge and social cohesion determining the degree of connectivity of or within a destination (Miossec 1977) as well as the opportunities and experiences for tourists. Hence, space is understood as "relatedness", based on the interaction between environment (the "spatial fix") and users (visitors)—scapes and flows (Williams 2013)—, as theorised in the Lefebvre's production of space theory.

Within the mobility space, journey experiences are addressed by making reference to the theoretical frameworks developed in the experience economy literature and emotions are measured based on the techniques developed in affective science. According to Pine and Gilmore, experiences are the result of a set of physical, emotional, spiritual and/or intellectual impressions (Pine and Gilmore 1999) staged for, and subjectively perceived by, individuals. This approach is reflected in the orchestra model of tourist experience by Pearce (2011), where tourist experiences are pivotal constructs based on sensory, affective, cognitive, behavioural and relationship components. Adapting both these definitions to the context of travel and tourism, journey experiences are then defined as tourist experiences on the move "made up of processes (social, emotional, sensory and physical)" (Delaney 2016, p. 6). Tourist journey experiences, and particularly those where an active ride is needed, tend also to be active experiences with a full immersion in the environmental context, i.e. the "escapist" component of the experience seems to prevail over the aesthetic, educational or entertaining ones (Pine and Gilmore 1999). The dissertation assesses these experiential processes and compares them among individuals and travel modes in one mobility space, with particular attention to their emotional aspects.

Emotions are referred to as "complex psychological states that involve three distinct components: a subjective experience, a physiological response, and an expressive response" (Hockenbury and Hockenbury 2007, p. 117). Emotions are subjective and dynamic psychological states, and, therefore, their measurement can hardly be quantitative only. Depending on the theory used to assess them, self-report or observation techniques are used to measure their levels of arousal and intensity (Scuttari and Pechlaner 2017). More recent approaches in tourism have used a combination of physiological and expressive responses, together with more old-fashioned self-reporting techniques, to gain a deeper and more comprehensive view of the emotional states. This combination of quantitative measures and subjective reports is also adopted in this dissertation, since it allows the triangulation of results and minimises distortions.

1.2 Research Aims and Research Questions

The dissertation's main aim is to address mobility as an experience maker in mobility spaces. Thus, the dissertation focuses on those cases where mobility works as (part of) tourism: it considers those environments, modes and travel motivations that have less utilitarian value and more experiential value (Scuttari et al. 2019). Moreover, it focuses on those means of transport where tourism research has not yet developed a body of knowledge. The aim is thereby to increase knowledge about ground transport, a quite underexplored domain with regard to tourists' experiences on the move (Jensen 2010). To achieve this goal, the dissertation focuses on panoramic roads within tourism intensive and sensitive areas; concerning modes, a comparison is made between human powered and motorised mobility on two wheels (motorcycles and bicycles); regarding travel motivations, the dissertation mainly selects those journeys that—in the continuum between utilitarian and undirected travel—are (mostly) made "for the fun of it" (Mokhtarian and Salomon 2001, p. 708). This kind of journey experience, both on human-powered means of transport (bicycles) and on motorized means of transport (motorcycles) are assessed in community-type destinations belonging to the eastern part of the Alpine area, which makes them particularly interesting because of their contribution to regional traffic and tourism management policies. Both type of experiences are expected to involve drivers actively, and to let them experience a type of immersion into the landscape. They are expected to produce both utilitarian value to guests (i.e. the opportunity to reach the desired destination), but also non-utilitarian effects, related to the peculiar "fun" of travelling (Mokhtarian and Salomon 2001). Compared to cars, these means of transport seem to generate more experiential value to users (Scuttari et al. 2019), rather than other vehicles. They are also open means of transport, where drivers are not isolated in a cabin and therefore tend to have deeper involvement of the senses, and less disturbance related to internal settings (e.g. stereo, air conditioning, etc.). Finally, they are mostly individual means of transport, which means that the rider has active control over the ride and interacts with other vehicles or individual as a single person. These are very independent travellers.

Based on these considerations and assumptions, and on the dissertation's aim to investigate the social, emotional, sensory, and physical processes with which tourists consciously and subconsciously engage while travelling on bicycles and motorcycles, the following research questions are formulated:

1. How to describe and how to measure the visitors' mobile journey experiences and their physical, sensory, emotional and social features in space and time?

    - What are the physical features of visitors' mobile journey experiences and what is their relationship to the *spatial fix*?

- What are the sensory features?
- What are the affective features?
- How does the negotiation of space in motion happen and how does social interaction happen in space and time?

2. How does travel mode—i.e. cycling versus motorcycling—shape journey experiences?

   - How do physical, sensory, affective and social features relate to mode of transport?

3. How to develop personas to address motorcyclists and cyclists in mobility spaces?

   - How to define common features among users of the same means of transport?
   - How much variety is there among users of the same means of transport?

Following the above research questions, the dissertation has both a descriptive and analytical-empirical objective. The overall aim is to fill the knowledge gap found in the relatively few studies on sociological aspects related to mobility. The specific aims of the dissertation are outlined below:

1. to add to current knowledge and critically reflect upon the construct of tourist mobility and mobility spaces;
2. to analytically and systematically describe journey experiences in mobility spaces;
3. to make a methodological contribution to the field of mobile methods on how to measure journey experiences using visual, sensory and self-reported data;
4. to make a practical contribution by understanding the motives and personas of motorcyclists and cyclists in Alpine mobility spaces, in order to refine and improve traffic management measures.

To achieve these goals, the dissertation takes a critical realist approach (Bhaskar 2008), i.e. a middle ground between positivism and constructivism (Robson 2002). If positivism assumes that "positive knowledge is based upon natural phenomena, their properties and relations as verified by science" (Savin Baden and Howell Major 2013, p. 63), constructivism asserts conversely that knowledge is socially constructed and an objective reality cannot be discovered and known. Indeed, in constructivist approaches, reality is "an internal construction where individuals assign meaning to experiences and ideas" (Savin Baden and Howell Major 2013, p. 63) and objectivity is unachievable. As middle ground between positivism and constructivism, the critical realist approach taken by this dissertation accepts that knowledge is influenced by the individual's interpretations of it; however, it also claims that "reality" and knowledge exist independent of human thought.

1.3 Research Design

Given the ontological and epistemological considerations explained above, and considering the place-specificity of mobility spaces, the adopted methodology to conduct research on the experiential value of undirected tourism travel is case study research (Yin 2006) which is both single and exploratory. The rationale for the selection of a single case study is the fact that it "represents an extreme case or a unique case" (Yin 2006, p. 40) to allow a rich experiential consumption of tourist experiences on the move.

The selected case study is Passo Sella/Sellajoch, a mountain Pass on the border between the Autonomous Provinces of Bolzano and Trento in Italy, which is characterised by high intensity tourism traffic (both of bikes and motorcycles) and spectacular landscape views of the Dolomites, parts of which are recognised as a UNESCO World Heritage Site. Its uniqueness relies in the high tourism intensity and sensitiveness of the environment, as well as the several attempts to implement pioneering experiments with traffic management measures to reduce tourism transport impacts. Indeed, for more than a decade studies and analyses were developed for traffic calming in the area and at the time the case study area was selected, no real action had taken place to implement traffic management. Later, during summer 2017, a pilot traffic management project, with a partial road closure to non-electric motorized transport—and a series of incentives for cycle transport—was implemented and in the future similar initiatives are planned, with suitable adjustments. Therefore, data and outcomes from the case study might help in understanding the effects of the implemented mobility measures, as well as providing ideas for future traffic and mobility management initiatives. Primary data collection refers to the behavioural and emotional components of journey experience on site, in relation to the available transport infrastructure and operational aspects in the existing environment. Data and method triangulation is achieved by using—within a framework of mobile video ethnography (Pink 2007; Spinney 2011)—both visual content, physical biometric data, as well as using self-reported and observation techniques for emotion measurement (Isomursu et al. 2007). Data was collected in summer 2016 by involving real visitors to the pass, i.e. by measuring their own journey experiences. Action cameras and sensors were placed on visitors' helmets to record videos and collect biometric data about their journey experience, including pass climb, stops and descent. After taking the tour, tourists were debriefed and asked to fill in a questionnaire for self-assessment of perceived emotions. In parallel, a video elicitation technique (Zehe and Belz 2016) was used to measure the emotions associated to the journey experience using a software for facial action coding (SHORE™, i.e. Sophisticated High-speed Object Recognition Engine) (Wierzbicki et al. 2013), which measures the extent of four basic emotions (happiness, sadness, anger and surprise) in relation to the journey experience. Videos were then encoded using NVivo Pro 11™ software through video content analysis (Ying and Jay Kuo 2003), while data from biometric sensors, emotions and questionnaires were analysed through Excel and mapped in the mobility space through ArcGis™ software. Sensory data, video data and emotion measurements are then related to understand and describe journey experiences at individual level and in form of personas.

1.4 Thesis Outline

The dissertation is structured into seven chapters (see Fig. 1.2). These are briefly outlined below. The next chapter, Chap. 2, sets out the interdisciplinary theoretical framework to assess mobility spaces and journey experiences in the tourism context. It reviews the transport geography literature, which relies on system theories, and the mobilities geography literature, based on Lefebvre's production of space theory. It further summarises existing literature on tourist experiences, as well as the important conceptualisation in business studies of the experience economy, and its theorisation of four realms to assess experience measurement. Further, it focuses on the emotional features of tourist experiences and on techniques and methods to understand and measure them in tourism terms. It concludes by setting the basis for the interdisciplinary framework of mobility space, and contextualising journey experiences within it. Chapter 2 is long: it is by far the longest chapter in this dissertation. It is necessarily long because the background to the discussions undertaken in the dissertation is both historically long (dating back to the nineteenth century) and extremely wide in its scope. Furthermore, the subject areas that are involved have grown in number and complexity over the last few years, and they continue to grow. Readers are asked to bear with this length: it is necessary to fully set in context, to understand the research work carried out and the roles and significance of the research findings produced for business, for tourists, for heritage of all kinds, natural and man-made, for the management of both transport systems and organizations and for the destinations along those transport routes.

Following on from this initial conceptualization of mobility space and journey experiences, Chap. 3 discusses the methodology of the research. It includes the research strategy, encompassing both the epistemological and ontological setting of the research, as well as the research design. Rooted in a critical realist approach, the research design uses an exploratory case study and concurrent mixed methods—QUAN + QUAL. The method description refers to three main steps: documentation and secondary data analysis; mobile video ethnography; and emotion measurement. Finally, quantitative and qualitative data are related and integrated using a common platform to show how the empirical evidence converges. Each methodological step is described explaining rationale, data collection strategy, recruitment procedures used to find the visitors that were studied, and data analysis. A consideration of the challenges faced by implementing each of the methods is presented, together with a reflection on the methodological process as a whole.

Chapters 4 and 5 present the empirical findings from the case study. Chapter 4 uses aggregate data coming from all participants and it aims at: (a) *describing the features* of journey experiences in their territorial context; (b) *highlighting the differences* between travel modes. By means of tables, diagrams, network graphs

1.4 Thesis Outline

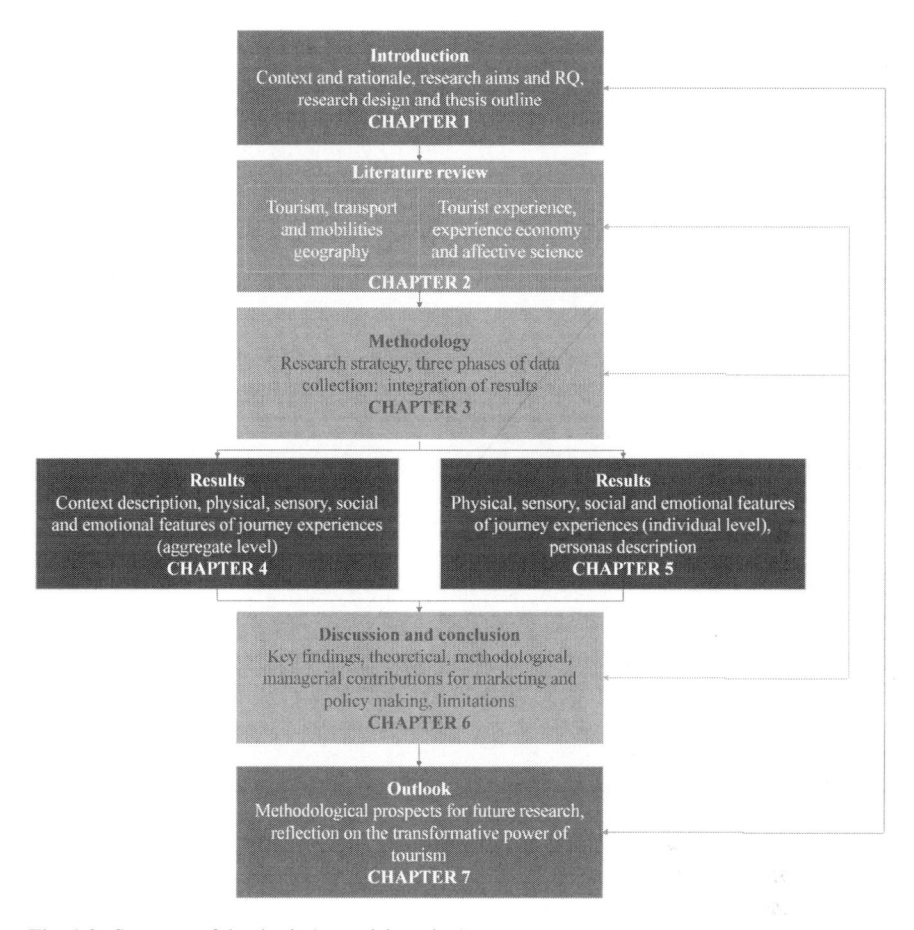

Fig. 1.2 Structure of the thesis (own elaboration)

and video stills and clips, it describes the technical and demand-related features of the transport system of the Sella Pass, it drafts the mobility space and its spatial and temporal dimensions, and finally it analyses the type and spatio-temporal patterns of physical, social, sensory and emotional features of journey experiences. It concludes by offering a first overall picture of journey experiences and their features, in a juxtaposition between motorcycles and bicycles.

Chapter 5 increases the granularity of data items studied, because it focusses on selected individual journey experiences. Based on the assumption that experiences and emotions are profoundly subjective, time- and space-specific, the study of single individuals in precise contextual conditions helps to generate convergence of evidence based on linking multiple data sources for one participant—rather than comparing the same data source for multiple participants (as it is done in Chap. 4). Two motorcyclists and three cyclists are selected for the thick description, applying the following criteria: (i) the avoidance of redundancy in results; (ii) the inclusion of both overnight tourists and day visitors; (iii) the inclusion of both first-time and repeat visitors; (iv) the (sensor) data quality. Results are presented by showing individual coding schemes of the video footage, diagrams, video stills, video clips and sensor-based maps. Evidence resulting from this chapter is merged—by using the generative process of personas description—with the overall descriptive picture created in Chap. 4. Four personas are presented, that enable the description of typified mobility, activity, social and emotional patterns along the mobility space. The creation of personas is a crucial linking element between the descriptive activity of experience analysis and the policy-driven activity of tourism and transport planning, management and marketing.

Chapter 6 presents a discussion of these research findings in the context of the literature outlined in Chap. 2. Specific issues are addressed in this chapter to outline the contribution to knowledge provided by this research. For instance, the key issues include: speed and its variation as a mediator for individual actions and perceptions; contextual conditions, velo-formations and encounters as crucial aspects of the journey experience; individual attitudes and behaviours as leverages to reconstruct space. Further, the equally important theoretical, methodological and managerial contribution of the dissertation are outlined, making reference to how the present work has the potential to extend and improve the existing theories on tourism mobility, the methodological designs using mobile methods and the destination practices of integrated tourism and transport planning, management and marketing. Detailed recommendations are provided for rethinking traffic management measures from the visitors' perspective and exploring possible side-effects of traffic regulation on specific types of users. Finally, a separate section is also provided in which research limitations are discussed.

A concluding set of discussions is then presented in Chap. 7, offering details on methodological prospects for future research and a final reflection on the transformational power of tourism for destinations. Methodological prospect discussions particularly address the field of mobile and bio-sensing as well as visual and psychophysiological methods, assessing ethical issues related to new ways of analysing consumer behaviour. The dissertation finishes with thoughtful reflections on the transformational power of tourism towards human behaviour, societies and regions, and finally towards scientific research.

References

Banister D (2008) The sustainable mobility paradigm. Transp Policy 15(2):73–80
Becken S, Simmons D, Frampton C (2003) Segmenting tourists by their travel pattern for insights into achieving energy efficiency. J Travel Res 42(1):48–56. https://doi.org/10.1177/0047287503253938
von Bertalanffy L (1968) General system theory. Braziller, New York
Bhaskar R (2008) A realist theory of science. Routledge, London

References

Bieger T, Wittmer A (2006) Air transport and tourism—perspectives and challenges for destinations, airlines and governments. J Air Transp Manag 12(1):40–46. https://doi.org/10.1016/j.jairtraman.2005.09.007

Campbell CK (1967) An approach to research in recreational geography. BC Occasional Papers, Department of Geography, University of British Columbia, Vancouver, Canada (7):85–90

Canzler W, Knie A (2002) New Mobility? Mobilität und Verkehr als soziale Praxis ["New mobility"? Mobility and transport as social practices]. Politik und Zeitgeschichte B(45-46/2000)

Clawson M, Knetsch J (1966) Economics of outdoor recreation. John Hopkins University Press, Baltimore

Culler J (1981) Semiotics of tourism. Am J Semiot 1(1):127–140

Currie C, Falconer P (2014) Maintaining sustainable island destinations in Scotland: the role of the transport–tourism relationship. J Destin Mark Manag 3(3):162–172. https://doi.org/10.1016/j.jdmm.2013.10.005

Delaney H (2016) Walking and cycling interactions on shared-use paths. Doctorate Thesis (Doctorate), University of the West of England

Dickinson J, Lumsdon L (2010) Slow travel and tourism. Tourism, environment and development. Earthscan, Washington DC

Dickinson JE, Robbins D (2007) Using the car in a fragile rural tourist destination: a social representations perspective. J Transp Geogr 15(2):116–126. https://doi.org/10.1016/j.jtrangeo.2006.11.002

Dickinson JE, Robbins D (2008) Representations of tourism transport problems in a rural destination. Tour Manag 29(6):1110–1121. https://doi.org/10.1016/j.tourman.2008.02.003

Duval DT (2007) Tourism and transport: modes, networks, and flows. Aspects of tourism text books. Channel View Publications, Clevedon, England, Buffalo, NY

Fincham B, McGuinness M, Murray L (eds) (2010) Mobile Methodologies. Palgrave Macmillan, London, UK

Flagestad A, Hope CA (2001) Strategic success in winter sports destinations: a sustainable value creation perspective. Tour Manag 22(5):445–461. https://doi.org/10.1016/S0261-5177(01)00010-3

Flognfeldt T (2005) The tourist route system—models of travelling patterns: Le système de l'itinéraire touristique—modèles de schémas de voyage. Belgeo 1–2:35–58. https://doi.org/10.4000/belgeo.12406

Gunn CA (1994) Tourism planning: basics, concepts, cases. Taylor and Francis, Washington DC

Hagen S, Boyes M (2016) Affective ride experiences on mountain bike terrain. J Outdoor Recreat Tour 15:89–98. https://doi.org/10.1016/j.jort.2016.07.006

Hannam K, Sheller M, Urry J (2006) Editorial: mobilities, immobilities and moorings. Mobilities 1(1):1–22. https://doi.org/10.1080/17450100500489189

Hockenbury DH, Hockenbury SE (2007) Discovering psychology, 4th edn. Worth Publishers, New York

Holding DM (2001) The Sanfte Mobilitaet project: achieving reduced car-dependence in European resort areas. Tour Manag 22(4):411–417. https://doi.org/10.1016/S0261-5177(00)00071-6

Hosany S, Witham M (2009) Dimensions of cruisers' experiences, satisfaction, and intention to recommend. J Travel Res 49(3):351–364. https://doi.org/10.1177/0047287509346859

Isomursu M, Tähti M, Väinämö S, Kuutti K (2007) Experimental evaluation of five methods for collecting emotions in field settings with mobile applications. Int J Hum Comput Stud 65(4):404–418. https://doi.org/10.1016/j.ijhcs.2006.11.007

Jensen OB (2010) Negotiation in motion: unpacking a geography of mobility. Space Cult 13(4):389–402. https://doi.org/10.1177/1206331210374149

Kaul RN (1985) Dynamics of tourism: a trilogy transportation and marketing. Sterling Publishers, New Delhi

Khadaroo AJ, Seetanah B (2007) Transport infrastructure and tourism development. Ann Tour Res 34(4):1021–1032. https://doi.org/10.1016/j.annals.2007.05.010

Khadaroo AJ, Seetanah B (2010) Transport infrastructure and foreign direct investment. J Int Dev 22(1):103–123. https://doi.org/10.1002/jid.1506

Kim J, Fesenmaier DR (2015) Measuring emotions in real time: implications for tourism experience design. J Travel Res 54(4):419–429. https://doi.org/10.1177/0047287514550100

Kozak M, Rimmington M (1999) Measuring tourist destination competitiveness: conceptual considerations and empirical findings. Int J Hosp Manag 18(3):273–283. https://doi.org/10.1016/S0278-4319(99)00034-1

Larsen GR, Guiver JW (2013) Understanding tourists' perceptions of distance: a key to reducing the environmental impacts of tourism mobility. J Sustain Tour 7(21):968–981. https://doi.org/10.1080/09669582.2013.819878

Larsen J (2001) Tourism mobilities and the travel glance: experiences of being on the move. Scand J Hosp Tour 1(2):80–98. https://doi.org/10.1080/150222501317244010

Lefebvre H (1991) The production of space. Blackwell, Malden, MA

Lohmann G, Pearce DG (2012) Tourism and transport relationships: the suppliers' perspective in gateway destinations in New Zealand. Asia Pac J Tour Res 17(1):14–29. https://doi.org/10.1080/10941665.2011.613211

Luhmann N (1984) Soziale Systeme: Grundriss einer allgemeinen Theorie [Social Systems. Outline of a General Theory]. Suhrkamp, Frankfurt

Lumsdon L, Page S (eds) (2004) Tourism and transport: issues and agenda for the new millennium. Advances in tourism research. Elsevier, Amsterdam, San Diego

Lumsdon LM, McGrath P (2011) Developing a conceptual framework for slow travel: a grounded theory approach. J Sustain Tour 19(3):265–279. https://doi.org/10.1080/09669582.2010.519438

Mills B, Andrey J (2002) Climate change and transportation: potential interactions and impacts. The potential impacts of climate change on transportation (Summary and Discussion Papers). https://climate.dot.gov/documents/workshop1002/workshop.pdf. Accessed 5 Jan 2018

Miossec J (1977) Un modèle de l'espace touristique [A model of the tourist space]. Espace géographique 6(1):41–48

Mokhtarian PL, Salomon I (2001) How derived is the demand for travel? Some conceptual and measurement considerations. Transp Res Part A Policy Pract 35(8):695–719. https://doi.org/10.1016/S0965-8564(00)00013-6

Moscardo G, Pearce PL (2004) Life cycle, tourist motivation and transport: some consequences for the tourist experience. In: Lumsdon L, Page S (eds) Tourism and transport: issues and agenda for the new millennium. Elsevier, Amsterdam, San Diego, pp 29–43

Page SJ (2008) Transport and tourism: global perspectives, 2nd edn. Themes in Tourism. Pearson Prentice Hall, Harlow

Pearce PL (2011) Tourist behaviour and the contemporary world. Channel View Publications, Bristol

Pechlaner H, Pichler S, Herntrei M (2012) From mobility space towards experience space: implications for the competitiveness of destinations. Tour Rev 67(2):34–44. https://doi.org/10.1108/16605371211236150

Peeters P, Szimba E, Duijnisveld M (2007) Major environmental impacts of European tourist transport. J Transp Geogr 15(2):83–93. https://doi.org/10.1016/j.jtrangeo.2006.12.007

Pine BJ, Gilmore JH (1999) The experience economy, Updated edn. Harvard Business Review Press, Boston, Mass

Pink S (2007) Doing visual ethnography. Sage, London

Prideaux B (2000) The role of the transport system in destination development. Tour Manag 21(1):53–63. https://doi.org/10.1016/S0261-5177(99)00079-5

Rey B, Myro RL, Galera A (2011) Effect of low-cost airlines on tourism in Spain. A dynamic panel data model. J Air Transp Manag 17(3):163–167. https://doi.org/10.1016/j.jairtraman.2010.12.004

Robson C (2002) Real world research. Blackwell Publishing, Oxford

Savin Baden M, Howell Major C (2013) Qualitative research: the essential guide to theory and practice. Routledge, Abingdon

Schiefelbusch M, Jain A, Schäfer T, Müller D (2007) Transport and tourism: roadmap to integrated planning developing and assessing integrated travel chains. J Transp Geogr 15(2):94–103. https://doi.org/10.1016/j.jtrangeo.2006.12.009

References

Scuttari A, Della Lucia M, Martini U (2013) Integrated planning for sustainable tourism and mobility. A tourism traffic analysis in Italy's South Tyrol region. J Sustain Tour 21(4):614–637. https://doi.org/10.1080/09669582.2013.786083

Scuttari A, Della Lucia M (2015) Managing sustainable mobility in natural areas: the case of South Tyrol (Italy). In: Orsi F (ed) Sustainable transportation in natural and protected areas. Routledge/Taylor & Francis Group; Earthscan from Routledge, London, New York, pp 99–114

Scuttari A, Orsi F, Bassani R (2019) Assessing the tourism-traffic paradox in mountain destinations. A stated preference survey on the Dolomites' passes (Italy). J Sustain Tour 27(2):241–257. https://doi.org/10.1080/09669582.2018.1428336

Scuttari A, Pechlaner H (2017) Emotions in tourism: from consumer behavior to destination management. In: Fesenmaier DR, Xiang Z (eds) Design science in tourism: foundations of destination management. Springer, Cham, CH, pp 41–54

Seetanah B, Khadaroo J (2009) An analysis of the relationship between transport capital and tourism development in a dynamic framework. Tour Econ 15(4):785–802. https://doi.org/10.5367/000000009789955215

Siddall WR (1987) Transportation and the experience of travel. Geogr Rev 77(3):309. https://doi.org/10.2307/214122

Spinney J (2011) A chance to catch a breath: using mobile video ethnography in cycling research. Mobilities 6(2):161–182. https://doi.org/10.1080/17450101.2011.552771

Teal RF, Becker AJ (2011) Business strategies and technology for access by transit in lower density environments. Res Transp Bus Manag 2:57–64. https://doi.org/10.1016/j.rtbm.2011.08.003

Thompson K, Schofield P (2007) An investigation of the relationship between public transport performance and destination satisfaction. J Transp Geogr 15(2):136–144. https://doi.org/10.1016/j.jtrangeo.2006.11.004

Tolley RS, Turton BJ (1995) Transport systems, policy, and planning: a geographical approach. Routledge, Oxford, New York

Urry J (2007) Mobilities. Polity Press, Cambridge, Malden, MA. Reprinted

Urry J, Larsen J (2011) The tourist gaze 3.0. Sage Publications Ltd., London

Volo S (2017) Emotions in tourism: from exploration to design. In: Fesenmaier DR, Xiang Z (eds) Design science in tourism: foundations of destination management. Springer, Cham, CH, pp 31–40

Wattanacharoensil W, Schuckert M, Graham A (2016) An airport experience framework from a tourism perspective. Transp Rev 36(3):318–340. https://doi.org/10.1080/01441647.2015.1077287

Wattanacharoensil W, Schuckert M, Graham A, Dean A (2017) An analysis of the airport experience from an air traveler perspective. J Hosp Tour Manag 32:124–135. https://doi.org/10.1016/j.jhtm.2017.06.003

White HP, Senior ML (1991) Transport geography. Longman, Harlow. Reprint

Wierzbicki RJ, Tschoeppe C, Ruf T, Garbas J (2013) EDIS—emotion-driven interactive systems. In: Proceedings of the 5th international workshop on semantic ambient media experience (SAME). International SERIES on information systems and management in creative eMedia (CreMedia), vol 1, pp 59–68

Williams AM (2013) Mobilities and sustainable tourism: path-creating or path-dependent relationships? J Sustain Tour 21(4):511–531. https://doi.org/10.1080/09669582.2013.768252

Yin RK (2006) Case study research: design and methods, 3rd edn. Applied social research methods series, vol 5. Sage, Thousand Oaks, CA

Ying L, Jay Kuo C (2003) Video content analysis using multimodal information. For Movie Content Extraction, Indexing and Representation. Springer US, New York

Zakrisson I, Zillinger M (2012) Emotions in motion: tourist experiences in time and space. Curr Issues Tour 15(6):505–523. https://doi.org/10.1080/13683500.2011.615391

Zehe AK, Belz F (2016) Video elicitation interviews in organizational and management research. Application in a field study. In: Paper presented at 16th conference on the European academy of management (EURAM), 1–4 June 2016, Paris

Chapter 2
Tourist Mobility as an Experience Maker: Understanding the Blank Space

> *Mobility [...] is more central to both the world and our understanding of it than ever before. And yet mobility itself, and what it means, remains [sic] unspecified. It is a kind of blank space that stands as an alternative to place, boundedness, foundations, and stability. This space needs examining.*
> Tim Cresswell (2006)

Abstract This chapter introduces the necessary definitions, assumptions and delimitations on mobility, experience and affect. It presents the main theories behind their conceptualisation. Four streams of literature are reconstructed for this purpose: transport and mobilities geographies, experience economy and affective science. The interdisciplinary integration of these four perspectives allows the assessment of mobility as an experience-maker in tourism and introduces the theoretical framework of the mobility space and journey experiences.

2.1 Introduction

This chapter is devoted to the understanding of tourist mobility as an experience maker and to develop an interdisciplinary conceptual framework—the mobility space– to assess journey experiences. Repko (2006) provides a step-based approach to operationalizing the interdisciplinary research process. The first step refers to the definition of disciplinary insights. In this phase, it is crucial to justify the need for using an interdisciplinary approach, for conducting an interdisciplinary literature review and thereby develop adequacy in each relevant discipline, with the aim to analyse the specific problem addressed. The second crucial step refers to the integration of insights and production of an interdisciplinary understanding. The interdisciplinary understanding is based on the derivation of conflicts between different insights and the identification of some common ground. Both types of analysis help integrate insights and produce a more comprehensive view of the problem, which then needs to be tackled.

Theoretical interdisciplinarity is defined as the integration, interaction and collaboration among different disciplines (Thompson Klein 2010). "The outcomes include conceptual frameworks for analysis of particular problems, integration of propositions across disciplines, and new syntheses based on continuities between models and analogies" (Thompson Klein 2010, p. 20). Interdisciplinarity is at the core of mobilities studies (Merriman et al. 2013) and of this dissertation, because disciplines dealing with transport in tourism tend to omit the analysis of the experiential value of undirected travel and do not assess emotional features related to displacement in space. Tourist mobility is mainly studied through the lens of transport geography; however, the integration of newer approaches, such as mobilities geographies, might help to grasp the immaterial and emotional features of displacement, as well as its shades and contradictions. These emotional features can be better measured if the notion of *tourist experience* is enriched through the conceptual integration of the *experience economy* paradigm and if real-time measurement instruments for emotion research are used together with traditional self-reporting techniques.

This chapter, based on the integrated approach to the interdisciplinary research process by Repko (2006), introduces the necessary definitions, assumptions and delimitations on mobility, experience and affect, and presents the main theories behind their conceptualisation. Four streams of literature are reconstructed for this purpose: Two of them refer to transport and mobility (see Sect. 2.2), two to emotion and experience (see Sects. 2.3 and 2.4). Thereby, the interdisciplinary integration of these four perspectives—transport and mobilities geographies, experience economy and affective science—allows a deep assessment of the role of mobility as an experience-maker in tourism (see Fig. 2.1) and introduces the framework of the mobility space and journey experiences. The mobility space framework is an attempt to transform the "blank space" of mobility into a more structured space, overcoming different disciplinary boundaries and offering interesting multiple layers to describe mobile journey experiences. The conceptual framework of mobility space is then applied to practice in the empirical analysis (see Chaps. 3–5).

2.2 Tourist Mobility and Transport

Mobility is a precondition for tourism, yet its conceptualization in tourism research was slow and fragmented. A basic signifier of mobility is displacement, i.e. movement from A to B. Nevertheless, mobility is far more than displacement. Mobility can be defined based on the contrast with steadiness as "a kind of blank space that stands as an alternative to place, boundedness, foundations, and stability." (Cresswell 2006, p. 2). Indeed, mobility not only "describes the idea of an act of displacement that allows people to move between locations": it also considers "the type, strategies and social implications of that movement" (Cresswell 2006, pp. 2–3). Therefore, mobility in this dissertation is defined as displacement imbued with *meaning* and *power*: a "socially produced motion" (Cresswell 2006, pp. 2–3). The difference between mobility and transport lies in the embedded meanings and power relations that make

2.2 Tourist Mobility and Transport

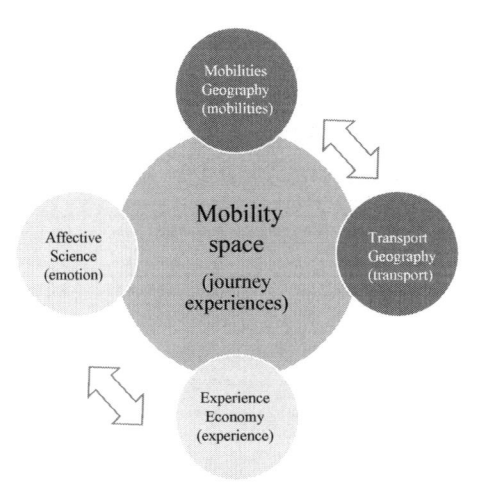

Fig. 2.1 Streams of literature considered for the theoretical framework (own elaboration)

transport work as a tool to enable displacement (Egger-Jenzer 2013), rather than as a signifier of it. A second difference lies in the hypothetical—more than performed—nature of displacement embedded in the idea of mobility. "Mobility is a property of things and of people", argues Urry (2007, p. 7): mobility is potential displacement in hypothetical spaces, whereas transport is real displacement in concrete spaces (Canzler and Knie 2002). Assessing the experiential value of mobility means, therefore, investigating the individual and subjective components of transport, although still relating them to a concrete asset of technical and technological transport settings.

After two decades of academic research by tourism scholars in the tourist mobility field, two main approaches stand out in academic writings to assess mobility: transport geography—a system-based and policy driven approach—and the new mobilities geography—a movement-based and experience driven approach (Shaw and Hesse 2010; Delaney 2016). Mobilities research is often understood as being in antagonism to transport geography, because "geographical knowledge often assumes a stable point of view, a world of places and boundaries and territories rooted in time and bounded in space" (Cresswell and Merriman 2016, p. 4). Conversely, mobilities research uses a dynamic perspective and attempts to establish a "a movement-driven social science" (Urry 2007, p. 18), which then applies to anthropology, cultural studies, geography, transport studies, sociology, etc.

Shaw and Hesse (2010), although acknowledging the main differences in mobilities and transport geography approaches, highlight that the perception of the two approaches as mutually exclusive is not appropriate: they have "exploitable commonalities" (p. 310) and should be perceived as two extremes of one same continuum, where a common agenda for future research brings "more to the study of movement overall" (p. 310). In the following sections, the main features of both approaches are presented to form a common basis of knowledge for the analysis of journey experiences of this dissertation. Table 2.1 introduces them.

Table 2.1 Similarities and differences among transport and mobilities geography (own elaboration based on Cresswell 2006; Hannam et al. 2006; Shaw and Hesse 2010; Tolley and Turton 1995; Urry 2007)

	Transport geography	Mobilities geography
Definition	A sub-discipline of geography concerned about the study of the spatial aspects of transport	A "movement-driven social science" (Urry 2007, p. 18)
Object of research	Transport	Mobilities
Core elements	Transport systems (networks, nodes and demand)	Multisensuous experiences (embodiment, kinaesthetics), negotiation in motion, materialities (objects and technologies), scapes and rhythms
Understanding of space	Space is a constraint for the construction of transportation networks and is referred to using distance and time (quantitative approach)	Space is a social flow, constructed by individuals in their interactions with the *spatial fix* (qualitative approach)
Understanding of travel	Travel is an opportunity cost	Travel is a gift
Understanding of the traveller	The traveller is a "rational mobile person" (Shaw 2012, p. 128)	The traveller is a bundle of senses that encounter objects and the physical world multi-sensuously.
Research agenda	Industry- and policy-driven (mostly supply-related)	Market- and experience-driven (mostly demand-related)

2.2.1 On Site: Transport Geography and the Tourist Transport System

Transport geography is a sub-discipline of geography, emerging in the second half of the twentieth century from economic geography. Adopting a restrictive definition, transport geography refers to "the study of the spatial aspects of transportation", including "the location, structure, environment and development of networks as well as the analysis and explanation of the interaction or movement of goods and people" (Goetz et al. 2004, p. 221). Transport geography is mainly aimed at understanding how to deal with the displacement of goods and services within a transportation system, in order to match demand and supply needs (Knowles et al. 2009).

Based on these key concepts, two aspects of the link between transport and geography have traditionally attracted the attention of transport geographers: the *geography of transport systems* and the *impact of transport on the distribution of social and economic activity* (Knowles et al. 2009). Both of them have been conceptually applied to the tourism context in the second half of the 20th century (Prideaux 2000; Kaul

1985; Miossec 1977), opening up a new and wide research agenda on accessibility as a powerful factor affecting and explaining destination development (e.g., Prideaux 2000; Bieger and Wittmer 2006; O'Connor 1995; Papatheodorou 2002; Rey et al. 2011).

Apart from these two core issues, a third main concern of transport geography was applied to tourism: the transport sectors' *contribution to global warming* (Knowles et al. 2009). This contribution was analysed and quantified firstly in the tourism and transport fields separately, and only later was it studied specifically from the tourism transport perspective. Transport's contribution to climate change was acknowledged worldwide in the late 1980s thanks to a series of scientific papers presented at the 1989 meeting of the European Conference of Ministers of Transport (ECMT) (Knowles et al. 2009). Ten years later, the UN Intergovernmental Panel on Climate Change (IPCC) Special Report on Climate Change and Aviation (Penner et al. 1999) was an important milestone in recognising transport's contribution to greenhouse gas (GHG) emissions; nevertheless, tourism was only marginally addressed as a possible contributor to transport's impacts, mainly because it was responsible for increases in travel demand. At the same time, but in a separate field, the sectoral contribution of tourism as a whole to climate change was also slowly being assessed worldwide. Scott and Becken (2010) provide an overview of the sectoral engagement of tourism scholars with climate change issues and identify the pioneering work by Wall et al. (1986) as the first contribution discussing the idea of tourism-driven climate change. But it was believed that tourism played a marginal role in the climate change discourse until at least 1995, when a lack of tourism-related knowledge was mentioned in the Second Assessment Report of the UN IPCC. To fill this gap, the first international conference on climate change and tourism was organized by UNWTO in 2003, where the *Djerba Declaration on Climate Change and Tourism* was signed. Sector-specific analyses on transport-related tourism impacts developed accordingly in later years (Becken et al. 2003; Peeters and Dubois 2010; Peeters et al. 2004, 2007) and a Special Issue on tourism transport was published by the *Journal of Sustainable Tourism* (JOST, Volume 14, Issue 2 of 2006, entitled: "Transport and Tourism. The Sustainability Dilemma"), merging the transport and the tourism sector under the common domain of sustainability. That Special Issue was followed almost immediately by JOST (14), 4, entitled "Tourism and its Interactions with Climate Change".

Applying transport modelling techniques and impact analysis, seminal works were produced to quantify and project flows and impacts related to tourist transport at the EU and global level (Peeters et al. 2004, 2007; Peeters 2017). Moreover, based on the three international workshops on tourist transport in the Black Forest of Freiburg, Germany (https://www.cstt.nl/freiburg2016), further Special Issues of JOST were published (Volume 21, Issue 7 of 2013, entitled "Psychological and Behavioral Approaches to Understanding and Governing Sustainable Mobility"; Volume 24, Issue 3 of 2016, entitled "Implementing sustainable mobility: bridging the science-policy gap"; and finally was Volume 27, Issue 2 of 2019, entitled "Desirable Tourism Transport Futures").

Along this process of tourism-transport integration under the common framework of sustainability (Scuttari et al. 2013), the application of transport geography to tourism was shaped by at least three main (text)books: *Transport and Tourism: Global Perspectives* by Stephen Page, first published in 1999 with multiple reprints; *Tourism and transport: Modes, networks and flows* by Duval (2007); and *Tourism and Transport: Issues and Agenda for the New Millennium*, edited by Lumsdon and Page (2004). These important milestones in tourism transport literature set—together with JOST Special Issues—the basis for the definition of the so-called *tourist transport system*. The following sub-sections will first provide a definition of the most important conceptual features of transport geography and later define the tourist transport system.

2.2.1.1 Transport Demand and Supply

Transport supply is "the expression of the capacity of transportation infrastructures and modes, generally over a geographically defined transport system and for a specific period of time" (Rodrigue et al. 2006, p. 54). It is expressed in terms of infrastructures (capacity), services (frequencies) and networks (hubs). Conversely, transport demand corresponds to the "expression of the transport needs" (Rodrigue et al. 2006, pp. 54–55), both those performed in reality and the potential ones. In the framework of transport geography, transport demand is assumed to be ancillary to the (economic or leisure) activities generating it, thereby it is treated (directly or indirectly) as derived demand. Passengers' volumes are the units of transport demand and are usually measured in terms of passenger-km, i.e. people per unit of time and space. Apart from the interplay of demand and supply, at least three additional concepts are crucial to framing the discipline of transport geography: transportation networks, transportation modes and the topological interpretation of space.

2.2.1.2 Transport Networks and Modes in the Topological Space

Transportation networks (or systems) are "the framework of routes within a system of locations, identified as nodes. A route is a single link between two nodes that are part of a larger network" (Rodrigue et al. 2006, p. 47). Each transport network is conceptualised as a system and is displayed by applying system theories (Bertalanffy 1968; Luhmann 1984). System theories rely on the definition of a system as "an integrated whole whose essential properties arise from the relationships between its constituent parts" and with the surrounding environment (Hall 2008a, p. 57). A system comprises: (a) a set of elements (sometimes called entities); (b) a set of relationships between the elements; and (c) a set of relationships between those elements and the environment (Hall 2008a, p. 57). Systems are embedded within other systems, therefore it is crucial to understand the scale at which we conceive system analysis—the so-called resolution level—and to define the boundaries of the system itself—normally set according to the problem to be solved. This means that transport networks can be abstracted through a composition of nodes (terminals/hubs) and edges (routes), at a certain scale. This interpretation of transport networks helps exemplify network complexity and allow for a clear representation of it through graph theory. Transport networks have a specific topology referring to their structure, based on network geometry and levels of connectivity. Finally, transport networks (and also their edges) have a physical capacity, corresponding to the volume of traffic they can support under normal conditions. The "load" of a network/edge "is the relation between the existing volume and the capacity. The closer it is to a full load (ratio of 1), the more congested it is." (Rodrigue et al. 2006, p. 51).

Transportation modes are the components of the transport system that allow people to achieve mobility. Each mode has its own specific features, but they tend to be grouped in three types, corresponding to the surfaces they are travelling over: land (road, rail and pipelines), water (shipping) and air (Rodrigue et al. 2006). The approaches to assess the role of transport modes in transport geography keep a predominantly classical spatial perspective (Knowles et al. 2009), whereas the focus on travel modes as experience-creators is still limited (Larsen 2001). For example, the following conceptualisation of the ideal transport mode excludes completely the experiential and social value of undirected travelling, reducing travel to a mere (direct or indirect) derived travel demand.

> The ideal transport mode would be instantaneous, free, have an unlimited capacity and always be available. It would render space obsolete. This is obviously not the case. Space is a constraint for the construction of transport networks. Transportation appears to be an economic activity different from the others. It trades space with time and thus money. (translated from Merlin 1992 by Rodrigue et al. 2006, p. 1)

In transport geography, geographical space located between two nodes is interpreted as a constraint to transportation systems in terms of modal choice set, service, costs and capacities (Rodrigue et al. 2006). Space is thereby an *obstacle* to overcome through displacement and it is bi- or three-dimensional depending on the mode of transport. Topography, hydrography and climate are the basic spatial constraints of the terrestrial space that can develop into absolute barriers (representing an obstacle that prevents movement, e.g. a river for ground transport) or relative barriers (geographical features that cause friction on movements, e.g. mountain ranges).

2.2.1.3 The Tourist Transport System

The tourist transport system was conceptualized based on the common approach of system theories (Bertalanffy 1968; Luhmann 1984) applied both in transport geography (White and Senior 1991; Tolley and Turton 1995; Fincham et al. 2010) and in tourism geography (Leiper 1990; Mill and Morrison 2013). As explained above, transport systems refer mainly to three aspects: infrastructure, operational services, and travel demand (Mills and Andrey 2002; Rodrigue et al. 2006). Further aspects such as historical development patterns, technological settings, economic, political and social factors also shape the transport system, but they are not at the core of geographical approaches to transport (White and Senior 1991). Moving on to tourism systems, they are conceptualized considering four basic elements: the generating region, the transit region or route, the destination region and finally the environment (Leiper 1990). Apart from these basic structures, several other elements such as landscape, culture, languages, and other facilities form part of the tourism system, even though they are not especially created or produced for tourists (Hall 2008a). The two theorizations of tourism and transport systems are so similar, that a systems approach to describe tourist transport is straightforward.

The tourist transport system is defined as "a framework which embodies the entire tourist experience of travelling on a particular form of transport" to or within a tourist destination (Page 2008, p. 19). It combines the transport and the tourism perspective and can be defined as "the physical movement of visitors using one or more forms of transport—the logistical component—and the travel experience—the experiential component" (Scuttari et al. 2013, p. 615). The logistical includes the infrastructure and the operational aspects of transport, e.g. the routes and hubs, the modes of transport and the flows. For instance, the routes include arterial roads and internal distribution, pedestrian paths, and specialized trails (e.g. bike and hiking trails) (Berardi 2007). The means of transport, can, in some cases, be the place where an entire holiday is spent, e.g. cruises or heritage railways with sleeping car trains (Page 2008). Flows generated on communication routes by different means of transport define different mobility forms:

> transit or access flows are the direct flows between origin and destination regions; internal (or intra-destination) mobility is the tourist movement in the destination during a holiday; travel itineraries are a sort of imaginary travel chain, where different means of transport are linked to one another (Schiefelbusch et al. 2007). Junctions or hubs—the locations where tourists change from one means of transport to another—play a fundamental role in travel itineraries and allow the development of intermodal travel, i.e. the use of multiple means of transport. (Scuttari et al. 2013, p. 616)

Over the years, the framework of the tourist transport system has been a valid background for traffic impact assessments (Peeters et al. 2004, 2007; Scuttari et al. 2013, 2019). The concept of the tourist transport system was applied in transport and tourism geography through the study of travel patterns and itineraries (Lew and McKercher 2002, 2006). Later on, the "mobilities turn" and the deeper consideration of the experiential component of transport have required new and more qualitative approaches to assess tourist mobility (Urry and Larsen 2011).

2.2.1.4 Tourists' Travel Patterns and Itineraries

The understanding of spatial patterns of tourist flows across space interested many tourism scholars, although with few reference to tourists' subjectivities, perceptions and interactions. The approach allows the creation of typologies of travel patterns. For instance, according to Flognfeldt (2005) tourist's trips can be: day trips (daily visits to attractions), resort trips (home to/from resort trips with no movement in the destination), base holiday trips (daily visits within the destination starting from the accommodation facility), round trips (circular routes from multiple accommodation facilities), passing through (linear) trips. Lew and McKercher (2006) further study itinerary patterns within a destination. Similarly to the typologies of Flognfeldt (2005), they propose to distinguish between point-to-point travel patterns (including single point-to-point, repetitive point-to-point and touring point-to-point), circular patterns (including circular loop and stem and petal) and finally complex patterns (including random exploratory and radiating hub). They further introduce a territorial classification of travel patterns, which indicates the different inclination of the individual to explore the surrounding space.

This recalls the more recent analyses of tourists' movement patterns by Zakrisson and Zillinger (2012) developed with modern Global Positioning System (GPS) technology and explaining how visitors can be grouped in clusters according to their attitudes towards discovering space. Lew and McKercher (2006) acknowledge that multiple factors can affect the choice of a travel route, related to both the transport system and the tourist. For instance, place knowledge, time budgets, personality types, and travel motivations are among the factors that influence the route selection and, consequently, the patterns of movement of a tourist in space. Based on this assumption, Lew and McKercher point out that transportation geography is not enough to explain tourist's mobility:

> The transportation geography of a place could be a sufficient planning tool if all tourists shared the same interests and sought to optimize their visits in the same way. However, their actual behavior in a destination can vary considerably, even if they might happen to share common motivations. (Lew and McKercher 2006, p. 408)

In doing so, the authors indirectly prepared the ground for mobilities geography, as explained below (see Sect. 2.2.2).

2.2.2 On the Move: The New Mobilities Geography

The new mobilities geography can work as a theoretical and methodological answer to the investigation of a more qualitative dimension for tourism mobility, but its importance for contemporary literature and practice goes far beyond just the tourism transport sector. Therefore, a brief outline of the key concepts related to the *new mobilities paradigm* is introduced in this section, and the relationship between mobilities and transport geography is explained as a second step.

The *new mobilities paradigm* is a paradigm shift introduced by Sheller and Urry in 2006, encompassing several disciplines within the social sciences: anthropology, cultural studies, geography, migration studies, science and technology studies, tourism and transport studies, and sociology. The *new mobilities paradigm* emerges as a critique of existing approaches to social science and it identifies a compromise between traditional "sedentarist" approaches and post-modern approaches assuming relentless change (Bauman 2000):

> both 'sedentarist' approaches […] that treat place, stability and dwelling as a natural steady-state, and 'deterritorialized' approaches that posit a new 'grand narrative' of mobility, fluidity or liquidity as a pervasive condition of postmodernity or globalization. (Hannam et al. 2006, p. 5)

As a response to these approaches, Hannam et al. (2006) introduce a new framework to analyse contemporary societies, assuming that objects, media, technologies and information are interrelated and "on the move" and therefore require "a movement driven social science" to be assessed (Urry 2007, p. 18). Applying theoretical frameworks borrowed from the socio-spatial theory of space by Lefebvre (1991), the *new mobilities paradigm* expands both on the concept of mobility and on the methods that could be used to analyse "issues of movement" (Sheller and Urry 2006, p. 208), as explained below. This is the point where the analysis of transport develops into a study of mobilities.

According to the *new mobilities paradigm*, mobility is far more than displacement from A to B: it is rather a constructive framework for modern society (Shaw and Hesse 2010). The concept of mobilities incorporates "both the large-scale movements of people, objects, capital and information across the world, as well as the more local processes of daily transportation, movement through public space and the travel of material things within everyday life" (Hannam et al. 2006, p. 1). More precisely, according to Urry (2007) the multiple mobilites to be assessed through this new paradigm are: (a) *corporeal travel,* both for business and for leisure, and with regular or occasional patterns; (b) *physical movement of objects*, for commercial or individual purposes; (c) *imaginative travel*, achieved in form of imaginative journeys inspired by print and visual media; (d) *communicative travel,* happening through traditional or digital media with the aim to exchange information; and finally (e) *virtual travel*, enabling Virtual Reality (VR) trips without physical displacement. Mobilities is explained and analysed as a "complex assemblage" (Urry 2007, p. 48) of these real or virtual displacements, as well as their individual and social meanings, and their links to the "spatial fix" (Williams 2013, p. 522). The paradigm shift introduced by the new mobilities turn affects not only theoretical approaches, but also methodological strategies in social sciences: based on the new mobilities paradigm, a wide range of methods was developed under the common name of mobile methods (Fincham et al. 2010; Buscher and Urry 2009). Mobile methods are the methodological innovation introduced by the new mobilities paradigm and they generally describe "any attempt to physically or metaphorically follow people/objects/ideas in order to support analysis of the experience/content/doing of, and interconnections between, immobility/mobility/flows/networks" (Spinney 2015, pp. 36–42). Further details on the application of mobile methods in mobilities studies is provided in Chap. 3, Sect. 3.4.

Within transport studies, the new mobilities paradigm was theoretically interpreted as a contrasting approach to tourism geography (Cresswell and Merriman 2016), but in practice it seemed to help "unpack" transport networks and systems traditionally developed in transport geography and concentrate the attention on "flows and spaces, to reveal nuanced or counterintuitive qualities of transport" (Knowles et al. 2009, p. 6). Due to this cross-disciplinary relationship, Shaw and Hesse (2010) understand mobilities geography more as a complementary than a substitutive approach to transport geography: the policy-driven research agenda of geographers should merge with the more experiential driven approach of mobilities geographers. This could encourage researchers both to broaden the disciplinary boundaries of transport geography and to explore the practical implications of mobilities geography.

It should be noticed here that the study of movement in geography is by no means new, but how movement is studied makes the difference across the two perspectives. For instance, transport geographers generally focussed on a "rational mobile person" displacing through nodes and networks between places (Shaw 2012, p. 128). Mobility geographers address bodily sensations, affective appraisals, emotional states while travelling and constructing space. Travel time in traditional approaches is conventionally referred to as a mere *opportunity cost* where the actual practices, spaces, subjects and meanings of movement are mostly neglected. Conversely, the mobilities geography problematizes the interpretation of travel time as an *opportunity cost* and suggests that time might be potentially a *gift* for passengers (Lyons et al. 2007). Policy implications deriving from this time-shift are relevant: high quality becomes more important than high speed, if travel time is a gift. The example of travel time shift shows how the mobilities geography is filling a gap in traditional transport geography, by addressing the framework conditions behind movement, the practices, spaces and subjects of movement, the experiential value of displacement, and finally its social, economic and political implications (Shaw and Hesse 2010; Shaw 2012). Mobilities geography and its discourse has also entered the tourism transport field with a dedicated special issue of JOST (Volume 21, Issue 4, entitled "Mobilities and Sustainable Tourism"), setting a first milestone to address qualitative and non-utilitarian aspects of travel.

The future research agenda in mobilities research addresses the analysis of the relation between mobility systems and infrastructural moorings—the so-called *spatial fix* (Williams 2013, p. 522)—and the investigation of visible and non-visible activities happening *on the move*—while travelling (Lyons and Urry 2005; Hannam et al. 2006; Jensen 2010). Related to this research fields, what has been termed "non-representational theory" (NRT) helps understand the "significance of practice and doing in the construction of meanings and networks. [...] NRT is concerned with phenomena—such as sensory and affective experience—that 'overflow' our ability to apprehend and represent them through language" (Spinney 2015, pp. 232). NRT is offering a new approach to develop mobile methods, capable of acquiring data on the move.

To better understand the new mobilities paradigm and its shades, the notions of space, place, embodiment and motion are introduced in the following sub-sections.

2.2.2.1 Space and Place

Space and place are two keystones of geography, but their meanings have varied across time and sub-disciplines (Shields 2006). Both space and place are crucial elements in the mobilities geography and therefore need some additional clarification in this work. A first remark is necessary here to compare the transport geography approach and mobilities geography: if transport geographers have limited their appreciation of space to a quantitative approach based on distance and time, mobilities theorists have introduced a notion of space as a qualitative context where multiple behaviours and actions take place (Shields 2006).

Cooper (2008) identifies two main lines of spatial thought: the *poetics of space*, which emerges out of Heideggerian phenomenology; and the *production of space*, which is based on the Marxist cultural analysis of Henri Lefebvre. The main distinguishing factor between the two is that Heidegger (1927) identifies the roots of place in dwelling—i.e. in the fixity and stability of the so-called *Dasein-*, whereas Lefebvre focusses on the dynamic and multi-layered nature of space. Lefevbre's line of thought inspires the new mobilities paradigm and is further explained here.

Lefebvre in his essay *The production of space* argues that "[s]pace is not a static container, but the network of relations that composes a block of space-time" (Mommersteeg 2014, pp. 2–3). Space is a mental and material product, "conceived not as a completed reality or an abstract totality, but as a set of possibilities in the process of being realized" (Lefebvre 1991, p. 134). In this sense, Lefebvre "gives space an agency of its own" (Mommersteeg 2014, p. 8), because space shapes de facto the possibility to act.

> [A]ctivity in space is restricted by that space; space 'decides' what activity may occur, but even this 'decision' has limits placed upon it. Space lays down the law because it implies a certain order — and hence also a certain disorder [...]. Space commands bodies, prescribing or proscribing gestures, routes and distances. (Lefebvre 1991, p. 143)

Space is further explained through three dialectically interconnected dimensions: *spatial practice* (everyday social practices, routines), *representation of space* (abstract knowledge or discourses about space constructed by professionals) and *spaces of representation* (space as it is lived) (Lefebvre 1991, pp. 38–39). A binary distinction between subjectivity and materialities is therefore not given in this theory of space, thanks to the conceptualisation of the third space, i.e. the space where subjectivity and objectivity, abstract and concrete meet (Saar and Palang 2009).

If space is a social flow, then place in Lefevbre's theories is defined as the momentary suspension of this social flow (Vermeulen 2015). According to his dialectically materialist thought, place is where the perceived-conceived-lived triad of space gets concrete and tangible, it is a moment in and of space. Lefevbre's socio-spatial theory is rooted in Michel de Certeau's post-structuralist theory of "space as a 'practiced place'" (Certeau 1984, p. 117) and it inspired later conceptualisations, e.g. Tuan's according to which "if we think of space as that which allows movement, then place is pause; each pause in movement makes it possible for location to be transformed into place" (Tuan 1977, p. 6). It is also argued that sometimes places can act as important markers in people's lives, acquiring particular meanings "through significant experiences (trauma, loss) and through the experiences of change and transition (moving)" (Saar and Palang 2009, p. 11). Hillier and Hanson, who contextualised the Lefevbrian notion of space to the built (and not to the social) environment (Hillier et al. 1976) also argued that mobility can work as a co-creator of place, analysed as a network of choices within a spatial environment.

The new mobilities paradigm builds upon the Lefevbrian discourse on spatiality and directly assesses the post-Lefebvrian spatial theorists (Soja 2009), as well as those focussing on the relationality and circulation of objects (Pyyhtinen 2010; Latour 1992). Both streams of thought help to move beyond bipolar logics of material and immaterial, mobile and immobile, as described by (Hannam et al. 2006, p. 13):

> The emerging mobilities paradigm argues against the ontology of distinct 'places' and 'people'. [...] the places travelled to depend in part upon what is practised within them (Gogia 2004). [...] Places are thus not so much fixed but are implicated within complex networks by which 'hosts, guests, buildings, objects and machines' are contingently brought together to produce certain performances in certain places at certain times. [...] Places are indeed dynamic—'places of movement' according to Hetherington (1997). Places are like ships, moving around and not necessarily staying in one location. In the emerging mobilities paradigm, places themselves can be seen as becoming or traveling, slowly or quickly, through greater or shorter distances and within networks of both human and non-human agents. Places are about relationships, about the placing of peoples, materials, images and the systems of difference that they perform. We understand 'where' we are through 'vision in motion' (Büscher 2006) practiced through the alignment of material objects, maps, images and a moving gaze (see also Kaplan 2006).

Places are like ships because they are on the move, but they are still based on a dynamic dialectic between material and immaterial, not necessarily staying in one place. The mobilities geography introduces therefore the possibility of a *dwelling-in-motion* and thereby questions the Heideggerian interpretation of place as dwelling. Places remain instantaneous and contingent expressions of space, but are not interpreted as only as *pauses*, but also as moving flows.

2.2.2.2 Embodiment, Sensory Perceptions and Kinaesthetic Sensation

Research within mobilities geography studies the embodied nature of travel experience (Hannam et al. 2006), comparing different modes of travel both as "forms of material and sociable dwelling-in-motion" (Sheller and Urry 2006, p. 214), and as real places where various activities are performed (see e.g., Veijola and Jokinen 1994; Crouch 2000; Featherstone 2016). Automobility (Featherstone 2016) and aeromobility (Urry 2007) have received the most attention so far, but cycling is raising scholars' interests (Brown and Spinney 2010; Delaney 2016; Spinney 2009, 2011), as well, particularly because of the importance of embodiment and kinaesthetics. Embodiment is defined as "the way in which the body experiences, perceives and engages in the world" (Delaney 2016, p. 33). Journey experiences, and particularly those where riding is required, are therefore unique because they actively involve bodies in generating or controlling movement. Given this connection between embodiment and sensations, journey experiences are difficult to observe from an external point of view: they are about the non-visible, the immaterial and the internal aspects connected to the body governing movement across space. They are *glimpses* and *breaths* (Spinney 2011; Brown and Spinney 2010), subjective experiences, feelings and sensations (Adey 2010), they are connected to motion, but transcend the observation of displacement as simple motion from A to B. They are multi-sensory, subjective and dynamic experiences on the move.

> The body is a bundle of senses that encounter objects and the physical world multi-sensuously. […] In particular, the body senses as it moves. Bodies are endowed with kinesthetics, the sixth sense which informs one of what the body is doing in space through the sensation of movement registered in the body's joints, muscles, tendons and so on. Especially important in that sense of movement, […] is that of touch, of the hands as on a rock-face but especially of the feet as people move in and over nature. (Urry 2001, p. 243)

Exploring the act of moving itself (Adey 2010) provides interesting information about the sensory and kinaesthetic sensations associated to different means of transport. According to Taylor (2016), who analysed the perceived traffic in urban areas, the experience of traffic is multisensory, kinaesthetic and vicarious. It is multisensory because all senses (with limited involvement of taste) are involved in the perception of space and movement and help evaluate them. It is kinaesthetic because it is usually perceived as a flowing and dynamic combination of sight and touch (and a minor contribution of sounds and smells) on the move. Finally, it is vicarious because usually the concentration of the subject that is moving is directed to the action of moving, riding or driving, and to the path, whereas the perception of the "other", the surrounding world, is often incidental. Therefore, when describing driving or riding experiences a distinction is made between main tasks—related to the "physical and/or mental resources to execute different kinds of driving tasks" (Rodrick et al. 2013, p. 560)—and secondary tasks—often related to the use of technology. The sensory experience of traffic is also different based on the perspective of users: the point of view and the perceptions inside motor vehicles are significantly other than the ones of those outside the motor vehicles, e.g. walking or cycling activities (Taylor 2016). Differences occur also among non-motorised means of transport: cycling stimulates more kinaesthetic senses, while walking seems to activate more the visual senses (Edensor 2010; Spinney 2009, 2011). Finally, speed is also mediating perceptions: at faster speeds, the angle of vision of drivers narrows down and concentrates mostly on points of decision (Taylor 2016). Depending on the spatial setting, on the type of mobile activity and also on speed, individuals can perceive also situations of "sensory overload" (Delaney 2016, p. 35), to which they might react by "filtering" substantial information (Kellerman 2006, p. 44).

Once again, sensory data is intermediated through "the corporeal body as an affective vehicle" (Sheller and Urry 2006, p. 216) and is by no means objective, but rather cognitively processed and influenced by the contingent situation and the process of displacement. Some additional factors also affect sensory data perception: technical knowledge on transport means, expectations about traffic, and socio-cultural characteristics (Taylor 2016). Nevertheless, even acknowledging the subjective nature of sensory perceptions, there is evidence that the same sensory material processed by different subjects is not completely different: there is rather a common perceptual ground with individual and subjective shades (Taylor 2016).

Kinaesthetic and perceptual experiences, as well as cognitive capacities are important for individuals to sense and understand space and develop spatial abilities (Tuan 1977). This is particularly interesting in the tourism context, where the spatial practice is oriented to the discovery of geographical locations mostly unknown to visitors, but at the same time packaged and prepared by tourism managers to facilitate their consumption, the *touristscapes* (Edensor 2007).

2.2.2.3 Materialities and Scapes

The concept of materiality by Latour (1992) introduces the need to address the "nonhuman" elements in social interactions, including objects as crucial aspects of socio-technical systems. He argues that "artefacts can be deliberately designed to both replace human action and constrain and shape the actions of other humans" (Latour 1992, p. 151). Thereby, materiality, together with embodiment, helps describe the ways in which "things"—e.g. objects, equipment—affect journey experiences.

According to Spinney et al. (2015, p. 334), the interaction between objects or technologies and humans in motion defines "socio-technical processes and systems", which need to be addressed to explain mobilities. Objects—e.g. traffic lights (Hornsey 2010), safety technology tools (Spinney et al. 2015) or even walking boots (Michael 2000), affect bodily perception of space and sometimes can reshape information and influence human action. The interaction of bodies and materialities also produces rhythmical patterns while on the move, which is addressed in more detail in the next section. The way objects and artefacts can limit and shape human actions, as well as generate rhythms is evident in this example by Latour (1992, pp. 151–152):

> Early this morning, I was in a bad mood and decided to break a law and start my car without buckling my seat belt. My car usually does not want to start before I buckle the belt. It first flashes a red light "FASTEN YOUR SEAT BELT!," then an alarm sounds; it is so high pitched, so relentless, so repetitive, that I cannot stand it. After ten seconds I swear and put on the belt. […T]his assembly of a driver and a car obeys the law in such a way that it is impossible for a car to be at the same time moving AND to have the driver without the belt on. A *law of the excluded middle* has been built, rendering logically inconceivable as well as morally unbearable a driver without a seat belt.

Several layers can be used to analyse human interactions with the "nonhuman". Within this example, personification is used rhetorically to describe the car as a human being, who is caring for the driver's safety conditions and is pushing the driver towards a kind of "assembly", which in turn causes the emergence of a "law", the "law of the excluded middle". The design of the object, indeed, is shaping its users' minds and forcing their behaviour.

A further example of an object that can influence human behaviour at different levels is the one of walking boots for hikers (Michael 2000). Walking boots are far more than objects, but rather mediators of the meaning of the journey experience. They can be looked at mechanically—as instruments in which to walk—, or socially—as tools to express a specific social identity, or even as technological means of damage to nature (Michael 2000).

Finally, information processing technologies are even more powerful in shaping journey experience, since they can distort space-time perception and therefore influence behaviour significantly. For instance, safety technology systems on HGVs

(Heavy Goods Vehicles) shape the interactions between HGV drivers and cyclist, introducing new information useful to increase safety.

Technology and objects, indeed, are not just "innocent mediums": they rather shape the dynamics of interactions and mobile experiences (Latour 1992). Their influence on individuals and societies is such that behavioural changes in mobility can be encouraged or restrained by the *spatial fix* (Williams 2013, p. 522). Spatial, infrastructural and institutional moorings shape space and time through rhythms, i.e. "networks of machines, technologies, organisations, texts and actors, constitute scapes: various interconnected nodes along which the flows can be relayed. Such scapes reconfigure the dimensions of time and space" (Urry 2000, p. 36).

2.2.2.4 Encounters and Negotiations in Space

Journey experiences are "hybrid systems made up of different processes involving: objects, technologies, and socialities" (Sheller and Urry 2006, p. 214). The analysis of socialities includes encounters and negotiations in space and provides an additional layer from which to explore interactions. Two main issues besides verbal interaction are crucial in the encounters while on the move: corporeal tactics (Symes 2013) of negotiation in motion (Jensen 2010) and tactics of self-presentation (Delaney 2016). Corporeal tactics of negotiation in motion—such as the continuous selection of routes in overcrowded areas or the nonverbal signals among subjects in motion—are important signs of interaction, because in mobile encounters there are often no words exchanged, no obvious interactions taking place, but rather body gestures, nonverbal language or facial expressions (Delaney 2016). To explore this type of interactions, (Seamon 1979) developed the *awareness continuum*, which describes different intensities of mobile encounters. He argues that individuals have different inclinations to engage or not engage in an interaction. Therefore, his scale of possible encounters encompasses multiple levels: obliviousness, watching, noticing, heightened contact, basic contact, and at-homeness. Jensen (2010), observing flows of traffic in the urban setting of Aalborg, conceptualized three types of meeting between street users: frontal meetings, orthogonal meetings, and parallel meetings (typically, overtaking). Corporeal tactics to manage these meetings are expressed in the form of movement patterns and facial expressions, and can be seen as more than movements: they are rather complex choreographies in space performed to avoid contacts between bodies or vehicles on the move (Symes 2013; Jensen 2010).

The concepts of *personal space* and *use space* introduced by Goffman (1972, pp. 29–35) offer a powerful perspective to understand these spatial negotiations in constrained spaces. *Personal space* "is the space surrounding an individual, anywhere within which an entering by others causes the individual to feel encroached upon", whereas *use space* is "the territory immediately around or in front of an individual, his claim to which is respected because of apparent instrumental needs" (Goffman 1972, pp. 29–35). These spaces are not objectively determined: they are perceived by individuals in relationship to the perception of self, the speed and the intruding object (Delaney 2016). For instance, cyclists vary their route around pedestrians depending on their speed, keeping more distance if they travel quicker and less distance if their speed is low.

Negotiations and encounters in space vary also according to tactics of individuals' self-presentation, since once again the nonverbal language is prevailing on the verbal language, especially for those motorised vehicles where individuals are isolated in their cabin. Therefore, in a sort of dramaturgical performance on the road, drivers and riders act like characters and they express themselves through clothing, positions, attitudes, that reveal their identity without the need of verbal interaction (Delaney 2016). Walking boots or the uniform of a cyclist, for instance, can both work as technical equipment and identity markers, since they express individual lifestyle and community belonging.

Finally, verbal interactions in encounters among mobile individuals are possible in some particular modes of transport, e.g. cycling, where there is no physical barrier to communication through cabins or equipment. Encounters between cyclists can happen by chance or even by intention, but they have in common the fact that they express the concept of being *mobile with*, i.e. being mobile in a group (Jensen 2010, p. 341). As argued by McIlvenny (2014, p. 137) "[c]ycling is not just a skilled accomplishment by individual cyclists, it can also be social." From side-by-side arrangements to the so-called Vélomobile Formations-in-action (or velo-formations)—i.e. "specific arrangements of bodies on bikes and configurations of a 'vélomobile with'" (McIlvenny 2014, p. 137)—, different spatial configurations of cyclists in road space are possible and are negotiated with respect to each other's cycling abilities and to the current environment (Oldenburg 2015). Even if cyclists engage in real verbal conversations, several nonverbal micro-interactions still shape their encounters: "For example a negotiation of space when trying to pass another cyclist; for example, a mutual, silent appreciation of each other's bicycle; or, for example, a demonstration of physical stamina when overtaking someone else with high speed on an upward slope" (Oldenburg 2015, p. 9).

2.2.2.5 Rhythm and Flow

Based on individual elaborations of spatio-temporal world, the so-called rhythmanalysis (Lefebvre 2004) studies the relatedness between time and space in life, and between motion and its interruption in journey experiences. Indeed, if the uninterrupted sensory experience of motion—the flow—is typically pleasing, the constant interruption of forward movement is typically felt as displeasing and frustrating (Taylor 2016). The analysis of rhythms goes in pair with the Lefebvrian notion of space as a product of interaction—and not an empty container. Rhythmanalysis is, therefore, an attempt to include the dimension of time in the above mentioned conceptualisation of Lefebvrian space (Lefebvre 2004). Several contradicting concepts can help understand rhythm according to Lefevbre: repetition versus difference, mechanical versus organic, discovery versus creation, cyclical versus linear, continuous versus discontinuous, and finally quantitative versus qualitative. "Rhythm appears as regulated time, governed by rational laws, but in contact with what is least rational in human being: the lived, the carnal, the body" (Lefebvre 2004, p. 9). Lefebvre asserts how the everyday life is based on intersecting rhythms, including isorhythmic (repetitive), arhythmical (irregular). Bodies normally present numerous rhythms (ear beat, breath, etc.): this is the so-called polirhythmia. When in a good state of health, they show a harmony of rhythms: eurhythmia. Rhythms have the quality of evoking a phenomenology of mobility as "simultaneously organic, lived, and endogenous and exterior, imposed, and mechanical" (Cresswell 2010, p. 24). Rhythms help designing space, as explained by Edensor and Holloway (2008, p. 485) by quoting Crang (2007, pp. 189–190):

> some long run, some short term, some frequent, some rare, some collective, some personal, some large scale, some hardly noticed—the urban [or rural] place or site is composed and characterised through patterns of these multiple beats.

By exploring the multiple rhythms of coach tourists, Edensor and Holloway (2008, p. 485) argue that "tourism is typically constituted by a blend of placed and mobile rhythms, yet so diverse are contemporary tourist practices that such rhythms are multiple, ever-changing and place and time specific" (Edensor and Holloway 2008, p. 486). Tourist rhythms might be repetitive and predictable, but can also be disorderly and disruptive (or even transgressive), depending on travel motivations and practices. Modes of transport in rhythmanalysis turn into modes of spatio-temporal ordering, since speed and style of motion work both as mediators of time and space perception, defining thereby different rhythms. Rhythms emerge in journey experiences also in relation to the external environment, where "sights and signs recur like musical notations" (Edensor and Holloway 2008, p. 488): road signs, stations, roadside embankments and other vehicles travelling are like the notes of this music, which is perceived both as soundscape and landscape by the traveller. Soundscapes—or sonic spaces—are more than a rhythm of sound within a specific environment, but rather sonorous subjects characterising a specific place, with the same richness of descriptive information as landscapes (Blesser and Salter 2007).

Further, social interactions or their absence might affect journey rhythms. According to Edensor and Holloway (2008) the drivers' or passengers' narratives and—conversely—their moments of silence stimulate different rhythms, because they activate different affectual registers by introducing an additional mediation between (visual) expectations, perceptions, and surprises. These patterns often intersect with non-tourist social rhythms, both "embodied" and natural rhythms which characterise the destination. All these rhythmic perceptions constitute the so-called "rhythmic cartographies of motorized travel" (Edensor and Holloway 2008, p. 496).

Rhythmic cartographies of motorized travel interact with the materialities around them, mainly technological settings of the transport modes and infrastructural assets of the transport network. This means that, e.g. engine capacity, suspension, speed, manoeuvrability and seat comfort of the transport mode affects human bodies' perceptions and, in their interaction with road conditions, landscapes and soundscapes, define smooth mobile rhythms or disorderly and arrhythmic disruptions. Rough/pulsed accelerations and strong/mild braking affect travellers' bodies and their kinaesthetic sensations, as well as the activities practiced on the move. Although several rhythms co-exist in one single journey experience, Edensor and Holloway (2008, p. 497) assert that the linear vehicular progress motion tends to "sensually eclipse the numerous rhythms of other mobile flows that intersect with this movement": the flow catches sensory attention, and the pauses activate other sensory perceptions.

Rythmanalysis is a powerful tool to combine spatial and temporal analysis of embodied experiences. So far, it has been only rarely applied to tourism research (Dickinson et al. 2013; Jensen et al. 2015a; Edensor 2007; Edensor and Holloway 2008) and even more rarely associated with emotional arousal.

2.3 Tourist Experiences

Mobilities geography has partly introduced the notion of experience, by addressing the individual and subjective nature of space and time perception and the multi-sensuous abilities of the human body. This section is devoted to a deeper understanding of the experience construct, particularly in the tourism field.

Experiences are the result of a set of physical, emotional, spiritual and/or intellectual impressions staged for, and subjectively perceived by, individuals (Pine and Gilmore 1999). More precisely, the word experience stands for:

> a cover-all term for the various modes through which a person knows and constructs realty. These modes range from the more direct and passive senses of smell, taste, and touch, to active visual perception and the indirect mode of symbolization. [...] Experience has a connotation of passivity [...]; Experience [...] implies the ability to learn from what one has undergone. To experience is to learn; it means acting on the given and creating out of the given. [...] Experience is the overcoming of perils. The word "experience" shares a common root (per) with "experiment", "expert" and "perilous". To experience in the active sense requires that one venture forth into the unfamiliar and experiment with the elusive and uncertain. To become an expert one must dare to confront the perils of the new (Heisenberg 1972, p. 8).

Thus, experience includes both passive and active sensing of reality, involvement and learning in unfamiliar environments. This description deeply recalls tourists' activities and perfectly fits to the tourism industry.

Pine and Gilmore's seminal proposition on the experience economy was *not* the first conceptualization of experiences in the tourism field: the tourist experience has been studied in tourism research since the 1960s (Uriely 2005) and it still has multiple embedded meanings (Neuhofer 2014). After the first conceptualisations by MacCannell (1973), and Cohen (1979), at the turn of the 21st century, the concept has been revisited, focussing on the quality, extraordinary and satisfactory nature of experiences (Csikszentmihalyi 1990; Arnould and Price 1993; Ryan 1995, 1997), as well as on their memorability (Kim et al. 2010, 2011; Tung and Ritchie 2011). Nevertheless, as stated by Chhetri et al. (2004, p. 34), after decades of research there is still no single theory defining tourist experience:

There is no single theory that defines the meaning and extent of tourist experiences, although a number of authors have made attempts to formulate models by generalizing and aggregating information.

Based on this, Neuhofer states that "the tourist experience needs to be understood as a broad theoretical framework, rather than a theory", because "[i]t is composed of theoretical fragments that have emerged through multiple disciplines and have collectively contributed to the development of a comprehensive framework over the past five decades" (2014, p. 16). Among the disciplines theorising the tourist experience are philosophy, anthropology, sociology, psychology and geography (Frochot and Batat 2013).

After the seminal work by Pine and Gilmore on the experience economy (Pine and Gilmore 1999), tourist experience literature made reference to this paradigm (see, e.g. Mehmetoglu and Engen 2011; Oh et al. 2007), but at the same time continued to apply the sociological phenomenology of tourist experience by Cohen (see e.g. Pearce and Zare 2017; Gnoth and Matteucci 2014), as well. Notwithstanding these two important milestones, after several decades, the tourist experience literature remains a domain with "a wide-range and perplexing set of definitions and theoretical meanings" (Jensen et al. 2015b, p. 1). Since the literature on tourist experiences is vast and contradictory, the definition of the concept for this work is based on a review of the seminal contributions to tourism research, particularly on the early contributors (in the 1960s), on later contributions (around the 1990s) and finally on the experience economy turn and the digitalisation shift, both with perceivable impacts onto the tourist experience literature (see Fig. 2.2).

The most recent reviews of conceptual developments around tourist experience in the tourism field (Jensen et al. 2015b; Dann 2014; McCabe 2005; Uriely 2005; Walls et al. 2011; Neuhofer 2014) were enlightening sources of categorisation of the existing vast body of literature. Table 2.2, adapted from Neuhofer (2014) reports a series of definitions of the tourist experience that can work as a point of reference to define journey experiences later on.

Based on the above mentioned seminal works, a review of the literature on tourist experience is briefly reconstructed here; the definitory framework for empirical research is then set.

1970s-1990s	1990s-2000s	2000s-today
Peak experience and the first taxonomy of tourist experience	Satisfactory/ extraordinary experience and the experience economy paradigm	Multidimensional and memorable experiences and the digital transformation
Phenomenological approach	Definitional approach	Descriptive approach

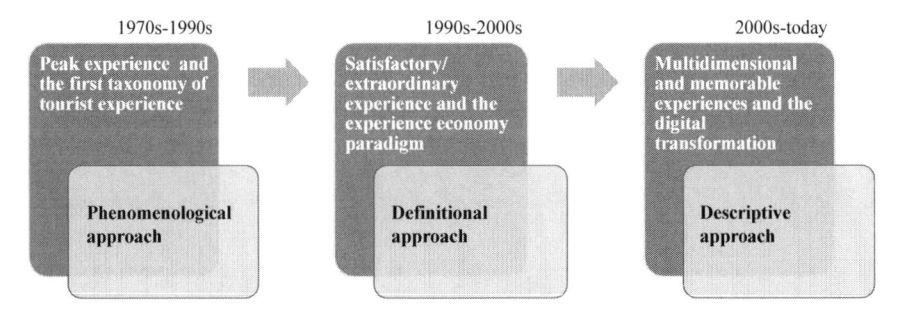

Fig. 2.2 Phases and approaches of tourist experience study (own elaboration)

2.3 Tourist Experiences

Table 2.2 Overview of tourist experience definitions (adapted from Neuhofer 2014)

Author (Year)	Definition
Kang and Gretzel (2012)	"A constant flow of thoughts and feelings during moments of consciousness (Carlson 1997) which occur through highly complex psychological, sociological, and cognitive interaction processes" (p. 442)
Kim et al. (2011)	A memorable tourism experience is "a tourism experience positively remembered and recalled after the event has occurred" (p. 2)
Tung and Ritchie (2011)	"An individual's subjective evaluation and undergoing (i.e., affective, cognitive, and behavioural) of events related to his/her tourist activities which begins before (i.e., planning and preparation), during (i.e., at the destination), and after the trip (i.e., recollection)" (p. 3)
Chen and Chen (2010)	Service experience can be defined as the subjective personal reactions and feelings that are felt by consumers when consuming or using a service (p. 29)
Quinlan Cutler and Carmichael (2010)	Experience in the context of tourism can be regarded as a complex psychological construct
Gopalan and Narayan (2010)	"The 'customer experience' in tourism consists of an assorted bundle of experiences, starting with the immigration desk and customs clearance at the airport." (p. 102)
Tussyadiah and Fesenmaier (2009)	The tourist experience constitutes a socially constructed term which is informed by multiple meanings of social, environmental or activity dimensions of the experience
Volo (2009)	"A tourist experience can be defined as any occurrence that happens to a person outside the 'usual environment' and the "contracted time" for which a sequence of the following events happens: energy reflecting the state of the environment impinges on sensory organs, the energy pattern is transmitted centrally and is interpreted and categorized according to one's knowledge acquired through time and is integrated and may be stored in the form of memory under some conditions (and thus some learning will occur)" (pp. 119–120)
Andersson (2007)	The moment when tourism consumption and tourism production meet. The moment when value is created and resources are consumed
Larsen (2007)	A tourist experience could be viewed as "a function of individual psychological processes. Such a perspective implies that the concept of tourist experience presupposes the individual" and "A past-travel related event which was significant enough to be stored in long-term memory" (p. 15)

(continued)

Table 2.2 (continued)

Author (Year)	Definition
Mossberg (2007)	"An experience is made up inside a person and the outcome depends on how an individual, in a specific mood and state of mind, reacts to the interaction with the staged event" (p. 60)
O'Dell (2007)	"Tourist experiences can be more than a simple continuation of everyday life, physically affecting us and leaving us with the perception that we have just participated in something extraordinary. And this aspect of the production, consumption, and staging of experiences needs to be understood" (p. 41)
O'Dell (2007)	"Experiences are highly subjective, intangible, continuous and highly personal phenomena" (p. 38)
O'Dell (2005)	Experiences occur "in an endless array of specific places, such as stores, museums, cities, sporting arenas, shopping centers, neighbourhood parks and well-known tourist attractions. At the same time they do not need to be limited to any single place" (p. 15)
Uriely (2005)	The tourist experience is currently depicted as an obscure and diverse phenomenon, which is mostly constituted by the individual consumer
Quan and Wang (2004)	The tourist experience is the experience in sharp contrast or opposition to the daily experience (p. 300)
Stamboulis and Skayannis (2003)	"Experience emerges from the interaction between destinations and tourists—with destinations as 'theaters' at which experience takes place, and tourists as 'actors' who have to play their own role (depending on the extent of their immersion)" (p. 41)
Aho (2001)	Experience can be understood to cover all kind of things that a person has passed through, regardless of their mental, emotional or other relevance
Lewis and Chambers (2000)	An emergent phenomenon. It is the outcome of participation in a set of activities within a social context.
Ryan (2000)	"Tourist experiences are 'messy': they are messy at the place of delivery, they may be unclear in meaning when located within the totality of any individual's experiences, and are all the more messy because, paradoxically, tourist experiences can be rich, enriching and cathartic" (p. 122)
Botterill and Crompton (1996)	"A person's experience or thoughts about reality are regarded as tentative hypotheses that may or may not be true" (p. 59)
Otto and Ritchie (1996)	Subjective mental state felt by participants during a service encounter

(continued)

Table 2.2 (continued)

Author (Year)	Definition
Wearing and Wearing (1996)	"The reality of the tourist experience is the interaction that the tourist has within the tourist space, that is the tourist destination and the meaning that the tourist gives to this interaction" (p. 237)
Lee et al. (1994)	Leisure experiences are characterized as being multi-dimensional, transitory and multi-phased construct
Arnould and Price (1993)	Extraordinary experiences are characterized by high levels of emotional intensity and triggered by an unusual event
Cohen (1979)	"Tourist experience as either something essentially spurious and superficial, an extension of an alienated world, or as a serious search for authenticity, an effort to escape from an alienated world" (p. 179)

Tourist experience scholarship possibly started relating to the notion of peak experience by Maslow (1964), linking to the "moments of highest happiness and fulfilment" (Mannell and Iso-Ahola 1987, p. 314). Later, the tourist experience was juxtaposed to everyday life (MacCannell 1973), describing it as authentic and escapist in nature. Similarly, it was described as referring to the temporary distance from home and thereby from ordinary activities (Turner and Ash 1975).

Following this stream of thought, Cohen (1979) underlined the quest for novelty intrinsic in tourist experiences and the different ways of dealing with this novelty according to different types of tourists. In his seminal work "A phenomenology of tourists' experiences" he categorised these experiences according to tourists' different appreciation of culture, social life and natural environment. Five main modes of practicing tourism were thereby introduced: recreational, diversionary, experimental, experiential, and existential. The *recreational mode* refers to a form of mass-entertainment, where tourists look for the hedonic essence of their holiday and accept the make-believe without questioning authenticity or seeking any deeper, significant or spiritual content (Cohen 1979). *The diversionary mode* is a form of escapism from ordinary life, from the boredom and alienation of the routine. It differs from recreational tourism because it is not *meaningful*: it is not powerful enough to refresh tourists' minds, but helps only to escape. *The experiential* mode of tourism is motivated by some kind of modern post-religious quest for authenticity and refers to the attempt of disenchanted creatures of habits to "look for meanings in the life of others" (Cohen 1979, p. 185). Finally, the *experimental* mode of tourism is also experiential, but includes also participation and engagement in the authentic life of others as well. This classification is based mainly on travel motivations and, therefore, although it is worth mentioning because it is amongst the first taxonomies of tourist experiences, it might be only partly useful for the analysis of journey experiences. This conceptualisation was important for later academic discourse, since it introduced the idea of the subjectivity of tourist experiences.

Later conceptualisations were focussed on analysing features of the satisfactory or extraordinary experience and used a definitional approach (Csikszentmihalyi 1990). Csikszentmihalyi theorises that a state of consciousness called flow, based on a high level and a balance of challenges and skills perceived by individuals, which can make experiences become satisfying, facilitate learning and improve self-esteem. This feeling can include painful, risky or difficult efforts that stretch the person's capacity as well as elements of novelty or discovery. It is interesting to note that flow as a concept is relevant in mobilities literature, as well, when it comes to describe the pleasant (although sometimes painful) uninterrupted travelling continuum (Williams 2013; Taylor 2016).

In contrast to the balance between challenges and skills, Arnould and Price (1993) focus on extraordinary experiential moments. They study the chronological orders of experiences as multi-phasic phenomena with specific regard to the white water rafting experience. They report that extraordinary experiences are based on high levels of emotional intensity, typically occurring at the interface between tourist demand and supply and activated by an unusual event.

Two decades after the first conceptualisations of tourist experience, Pine and Gilmore coined the *experience economy paradigm*, without making direct reference to its application in tourism. In their classifications of experiences according to degree of participation and connection to the external environment, they borrowed several examples from the leisure and tourism field. For instance, sightseeing is rewarded as an aesthetic experience, whereas skiing is classified as an educational or even escapist experience. Pine and Gilmore's conceptualisation of experience offers interesting insights for the analysis of mobile journey experiences. Therefore, a deeper insight into the experience economy paradigm is provided below (see Sect. 2.3.2).

The increasing importance of experiences in tourism is proved by the recent pluralization and de-differentiation of academic work on it (Ek et al. 2008; Kim and Fesenmaier 2015b). Experiences are mostly analysed with reference to their spatio-temporal dimension, e.g. assessing pre-trip, on-trip and post-trip stages (Larsen 2007; Gretzel et al. 2006) and their consequences are expressed in terms of memorability, tourist satisfaction and loyalty (Lin and Kuo 2016). A geographical or place-based focus is also introduced, e.g. investigating tourists' spatial involvement and place attachment (Gross and Brown 2006). The exploration of the affective valence of tourist experiences reveals that they are mainly hedonic and related to joy, love and positive surprise (Hosany and Gilbert 2010). Digital technologies—smartphones and action cams—are increasingly explored as mediators of experiences both on-trip and post-trip (Tan 2017; Dickinson et al. 2016; Wang and Alasuutari 2017; Dinhopl and Gretzel 2016), or as tools to collect information in real time (Liu et al. 2016).

Examples of tourist experiences recently applied to aspects of tourism include the food sector (Quan and Wang 2004; Tsai 2016; Sthapit 2017), sport and leisure (Hagen and Boyes 2016; Brown 2015; Geffroy 2017; Tsiotsou 2016), as well as cultural tourism (Cetin and Bilgihan 2016), business travel (Unger et al. 2016) and mountain tourism (Milman and Zehrer 2017; Milman et al. 2017). Tourist transport experiences, as mentioned above (see Sect. 1.1), are studied mostly with reference to air travel (Wattanacharoensil et al. 2016, 2017), cruises (Hosany and Witham 2009; Kang et al. 2015; Quintano et al. 2017), walking (Quinlan Cutler et al. 2014) and other minor forms of travel, e.g. canal travel (Kaaristo and Rhoden 2016). Particularly sport experiences and walking experiences offer interesting insights for analysing mobile journeys: physical strain, pain, struggle, challenges and control are key elements of these kind of experiences, which—in contrast to other tourist experiences -do not always encompass positive affective states only (Quinlan Cutler et al. 2014). More recently it has been argued that the products of the tourism industry are always experiential (Oh et al. 2007; Williams 2006), which turns the tourism sector into a marketplace of (memorable) experiences (Volo 2009). What is common to all experiences is their multidimensional nature, the relationship with space and time through benchmarks and memories, to individual characteristics, to situational factors, and to social interactions (Walls et al. 2011; Milman et al. 2017).

Acknowledging these several shades in the definition and analysis of tourist experiences (see Fig. 2.2 and Table 2.2), this dissertation adopts the definition by Tung and Ritchie (2011, p. 3): A "tourist experience" is "an individual's *subjective* evaluation and undergoing of events (i.e., *affective*, cognitive, and behavioral) related to his/her tourist activities, before (i.e. planning and preparation), during (i.e. at the destination), and after the trip (i.e. recollection)". This reflects the prevalence of a micro-perspective on tourist experience (Jensen et al. 2015b), i.e. the aspect of journey experiences, as well as the consideration of the pre-, on- and post-trip phases. The tourist experience is, therefore, assessed as the result of a sequence of "micro" experiences (Tussyadiah and Zach 2012; Volo 2009), both "peak experiences" and other experiences (Quan and Wang 2004), related to a series of single events (Kim and Fesenmaier 2015b). To operationalise the description of tourists' journey experiences, the dissertation uses the grid of the *orchestra model* by Pearce (Pearce and Zare 2017; Pearce 2011), explained in the next section (see Sect. 2.3.1).

2.3.1 In a Harmony: The Orchestra Model of Tourist Experience

The definition used in this dissertation is further reflected in the *orchestra model of tourist experience* by Pearce (Pearce and Zare 2017; Pearce 2011), that "conceives of experience as the sum of the multiple facets of the individual's embodied and mental world available to consciousness and recall" (Pearce and Zare 2017, p. 58). Thereby, the tourist experience itself is a pivotal construct based on multiple sensory, affective, cognitive, behavioural and social components that are suitable to be orchestrated by experience designers and assume variable importance across time, including pre- and post- trip moments, and depending on a series of micro-events. This perspective is particularly important to highlight not only the components or features of journey experience, but also to understand them as the elements of an overall picture that should be developed in a harmony with the environment and the individual. Thus, the orchestra model is very helpful not only for descriptive purposes, but also in identifying possible sour notes in the overall experience and provide adequate responses on a tourism management level. It is argued by the authors (p. 59) that the way to approach experience design includes: an emic perspective—i.e. the perspective of the consumer, an other-centred approach; the accomplishment with the principles of sustainable development; the necessity to address commonalities amongst individuals, while still encompassing the subjectivity of the experience construct; the need to contextualise and monitor experiences in space and time, considering them as "social episodes with temporal, symbolic and spatial boundaries" (p. 60). Among the possible tools to analyse and track experience in space and time using a user-centered perspective are systematic observation, photo elicitation techniques, personas design and other tools. The research design of this dissertation was made by adapting these suggestions to the context of mobile journey experiences (see Sect. 2.5).

2.3.2 On the Stage: The Experience Economy and Its Implications for Tourism

The experience economy paradigm became popular in the late 1990s in the field of business studies through the contribution of Pine and Gilmore (Pine and Gilmore 1999) in their well-known book *The experience economy. Work is Theatre & Every Business a Stage*. As stated above, a deeper insight into this conceptualisation is necessary to better approach the analysis of tourists' journey experiences, and to appraise their non-utilitarian value. Pine and Gilmore proposed an interpretation of the history of economic progress, postulating a shift from the production of commodities to the staging of experiences. They explained this paradigm shift using the metaphor of the birthday cake:

> As a vestige of the agrarian economy, mothers made birthday cakes from scratch, mixing farm commodities (flour, sugar, butter, and eggs) that together cost mere dimes. As the goods-based industrial economy advanced, moms paid a dollar or two to Betty Crocker for premixed ingredients. Later, when the service economy took hold, busy parents ordered cakes from the bakery or grocery store, which, at $10 or $15, cost ten times as much as the packaged ingredients. Now, in the time-starved 1990s, parents neither make the birthday cake nor even throw the party. Instead, they spend $100 or more to "outsource" the entire event to Chuck E. Cheese's, the Discovery Zone, the Mining Company, or some other business that stages a memorable event for the kids—and often throws in the cake for free. Welcome to the emerging *experience economy* (Pine and Gilmore 1998, p. 131).

Pine and Gilmore argued that, in pre-industrial societies, commodities from the agrarian economy were the predominant economic offerings and they were relatively undifferentiated. With the industrialization process, factories started to produce goods in massive quantities, and manufactured products became the main economic offering. The standardization of the production system and the massive amount of goods in commerce determined a "commodification" of goods, which did not

2.3 Tourist Experiences

preserve their economic value. This was the turning point for the shift towards a service economy, where even intangible activities (e.g. cooking, hosting guests, cutting hair, etc.) were performed and sold onto the market, following a kind of *progression of economic value*, often becoming attributes to integrate tangible products (e.g. through contract warranties, repair programmes, etc.).

The next step in the progression of economic value according to the authors was the staging of unique experiences, which are "as real an offering as any service, good or commodity" (Pine and Gilmore 1998, p. 98). Experiences should not be "wrapped around" traditional offerings, they should be accurately designed, staged and sold. If this shift in the production of experiences happens, the service itself becomes simply the experience stage where the memorable event is performed. Thus, "[a]n experience occurs when a company intentionally uses services as the stage, and goods as props, to engage individual customers in a way that creates a memorable event" (Pine and Gilmore 1998, p. 98). Because of the lack of tangibility, the value of experiences relies in their memorability, in the engagement in *doing* something, rather than *having* something. In this sense, the price of the experience is an expression of the value of time its customers spend with it, or in other words "[t]ime is the primary currency for experiences" (Pine and Gilmore 2013, p. 38).

Given the commodification of products and services, experiences provide businesses with a new platform for value-(co)creation. They represent "a distinct form of economic output", resulting from the "mass customization of a service", just like services result from the mass customization of goods (Pine and Gilmore 2013, p. 22). Experiences—like goods and services—have their own distinctive characteristics and are challenging to design, stage and market. This has to do with the need to reach the "inside" of the customers, with sensations capable of evoking emotions, and not simply with unique features of objects providing some kind of practical utility. This feature has implications both on the supply side, influencing experience design, and on the demand side, affecting users' engagement.

A key aspect in experience design related to the emotional potential of experiences is *customization*, which enables a higher degree of customer engagement. With mass customization—i.e. "efficiently serving customers uniquely" (Pine and Gilmore 2013, p. 27)—the experience is efficiently produced as a commodity, but it is effectively customized as a tailor-made artefact. But who is mass-customizing experiences? Workers, with their performance ability. If businesses are theatres, then each and every aspect of interaction between user and stagers happens in the form of a performance: from stage costumes to settings, to interactions, every aspect should carefully shaped to enable the memorability of the experience. Authenticity, i.e. the idea of "purchasing on the basis of conformance to self- image" (Pine and Gilmore 2013, p. 29) should also be a guiding principle of experience creation: producers of experiences should care about the value-based correspondence of what they sell and what they are, because authenticity has become the new consumer sensibility (Xie and Lane 2006). Finally, if experiences are customized, well-staged and authentic, they can work as marketing tools to attract customers and to create economic value, by charging admissions.

2 Tourist Mobility as an Experience Maker …

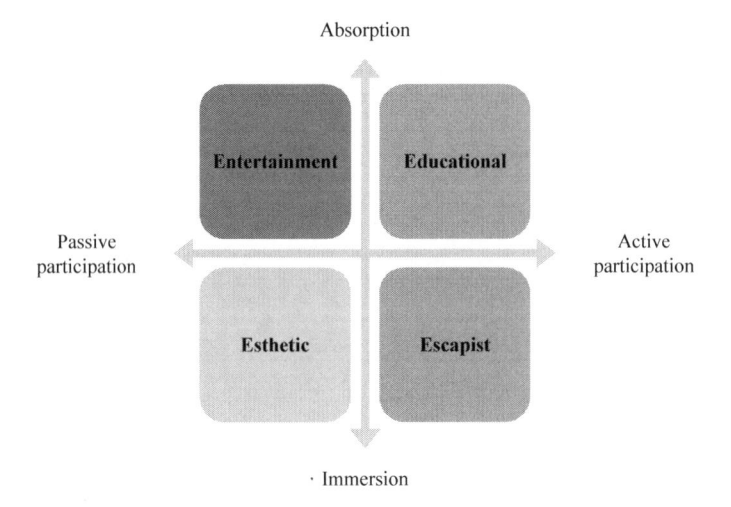

Fig. 2.3 The four realms of an experience (Pine and Gilmore 1999, p. 30)

The other side of the coin to mass customisation is *customers' involvement*. But how does this involvement happen? As indirectly mentioned by Heisenberg (1972), two main dimensions are important to understand tourist experiences and how customers are involved in their creation. The level of *participation*—from passive to active participation—relates to the degree of active engagement of the customer that can either be passively "listening to the performance" or actively "performing on the stage". For instance, Pine and Gilmore (1998) argue that skiing is an activity with high levels of customer participation, whereas watching television requires customers to participate less. The second variable to characterize experiences is *connection*—from absorption to immersion—, and it describes if customers are detached from the surrounding environment or immersed, with a higher (or lower) sensory activation. According to these two variables, a matrix to classify four realms of experience can be drawn (see Fig. 2.3). *Entertainment experiences* are those where contents are passively absorbed through the five senses (e.g. watching tv, listening to music, attending a theatre play); *educational experiences* are also absorptive, but tend to make individuals participate more actively and engage their minds (e.g. learning activities); *escapist experiences* involve both immersion and active participation in the performance (e.g. outdoor sport activities); finally, *aesthetic experiences* are those immersive experiences where there is a passive contemplative attitude and almost no active participation (e.g. admiring the beauty of a landscape or monument).

All these kind of experiences are complex constructs subjectively perceived through the senses and emotional arousal of customers, which makes them hard to perceive and to measure for the researcher. Being subjectively perceived by individuals (Pine and Gilmore 1999), experiences are "inherently personal, existing only in the mind of an individual who has been engaged on an emotional, physical, intellectual, or even spiritual level" (Pine and Gilmore 1998, p. 99). There is no repetition of the same experience, and there is no exactly identical experience for two people being "on the same stage". The uniqueness of each experience is kept in the interplay between: seller, who organizes the play just as if they were a stage director of a theatre play; actors, both producers and consumers, who perform the play and perceive it with their individual states of mind; and finally the environment, and its relationship with the actors. Measuring these several layers of experience and levels of customer engagement in relation to their tangible context is one of the challenges of this dissertation.

In assessing the more recent developments of the experience economy paradigm, Pine and Gilmore (2013) also assert that a further step towards a higher value generation of experiences is their ability to guide transformations within users, which could eventually cause enduring effects on users. This transformative capacity of new forms of commodities—which recalls much the existential mode of experience by Cohen (1979)—is acknowledged in this dissertation, and is linked to the capacity of generating behavioural change in tourists by staging attractive journey experiences, which may possibly encourage more sustainable behaviours. Such a transformational capacity is acknowledged also in the tourism field, and particularly in protected areas, where the design of experience might become a powerful tool for marketing and natural resource conservation (Wolf et al. 2017).

2.3.2.1 The Performance Turn

Although it is generally agreed that tourism experiences are socially and culturally produced (Kim and Fesenmaier 2015b; Larsen 2007; Tussyadiah and Fesenmaier 2009), the focus on tourist demand, and particularly on tourists themselves as experience producers is quite recent. One decade after the experience economy paradigm was designed, Ek et al. reported how "writings about and studies of 'the experience economy' have privileged the supply-side over the demand-side, the performances of the industry over consumers and tourists. As a consequence, consumers and tourists have been reduced to more or less passive spectators" (Ek et al. 2008, p. 123). Acknowledging this lack of interest towards the individuals, Ek et al. (2008) claim a "performance turn", putting into play dramaturgical metaphors to explain the tourist experience as some kind of performance with encounters and enactments. However, conversely to what is maintained in Pine and Gilmore (1998), tourists are not only co-designers of their own experiences, but also co-designers of places, by means of (online and/or visual) discourses about the visited places (Ek et al. 2008). Their consumption, indeed, might not necessarily be an economic activity, but it can become place consumption, or at least place sense-making.

The so-called "performance turn"—expressing somehow similarities to the "mobilities turn" (Sheller and Urry 2006)—stresses the corporeality and performative nature of tourist experiences. It overcomes the traditional perception of tourists as passive spectators of a service performance and turns them into creative, interactive agents (Richards and Wilson 2006) and as co-creators of tourist spaces (Mossberg 2007). The "performance turn" develops in opposition to the first conceptualization of the "tourist gaze" by Urry (1990), because it criticizes the notion of tourist experience as mainly visual and contemplative and claims for the analysis of sensory perceptions and activities. Tourist experiences are no longer visual-only experiences: they are multisensual experiences. Thus, "tourism demands new metaphors based more on being, doing, touching and seeing rather than just 'seeing'" (Perkins and Thorns 2001, p. 189) and tourism companies and organizations need to design places and events, and market them in ways that pleases all senses, not only the eye. Recalling Pine and Gilomre's dramaturgical metaphor, tourists are no longer looking at performances, they are stepping into them and shaping them, together with service providers and *significant others*—e.g., family, friends and relatives—, creating collaborative performances (Ek et al. 2008, p. 125). Travelers, together with their significant others are not passive information consumers, but rather information creators, editors, and distributors (Kim and Fesenmaier 2015b). Thereby, the performance turn stresses the creativity of tourists as active producers, who do not simply replicate pre-existing routes or tours, but rather create new experiences based on them and shape them through visual contents. These visuals "produce, reproduce and violate 'place myths' that tourism organizations have designed and promoted" (Ek et al. 2008, p. 126). Visual aspects and more in general, sensory aspects related to the so-called *atmospherics* (Mattila and Gao 2017), are prominent in this new interpretation of destination places. Namely, the more the active co-production of tourists is stressed, the wider the range perceptual engagements are considered in analysing tourist performances.

The distinction between tourist demand and supply is dissolved. Similarly, also the distinction between the individual and the social perspective to tourist experiences tends to blur, because it converges into a more holistic notion of tourist experience, in a continuum between the individual and the social, the micro and the macro-level, the sensory and the participative, demand and supply. As a result, the need to seek for authenticity emerges not only in relationship to the environment (the scene), but also in relation to human-to-human interactions (the performance). The quest for authentic places and events (Cohen 1979) goes thereby in pair with the search of authentic sociability (Wang 1999).

The consideration of a "performance turn" in tourism industry results in a shift of focus from supply-side to demand-side, even if it is claiming to blend the two sides. This happens because understanding the tourists' point of view is imperative for future assumptions in experience co-design. The understanding of tourist experience from the customers' point of view has several implications, among which the most relevant might be the new insights into consumers' values and perceptions and the resulting novel assumptions in later experience co-design and marketing (Tussyadiah 2014; Volo 2009).

Exploring the customers' point of view in depth implies recognizing that tourism is often an emotionally charged consumer action (Pearce 2009; Malone et al. 2014) This is exactly when the application of affective science to tourism begins.

2.4 Emotions in Tourism

An emotion is a complex construct borrowed from evolutionary and psychological studies and more recently explored in cognitive psychology (Scuttari and Pechlaner 2017). Hockenbury and Hockenbury (2007, p. 344) refer to an emotion as "a complex psychological state that involves three distinct components: a subjective experience, a physiological response, and an expressive response." Ekmann argues that some responses to subjective experiences may also be voluntarily inhibited, or, conversely there might be an artificial expressive response, which is not reflected in individuals' subjective experiences (Ekman 1999). Whichever, these (possible) responses occur in relation to external impulses, so that one common definition of emotion is "a valenced reaction to events, agents or objects" (Ortony et al. 1988, p. 202). Etymologically, the word emotion finds its roots in two Latin words ("ex-" and "movere"), meaning "to stir up" or "to disturb" (Donada and Nogatchewsky 2009). The nature and study of emotions is complex and not unambiguous in research (Bagozzi et al. 1999). In fact, depending on the referenced literature, emotions can be referred to as discrete units in continuous change over time (Ellsworth and Scherer 2009) or global feelings (Lee et al. 2007).

A critical issue worth clarifying here is the difference between the terms *affect*, *emotion* and *mood* (Hosany and Gilbert 2010). Indeed, *affect* is "an umbrella term" (Hosany and Gilbert 2010, p. 515) for mental feeling processes referring both to mood, emotion and feelings (Cohen and Areni 1991). *Moods* are considered to be of longer duration and of lower intensity than emotions (Bagozzi et al. 1999; Hosany and Gilbert 2010). Emotions *and* moods *are* affects. Marketing research distinguishes also between emotions and consumption emotions (Havlena and Holbrook 1986), where the last corresponds specifically to the affective responses generated during product usage or consumption experiences (Davidson et al. 2009; Han et al. 2009; Havlena and Holbrook 1986). Consumption emotions are supposed to be less intense than other emotions, but more specific in terms of characteristics (Han et al. 2009; Hosany and Gilbert 2010). The notion of "consumption emotion" is relevant because emotions are assumed to be part of consumer experiences (Pine and Gilmore 2013) and are also important features of tourist experiences (Aho 2001; Morgan et al. 2010).

The link between emotions and tourism is rooted in the fact that emotional responses occur all over the tourist experience in relation to different interactions and interfaces (Scuttari and Pechlaner 2017). Indeed, there is no single emotional state experienced in relation to an entire tourist experience, but rather "a sequence of emotions associated with the corresponding external stimuli" (Scuttari and Pechlaner 2017, p. 48) in a series of "micro experiences". Therefore, to understand the arousal of emotional responses in tourist experiences, it is worth analysing the possible nature of their elicitation through external impulses. The elicitation of emotions might occur in different contexts during the tourist experiences: during on-trip interactions with the landscape (Hosany 2012; Hosany and Gilbert 2010), related to artificial environments (Barsky 2002; Han et al. 2009) or as a response to human interactions (Hosany and Gilbert 2010). Moreover, actions taken in a post-trip phase, e.g.

through social sharing of vacation images (Kim and Fesenmaier 2015b) or through the recall of memories and nostalgia (Kim et al. 2011) can also work as stimuli for emotional arousal. Finally, the subjective experience, the physiological responses, and the expressive responses (Hockenbury and Hockenbury 2007) work as multiple individual and subjective affective reactions related to this emotional arousal.

Affective science and emotion measurement have increased their importance in the tourism discourse (Hosany and Prayag 2013) in the last decades. Nevertheless, they have been only sparsely applied to tourism (Nawijn et al. 2013). This gap might relate to the lack of well-structured (interdisciplinary) approaches and, as a consequence, the partial assessment of physiological and expressive responses to stimuli in real-time (Scuttari and Pechlaner 2017). This dissertation aims to fill this gap by exploring the physiological, expressive and cognitive nature of tourists' emotions, particularly those related to *micro-experiences* happening on the move: journey experiences. The main theoretical approaches to understand and measure emotion are addressed below (see Sect. 2.4.1).

2.4.1 Inside Out: Affective Science and Its Application to Tourism

Numerous emotion theories have developed in the affective science domain, dating back to Darwinism and evolutionary psychology (Adelmann and Zajonc 1989). However, only on modern psychology theories are reported here, because these have mostly influenced tourism research. They can be broadly classified into two groups, based on their reference to emotion content or emotion structure (Laros and Steenkamp 2005). Emotion content refers to "the relationship between different emotional states and their (possible) belonging to a general global feeling" (Scuttari and Pechlaner 2017, p. 43); in contrast, emotion content refers to "the nature or type of response (physiological, affective, expressive) to a stimulus and to the sequence of these types of responses across time" (Scuttari and Pechlaner 2017, p. 43).

2.4.1.1 Emotion Structure: Categorical and Dimensional Theories

Concerning emotion structure, there are two diverging frameworks: the *categorical* (or *modular*) theories of emotion (Allport 1924; Ekman and Friesen 1969; Izard 1971, 1977; Tomkins and Karon 1962; Woodworth 1938) and the *dimensional* theories (Wundt 1896; Plutchik 1962; Russell and Fernandez-Dols 1997; Schlosberg 1954).

Categorical theories (Hosany and Gilbert 2010) are based on Darwin's assumption on the discrete nature of emotions (Darwin 1872) and maintain that emotions correspond to a certain number of discrete entities and that they are unique experiential states stemming from distinct causes and present in humans from birth (Izard

1977). They are supposed to be generated without any interaction with cognition (Ellsworth and Scherer 2009) and they can only be experienced discretely, i.e. one separate from the other. Several scales are available to measure emotions as discrete entities: Plutchik's ten primary emotions (Plutchik 1980), Izard's Differential Emotion Scale (DES) (Izard 1977), Mehrabian and Russel's Pleasure, Arousal and Dominance (PAD) (Mehrabian and Russell 1974), and Watson's Positive Affect and Negative Affect Scales (PANAS) (Watson et al. 1988). More recently, the work of Ekman confirmed the existence of basic universal signals of emotions (based on facial expression or voice) (Ekman 2016) and developed and tested a scale to measure a basic set of facial expressions (the Facial Action Coding System—FACS) (Ekman et al. 2002), which developed a fundamental body of knowledge for facial recognition engines.

However, the interpretation of emotions as modular entities has been criticized, asserting that more than one emotion is possibly experienced simultaneously (Lee et al. 2007). This consideration set the ground for an alternative approach, the *dimensional* approach. Dimensional theories conceptualize emotions as both subjective experiences and global feelings. Namely, according to this perspective, emotions are not classifiable into a limited number of affective states, they rather result as a theoretically infinite set of assemblages of emotional states, evaluated according to a multidimensional perspective. Several dimensions are theorized to evaluate emotions according to these theories—e.g. valence and activation/arousal (Ellsworth and Scherer 2009) or alternatively pleasantness, excitement and tension (Wundt 1874). What is stressed is that "each emotion occupies a unique region in this multidimensional space" (Ellsworth and Scherer 2009, p. 574).

Finally, a more recent perspective on the structural classification of emotions—the hierarchical theory of emotions (Laros and Steenkamp 2005)—tries to reconcile categorical and dimensional theories. Based on this last perspective, there is a hierarchy of three levels, according to which emotions can be categorized: a superordinate level corresponding to positive versus negative affect, a basic level consisting in four basic positive and four basic negative emotional states; finally a subordinate level, encompassing 42 classified emotions.

This dissertation goes for the application of categorical theories of emotions, although it acknowledges that different categories of emotions can be experienced simultaneously, as it will be explained in the corresponding methodological section (see Sect. 3.5).

2.4.1.2 Emotion Content: Procedures of Elaborating Feelings

As explained above, the second possible way of classifying theories of affect is according to *content*. Theories dealing with emotion content have the purpose to understand the process of elaborating emotions: they investigate the relationship between the physiological, the expressive and the subjective reaction to stimuli. Cognitive theories hypothesize the involvement of cognition, other (non-cognitive) theories do not. Among cognitive theories, two have the widest application in market and tourism research: the appraisal theory of emotions (Roseman 1984, 1991; Lazarus 1966) and the affect-as-information theory (Clore and Huntsinger 2007).

The appraisal theory of emotions is rooted in the assumption that different subjects may react differently (or may not react at all) to the same stimulus (Bagozzi et al. 1999). The reason for this diversity among individuals is the fact that the interpretation (i.e. the appraisal) process, rather than the stimulus are supposed to determine the type and intensity of the emotional response. Appraisal might happen consciously or unconsciously and it can be influenced by different determinants, e.g. motivational or situational states, probability, legitimacy, and agency (Roseman 1984).

Based on these determinants and on the subsequent subjective appraisal process, an expressive response is generated, which is understood as part of the emotional response. As it was noticed in Scuttari and Pechlaner (2017, p. 44), the appraisal theory presents "some affinity with the cognitive-centered expectation-disconfirmation paradigm in customer satisfaction research (Oliver 1980)—where satisfaction results from the comparative process between expectation and performance—and it is seen as a complement to this theory (Han et al. 2009)". At the interface between appraisal theories of emotion and expectation-disconfirmation theories of customer satisfaction, the affective component of satisfaction was investigated (del Bosque Rodríguez and San Martín 2008).

In contrast to appraisal theories, affect as information theories hypothesise that "affect assigns value to whatever seems to be causing it" (Clore and Huntsinger 2007, p. 394). In other words, they postulate an opposite direction of the interaction between affective state and cognition: they assert that emotional states can shape cognitive processes, in that they create biases in the interpretation of external stimuli. Evidence generated in psychological experiments suggests that positive affective information encourages, and negative affective information hinders cognitive responses (Clore and Huntsinger 2007).

Finally, the James-Lange theory (James 1884) and the Cannon-Bard theory (Cannon 1927) can be cited in the wide variety of approaches to emotional research in modern psychology. Both exclude cognition from emotional response and focus on physiological/expressive responses to stimuli. The first postulates that subjective experiences arise as a reaction to physiological arousal, while the second argues that neither influences the other, but rather they happen simultaneously. Both theories have been used to check physiological reactions to stimuli (e.g. facial expression) (Adelmann and Zajonc 1989).

Several different measurement techniques and tools are used to measure emotions, according to the theoretical interpretation of the emotional construct. They are basically classified into self-reporting or observation techniques (Scuttari and Pechlaner 2017). These will be further assessed and explained in the methodological section, within Chap. 3, Sect. 3.5.

2.4.1.3 Affective Science in Tourism: Hedonia and Eudaimonia

Despite the importance of affect in tourism, and despite the cross-cutting nature of emotions during different stages of tourist experiences, affective science was initially applied to tourism by borrowing notions from marketing studies, which limited its application mostly to "customer satisfaction and customer loyalty issues" (Scuttari and Pechlaner 2017, p. 16). Emotion were initially used only as an "evaluative construct" (Malone et al. 2014, p. 243) associated to post-consumption satisfaction or behavioural choices. For instance, applying cognitive appraisal theories, it has been established that positive emotional states have an impact on customer satisfaction (del Bosque Rodríguez and San Martín 2008; Prayag et al. 2013; Hosany and Prayag 2013; Martínez Caro et al. 2007; Phillips and Baumgartner 2002), on loyalty (Barsky 2002; Han et al. 2009), on future behavioural intentions (Bigné et al. 2005) and on memorability (Tung and Ritchie 2011).

Pre-consumption and consumption behaviour have been addressed in very few academic contributions (Scuttari and Pechlaner 2017). For instance, Hosany and colleagues applied affective science to tourism destinations to study the affective value of locations (Hosany and Gilbert 2010; Hosany 2012; Hosany and Prayag 2013); Kim and Fesenmaier (2015a) elaborated "emotion maps" based on real-time measurement of dermal responses during tourist experiences. Further interesting applications of affective science in tourism can be found in Malone and her colleagues (Malone et al. 2014), who assessed the role of pre-consumption emotions as facilitators for choosing ethical tourism holidays. Similarly, Sirakaya and his colleagues uncovered how mood can mediate emotional and cognitive responses to a holiday experience (Sirakaya et al. 2004). Both findings support the affect as information theory, according to which mood and affect can shape reactions to external stimuli. Some scholars explored the potential to design emotional exchanges in tourism (rather than organize service encounters), asserting that service providers can shape affective connections (and not simply construct formal relations) with the consumer (Tussyadiah 2014).

Finally, Hosany (2012) theorised three appraisal determinants of tourists' emotional responses (pleasantness, goal congruence, and internal self-compatibility) and three main emotional states (joy, love, and positive surprise). Postulating that *positive* feelings are related to tourism, Hosany introduced the notion of hedonism and hedonic enjoyment in tourist experience. Nawijn and colleagues confirmed the hedonic nature of holiday experiences (Nawijn et al. 2013) and explored their dynamic development across time. However, Knobloch et al. (2016) problematize the notion of tourist experiences as hedonic moments and maintain that an oversimplification of affective states should be avoided. They recall examples of deliberately negative feelings perceived by tourists, e.g. in the field of dark tourism, and introduce the concept of eudaimonia, which should better fit the investigation of affect in tourism. They argue that (Knobloch et al. 2016, p. 653):

> While hedonia is generally equated with pleasure, eudaimonic well-being is related to the feeling that one's activities are meaningful and valuable; a sense of being inspired, enriched, and raised to a higher or broader level of functioning; experiencing feelings of awe and wonder and connection with, awareness of, and harmony with oneself and one's activities; feeling alive and present; feeling fulfilled and complete; and experiencing competence and mastery in life's important domains (Huta 2013). Another important distinction is that hedonia is about feeling good while engaging in an activity, while eudaimonic effects can result from activities that are not particularly pleasant at the time, but may have delayed positive effects that occur when results are achieved, such as increased skill level, or reaching a goal (Huta and Ryan 2010), resulting in personal growth and development (Waterman 1993).

The eudaimonic well-being concept fits with the results on emotional states associated with hiking found by Quinlan Cutler et al. (2014): pain has a relevant role in defining the memorability and the affective valence of tourist mobile experiences, but it remains an underexplored domain.

2.5 Mobile Journey Experiences: An Interdisciplinary Framework

Previous sections outlined several theoretical approaches to mobility, transport, experience and emotion and defined these concepts. The present section aims to create a first interdisciplinary conceptual framework to integrate these approaches, which will work as a guiding reference to analyse empirical data. As suggested in Repko (2006), to define an interdisciplinary framework, a first step relies in the definition of commonalities and differences among different theories, in order to establish common ground to work with. Figure 2.4 provides an overview of the commonalities and differences of the four presented approaches and works as background knowledge for the definition of the mobility space.

As stated in the previous sections, two important shifts have taken place in the mobility and in the experience research fields: respectively, the "mobilities" turn and the "performance" turn. Both advocated renewed attention towards the individual,

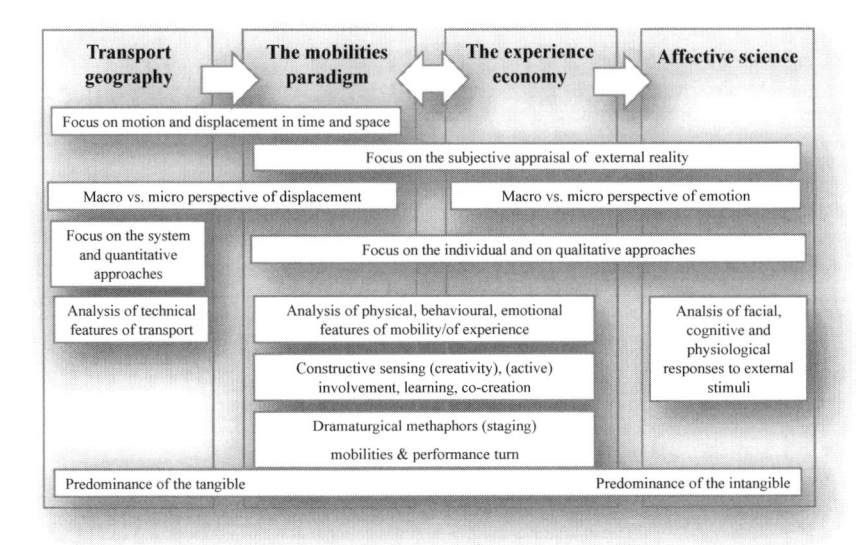

Fig. 2.4 Commonalities and differences in disciplinary approaches to mobility and experience (own elaboration)

and particularly the tourist, with his/her sensing abilities and emotional responses. Both stressed the importance of time and space as mediators of processes and sensing activities. Finally, both introduced the concept of co-production, meaning an active shaping of experiences through relational processes at the interface between demand and supply. Nevertheless, while experience theories have their roots in tourism literature and have only further developed through the introduction of the experience economy framework, mobility and transport theories remained detached from tourism literature for long time, and were introduced into tourism studies mainly to provide a response to the quests for the environmental impact assessment of tourism. This primary function of transport literature in tourism made it easier to embrace transport geography frameworks, and overlook the sociological approaches of the mobilities literature. The resulting gap is that, notwithstanding the acknowledgement of the tourism sector as a marketplace of (memorable) experiences (Volo 2009), tourist transport facilities are still considered as services and their experiential and emotional value is only rarely assessed. Claims to consider the psychological and behavioural aspects related to tourist transport were made when the scientific evidence came that high transport service quality is necessary but not sufficient to encourage sustainable mobility behaviour (Cohen et al. 2014). Notwithstanding the Special Issue of the Journal of Sustainable Tourism edited by Cohen, Higham, Gössling and Peeters in 2013 (Volume 21, Issue 7 of 2013, entitled "Psychological and Behavioral Approaches to Understanding and Governing Sustainable Mobility"), and the parallel book on the same subject with the same material, psychological and behavioural approaches to understand mobility lack a common framework. In order to design that framework, an interdisciplinary perspective is needed, which integrates principles of the experience economy and mobilities geography, on the background of tourist transport systems, and particularly stressing the sensory and emotional values of travelling. This translates into an attempt to define and describe tourist journey experiences through the theoretical framework of the mobility space.

2.5.1 Mobile Journey Experience

Adapting the definition of experiences by Tung and Ritchie (2011, p. 3) (see Sect. 2.3) to the context of travel and tourism, journey experiences are described as *tourist experiences on the move* "made up of processes (social, emotional, sensory and physical)" (Delaney 2016, p. 6). Physical processes include embodiment, i.e. "the way in which the body experiences, perceives and engages in the world" (Delaney 2016, p. 33), rhythm and fluidity of movement; sensory processes include the way the five senses are stimulated during the journey (Agapito et al. 2014) and the kinaesthetic sensation of driving/riding (i.e. the tactile sensation of motion); emotional processes are related to the interaction of the individuals with the external environment, both human and non-human; finally, social processes refer to the interactions of individuals with other human beings along the trip.

According to the transport mode, the experiential value of a journey experience might be higher or lower (Page 2008), but actually there is not a shared framework to understand the reasons behind a high or low experiential value associated to a specific mode of transport. But, space/time relationships and perceptions are supposed to have a key role. Indeed, on the one hand, *human-powered, slow mobility* is acknowledged to have a high experiential value in tourism (Dickinson and Lumsdon 2010; Lumsdon and Mitchell 1999), but on the other hand even air transport (Schuckert and Müller 2006) and cruise ship transport (Hall 2008b) are stimulating discourse on travel experiences, which makes the relationship between speed and experience increasingly attractive (Ram et al. 2013). Indeed, speed is acknowledged as a driver of journey experience (Mokhtarian and Salomon 2001), together with other more subjective drivers, e.g. curiosity, variety-, novelty-, and/or adventure-seeking. Nevertheless, the *thrill of speed* and its ability to elicit emotions has been only rarely assessed in tourism literature (Germann Molz 2009).

Similarly, research has only rarely examined the affective elements of a journey, even in a non-tourism field. Some insights at the interface between transport and psychology are provided in the studies on commuting practices or on commuter stress (Gatersleben and Uzzell 2007; Spinney 2011). There, factors determining stress for car users are related to the behaviour of other road users (e.g., Gulian et al. 1989; Rasmussen et al. 2000) and the possible delays in their journey (e.g., Koslowsky and Krausz 1993; Novaco et al. 1990; Schaeffer et al. 1988; Stokols et al. 1978). Factors determining stress for users of public transport are unpredictability (e.g., Evans et al. 2002) and travel time (e.g., Wener et al. 2004). Additionally, mediators of travel stress are the perceived control of the journey (Evans and Carrère 1991) and the roadside aesthetics (Parsons et al. 1998). Aesthetics (i.e. an aesthetically pleasing environment) might also work as a mediator of speed (Drottenborg 1999). Further, the way tourists deal with routes, itineraries and the *hybrid system* (Sheller and Urry 2006) of a tourist journey experience is not assumed to be identical to day-to-day routines in ordinary life, therefore additional insights are needed. What is more, journey experiences are "made up and constructed by both the immaterial and the material" (Delaney 2016, p. 34), but their relationships have been not investigated so far.

Literature on the classification of experiences explained in previous sections might be also helpful in assessing the hybrid nature of journey experiences and the polyvalent experiential value they might offer. Indeed, tourist journey experiences, like any other experience, are classifiable according to four realms (see Sect. 2.3.4.2)—Entertainment, Escapist, Esthetic, Educational (Pine and Gilmore 2013)—based on the degree of immersion/absorption and the active involvement. This framework helps because it offers a palette of different "kinds" of experiential value, which goes far beyond the simple high/low scale used in contemporary tourist transport literature (Scuttari et al. 2019). Applying the four realms of experience to tourist transport, we could argue that a main distinction can be made between active drivers/riders and passengers. Passengers' experiences tend to be less active than riders', and, therefore, are more likely to have an entertainment or aesthetic realm, whereas drivers' and riders' experiences tend to me more active, mostly requiring a certain degree of immersion in the context, therefore they are likely to be understood as escapist experiences. "Educational" experiences are hardly imaginable in the tourist transport domain, but still some educational shades might be added to the "escapist" experience of driving/riding (e.g. cycling training activity). Also passengers might experience "educational" moments on the move, particularly if their entertainment or aesthetic experience is coupled with some kind of knowledge transfer (e.g. guided tours in buses, reading educational signs, following landscape/heritage interpretive programmes on smart phones). There might also be moments of "aesthetic" experiences, related to the contemplation of landscape after simply reaching a particularly prominent point (e.g. mountain peak, mountain passes, sea views). All these experiences represent displacement possibilities and practices imbued with meaning and capable of transferring and transforming meanings of places. This melting pot of possible displacement options with different experiential and emotional charge and various constraints related to the spatial fix of the tourist transport system construct the mobility space, as explained below.

2.5.2 The Mobility Space

In contextualizing and understanding mobility space in tourism, the framework introduced by Pechlaner et al. (2009) and empirically tested by Pechlaner et al. (2012 and 2013) offers interesting insights. According to their perspectives, tourist destinations can be seen as the result of the interplay between resources, activities and experiences within a dynamic system. Based on their contribution, three typologies of spaces can be conceptualised in tourism: the resource space, the activity space and the experience space (see Fig. 2.5).

The *resource space* of the destination corresponds to its natural resources, the tourism and transport infrastructure, and its points of interest or attractions. It offers "the basic physical equipment for locals and guests" (Pechlaner et al. 2009, p. 292) and could be associated to the concept of "spatial fix" (Williams 2013, p. 522) used by mobilities geographers, i.e. spatial, infrastructural and institutional moorings that configure and enable mobility (Hannam et al. 2006).

The *activity space* of the destination is "the space the visitor will open on his/her own during the holiday stay […] by making use of products and services along the chain of tourism services" (Pechlaner et al. 2009, p. 292). The limits of the activity space are set by spatial planning, that facilitates certain activities in certain areas of the destination, but at the same time defines "negative activity spaces (no go areas)" (Pechlaner et al. 2009, p. 292) to set a limit to territorial consumption. According to Pechlaner et al. (2009), spatial planning, in defining the shape and distribution of the infrastructure and built environment, is conceived as a strategic partner for product development in tourism, because it influences the space that visitors can (and cannot) cross and experience during their holiday, i.e. the *activity* space.

Finally, the *experience* space is the space "in which experiences are provided and consumed" (Pechlaner et al. 2009, p. 292). The experience space does not only

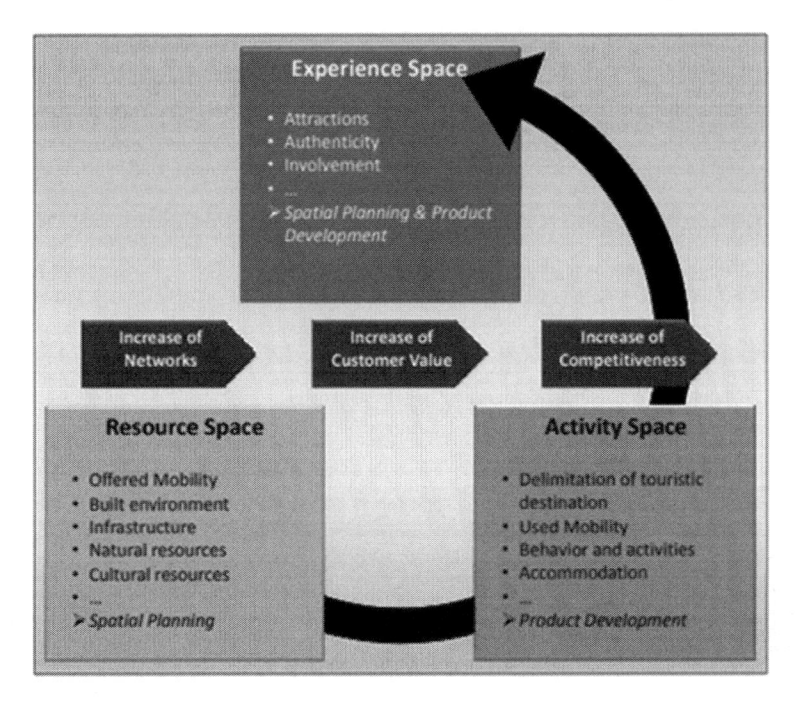

Fig. 2.5 Typologies of spaces in tourism (Pechlaner et al. 2009, p. 291)

refer to the resources used or the geographical areas crossed. Rather, it links to the moments of subjective experience consumption, which should ideally be designed in a "continuous, positive experience flow" (Pechlaner et al. 2009, p. 292). The idea of the experience space therefore introduces a time perspective in the conceptualisation of space, which might be associated to the concept of *spaces of representation* (space as it is lived) developed by Lefebvre (1991). The materialities and subjectivities of this space are intertwined and non-detachable; experiences are designed at the interface between spatial planning and tourism product development and between individual challenges and skills.

Within this framework, Pechlaner et al. (2009) dedicate a section to the discussion of the role of mobility in the three types of spaces and make a claim for the consideration of an experience space between the attractions:

> Tourist's' mobility between the attractions is part of the service chain, the destination space and the resource space, respectively. Thus, the experience chain with its experience flow should be extended to the space between the attractions; in particular, to avoid negative impressions, which can influence the experience value of the attractions. The quality of experiences need not only to be measured and managed at the tourism attractions but also within the whole resource space, the space in which the tourist is moving during his stay (Pechlaner et al. 2009, p. 289)

Nevertheless, in a later contribution on the tourism spaces concept, Pechlaner et al. (2012) connect the mobility space mainly with the resource space and avoid considering the experiential value of transport. In fact, the conceptualisation of the *mobility space* substitutes that of the resource space, and is mainly associated with the transport infrastructure and operational network, which reflects part of the transport system, i.e. its network and nodes. The mobility space in Pechlaner et al. (2012) defines the *quality of access* of the destination. Transportation is regarded, as usual in transport geography approaches, as an "opportunity cost". The *activity space* (and the related *quality of activities* in it) is the *operationalized* mobility space and comprises the physical environment in which tourism activities occur, as well as their function and use. The activity space does not explicitly include activities undertaken "on the move", but rather stationary activities, accessed by the transport system and services. Seen via the lens of the transport geographers, this would represent the tourist activities performed by the *demand*. Finally, the *experience space* (and the *quality of experience*) refers to the staging and consuming of tourist experiences, which, again, are *not* explicitly imagined on the move. This level of analysis is normally not included in transport geographers' research interests, whereas it is at the core of mobile geographers' analyses (see Fig. 2.4). What is interesting in the operationalization of the concept of tourism spaces by Pechlaner et al. (2012) is that—in contrast to what Pechlaner et al. (2009) maintained—transport and mobility seem to be something detached from tourist activities and tourist experiences, yet they can still influence them. The results in that 2012 paper also show that the three spaces are significantly interrelated, and that the experience space is the one that mainly contributes to the overall satisfaction with the destination. Transport is understood as a non-experiential factor of tourist destinations, which nevertheless serves as a basis for the creation of tourist experiences. But what if experiences happen on the move? And what happens if those one transport experiences are important for the tourists involved?

This dissertation expands on the analysis of the mobility space based on Pechlaner et al. (2009, 2012) by hypothesising that journeys *are* tourist activities and the experience associated with them *can* have an emotional value for travellers. Thereby, the subjective and non-material analyses of mobility proposed by the mobilities theorists integrate the objective measurements of the transport system, designing an interdisciplinary, experience-based framework to assess tourist transport. The reinterpretation of the mobility space in this approach embodies a shift from the idea of transport *for* tourism towards the idea of transport *as* tourism (Page 2008) as well as the integration of the *performance turn* and the *mobilities turn* in the tourism mobility discourse.

This reinterpretation results in the fact that the mobility space is not the precondition to develop experiences, it is rather a space where tourists and tourism providers co-produce tourism experiences, even on the move: the tourist journey experiences. The mobility space is also shaped by these tourist (journey) experiences, because they convey a *meaning* to the transport network, to nodes and flows. The mobility space in this analysis includes not only the "transport infrastructures and social relationships as the structural and material fundamentals of movement within space" (Pechlaner et al. 2012, p. 37), but also the integrated and technologically innovative transport services and the cultural values behind them, and the individuals involved as main actors in subjectively sensing and shaping the space.

The tourist transport system is only part of the mobility space; it represents the space as it is perceived by the subject (individual) in motion. If the transport network can be graphically rendered with a map, the mobility space might need an additional layer of explanation through sensory and emotional data, e.g. through video material, which is capable of rendering contingent and subjective multisensory experience (Dinhopl and Gretzel 2016). The importance of the individual actors in the mobility space goes so far, that the mobility space as conceptualized here corresponds to a unique and subjective set of perceptual impressions of the spatial fix—i.e. infrastructures and services of the transportation network and nodes—, in some precise spatial/temporal context of movement and with a precise technological setting—e.g. smartphone Apps, GPS data etc.—and in the development of contingent social interactions with others. Thus, no traveller is identical to the other, and no experience perfectly replicates another, although it might be in the same geographical area. The mobility space enables the spatial fix to be imbued with meaning through sensations collected by the body in motion, information from the available technological settings and interactions with (significant) others. There is a continuum in the mobility space between objective measurements of infrastructure, service and flow, and subjective measure of sensations, interactions and feelings. As was argued by Pechlaner et al. (2012, p. 36), infrastructures enable tourist activities and stimulate tourist experiences, but, it is argued here, experiences are not detached from infrastructures or tourist activities: they are co-designed and co-exist in one mobility space.

Finally, it is possible to conclude that the mobility space is a space of travel opportunities and experiences (Canzler and Knie 2002), which relies on existing infrastructures and transportation networks and modes (Lew and McKercher 2006), but is mediated by individuals' actions, perceptions and interactions.

2.6 Chapter Summary

This chapter has identified a number of disciplines and streams of thought which will be taken into consideration throughout this thesis. By drawing on the apparent contradiction of transport and mobilities geographies viewpoints, this chapter supports Shaw and Hesse (2010) in their interpretation of possible common aims and areas of research between the two disciplines. Using an interdisciplinary perspective broadens the disciplinary boundaries of transport geography and so offers policy oriented implementation possibilities to mobilites' abstract conceptualizations. This chapter argues that tourist experiences are key concepts of tourism literature, where they have been discussed over the past 70 years. It is also argued that their conceptualization was enriched by the experience economy paradigm and only very lately and scarcely applied to transport and mobility. For instance, there are mobilites studies on sensory and kinaesthetic perceptions on the move, but they are not related to tourism. At the same time, there are several analyses of tourist experiences, but with almost no connection to mobility and transport. It seems that the experiential component of life has entered both the tourist and the transport domain (respectively through the mobilities and the performance turn), but it has still not entered the tourism mobility domain. Moreover, the emotional valence of experience remains quite underexplored in both areas of research. By drawing on this literature and bringing together aspects of transport geography, the mobilities geography, experience economy and affective science, this thesis sets out the theoretical framework for this research: the mobility space. "A dynamic view on the tourist experience requires a dynamic view on time and space and vice versa" (Ek et al. 2008, p. 124). Therefore, the next chapter will focus on methods and approaches to "catch the glimpse" (Brown and Spinney 2010, p. 130) of mobile journey experiences.

References

Adelmann PK, Zajonc RB (1989) Facial efference and the experience of emotion. Annu Rev Psychol 40:249–280
Adey P (2010) Mobility. Key ideas in geography, vol 9. Routledge, Abingdon
Agapito D, Valle P, Mendes J (2014) The sensory dimension of tourist experiences: capturing meaningful sensory-informed themes in Southwest Portugal. Tour Manag 42:224–237. https://doi.org/10.1016/j.tourman.2013.11.011
Aho SK (2001) Towards a general theory of touristic experiences: modelling experience process in tourism. Tour Rev 56(3/4):33–37. https://doi.org/10.1108/eb058368
Allport F (1924) Social psychology. Houghton Mifflin, Boston, MA
Andersson TD (2007) The tourist in the experience economy. Scand J Hosp Tour 7(1):46–58. https://doi.org/10.1080/15022250701224035
Arnould EJ, Price LL (1993) Rivermagic: extraordinary experience and the extended services encounter. J CONSUM RES 20(1):24–45
Bagozzi RP, Gopinath M, Nyer P (1999) The role of emotion in marketing. J Acad Mark Sci 27(2):184–206
Barsky J (2002) Evoking emotion: affective keys to hotel loyalty. Cornell Hotel Restaur Adm Q 43(1):39–46. https://doi.org/10.1016/S0010-8804(02)80007-6
Bauman Z (2000) Liquid modernity. Polity Press, Cambridge
Becken S, Simmons D, Frampton C (2003) Segmenting tourists by their travel pattern for insights into achieving energy efficiency. J Travel Res 42(1):48–56. https://doi.org/10.1177/0047287503253938
Berardi S (2007) Principi economici ed ecologici per la pianificazione di uno sviluppo turistico sostenibile [Economic and ecological principles for sustainable tourism development planning]. Franco Angeli, Milano
von Bertalanffy L (1968) General system theory. Braziller, New York
Bieger T, Wittmer A (2006) Air transport and tourism—perspectives and challenges for destinations, airlines and governments. J Air Transp Manag 12(1):40–46. https://doi.org/10.1016/j.jairtraman.2005.09.007
Bigné JE, Andreu L, Gnoth J (2005) The theme park experience: an analysis of pleasure, arousal and satisfaction. Tour Manag 26(6):833–844. https://doi.org/10.1016/j.tourman.2004.05.006
Blesser B, Salter L (2007) Spaces speak, are you listening?: experiencing aural architecture. MIT Press, Cambridge, Mass
Botterill DT, Crompton JL (1996) Two case studies exploring the nature of the tourist's experience. J Leis Res 28(1):57–82
Brown K, Spinney J (2010) Catching a glimpse: the value of video in evoking, understanding and representing the practice of cycling. In: Fincham B, McGuinness M, Murray L (eds) Mobile methodologies. Palgrave Macmillan, London, UK, pp 130–151

Brown KM (2015) Leave only footprints? How traces of movement shape the appropriation of space. Cult Geogr 22(4):659–687. https://doi.org/10.1177/1474474014558987

Buscher M, Urry J (2009) Mobile methods and the empirical. Eur J Soc Theory 12(1):99–116. https://doi.org/10.1177/1368431008099642

Büscher M (2006) Vision in motion. Environ Plann A 38(2):281–299

Cannon WB (1927) The james-lange theory of emotions: a critical examination and an alternative theory. Am J Psychol 39(1/4):106. https://doi.org/10.2307/1415404

Canzler W, Knie A (2002) New Mobility? Mobilität und Verkehr als soziale Praxis ["New mobility"? Mobility and transport as social practices]. Politik und Zeitgeschichte B(45-46/2000)

Carlson R (1997) Experienced cognition. Lawrence Erlbaum Associates, New York

Certeau M (1984) The practice of everyday life. University of California Press, Berkeley

Cetin G, Bilgihan A (2016) Components of cultural tourists' experiences in destinations. Curr Issues Tour 19(2):137–154. https://doi.org/10.1080/13683500.2014.994595

Chen C, Chen F (2010) Experience quality, perceived value, satisfaction and behavioral intentions for heritage tourists. Tour Manag 31(1):29–35

Chhetri P, Arrowsmith C, Jackson M (2004) Determining hiking experiences in nature-based tourist destinations. Tour Manag 25(1):31–43

Clore GL, Huntsinger JR (2007) How emotions inform judgment and regulate thought. Trends Cogn Sci (Regul Ed) 11(9):393–399. https://doi.org/10.1016/j.tics.2007.08.005

Cohen E (1979) A phenomenology of tourist experiences. Sociology 13(2):179–201. https://doi.org/10.1177/003803857901300203

Cohen JB, Areni C (1991) Affect and consumer behaviour. In: Robertson ST, Kassarjian HH (eds) Handbook of consumer behaviour. Prentice Hall, Englewood Cliffs, NJ, pp 188–240

Cohen SA, Higham JE, Gössling S, Paul Peeters (eds) (2014) understanding and governing sustainable tourism mobility: psychological and behavioural approaches. Routledge, London

Cooper D (2008) the poetics of place and space: wordsworth, Norman Nicholson and the Lake District. Lit Compass 5(4):807–821. https://doi.org/10.1111/j.1741-4113.2008.00555.x

Crang M (2007) Rhythms of the city: temporalised space and motion. In: May J, Thrift N (eds) Timespace: geographies of temporality, transferred to digital printing. Routledge, London, pp 187–208

Cresswell T (2006) On the move: mobility in the modern Western world. Routledge, New York

Cresswell T (2010) Towards a politics of mobility. Environ Plan D 28(1):17–31. https://doi.org/10.1068/d11407

Cresswell T, Merriman P (2016) Geographies of mobilities: practices, spaces, subjects. Routledge, London

Crouch D (2000) Places around us: embodied lay geographies in leisure and tourism. Leis Stud 19(2):63–76. https://doi.org/10.1080/026143600374752

Csikszentmihalyi M (1990) Flow: the psychology of optimal experience. Harper & Row, New York

Dann G (2014) Why, oh why, oh why, do people travel abroad? In: Prebensen NK, Chen JS, Uysal M (eds) Creating experience value in tourism. CABI, Wallingford, pp 48–62

Darwin C (1872) The expression of the emotions in man and animals. John Murray, London, England

Davidson RJ, Scherer KR, Goldsmith HH (eds) (2009) Handbook of affective sciences. Series in affective science. Oxford University Press, New York

del Bosque Rodríguez I, San Martín H (2008) Tourist satisfaction a cognitive-affective model. Ann Tour Res 35(2):551–573. https://doi.org/10.1016/j.annals.2008.02.006

Delaney H (2016) Walking and cycling interactions on shared-use paths. Doctorate Thesis (Doctorate), University of the West of England

Dickinson J, Lumsdon L (2010) Slow travel and tourism. Tourism, environment and development. Earthscan, Washington DC

Dickinson JE, Filimonau V, Cherrett T, Davies N, Norgate S, Speed C, Winstanley C (2013) Understanding temporal rhythms and travel behaviour at destinations: potential ways to achieve

References

more sustainable travel. J Sustain Tour 21(7):1070–1090. https://doi.org/10.1080/09669582.2013.802328

Dickinson JE, Hibbert JF, Filimonau V (2016) Mobile technology and the tourist experience: (Dis)connection at the campsite. Tour Manag 57:193–201. https://doi.org/10.1016/j.tourman.2016.06.005

Dinhopl A, Gretzel U (2016) Conceptualizing tourist videography. Inf Technol Tour 15(4):395–410. https://doi.org/10.1007/s40558-015-0039-7

Donada C, Nogatchewsky G (2009) Emotions in outsourcing. An empirical study in the hotel industry. Int J Hosp Manag 28(3):367–373. https://doi.org/10.1016/j.ijhm.2008.10.005

Drottenborg H (1999) Aesthetics and safety in traffic environments: unpublished doctoral thesis, School of Architecture, Lund Institute of Technology, Lund

Duval DT (2007) Tourism and transport: modes, networks, and flows. Aspects of tourism text books. Channel View Publications, Clevedon, England, Buffalo NY

Edensor T (2007) Mundane mobilities, performances and spaces of tourism. Soc Cult Geogr 8(2):199–215. https://doi.org/10.1080/14649360701360089

Edensor T, Holloway J (2008) Rhythmanalysing the coach tour: the Ring of Kerry, Ireland. Trans Inst Br Geogr 33(4):483–501. https://doi.org/10.1111/j.1475-5661.2008.00318.x

Edensor T (ed) (2010) Geographies of rhythm: nature, place, mobilities and bodies. Ashgate, Farnham, UK

Egger-Jenzer B (2013) Mobilität der Zukunft: Wie sind wir in Zukunft mobil?—Berner Verkehrstag 2013 [Future Mobility: How will we be mobile in the future?—Transport Day of Bern 2013]. Berner Verkehrstag 2013 (Bern)

Ek R, Larsen J, Hornskov SB, Mansfeldt OK (2008) A dynamic framework of tourist experiences: space-time and performances in the experience economy. Scand J Hosp Tour 8(2):122–140. https://doi.org/10.1080/15022250802110091

Ekman P, Friesen WV (1969) The repertoire of nonverbal behavior: categories, origins, usage, and coding. Semiotica 1(1):49–98. https://doi.org/10.1515/semi.1969.1.1.49

Ekman P (1999) Basic Emotions. In: Dalgleish T, Power MJ (eds) Handbook of cognition and emotion. Wiley, New York, NY, pp 45–60

Ekman P, Friesen WV, Hager JC (2002) Facial action coding system. Manual and investigator's guide. Research Nexus, Salt Lake City, UT

Ekman P (2016) What scientists who study emotion agree about. Perspect Psychol Sci 11(1):31–34. https://doi.org/10.1177/1745691615596992

Ellsworth PC, Scherer KR (2009) Appraisal process in emotion. In: Davidson RJ, Scherer KR, Goldsmith HH (eds) Handbook of affective sciences. Oxford University Press, New York, pp 572–595

Evans GW, Carrère S (1991) Traffic congestion, perceived control, and psychophysiological stress among urban bus drivers. J Appl Psychol 76(5):658–663

Evans GW, Wener RE, Phillips D (2002) The morning rush hour. Environ Behav 34(4):521–530. https://doi.org/10.1177/00116502034004007

Featherstone M (2016) Automobilities. Theory Cult Soc 21(4–5):1–24. https://doi.org/10.1177/0263276404046058

Fincham B, McGuinness M, Murray L (eds) (2010) Mobile methodologies. Palgrave Macmillan, London, UK

Flognfeldt T (2005) The tourist route system—models of travelling patterns: Le système de l'itinéraire touristique—modèles de schémas de voyage. Belgeo 1–2:35–58. https://doi.org/10.4000/belgeo.12406

Frochot I, Batat W (2013) Marketing and designing the tourist experience. Goodfellow Publishers, Oxford

Gatersleben B, Uzzell D (2007) Affective appraisals of the daily commute: comparing perceptions of drivers, cyclists, walkers, and users of public transport. Environ Behav 39(3):416–431. https://doi.org/10.1177/0013916506294032

Geffroy V (2017) 'Playing with space': a conceptual basis for investigating active sport tourism practices. J Sport Tour 21(2):95–113. https://doi.org/10.1080/14775085.2016.1271349

Germann Molz J (2009) Representing pace in tourism mobilities: staycations, slow travel and the amazing race. J Tour Cult Chang 7(4):270–286

Gnoth J, Matteucci X (2014) A phenomenological view of the behavioural tourism research literature. Int J Culture Tourism Hosp Res 8(1):3–21. https://doi.org/10.1108/IJCTHR-01-2014-0005

Goetz AR, Ralston B, Stutz F, Leinbach TR (2004) Transportation geography. In: Gaile G, Wilmott C (eds) Geography in America at the dawn of the 21st century. Oxford University Press, Oxford, pp 221–236

Goffman E (1972) Relations in public: micro studies of the public order. Penguin, Harmondsworth

Gogia N (2004) Bodies on the move: the poetics and politics of corporeal mobility: paper presented at the conference alternative mobility futures, 9–11 January

Gopalan R, Narayan B (2010) Improving customer experience in tourism: a framework for stakeholder collaboration. Socio-Econ Plan Sciences Socio-Econ Plan Sci 44(2):100–112

Gretzel U, Fesenmaier DR, O'Leary J (2006) The transformation of consumer behaviour. In: Buhalis D, Costa C (eds) Tourism business frontiers: consumers, products and industry. Elsevier, Burlington, MA, pp 9–18

Gross MJ, Brown G (2006) Tourism experiences in a lifestyle destination setting: the roles of involvement and place attachment. J Bus Res 59(6):696–700. https://doi.org/10.1016/j.jbusres.2005.12.002

Gulian EA, Matthews GA, Glendon AIA, Davies DR, Debney LM (1989) Dimensions of driver stress. Ergonomics 32(6):585–602. https://doi.org/10.1080/00140138908966134

Hagen S, Boyes M (2016) Affective ride experiences on mountain bike terrain. J Outdoor Recreat Tour 15:89–98. https://doi.org/10.1016/j.jort.2016.07.006

Hall CM (2008a) Tourism: rethinking the social science of mobility. Prentice Hall, Harlow. 3. print

Hall D (2008b) Transport and tourism: some policy issues. Scott Geogr J 120(4):311–325. https://doi.org/10.1080/00369220418737214

Han H, Back K, Barrett B (2009) Influencing factors on restaurant customers' revisit intention: the roles of emotions and switching barriers. Int J Hosp Manag 28(4):563–572. https://doi.org/10.1016/j.ijhm.2009.03.005

Hannam K, Sheller M, Urry J (2006) Editorial: mobilities, immobilities and moorings. Mobilities 1(1):1–22. https://doi.org/10.1080/17450100500489189

Havlena WJ, Holbrook MB (1986) the varieties of consumption experience: comparing two typologies of emotion in consumer behavior. J Consum Res 13(3):394. https://doi.org/10.1086/209078

Heidegger M (1927) Being and time. HarperOne, New York

Heisenberg W (1972) Physics and beyond: encounters and conversations. Harper Torchbook, New York

Hetherington K (1997) In place of geometry: the materiality of place. In: Hetherington K, Munro R (eds) Ideas of difference. Blackwell, Oxford, pp 183–199

Hillier B, Leaman A, Stansall P, Bedford M (1976) Space syntax. Environ Plan B Urban Anal City Sci 3(2):147–185. https://doi.org/10.1068/b030147

Hockenbury DH, Hockenbury SE (2007) Discovering psychology, 4th edn. Worth Publishers, New York

Hornsey R (2010) 'He who thinks, in modern traffic, is lost': automation and the pedestrian rhythms of interwar London. In: Edensor T (ed) Geographies of rhythm: nature, place, mobilities and bodies. Ashgate, Farnham, UK

Hosany S, Gilbert D (2010) Measuring tourists' emotional experiences toward hedonic holiday destinations. J Travel Res 49(4):513–526. https://doi.org/10.1177/0047287509349267

Hosany S, Prayag G (2013) Patterns of tourists' emotional responses, satisfaction, and intention to recommend. J Bus Res 66(6):730–737. https://doi.org/10.1016/j.jbusres.2011.09.011

Hosany S, Witham M (2009) Dimensions of cruisers' experiences, satisfaction, and intention to recommend. J Travel Res 49(3):351–364. https://doi.org/10.1177/0047287509346859

References

Hosany S (2012) appraisal determinants of tourist emotional responses. J Travel Res 51(3):303–314. https://doi.org/10.1177/0047287511410320

Huta V, Ryan R (2010) Pursuing pleasure or virtue: the differential and overlapping well-being benefits of hedonic and eudaimonic motives. J Happiness Stud 11:735–762

Huta V (2013) Eudaimonia. In: David S, Boniwell I, Ayers AC (eds) Oxford handbook of happiness. Oxford University Press, Oxford, pp 201–213

Izard CE (1971) The face of emotion. Century psychology series, vol 1969. Appleton-Century-Crofts, New York

Izard CE (1977) Human emotions. Emotions, personality, and psychotherapy. Plenum Press, New York

James W (1884) What is an emotion? Mind os-IX(34):188–205. https://doi.org/10.1093/mind/os-ix.34.188

Jensen MT, Scarles C, Cohen SA (2015a) A multisensory phenomenology of interrail mobilities. Annals of Tourism Research 53:61–76. https://doi.org/10.1016/j.annals.2015.04.002

Jensen Ø, Lindberg F, Østergaard P (2015b) How can consumer research contribute to increased understanding of tourist experiences?: a conceptual review. Scand J Hosp Tour 15(sup1):9–27. https://doi.org/10.1080/15022250.2015.1065591

Jensen OB (2010) Negotiation in motion: unpacking a geography of mobility. Space Cult 13(4):389–402. https://doi.org/10.1177/1206331210374149

Kaaristo M, Rhoden S (2016) Everyday life and water tourism mobilities: mundane aspects of canal travel. Tour Geogr 19(1):78–95. https://doi.org/10.1080/14616688.2016.1230647

Kang J, Manthiou A, Kim I, Hyun SS (2015) Recollection of the sea cruise: the role of cruise photos and other passengers on the ship. J Travel Tour Mark 33(9):1286–1308. https://doi.org/10.1080/10548408.2015.1117409

Kang M, Gretzel U (2012) Perceptions of museum podcast tours: effects of consumer innovativeness, Internet familiarity and podcasting affinity on performance expectancies. Tour Manag Perspect 4:155–163

Kaplan C (2006) Mobility and war: the 'cosmic view' of air power. Environ Plann A 38(2):395–407 (forthcoming)

Kaul RN (1985) Dynamics of tourism: a trilogy transportation and marketing. Sterling Publishers, New Delhi

Kellerman A (2006) Personal mobilities. The networked cities series. Routledge, New York

Kim J, Fesenmaier DR (2015a) Measuring emotions in real time: implications for tourism experience design. J Travel Res 54(4):419–429. https://doi.org/10.1177/0047287514550100

Kim J, Fesenmaier DR (2015b) Sharing tourism experiences: the posttrip experience. J Travel Res, 28–40. https://doi.org/10.1177/0047287515620491

Kim J, Ritchie JRB, McCormick B (2011) Development of a scale to measure memorable tourism experiences. J Travel Res 51(1):12–25. https://doi.org/10.1177/0047287510385467

Kim J, Ritchie JRB, Tung VWS (2010) The effect of memorable experience on behavioral intentions in tourism: a structural equation modeling approach. Tour Anal 15(6):637–648. https://doi.org/10.3727/108354210X12904412049776

Knobloch U, Robertson K, Aitken R (2016) Experience, emotion, and eudaimonia: a consideration of tourist experiences and well-being. J Travel Res 56(5):651–662. https://doi.org/10.1177/0047287516650937

Knowles R, Shaw J, Docherty I (eds) (2009) Transport geographies: mobilities, flows, and spaces. Blackwell Publishing, Malden, MA

Koslowsky M, Krausz M (1993) On the relationship between commuting, stress symptoms, and attitudinal measures: a LISREL application. J Appl Behav Sci 29(4):485–492. https://doi.org/10.1177/0021886393294007

Laros FJ, Steenkamp JE (2005) Emotions in consumer behavior: a hierarchical approach. J Bus Res 58(10):1437–1445. https://doi.org/10.1016/j.jbusres.2003.09.013

Larsen J (2001) tourism mobilities and the travel glance: experiences of being on the move. Scand J Hosp Tour 1(2):80–98. https://doi.org/10.1080/150222501317244010

Larsen S (2007) Aspects of a psychology of the tourist experience. J Hosp Tour 7(1):7–18

Latour B (1992) Where are the missing masses? The sociology of a few mundane artifacts. In: Bijker WE, Law J (eds) Shaping technology/building society: studies in sociotechnical change, [Nachdr.]. MIT Press, Cambridge, MA [u.a.], pp 151–180

Lazarus RS (1966) Psychological stress and the coping process. McGrawHill, New York

Lee N, Chamberlain L, Broderick AJ (2007) The application of physiological observation methods to emotion research. Qual Mrkt Res Int J 10(2):199–216. https://doi.org/10.1108/13522750710740853

Lee Y, Dattilo J, Howard D (1994) The complex and dynamic nature of leisure experience. J Leis Res 26(3):195–211

Lefebvre H (1991) The production of space. Blackwell, Malden, MA

Lefebvre H (2004) Rhythmanalysis: space, time and everyday life. Continuum International Publishing Group Ltd., London

Leiper N (1990) Tourism systems: an interdisciplinary perspective. Occasional papers, vol 2. Massey University, Business Studies Faculty, Palmerston North, New Zealand

Lew A, McKercher B (2006) Modeling tourist movements. Ann Tour Res 33(2):403–423. https://doi.org/10.1016/j.annals.2005.12.002

Lew AA, McKercher B (2002) Trip destinations, gateways and itineraries: the example of Hong Kong. Tour Manag 23(6):609–621. https://doi.org/10.1016/S0261-5177(02)00026-2

Lewis RC, Chambers RE (2000) Marketing leadership in hospitality. Wiley, New York

Lin C, Kuo BZ (2016) The behavioral consequences of tourist experience. Tour Manag Perspect 18:84–91. https://doi.org/10.1016/j.tmp.2015.12.017

Liu W, Sparks B, Coghlan A (2016) Measuring customer experience in situ: the link between appraisals, emotions and overall assessments. Int J Hosp Manag 59:42–49. https://doi.org/10.1016/j.ijhm.2016.09.003

Luhmann N (1984) Soziale Systeme: Grundriss einer allgemeinen Theorie [Social Systems. Outline of a General Theory]. Suhrkamp, Frankfurt

Lumsdon L, Mitchell J (1999) Walking, transport and health: do we have the right prescription? Health Promot Int 14(3):271–280. https://doi.org/10.1093/heapro/14.3.271

Lumsdon L, Page S (eds) (2004) Tourism and transport: issues and agenda for the new millennium. Advances in tourism research. Elsevier, Amsterdam, San Diego

Lyons G, Jain J, Holley D (2007) The use of travel time by rail passengers in Great Britain. Transp Res Part A Policy Pract 41(1):107–120. https://doi.org/10.1016/j.tra.2006.05.012

Lyons G, Urry J (2005) Travel time use in the information age. Transp Res Part A Policy Pract 39(2–3):257–276. https://doi.org/10.1016/j.tra.2004.09.004

MacCannell D (1973) Staged authenticity: arrangements of social space in tourist settings. Am J Sociol 79(3):589–603

Malone S, McCabe S, Smith AP (2014) The role of hedonism in ethical tourism. Ann Tour Res 44:241–254. https://doi.org/10.1016/j.annals.2013.10.005

Mannell RC, Iso-Ahola S (1987) The psychological nature of leisure and tourism experience. Ann Tour Res 14:314–331

Martínez Caro L, Martínez García, José Antonio (2007) Cognitive–affective model of consumer satisfaction. An exploratory study within the framework of a sporting event. J Bus Res 60(2):108–114. https://doi.org/10.1016/j.jbusres.2006.10.008

Maslow A (1964) Religions, values and peak-experiences. Ohio State University Press, Columbus, OH

Mattila AS, Gao LY (2017) Atmospherics and the touristic experience. In: Fesenmaier DR, Xiang Z (eds) Design science in tourism: foundations of destination management. Springer, Cham, CH, pp 151–160

McCabe S (2005) 'Who is a tourist?': a critical review. Tour Stud 5(1):85–106. https://doi.org/10.1177/1468797605062716

McIlvenny P (2014) Vélomobile Formations-in-Action. Space Cult 17(2):137–156. https://doi.org/10.1177/1206331213508494

Mehmetoglu M, Engen M (2011) Pine and Gilmore's concept of experience economy and its dimensions: an empirical examination in tourism. J Qual Assur Hosp Tour 12(4):237–255. https://doi.org/10.1080/1528008X.2011.541847

Mehrabian A, Russell JA (1974) An approach to environmental psychology. The Mit Press, Cambridge, Mass

Merlin P (1992) Géographie des Transports, Que sais-je? [Transport Geography. What do we know?]. Presses Universitaires de France, Paris

Merriman P, Jones R, Cresswell T, Divall C, Mom G, Sheller M, Urry J (2013) Mobility: geographies, histories, sociologies. Transfers 3(1). https://doi.org/10.3167/trans.2013.030111

Michael M (2000) These boots are made for walking…: mundane technology, the body and human-environment relations. Body Soc 6(3–4):107–126

Mill RC, Morrison AM (2013) The tourism system, 7th edn. Kendall/Hunt, Dubuque

Mills B, Andrey J (2002) Climate change and transportation: potential interactions and impacts. In: The potential impacts of climate change on transportation (Summary and Discussion Papers). https://climate.dot.gov/documents/workshop1002/workshop.pdf. Accessed 5 January 2018

Milman A, Zehrer A (2017) Exploring visitor experience at a mountain attraction. J Vacat Mark 5(4):172–186

Milman A, Zehrer A, Tasci AD (2017) Measuring the components of visitor experience on a mountain attraction: the case of the Nordkette, Tyrol, Austria. Tour Rev 72(4):429–447. https://doi.org/10.1108/TR-03-2017-0060

Miossec J (1977) Un modèle de l'espace touristique [A model of the tourist space]. Espace géographique 6(1):41–48

Mokhtarian PL, Salomon I (2001) How derived is the demand for travel? Some conceptual and measurement considerations. Transp Res Part A Policy Pract 35(8):695–719. https://doi.org/10.1016/S0965-8564(00)00013-6

Mommersteeg B (2014) Space, territory, occupy: towards a non-phenomenological dwelling. The University of Western Ontario

Morgan M, Lugosi P, Ritchie B (eds) (2010) The tourism and leisure experience: consumer and managerial perspectives. Channel View, Bristol

Mossberg L (2007) A marketing approach to the tourist experience. Scand J Hosp Tour 7(1):59–74. https://doi.org/10.1080/15022250701231915

Nawijn J, Mitas O, Lin Y, Kerstetter D (2013) How do we feel on vacation? A closer look at how emotions change over the course of a trip. J Travel Res 52(2):265–274. https://doi.org/10.1177/0047287512465961

Neuhofer BE (2014) An exploration of the technology enhanced tourist experience. Doctorate Thesis (Doctorate), Bournemouth University

Novaco RW, Stokols D, Milanesi L (1990) Objective and subjective dimensions of travel impedance as determinants of commuting stress. Am J Community Psychol 18(2):231–257

O'Dell T (2005) Experiencescapes: blurring borders and testing connections. In: O'Dell T, Billing P (eds) Experiencescapes: tourism, culture, and economy. Copenhagen Business School Press, Copenhagen, pp 11–34

O'Connor K (1995) Airport development in Southeast Asia. J Transp Geogr 3(4):269–279. https://doi.org/10.1016/0966-6923(95)00032-1

O'Dell T (2007) Tourist experiences and academic junctures. Scand J Hosp Tour 7(1):34–45

Oh H, Fiore AM, Jeoung M (2007) Measuring experience economy concepts: tourism applications. J Travel Res 46(2):119–132. https://doi.org/10.1177/0047287507304039

Oldenburg T von (2015) Representing bicycle-based interaction: an interaction design exploration into bicycling research, Malmö University

Oliver RL (1980) A cognitive model of the antecedents and consequences of satisfaction decisions. J Mark Res 17(4):460. https://doi.org/10.2307/3150499

Ortony A, Clore GL, Collins A (1988) The cognitive structure of emotions. Cambridge University Press, Cambridge, UK and New York

Otto JE, Ritchie JRB (1996) The service experience in tourism. Tour Manag 17(3):165–174

Page SJ (2008) Transport and tourism: global perspectives, 2nd edn. Themes in Tourism. Pearson Prentice Hall, Harlow

Papatheodorou A (2002) Civil aviation regimes and leisure tourism in Europe. J Air Transp Manag 8(6):381–388. https://doi.org/10.1016/S0969-6997(02)00019-4

Parsons R, Tassinary LG, Ulrich RS, Hebl MR, Grossman-Alexander M (1998) The view from the road: implications for stress recovery and immunization. J Environ Psychol 18(2):113–140. https://doi.org/10.1006/jevp.1998.0086

Pearce PL (2009) The relationship between positive psychology and tourist behavior studies. Tour Anal 14(1):37–48. https://doi.org/10.3727/108354209788970153

Pearce PL (2011) Tourist behaviour and the contemporary world. Channel View Publications, Bristol

Pearce PL, Zare S (2017) The orchestra model as the basis for teaching tourism experience design. J Hosp Tour Manag 30:55–64. https://doi.org/10.1016/j.jhtm.2017.01.004

Pechlaner H, Dal Bò G, Pichler S (2013) Differences in perceived destination image and event satisfaction among cultural visitors: the case of the european biennial of contemporary art "Manifesta 7". Event Management 17(2):123–133

Pechlaner H, Herntrei M, Kofink L (2009) Growth strategies in mature destinations: linking spatial planning with product development. Tour Int Interdiscip J 57(3):285–307

Pechlaner H, Pichler S, Herntrei M (2012) From mobility space towards experience space: implications for the competitiveness of destinations. Tour Rev 67(2):34–44. https://doi.org/10.1108/16605371211236150

Peeters P, Dubois G (2010) Tourism travel under climate change mitigation constraints. J Transp Geogr 18(3):447–457. https://doi.org/10.1016/j.jtrangeo.2009.09.003

Peeters P, Szimba E, Duijnisveld M (2007) Major environmental impacts of European tourist transport. J Transp Geogr 15(2):83–93. https://doi.org/10.1016/j.jtrangeo.2006.12.007

Peeters P, van Egmond T, Visser N (2004) European tourism, transport and environment. Breda

Peeters P (2017) Tourism's impact on climate change and its mitigation challenges. How can tourism become 'climatically sustainable'? Doctorate Thesis (Doctorate), TU Delft

Penner JE, Lister D, Griggs DJ, Dokken DJ, McFarland M (1999) Aviation and the global atmosphere. Cambridge University Press, Cambridge

Perkins HC, Thorns DC (2001) Gazing or performing? Reflections on Urry's tourist gaze in the context of contemporary experience in the antipodes. Int Sociol 16(2):185–204

Phillips DM, Baumgartner H (2002) The role of consumption emotions in the satisfaction response. J Consum Psychol 12(3):243–252

Pine BJ, Gilmore JH (1998) Welcome to the experience economy. Harvard Bus Rev 76(4):97–105

Pine BJ, Gilmore JH (1999) The experience economy, Updated edn. Harvard Business Review Press, Boston, Mass

Pine BJ, Gilmore JH (2013) The experience economy: past, present and future. In: Sundbo J, Sørensen F (eds) Handbook on the experience economy. Edward Elgar Publishing, Cheltenham, UK, pp 21–44

Plutchik R (1962) The emotions: facts, theories, and a new model. Random House, New York, NY

Plutchik R (1980) Emotion, a psychoevolutionary synthesis. Harper & Row, New York

Prayag G, Hosany S, Odeh K (2013) The role of tourists' emotional experiences and satisfaction in understanding behavioral intentions. J Destin Mark Manag 2(2):118–127. https://doi.org/10.1016/j.jdmm.2013.05.001

Prideaux B (2000) The role of the transport system in destination development. Tour Manag 21(1):53–63. https://doi.org/10.1016/S0261-5177(99)00079-5

Pyyhtinen O (2010) Relations and circulating objects. In: Pyyhtinen O (ed) Simmel and 'the Social'. Palgarve Macmillan, London, pp 110–132

Quan S, Wang N (2004) Towards a structural model of the tourist experience: an illustration from food experiences in tourism. Tour Manag 25(3):297–305. https://doi.org/10.1016/S0261-5177(03)00130-4

Quinlan Cutler S, Carmichael B, Doherty S (2014) The Inca Trail experience: does the journey matter? Ann Tour Res 45:152–166. https://doi.org/10.1016/j.annals.2013.12.016

References

Quinlan Cutler QS, Carmichael B (2010) The dimensions of the tourist experience. In: Morgan M, Lugosi P, Ritchie B (eds) The tourism and leisure experience: consumer and managerial perspectives. Channel View, Bristol, pp 3–26

Quintano M, Risitano M, Sorrentino A (2017) Understanding the role of the service experience in the cruise industry. IJTP 7(4):289. https://doi.org/10.1504/IJTP.2017.10009392

Ram Y, Nawijn J, Peeters PM (2013) Happiness and limits to sustainable tourism mobility: a new conceptual model. J Sustain Tour 21(7):1017–1035. https://doi.org/10.1080/09669582.2013.826233

Rasmussen C, Knapp TJ, Garner L (2000) Driving-induced stress in urban college students. Percept Mot Skills 90(2):437–443. https://doi.org/10.2466/pms.2000.90.2.437

Repko AF (2006) Disciplining Inerdisciplinarity: the case for textbooks. Issues Integr Stud 24:112–142

Rey B, Myro RL, Galera A (2011) Effect of low-cost airlines on tourism in Spain. A dynamic panel data model. J Air Transp Manag 17(3):163–167. https://doi.org/10.1016/j.jairtraman.2010.12.004

Richards G, Wilson J (2006) Developing creativity in tourist experiences: a solution to the serial reproduction of culture? Tour Manag 27(6):1209–1223. https://doi.org/10.1016/j.tourman.2005.06.002

Rodrick D, Bhise V, Jothi V (2013) Effects of driver and secondary task characteristics on lane change test performance. Hum Factors Ergon Manuf Serv Ind 23(6):560–572

Rodrigue J, Comtois C, Slack B (2006) The geography of transport systems. Routledge/Taylor & Francis Group, London and New York

Roseman IJ (1984) Cognitive determinants of emotions: a structural theory. In: Shaver P (ed) Review of personality and social psychology, vol 5. Sage, London

Roseman IJ (1991) Appraisal determinants of discrete emotions. Cogn Emot 5(3):161–200. https://doi.org/10.1080/02699939108411034

Russell JA, Fernandez-Dols JM (eds) (1997) The psychology of facial expression. Cambridge University Press, New York, NY

Ryan C (1995) Researching tourist satisfaction: issues, concepts, problems. Routledge, London

Ryan C (1997) The tourist experience: a new introduction. Cassell, London

Ryan C (2000) Tourist experiences, phenomenographic analysis, post-positivism and neural network software. Int J Tourism Res 2:119–131

Saar M, Palang H (2009) The dimensions of place meanings. Living Rev Landsc Res 3(3). https://doi.org/10.12942/lrlr-2009-3

Schiefelbusch M, Jain A, Schäfer T, Müller D (2007) Transport and tourism: roadmap to integrated planning developing and assessing integrated travel chains. J Transp Geogr 15(2):94–103

Schaeffer MH, Street SW, Singer JE, Baum A (1988) Effects of control on the stress reactions of commuters[1]. J Appl Soc Pyschol 18(11):944–957. https://doi.org/10.1111/j.1559-1816.1988.tb01185.x

Schlosberg H (1954) Three dimensions of emotion. Psychol Rev 61(2):81–88. https://doi.org/10.1037/h0054570

Schuckert M, Müller S (2006) Erlebnisorientierung im touristischen Transport am Beispiel des Personenluftverkehrs [Experience orientation in tourism transport. The example of air transport]. In: Weiermair K, Brunner-Sperdin A, Grötsch K (eds) Erlebnisinszenierung im Tourismus: Erfolgreich mit emotionalen Produkten und Dienstleistungen [Experience orientation in tourism. Successful management of emotional products and experiences]. Erich Schmidt Verlag, Berlin, pp 153–166

Scott D, Becken S (2010) Adapting to climate change and climate policy: progress, problems and potentials. J Sustain Tour 18(3):283–295

Scuttari A, Della Lucia M, Martini U (2013) Integrated planning for sustainable tourism and mobility. A tourism traffic analysis in Italy's South Tyrol region. J Sustain Tour 21(4):614–637. https://doi.org/10.1080/09669582.2013.786083

Scuttari A, Orsi F, Bassani R (2019) Assessing the tourism-traffic paradox in mountain destinations. A stated preference survey on the Dolomites' passes (Italy). J Sustain Tour 27(2):241–257. https://doi.org/10.1080/09669582.2018.1428336

Scuttari A, Pechlaner H (2017) emotions in tourism: from consumer behavior to destination management. In: Fesenmaier DR, Xiang Z (eds) Design science in tourism: foundations of destination management. Springer, Cham, CH, pp 41–54

Seamon D (1979) Geography of the lifeworld: movement, rest and encounter. Croom Helm, London

Shaw J, Hesse M (2010) Transport, geography and the 'new' mobilities. Trans Inst Br Geogr 35(3):305–312. https://doi.org/10.1111/j.1475-5661.2010.00382.x

Shaw J (2012) Geographies of mobilities: practices, spaces, subjects. Area 44(1):128–129. https://doi.org/10.1111/j.1475-4762.2011.01046.x Edited by Tim Cresswell and Peter Merriman

Sheller M, Urry J (2006) The new mobilities paradigm. Environ Plann A 38(2):207–226. https://doi.org/10.1068/a37268

Shields R (2006) Knowing space. Theory, Cult Soc 23(2–3):147–149. https://doi.org/10.1177/026327640602300223

Sirakaya E, Petrick J, Choi H (2004) The role of mood on tourism product evaluations. Ann Tour Res 31(3):517–539. https://doi.org/10.1016/j.annals.2004.01.009

Soja EW (2009) Postmodern geographies: the reassertion of space in critical social theory. Verso, London [u.a.]

Spinney J (2009) Cycling the city: movement, meaning and method. Geogr Compass 3(2):817–835. https://doi.org/10.1111/j.1749-8198.2008.00211.x

Spinney J (2011) A chance to catch a breath: using mobile video ethnography in cycling research. Mobilities 6(2):161–182. https://doi.org/10.1080/17450101.2011.552771

Spinney J (2015) Close encounters? Mobile methods, (post)phenomenology and affect. Cult Geogr 22(2):231–246. https://doi.org/10.1177/1474474014558988

Spinney J, Kullman K, Golbuff L (2015) Driving the 'Starship Enterprise' through London: constructing the im/moral driver-citizen through HGV safety technology. Geoforum 64:333–341. https://doi.org/10.1016/j.geoforum.2015.04.014

Stamboulis Y, Skayannis P (2003) Innovation strategies and technology for experience-based tourism. Tour Manag 24(1):35–43

Sthapit E (2017) Exploring tourists' memorable food experiences: a study of visitors to Santa's official hometown. Anatolia 28(3):404–421. https://doi.org/10.1080/13032917.2017.1328607

Stokols D, Novaco RW, Stokols J, Campbell J (1978) Traffic congestion, type a behavior, and stress. J Appl Psychol 63(4):467–480. https://doi.org/10.1037/0021-9010.63.4.467

Symes C (2013) Entr'acte: mobile Choreography and Sydney Rail commuters. Mobilities 8(4):542–559. https://doi.org/10.1080/17450101.2012.724840

Tan W (2017) The relationship between smartphone usage, tourist experience and trip satisfaction in the context of a nature-based destination. Telemat Inf 34(2):614–627. https://doi.org/10.1016/j.tele.2016.10.004

Taylor N (2016) The aesthetic experience of traffic in the modern city. Urban Stud 40(8):1609–1625. https://doi.org/10.1080/0042098032000094450

Thompson Klein J (2010) A taxonomy of interdisciplinarity. In: Frodeman R, Thompson Klein J, Mitcham C (eds) The Oxford handbook of interdisciplinarity. Oxford University Press, Oxford, New York, pp 15–30

Tolley RS, Turton BJ (1995) Transport systems, policy, and planning: a geographical approach. Routledge, Oxford, New York

Tomkins SS, Karon BP (1962) Volume I, the positive affects. Affect imagery consciousness, the complete edition/Silvan S. Tomkins. With ed. Assistance of Bertram P. Karon; Book 1. Springer, New York, NY

Tsai CS (2016) Memorable tourist experiences and place attachment when consuming local food. Int J Tour Res 18(6):536–548. https://doi.org/10.1002/jtr.2070

Tsiotsou RH (2016) A service ecosystem experience-based framework for sport marketing. Serv Ind J 36(11–12):478–509. https://doi.org/10.1080/02642069.2016.1255731

Tuan Y (1977) Space and place: the perspective of experience. University of Minnesota Press, Minneapolis, MN

Tung VWS, Ritchie JB (2011) Exploring the essence of memorable tourism experiences. Ann Tour Res 38(4):1367–1386. https://doi.org/10.1016/j.annals.2011.03.009

Turner L, Ash J (1975) The golden hordes. Constable, London

Tussyadiah IP, Fesenmaier DR (2009) Mediating the tourist experiences: access to places via shared videos. Ann Tour Res 36(1):24–40

Tussyadiah IP, Zach FJ (2012) The role of geo-based technology in place experiences. Ann Tour Res 39(2):780–800. https://doi.org/10.1016/j.annals.2011.10.003

Tussyadiah IP (2014) Toward a theoretical foundation for experience design in tourism. J Travel Res 53(5):543–564. https://doi.org/10.1177/0047287513513172

Unger O, Uriely N, Fuchs G (2016) The business travel experience. Ann Tour Res 61:142–156. https://doi.org/10.1016/j.annals.2016.10.003

Uriely N (2005) The tourist experience. Ann Tour Res 32(1):199–216. https://doi.org/10.1016/j.annals.2004.07.008

Urry J (1990) The tourist gaze: leisure and travel in contemporary societies. Sage, London Repr. Theory, culture and society

Urry J (2000) Sociology beyond societies: mobilities for the twenty first century. Routledge, London

Urry J (2001) Transports of delight. Leis Stud 20(4):237–245. https://doi.org/10.1080/02614360110090449

Urry J (2007) Mobilities. Polity Press, Cambridge, Malden, MA Reprinted

Urry J, Larsen J (2011) The tourist gaze 3.0. SAGE Publications Ltd., London

Veijola S, Jokinen E (1994) The body in tourism. Theory, Cult Soc 11(3):125–151. https://doi.org/10.1177/026327694011003006

Vermeulen T (2015) Space is the place. https://frieze.com/article/space-place. Accessed 15 Jan 2018

Volo S (2009) Conceptualizing experience: a tourist based approach. J Hosp Mark Manag 18(2–3):111–126. https://doi.org/10.1080/19368620802590134

Wall G, Harrison R, Kinnaird V, McBoyle G, Quinlan C (1986) The implications of climatic change for camping in Ontario. Recreat Res Rev 13(1):50–60

Walls AR, Okumus F, Wang Y, Kwun DJ (2011) An epistemological view of consumer experiences. Int J Hosp Manag 30(1):10–21. https://doi.org/10.1016/j.ijhm.2010.03.008

Wang L, Alasuutari P (2017) Co-construction of the tourist experience in social networking sites: two forms of authenticity intertwined. Tour Stud 35:388–405. https://doi.org/10.1177/1468797616687559

Wang N (1999) Rethinking authenticity in tourism experience. Ann Tour Res 26(2):349–370. https://doi.org/10.1016/S0160-7383(98)00103-0

Waterman A (1993) Two conceptions of happiness: contrasts of personal expressiveness (Eudaimonia) and hedonic enjoyment. J Pers Soc Psychol 64(4):678–691

Watson D, Clark LA, Tellegen A (1988) Development and validation of brief measures of positive and negative affect: the PANAS scales. J Pers Soc Psychol 54(6):1063–1070. https://doi.org/10.1037/0022-3514.54.6.1063

Wattanacharoensil W, Schuckert M, Graham A (2016) An airport experience framework from a tourism perspective. Transp Rev 36(3):318–340. https://doi.org/10.1080/01441647.2015.1077287

Wattanacharoensil W, Schuckert M, Graham A, Dean A (2017) An analysis of the airport experience from an air traveler perspective. J Hosp Tour Manag 32:124–135. https://doi.org/10.1016/j.jhtm.2017.06.003

Wearing B, Wearing S (1996) Refocusing the tourist experience: the flâneur and the choraster. Leis Stud 15:229–243

Wener R, Evans G, Philips D, Nadler N (2004) Running for the 7:45: the effects of public transit improvements on commuter stress. Transportation 30:203–220. https://doi.org/10.1023/A:1022516221808

White HP, Senior ML (1991) Transport geography. Longman, Harlow Reprint

Williams A (2006) Tourism and hospitality marketing: fantasy, feeling and fun. Int J Contemp Hospitality Mngt 18(6):482–495. https://doi.org/10.1108/09596110610681520

Williams AM (2013) Mobilities and sustainable tourism: path-creating or path-dependent relationships? J Sustain Tour 21(4):511–531. https://doi.org/10.1080/09669582.2013.768252

Wolf ID, Ainsworth GB, Crowley J (2017) Transformative travel as a sustainable market niche for protected areas: a new development, marketing and conservation model. J Sustain Tour 25(11):1650–1673

Woodworth RS (1938) Experimental psychology. Henry Holt, New York, NY

Wundt W (1874) Grundzüge der physiologischen Psychologie. [Fundamentals of Physiological Psychology]. Engelmann, Leipzig

Wundt W (1896) Emotions. In: Grundriss der Psychologie [Emotions. Fundamentals of Psychology]. Engelmann, Leipzig, Germany

Xie PF, Lane B (2006) A life cycle model for aboriginal arts performance in tourism: perspectives on authenticity. J Sustain Tour 14(6):545–561. https://doi.org/10.2167/jost601.0

Zakrisson I, Zillinger M (2012) Emotions in motion: tourist experiences in time and space. Curr Issues Tour 15(6):505–523. https://doi.org/10.1080/13683500.2011.615391

Chapter 3
Methodology

My foregrounds are imaginary, my backgrounds real.
Gustave Flaubert (1821–1880 attributed)

Abstract This chapter discusses the methodological framework for the empirical research on cycling and motorcycling tourism. Taking a critical realist approach to create knowledge, it illustrates the four-phased, mixed-method strategy later used to collect empirical evidence. It reflects upon the rationale for every methodological choice, illustrates the data collection process and reflects upon the strengths and weaknesses of quantitative, qualitative and mixed research methods. Several of these methods are critically presented: case study research, mobile video ethnography, ride-alongs, bio-sensing techniques, and self-report and observation techniques for emotion measurement, including facial action coding systems. Finally, the introduction of thick description and personas design as tools to integrate quantitative and qualitative data allows for a structured planning of the convergence of evidence from the multiple methodological sources.

3.1 Introduction

This chapter presents a discussion of the theoretical and methodological approach used in this research. Further, it illustrates the four step data collection methods used: the first involved documentation on the case study site; the second entailed the qualitative method of mobile video ethnography using action-cameras and bio-sensing to record the participants' journey experiences; the third and fourth entailed video elicitation techniques using facial action coding systems to observe emotional reactions to journeys and in parallel used questionnaires to describe emotional and sensory aspects of the same experience.

Section 3.2 focuses on the research strategy: in Sect. 3.2.1 the overarching theoretical perspective is outlined, discussing the ontological and epistemological considerations taken for this research; the methodological strategy is then presented in Sect. 3.2.2, explaining the rationale for choosing mixed methods approaches. A discussion of the case study approach and details of the case study area are presented in Sect. 3.2.3. Section 3.2.4 connects the research questions with the associated methods and explains the linkages between the two. Sections 3.3, 3.4 and 3.5 outline the details of each of the methods and phases of data collection. For each method, the overall rationale is discussed, data collection challenges and limitations are described and the design is presented. Finally, a reflection is provided in Sect. 3.6 on the challenges, risks and advantages of implementing these methods, opening up a discussion about future research, which will be further addressed in Chap. 7.

3.2 Research Strategy

This section discusses the research strategy implemented for this research. The theoretical perspective is presented through a discussion of the ontological and epistemological considerations based on which knowledge is generated through the empirical data. A presentation of the methodological strategy follows, discussing the qualitative approach of this research and its exploratory nature. Finally, a critical presentation of the case study approach and case study site chosen for this thesis closes the section.

3.2.1 Theoretical Perspective

This thesis takes a critical realist approach (Bhaskar 2008): a compromise between positivism and constructivism (Robson 2002). "Positivism is associated with natural sciences and holds that positive knowledge is based upon natural phenomena, their properties and relations as verified by science" (Savin Baden and Howell Major 2013, p. 18). Conversely the constructivist approach sees that knowledge is socially created and "reality is an internal construction where individuals assign meaning to experiences and ideas" (Savin Baden and Howell Major 2013, p. 63). Objectivity is at the core of positivist perspective, whereas it cannot be reached in constructivist approaches, believing that reality is interpreted and perceived in multiple ways by different individuals, according to their value systems. This translates on the one hand into the positivist attempt to "neutralise the researchers, or to reduce or eliminate as far as possible their influence on the researched" (Robson 2002, p. 23), and on the other hand to the constructivist acknowledgement of the influences of researchers in shaping scientific research.

Being a compromise between positivism and constructivism, the critical realist approach admits that knowledge is a social construct, influenced by the individual's interpretation of it; however, it does also accept that "reality" and knowledge exist independently of human thought (Delaney 2016; Robson 2002). Indeed, Bhaskar (2008, pp. 5–6) argues "that knowledge is a social product, produced by means of antecedent social products; but that the object of which, in the social activity of science, knowledge comes to be produced, exist and act quite independently of men."

The critical realist approach has been already used in mobilities studies and particularly in using mobile methods to analyse cycling and walking activities outside the tourism field (Delaney 2016). In this previous research, the critical realist approach was based on the acknowledgement that transport networks and infrastructures exist independently of human experiences and perceptions of these spaces; however, these infrastructures and networks are interpreted and framed according to the individual perceptions of travellers during journey experiences in time and space. Accordingly, it is possible to objectively describe transport networks, hubs, and infrastructural characteristics. But in order to describe travel experiences more profoundly and access spatial interpretations and realities, one must embrace subjectivity, i.e. one must "concern themselves with the inner world of their subjects" (Robson 2002, p. 25). To dig into subjective interpretations of tangible objects implies that fact that the knowledge produced is no longer objective. Thereby, especially those considerations connected to the affective meanings of travel admit "the possibility of alternative valid accounts" (Maxwell 2012, p. 59).

By accepting this dual objective and subjective perspective to construct knowledge on journey experiences, it is accepted also that the researcher will have a certain amount of influence on the knowledge produced, since the researcher can never only "give voice" to their participants (Braun and Clarke 2006) and avoid completely subjective interpretations. As suggested by Braun and Clarke (2006) and also acknowledged by Delaney (2016), the researcher will always have some kind of control and influence on knowledge produced. Hence, it is important to highlight here that the researcher is a female motorcyclist who has experienced tourist journeys both on a motorbike and on a bicycle, although she has been travelling within the case study area only by motorbike so far.

In summary, similarly to Delaney's (2016) work, this thesis assumes that the world exists independently of human thought (ontological realism), but it develops knowledge on journey experiences based on the fact that there are multiple understandings and realities of the world (critical realist epistemological approach). This theoretical perspective inspired the design and the methodological choices for this research, as further explained in the coming sections.

3.2.2 Methodological Strategy

This thesis has implemented a four phased mixed method strategy; this was developed based on the theoretical perspective and research questions outlined in the previous sections. Mixed methods research can be defined as:

> the type of research in which a researcher or team of researchers combines elements of qualitative and quantitative research approaches (e.g., use of qualitative and quantitative research viewpoints, data collection, analysis, inference techniques) for the purposes of breadth and depth of understanding and corroboration (Johnson et al. 2007, p. 123)

The selection of a mixed method research design is motivated both by the research problem and by the research questions. Concerning the problem, the phenomenon of tourist mobility is rooted in quantitative research approaches, but the social science perspective is gaining an increasing importance and is bringing qualitative research approaches to mobility and transport research. The mobilities theory advocates methodological innovation, as well as a combination of quantitative and qualitative research for understanding displacement and its multiple shades (Delaney 2016). Integrating a qualitative research angle—mobilities geography—into a predominantly quantitative-based research field—tourist transport geography—requires exploratory research first, because the field of research is relatively new. These are the reasons why a concurrent research design was chosen, where the quantitative (QUAN) approach and the qualitative (QUAL) approach occur at the same time and the complementary QUAL + QUAN perspectives are explored to answer the same research questions. Also the nature of these research questions provides good ground for mixed methods research: the need to describe and compare experiences stimulates both subjective and objective knowledge generation, providing again complementary and diverse perspectives on individual journeys.

According to Greene (2007), the typology of mixed method research designs differs according to: the *degree of independence or interaction* among methods; the *status*, i.e. the priority or dominance given to one method with respect to the other method (or methods) used; and the *timing* of their implementation, concurrent or in sequence. Based on these classifications, it can be argued in this research that the mixed method design can be notated as QUAL + QUAN, with a high level of interaction among methods and no dominance of one type of methods. Further, the data collection is concurrent and often quantitative and qualitative data can be synchronised on a second-by-second base. Mobile video ethnography is the overall framework implemented and it defines the methodological context of the mixed method design, rooted in the interdisciplinary mobilities theory. Other methods complement the research design by introducing additional tools and strategies to understand and study journey experiences from a holistic perspective.

Qualitative and quantitative approaches are integrated to define subjective and objective descriptions of journey experiences. In fact, the qualitative approaches "seek to establish the meaning of a phenomenon from the views of participants. This means identifying a culture-sharing group and studying how it develops shared patterns or behaviours over time" (Creswell 2013, p. 16). The culture-sharing groups addressed in this dissertation are road cyclists and motorcyclists on a daily trip or tourist excursion and the aim is to understand the experiential (and thereby subjective) value of their mobility, in relationship with the mobility space they are travelling along. Quantitative approaches help to grasp the objective nature of transport systems, the specific features of modes and roads, and to quantify emotions in terms of their intensity through facial and biometric responses. The integration and combination of these perspectives offers a valid picture of experiences, and enables their contextualisation, comparison and typification.

3.2.3 Case Study

The research strategy outlined above has been set within a case study approach. Case studies are generally chosen from a plethora of research strategies based on three criteria (Yin 2006): the *typology of the research question*, the *extent of control* over the behavioural events and finally the *focus on contemporary* versus past *events*.

"How" and "Why" questions, as well as exploratory "What" questions are more likely to suit case study approaches. This relates to the fact that case studies deliberately cover contextual conditions, believing that these are not completely discernible from the object of research. In this sense, case studies differ completely from experiments. Indeed, an experiment (and more specifically a laboratory experiment) deliberately divorces a phenomenon from its context, and tends always to isolate some few variables. Conversely, case studies are appropriate when the isolation of specific variables is not possible, because the phenomenon must be holistically analysed in its context from diverse perspectives and through multiple data sources. Finally, an ultimate distinctive feature of case studies is the little control of researchers on research objects or behavioural events, a feature that is conversely crucial in experimental settings.

Based on these considerations, a case study can be defined as:

> an empirical inquiry that investigates a contemporary phenomenon within its real-life context, especially when the boundaries between phenomenon and context are not clearly evident. [...] The case study inquiry copes with the technically distinctive situation in which there will be many more variables of interests than data points, and as one result relies on multiple sources of evidence, with data needing to converge in a triangulating fashion, and as another result benefits from the prior development of theoretical propositions to guide data collection and analysis (Yin 2006, pp. 13–14).

Case study as a research approach have been often criticized. Critical aspects of case study research are related both to the lack of rigor in proceeding during data collection, and in the lack of a basis for scientific generalization (Yin 2006). While the first issue can be easily solved through the use of a structured research design and a rigorous data collection procedure and analysis, the second requires some additional explanation. Indeed, Yin (2006) argues that neither case studies nor experiments can provide a statistical generalization of the phenomenon, i.e. one that is reporting samples to the corresponding universe. Anyway, both are generalizable to theoretical propositions that can work as guidelines to contextualise in other case study areas.

In summary, case studies are appropriate when "a 'how' or 'why' question is being asked about a contemporary set of events, over which the investigator has little or no control." (Yin 2006, p. 9). Hence, a case study approach is generally most appropriate for a research project that seeks to understand, in detail, a real-life phenomenon; and where the specific context of that phenomenon is relevant to the research aims. It is well acknowledged that a case study will not produce statistically significant data, but it is believed that it will contribute to creating generalizable theoretical propositions to be contextualized elsewhere.

This dissertation profits from the use of case study design for several reasons. Firstly, it is dealing with the experiential value of mobility on holiday, posing three "how" questions, that are mostly addressable through case studies. Secondly, its aim is to accurately describe the journey experiences in their relationship with contextual space and time, comparing different means of transport. The case study approach enables the implementation of in-depth data collection, focusing on the details and complexities of journey experiences, modes and tourist transport systems. Thirdly, knowledge of journey experiences must be produced in a real-life context, because mobility patterns of tourists are place-specific (Scuttari et al. 2013) and in various ways constrained by the *spatial fix* of the mobility space (Williams 2013). Finally, the type of knowledge produced is not supposed to be statistically significant, but rather generalizable and able to offer some theoretical propositions to inform future traffic policies.

3.2.3.1 Case Study Design

According to Yin (2006, p. 21), five components of research design are especially important in preparing a case study: "(a) a study's question; (b) its proposition, if any; (c) its unit(s) of analysis; (d) the logic linking the data to the proposition; (e) the criteria for interpreting the findings". Table 3.1 contextualizes these components for this research. It works as a tool to guide the case study design and, later, on the data collection and analysis.

Starting from the research questions and based on the theoretical framework and perspective explained in previous sections (see Chap. 2), three *study propositions*

Table 3.1 Components of case study research design (own elaboration)

Research questions	How to describe and how to measure visitors' journey experiences in a mobility space? How does travel mode shape journey experiences? How to develop personas for journey experiences in mobility spaces?
Study propositions	Journey experiences are made up of physical, sensory, social and emotional features. Travel mode might influence those features. These features might be generalizable to personas
Units of analysis	One mobility space. A sample of visitors doing a journey experience on their pedal cycle/motorcycle in one same mobility space
Logic linking (data–propositions)	Collection of data on physical, sensory, social and emotional features of journey experience on different modes
Criteria for interpreting the findings	Qualitative patterns of similarity/contrast among users of the same/different transport modes

3.2 Research Strategy

were developed. The first refers to the configuration of journey experiences, consisting of physical, sensory, social and emotional features (Delaney 2016). The second refers to the ability of travel modes to influence those features, as reported in the literature through speed or emotional value (Lumsdon and McGrath 2011). Finally, the third proposes a theoretical generalization of visitors' journey experiences according to mode of transport.

The *units of analysis* of the case study are individuals on holiday or on a daily visit within one single mobility space, to facilitate the analysis of experiential features while keeping the touristic environment as constant as possible. These individuals are selected based on the means of transport used, focussing on two means of transport: the road bicycle and the motorbike. These two means of transport are selected because they share interesting commonalities (e.g. the riding experience, the absence of a cabin, the individual nature, and the space occupied in roads), but they also have evident differences (e.g. speed, human versus motorized propulsion, possibility versus impossibility to carry someone else on board). Data collection is closely linked to study proposition and provides, for each individual, a description of the physical, sensory, social and emotional features of the journey experience in the selected mobility space.

The necessity to analyse multiple units of analysis in one single mobility space is the reason for choosing a single exploratory case study with multiple embedded units (Baxter and Jack 2008). The rationale for the selection of a single case study is the fact that it "represents an extreme case or a unique case" (Yin 2006) to allow a rich experiential consumption of tourist experiences on the move. Indeed, the mobility space chosen is a panoramic road with a high touristic value close to a Natural Wold Heritage Site, where some pioneer initiatives to monitor and calm traffic have been developed in the last years, as will be explained below.

A three phased approach is used in the case study design. Phase I involved the preparatory analysis of the mobility space through *documentation and secondary data collection*; phase II refers to the real-time observation of the consumption experience through *mobile video ethnography* and particular sensors; phase III is about the post-consumption monitoring of the emotional features of tourist experiences through *self-reporting and observation techniques*–video elicitation combined with action coding systems and a self-reporting questionnaire. Finally, quantitative and qualitative data are related and integrated using NVivo Pro 11™ software as a platform to make empirical evidence converge.

The type and amount of data needed to describe journey experiences and perform cross-modal comparison justified the selection of mobile video ethnography as a method to develop in-depth individual analysis of the units of analysis; the need for reliable emotional information about the experience required a combination of self-reported and observation techniques for emotion measurement. Data was collected by involving real visitors to the pass, i.e. by measuring their own journey experiences (see Fig. 3.1) according to a precise *procedure*. Action cameras and sensors were placed on visitors' helmets to record videos and collect biometric data of their journey experience, including pass climb, stops and descent. After taking the tour, tourists were debriefed and asked to fill in a questionnaire for self-assessment of perceived emotions. In parallel, a video elicitation technique was used to measure the emotions associated with the journey experience using software for facial action coding (SHORE™, i.e. Sophisticated High-speed Object Recognition Engine) (Wierzbicki et al. 2013), which measures the extent of four basic emotions (happiness, sadness, anger and surprise) in relation to the journey experience.

Research design quality is ensured by making reference to the guidelines developed by Yin (2006) for exploratory case studies: construct validity, external validity, and reliability. *Construct validity*, i.e. the capacity to establish "correct operational measures for the concepts being studies" (Yin 2006, p. 35) is achieved through the use of multiple sources of evidence. This translates into a data and methodological triangulation (Patton 1987): combining different data sources and research methods to seek for convergence of evidence in results. More precisely, features of journey experience are analysed across different units of analysis (visitors), multiple data sources (e.g. video, transcript, questionnaire, sensor data), as well as using different methods (e.g. self-reporting vs observation techniques). Evidence from different units and methods is then triangulated to achieve final results.

External validity, i.e. the generalizability of findings beyond the specific case study, is pursued by making reference to pre-existing theoretical frameworks with the aim to broaden them. The main theories that support the case study propositions are: the non-utilitarian nature of travel theorized by Mokhtarian and Salomon (2001); the mediation effect of slow versus fast and motorised versus non-motorized travel modes introduced by Larsen (2001); finally, the compositional features of journey experiences found by Delaney (2016). Thanks to the pre-existence of these theoretical frameworks and making reference to them it is possible to achieve analytical generalization (Yin 2006) ascribing a particular set of results to a more general theory. Anyway, it is acknowledged that generalization is not a straightforward process, particularly in the case of single case studies (Yin 2006). However, the exploratory nature of this research required the selection of one single mobility space and multiple embedded units, offering possibilities to generalize from multiple individual journey experiences. It is acknowledged that journey experiences are very place-specific and, therefore, the future replication of the study in other case studies might provide stronger support for the theories, thanks to the accumulation of knowledge across different case studies. This critical aspect is addressed in the discussion and conclusion chapter (see Sect. 6.1.4).

The last element required to create a high quality design of the case study is *reliability*, i.e. the possibility of replicating the case study and achieving the same findings. The construction of a unique database to collect material on the case studies is a valid tool to reach reliability (Yin 2006). For this thesis, the dataset was created using NVivo 11 Pro™. The software allowed the storage of all documentary, textual and audio-visual material for one project with maximum transparency and replicability (see Sect. 3.4.3 and 3.4.4).

3.2 Research Strategy

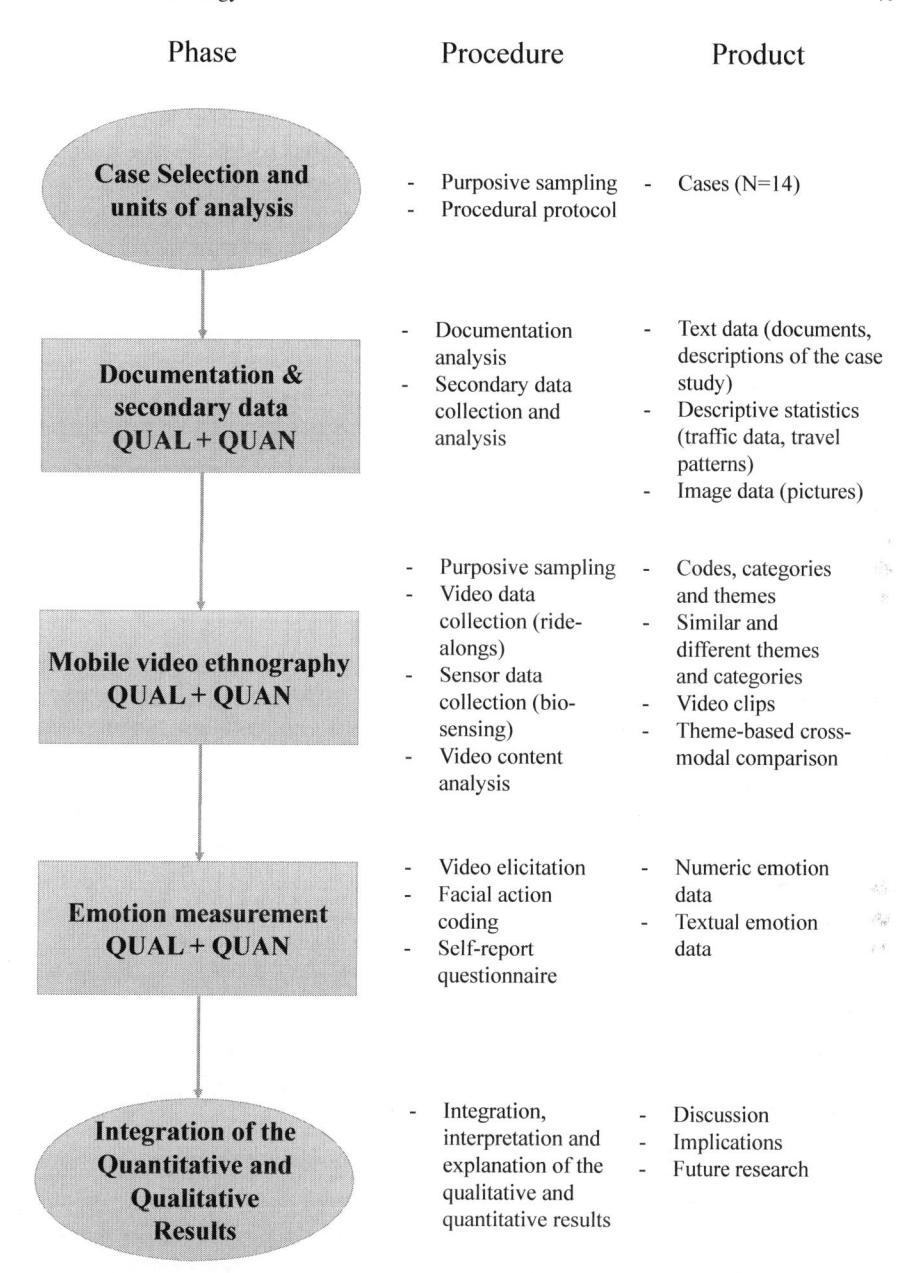

Phase	Procedure	Product
Case Selection and units of analysis	- Purposive sampling - Procedural protocol	- Cases (N=14)
Documentation & secondary data QUAL + QUAN	- Documentation analysis - Secondary data collection and analysis	- Text data (documents, descriptions of the case study) - Descriptive statistics (traffic data, travel patterns) - Image data (pictures)
Mobile video ethnography QUAL + QUAN	- Purposive sampling - Video data collection (ride-alongs) - Sensor data collection (bio-sensing) - Video content analysis	- Codes, categories and themes - Similar and different themes and categories - Video clips - Theme-based cross-modal comparison
Emotion measurement QUAL + QUAN	- Video elicitation - Facial action coding - Self-report questionnaire	- Numeric emotion data - Textual emotion data
Integration of the Quantitative and Qualitative Results	- Integration, interpretation and explanation of the qualitative and quantitative results	- Discussion - Implications - Future research

Fig. 3.1 Case study design process (own elaboration)

3.2.3.2 Case Study Description

The case study site selected for this thesis is Passo Sella (Sella Pass), Italy. The rationale behind this choice is outlined below. The Sella Pass is a tourism intensive attraction point situated within a panoramic road and surrounding the fossil archipelago of the Dolomites UNESCO World Heritage Site. From a tourist perspective, it was estimated that the whole WHS (i.e. 137 municipalities hosting the core or buffer zones of the WHS) is very tourism-intensive, since it welcomed around 4.9 million visitors per year at the time of the official WHS nomination in 2009 (Elmi and Wagner 2013). From a transport perspective, official counting stations measured traffic volumes that could reach 4,000 or more vehicles on main roads during summer peak days, mostly between 9 am and 5 pm (Scuttari and Bassani 2015).

Tourism-related road traffic in this wide area is, therefore, particularly intense, and extremely concentrated around some major passes. Among several passes surrounding the WHS, four—Passo Sella (2,240 m), Passo Gardena (2,136 m), Passo Campolongo (1,875 m) and Passo Pordoi (2,239 m)—stand out (Scuttari et al. 2019). These passes connect four valleys belonging to three different provinces and together constitute a circular tour (the Sellaronda ring) that encircles a spectacular rock formation (the Sella massif), offering astonishing views towards the Dolomites and crossing the borders of three different provinces. The Sellaronda tour is attractive for tourists using various means of transport: road bicycles, motorcycles, cars, travel busses, mountain bikes, and, during the winter, skis. Several events are organised to enhance the touristic attractiveness of the Sellaronda Tour, including car-free days. The Sellaronda passes are very important because they involve multiple touristic functions (Scuttari et al. 2019): they are important *departure points for hiking excursions*; they work as *panoramic terraces* from which to admire the landscape, and finally, they are *rest stops* to enjoy a meal at high elevation. Moreover, they also work as fundamental *logistical connections* between valleys, both for tourists and for residents. The multi-functionality of the pass and the multimodality of its users make this case unique and worth examining.

Notwithstanding the pioneering initiatives mentioned above, the impacts of traffic volumes, i.e. pollution, congestion, visual intrusion, noise and problems related to the use of parking space, are very substantial and possible traffic management solutions have been discussed for over 20 years, with the support of several research activities (Pechlaner et al. 2004; Pörnbacher 1995). After the UNESCO WHS nomination, the issue has gained more importance and has been increasingly looked at from a trans-regional perspective, with increased determination to take action and reduce individual motorized traffic. As regional administrations acknowledged the complexity of tourism and non-tourism traffic flows across Sellaronda Passes, further research was conducted to design a policy mix of efficient traffic management measures. A choice experiment was conducted in 2014 (Scuttari et al. 2019) on the most well-known pass of the Sella Ronda tour, the Sella Pass. This experiment revealed a strong inclination of car users to shift to bus transport, but only if there were high frequency and convenient of bus services. Based on this choice experiment, the first implementation of traffic management measures was done in 2017 on Sella Pass, with a road closure from 9 a.m. to 4 p.m. during nine Wednesdays in the summer months (Scuttari et al. 2018); a second series of closures was carried out in 2018. A qualitative monitoring of this 2017 initiative (Scuttari et al. 2018) revealed—as already acknowledged in the literature (Scuttari and Della Lucia 2015)—that traffic restrictions would also change the experiences on the route and represent at the same time an occasion for creating new travel experiences. The composition, the intensity and the types of vehicles on the move will change and a new and more sustainable equilibrium is desirable.

Motorcyclists are one of the categories mostly responsible for noise, whereas pedal cycles are among the most sustainable means of transport to reach the passes, although they are not usable without a high degree of fitness because of the steep climbs involved. They both represent means of transport where the experiential value is rather high, and possibly the trip is made to enjoy the journey, rather than to reach an end point. Investigating individual perceptions while riding on such spectacular roads plays a crucial role in understanding how to enhance these experiences, while minimising their impact on the environment, if possible. Understanding the value of these journey experiences may help destination managers and local administrations in leading this transition towards more sustainable mobility, because it might help planning new (and possibly more sustainable) experiences on the move in the future.

In conclusion, this research aims to provide an insight into cycling and motorcycling activities in a case study area that has collected a wide range of data and information on traffic flows, and has already experienced a pilot project for sustainability-oriented traffic management measures, in order to derive suggestions to better shape traffic management measures in the future.

3.2.4 Research Questions and Associated Methods

Now that the overall theoretical and methodological strategy of this thesis is set, each of the specific methods chosen is related to the corresponding research questions. It is important to highlight here that video ethnography combined with bio-sensing is the most innovative and rich source of information and knowledge in this thesis. Indeed, videos can work to "collapse the linearity of the tourist experience" (Dinhopl and Gretzel 2016, p. 13), enabling visual continuity, multiplicity of cues (audio-video), and ability to show motion. This is the reason why phase II (mobile video ethnography) is crucial to respond to all the research questions, whereas techniques to measure emotions explained in Phase III and IV (observation-based and self-reported) focus mainly on one aspect of journey experiences: their emotional features.

Table 3.2 illustrates the research questions and how they are related to the corresponding phases of the research design and methods. In the coming section, each of the specific methods is presented in detail, discussing the rationale for choosing it, the process of implementing it and how data was analysed. Since the methods used in phase III and IV are quite innovative, a brief reflection is presented for each of them.

Table 3.2 Research questions and associated methods (own elaboration)

Research questions	I Documentation	II Mobile video ethnography + sensors	III Video elicitation + facial action coding	IV Self-report questionnaire
How to describe and how to measure the visitors' mobile journeys and their physical, sensory, emotional and social features in relation to the "spatial fix"?	√	√	√	√
What are the physical features of visitors' mobile journey experiences?	√	√		
What are the sensory features?	√	√		√
What are the affective features?			√	√
How does the negotiation of space in motion happen and how does social interaction happen in space and time?	√	√		
How does travel mode—i.e. cycling versus motorcycling–shape journey experiences?		√	√	√
How do physical, sensory, affective and social features relate to mode of transport?		√	√	√
How to develop personas to address motorcyclists and cyclists in mobility spaces?	√	√	√	√
How to define common features among users of the same means of transport?	√	√	√	√
How much variety is there among users of the same means of transport?	√	√	√	√

3.3 Documentation and Secondary Data

Phase I of data collection will now be discussed. The rationale behind collecting documentation and secondary data will be presented, followed by a discussion about data analysis.

3.3.1 Rationale

Documentary information is crucial to contextualize the case study and it is probably relevant to every case study topic (Yin 2006). Documentation can take any form and it typically includes reports, administrative documents, formal studies or research projects, newspaper material, etc. Collecting documentation related to the case study site is crucial because this information is a stable point of reference along the primary data collection process, it is unobtrusive, because it was prepared outside the aims of the research project, and finally it offers a precise overview of the case study over a longer time span than the one observed (Yin 2006). In the specific case of Sella Pass, it was deemed as important to couple the documentation with the available secondary data, in order to describe the tourist transport system on which mobility experiences were recorded.

Among the critical aspects in using documentation to frame the case study data collection is the possibility of reporting biases from the documents collected, the risk of selecting only part of the available material and thereby have a biased overview of the status quo, and finally the difficulty in accessing these documents, that might be not retrievable or not publically accessible at all. The availability and accessibility of a wide range of documentary material, the participation of the researcher in earlier research projects on the case study site, as well as the rich database publicly available on traffic measurement helped to solve these possible difficulties in a very early stage. It was possible to review a wide range of documentary material and data, to better design the later data collection phase.

3.3.2 Documentation and Data Types

Several project reports and scientific publications were collected and examined in relation to the case study area. Some of them are related to tourism (e.g. Elmi and Perlik 2014; Scuttari and Della Lucia 2016; Della Lucia and Franch 2017), other are specific to mobilities on the mountain passes (Scuttari et al. 2019). Some of these documents were co-produced by the researcher herself in previous research projects, offering a good background information set for analysing journey experiences. Finally, internal records were provided to assess technical features related to transport impact, i.e. noise, Greenhouse Gas Emissions (GHG), and pollution.

Data surveys and census data help to describe the motivational and temporal patterns of travel experiences, as well as to quantify the intensity and timely distribution of traffic along the road across seasons, weekdays and daily hours. These aspects are very important as backup information when assessing single journey experiences from a subjective perspective. Table 3.3 lists the documentation and data accessed.

3.3.3 Analysis

The documentary material and secondary data was used to help understand the tourism and mobility phenomena in the mobile space and to contextualize journey experiences. This knowledge synthesis and contextualization was crucial before the primary data collection phase and it was also helpful during data analysis, in order to compare evidences from different sources and seek for evidence convergence. Studies and data mentioned in Table 3.3 were stored in one unique research project file through the software NVivo Pro 11™. This software allows the creation of cross-links between different types of sources and thereby enables the analysis of different data sources by using a pattern matching logic (Trochim 1989) and a hypothesis-generating process (Glaser and Strauss 1967).

More precisely, tourism studies and related data helped to define a profile of pass visitors and to understand their motivational and demographic aspects. Moreover, these sources were crucial in designing the details of primary data collection, e.g. framing the geographical area of the Sella Pass, identifying important tourism activities, understand temporal patterns of visits. Traffic-related data and projects were helpful in identifying the time frame for data collection, as well as understanding the mix of vehicles in transit, their origin and destination. It was, therefore, possible to derive different possible route patterns and cover them in the selection of the different journey experiences, as explained below (see Sect. 3.4.2). Finally, traffic data offered detailed information about hourly traffic and average vehicle speed at the counting station, which was then cross-checked with the individual features recorded through sensors during the whole journey experience.

3.3 Documentation and Secondary Data

Table 3.3 Documentation and data accessed (own elaboration)

Type of document	Authors (Year)	Title	Topic
Project reports	Pörnbacher (1995)	Verkehrsbefragung im Dolomitengebiet [Traffic survey in the Dolomites area]	Transport/Mobility
	Pechlaner et al. (2004)	Verkehrsentlastung Dolomitenpässe [Traffic calming in the Dolomites' passes]	Transport/Mobility
	Elmi and Wagner (2013)	Turismo sostenibile nelle Dolomiti. Una strategia per il Bene Patrimonio Mondiale UNESCO [Sustainable tourism in the Dolomites. A strategy for the Natural World Heritage Site Dolomites UNESCO]	Tourism
	Elmi (2014)	Turismo sostenibile nelle Dolomiti, approfondimento dell'analisi [Sustainable tourism in the Dolomites. In-depth analysis]	Tourism and transport/Mobility
	Scuttari and Bassani (2015)	I passi dolomitici: Analisi del traffico e dei suoi impatti e proposta di misure di gestione [Dolomites' passes. Traffic, its environmental impact and a proposal for traffic management measures]	Transport/Mobility
	Micheletti et al. (2015)	Strategia Generale di Gestione delle Dolomiti Patrimonio Naturale UNESCO [Overall Management Strategy of the UNESCO Dolomites World Heritage Site]	Tourism and transport/Mobility

(continued)

Table 3.3 (continued)

Type of document	Authors (Year)	Title	Topic
	Scuttari et al. (2018)	#Dolomitesvives. Vivere un'esperienza naturale sulle Dolomiti. Monitoring qualitativo [#Dolomitesvives. Experiencing nature naturally in the Dolomites. Qualitative monitoring]	Transport/Mobility
Scientific publications	Elmi and Perlik (2014)	From Tourism to multilocal residence?	Tourism
	Scuttari and Della Lucia (2016)	Principi di management delle aree protette e patrimonio naturale. L'efficacia della gestione integrata e partecipata delle Dolomiti UNESCO [Management principles for protected and natural heritage areas. The effectiveness of integrated and participatory management of the Dolomites UNESCO WHS]	Tourism
	Della Lucia and Franch (2017)	The effects of local context on World Heritage Site management: The Dolomites Natural World Heritage Site, Italy	Tourism
	Scuttari et al. (2019)	Assessing the Tourism-Traffic Paradox in Mountain Destinations. A Stated Preference Survey on the Dolomites' Passes (Italy)	Transport/Mobility

(continued)

Table 3.3 (continued)

Type of document	Authors (Year)	Title	Topic
Internal records	Autonomous Province of Bolzano—Provincial Environmental Agency (2014; 2017 available on demand)	Monitoraggio dell'impatto acustico del traffico sui passi dolomitici [Monitoring of traffic-related noise on the Dolomites' passes]	Transport/Mobility
	Autonomous Province of Trento—Office of Rail and Road (2018 available on demand)	Analisi sulla provenienza dei fruitori dei passi dolomitici [Analysis of the origin of users crossing Dolomites' passes]	Transport/Mobility
	Autonomous Province of Trento—Provincial Environmental Agency (2014 available on demand)	Monitoraggio dell'impatto ambientale del traffico sui passi dolomitici [Monitoring of traffic-related environmental impact on the Dolomites' passes]	Transport/Mobility
Other publications	Azienda "Musei provinciali" Touriseum–Museo Provinciale del Turismo, Merano (2017)	Il turismo alla conquista dei passi alpini. Catalogo della mostra "Sui passi, pronti, via!" [Tourism winning Alpine passes. Catalogue of the exhibition "Ready, steady, pass!"]	Tourism and transport/Mobility
Survey data	Elmi and Wagner (2013)	Dataset related to the sample survey developed in Elmi and Wagner (2013)	Tourism
	Elmi (2014)	Dataset related to the sample survey developed in Elmi (2014)	Tourism

(continued)

Table 3.3 (continued)

Type of document	Authors (Year)	Title	Topic
	Scuttari and Bassani (2015)	Dataset related to the sample survey developed in Scuttari and Bassani (2015)	Transport/Mobility
Census data	Provincial Institute for Statistics (ASTAT) of the Autonomous Province of Bolzano/Bozen	Census data on traffic counting stations, retrievable from: http://qlikview.services.siag.it/QvAJAXZfc/opendoc.htm?document=Traffico.qvw&host=QVS%40titan-a&anonymous=true	Transport/Mobility
Road-specific technical data	Autonomous Province of Bolzano/Bozen—Office of Road (2018 available on demand)	Technical data and shapefiles of the pass' road	Transport/Mobility

3.4 Mobile Video Ethnography: Ride-Alongs and Bio-Sensing

Phase II of data collection is now introduced. Firstly, the rationale behind using mobile video ethnography and bio-sensing will be presented, followed by a discussion about recruitment strategy, data collection and data analysis. Finally, there are reflections on the strengths and weaknesses of using mobile video ethnography and sensory data.

3.4.1 Rationale

There is a growing awareness in the mobilities literature that "a mobile subject demands a mobile method" (Cresswell 2012, p. 647), and that a traditional survey-based methods might "slow down and freeze experiences" (Fincham et al. 2010, p. 2) and might not work properly in exploring sensory and emotional features of travel journeys (Buscher and Urry 2009). By acknowledging these limitations, the mobilities turn calls for both a shift in the objectives (and the objects being researched) and the methods of that research (Sheller and Urry 2006), with the aim to bring the research process "as close to the mobile practice as possible" (Fincham et al. 2010, p. 4). There is some evidence that video technologies might offer unique chances to look closely at mobile practices, since videos as rich data sources enable visual continuity, multiplicity of cues (audio-video), and ability to show motion (Dinhopl and Gretzel 2016). Simultaneously, videos can grasp evidences of two of the most important senses involved in journey experiences: sight and hearing. These are the main reasons why this research uses *mobile video ethnography* as the main methodological framework to assess descriptions and cross-modal comparisons of journey experiences. Mobile video ethnography is rooted in both *visual ethnography* and *mobile methodologies,* and its results are a combination of the two. Therefore, a short description of these background methodologies is given before presenting a detailed explanation of the rationale for the selected method.

3.4.1.1 Visual Ethnography

Ethnography is the scientific description of peoples and cultures together with their customs, habits, and mutual differences. Ethnography is "a particular method or set of methods" that "involves the ethnographer participating, overtly or covertly, in people's daily lives for an extended period of time, watching what happens, listening to what is said, asking questions—in fact, collecting whatever data are available to throw light on the issues that are the focus of the research" (Hammersley and Atkinson 1995, p. 1). *Visual ethnography* is based on Sarah Pink's seminal work "*Doing visual ethnography*", published in 2007 and setting the theoretical and methodological backgrounds for using visuals—pictures, images or videos–in ethnographic research. Pink's definition of ethnography relates to "an approach to experiencing, interpreting and representing experience, culture, society and material and sensory environments that informs and is informed by sets of different disciplinary agendas and theoretical principles" (Pink 2007a, p. 34). Active participation and self-reflection are crucial aspects of this interpretation of ethnographic work. Visual ethnography allows the researcher to perform ethnographic research using visuals and is situated at the interdisciplinary interface between anthropological and sociological perspectives on the visuals.

> Visual Ethnography involves an approach that engages with audio-visual media and methods throughout its processes of research, analysis and representation. It is inevitably collaborative and to varying extents participatory. (Pink 2008, p. 1)

Moreover, visual ethnography is also "informed by recent theoretical turns to theories of place and space, practice, movement and the senses" (Pink 2007a, p. 17): the so-called "sensory turn" (Howes 2005) and the connected "nonrepresentational approaches" (Thrift 2008; Ingold 2011). Visual ethnography acknowledges thereby that sensory elements of experiences cannot be separated from visual ones and seeks to incorporate them in a holistic and integrative analysis. Visual ethnography is not only a practical tool for data collection through visuals, but it is rather a dynamic and self-reflective process of knowledge creation and interpretation: "a practice and way of knowing and learning in the world that might be equally analysed" (Pink 2007a, p. 17). Indeed, in visual ethnography the call for self-reflection on the researchers' individual visual practices and images is as important as the analysis of someone else's worlds through their visuals. This is because it is exactly the link between researchers' subjectivity and the subjectivities of research participants that produces a negotiated version of reality. Indeed, through visual ethnography it is not possible to achieve an "objective or truthful account of reality" (Pink 2007a, p. 35) but one can offer multiple (and not necessarily converging) versions of experiences of reality. Thereby, visual ethnography accepts subjectivity as "a central aspect of ethnographic knowledge, interpretation and representation" (Pink 2007a, p. 36) and not as a non-scientific way of approaching knowledge. In this sense, a realist use of the visuals, i.e. their understanding as objective visual records of environments, should be integrated by reflexive attitudes towards "the intentions behind such uses, the cultural conventions that frame them, their limits as regards the representation of truth, and the theoretical approaches that render them ambiguous" (Pink 2007a, p. 41). Subjectivity-related questions might go so far that they relate even to daily uses of visuals by researchers, and to how these practices can shape their approach to knowledge generation during data collection.

3.4.1.2 Video Ethnography

Video ethnography is a particular way of doing visual ethnography through video recording practices. Although video materials might seem realist representations of reality, once again if we examine them with the lenses of visual ethnography, they are also results of a subjective interpretation of the seen. They "are composed through not simply the capturing of what is in front of the camera lens. Rather, they are made in relation to what is behind and around the camera" (Pink 2007a, p. 40). This means that both what is seen and what is avoided to be seen are equally important for a visual ethnographer, who anyway negotiates the meaning of what he analyses together with participants. Indeed, for a (self-) reflection on the visual material once it is recorded, video ethnography relies on a tacit collaboration of researcher and participant: a so-called "collaborative encounter" (Pink 2007a, p. 61), which might also reduce the anxiety or stress related to the participation of the research project where video recordings are planned. Apart from causing stress or anxiety to participants, using video recordings as a method for data collection and knowledge generation might raise issues of participants' informed consent. Besides the possibility of having a consent form signed off at the beginning of the study, consent might need to be re-negotiated at different stages of the project to ensure that participants are fully informed of the different uses of visual material during data processing and later representations. Sometimes participants are also thanked with the restitution of some kind of recorded results or directly involved in their production through a co-creative platform of collaboration (Pink 2007a).

3.4.1.3 Mobile Ethnography

The second method that inspired mobile video ethnography is *mobile ethnography*, one of the possible applications of mobile methodologies in practice (Fincham et al. 2010). Mobile ethnography can be defined as "a mobile participant-observation with a particular focus on mobile phenomena" (Novoa 2015, p. 100). Indeed, mobile ethnography might involve *shadowing* (Czarniawska-Joerges 2007), other techniques to conduct fieldwork on the move, observing experiences while they are happening in a real space-time framework. The definition of mobile ethnography by Stickdorn et al. (2010) introduces a technological dimension of the data collection process, since mobile ethnography is defined as a "geographically independent ethnographic research for a specific subject matter through the utilisation of mobile devices" (Stickdorn et al. 2014, p. 495). The use of mobile devices enables different ways of observing the fieldwork on the move, based not only on the physical presence of researchers *shadowing* participants to collect data, but also on the handing over of tracking devices or the usage of participants' mobile phones (Stickdorn et al. 2014). Indeed, the adoption of mobile ethnography in the tourism field so far does not involve participant observation, but instead is mostly generating knowledge by integrating tourists as *active investigators*, typically using their mobile phones (Stickdorn et al. 2014; Stickdorn and Zehrer 2010; Muskat et al. 2013). This approach has been used to analyse end-to-end customer experiences, as well as to capture customer journeys from a user perspective (Stickdorn and Zehrer 2010). Mobile ethnography follows five basic principles (Stickdorn et al. 2014): (a) it is *user centred*, since it enables the viewing of service experiences from the customer's perspective; (b) it is *co-creative*, because it integrates real-life customers–but potentially also other stakeholders–actively as investigators; (c) it is *sequencing*, in that it collects customer journeys as a sequence of touchpoints; (d) it is *evidencing*, by permitting participants to document both intangible and tangible aspects of their experiences; (e) finally, it is *holistic*: it enables customers to record their whole customer journey. Thereby, mobile ethnography seems appropriate to collect subjective evidences on journey experiences and to analyse their physical, emotional, social and sensory features.

3.4.1.4 Mobile Video Ethnography

Theoretically rooted in the *new mobilities paradigm* (Sheller and Urry 2006), *mobile video ethnography* developed as an approach at the border between visual and mobile ethnography. In contrast to mobile ethnography, mobile video ethnography has been very rarely applied to tourism so far, even though some analyses on leisure mobilities exist already (Brown 2015, 2017). Mobile video ethnography has largely been used to integrate "orthodox instruments of transport geographers", such as stated preference surveys or traffic counts, with more innovative tools, aimed at unlocking "the more 'unspeakable' and 'non-relational(ised) meanings'" of mobility, instead of its rational motivations (Spinney 2011, p. 163). Justin Spinney—one of the initiators of the method points out that mobile video ethnography is a way of providing "an insight into the situated and contextual nature of knowledges and practices" as well as an attempt to focus on "experiential, affective and material aspects of practice which are often marginalized in less participative modes such as surveys" (Spinney 2011, p. 165). Anyway, even if mobile methods "can vibrantly apprehend mobile worlds" (DeLyser and Sui 2013, p. 297), Spinney partly acknowledges that also other methods, such as textual and historical sources, might be valid to (re-)collect journey experiences. The difference between mobile methods and more traditional methods relies in the fact that, by using mobile video ethnography, it is possible to also derive affective values of experiences related to contingent time-space situations, because it is possible to investigate "what people are feeling on a second-by-second basis in response to environmental stimuli" (Spinney 2015, p. 235). Mobile video ethnography and all mobile methods should not become "the new orthodoxy with which to interrogate and understand mobilities" (Bissel 2010, p. 56). They can and should be combined with traditional methods and with innovative data collection tools to provide the most complete view of mobility possible. In this sense, Spinney also identifies quantitative techniques of bio-sensing as valuable tools to enrich ethnographic research approaches, because they enable "the bodies to 'speak for themselves'" (Spinney 2015, p. 239) in relation to contingencies.

Several "on the move" inquiries come under the framework of mobile video ethnographic approaches. This research examines go-along and ride-along methods (Büscher et al. 2011), i.e. participant observation techniques with the support of action cameras. It is acknowledged that these methods can provide a deeper knowledge of "the identities, moralities, values, beliefs and concerns of the people they do their research with" (Pink 2007b, p. 244). Go-along methods using action cameras developed when the evolution of digital video technologies, with their portability and their relatively low cost, opened up the possibility of making *video ethnography on the move,* with the initial interest to study walking routes and their diverse representations of one same (urban) environment (Pink 2007b, 2008; Spinney 2011; Pink). They have later developed into *ride-along* techniques, with the investigation of urban cycling routes (Brown and Spinney 2010). The shift from walking to using a bicycle while doing visual ethnographic research needed some adaptations in the data collection, since in certain contexts, e.g. in metropolitan areas, the ride-along procedure with a physically present accompanying researcher was either technically impossible due to different riding skills, or even dangerous for safety reasons. Moreover, the *there-ness* of the researcher during the participants' journeys was perceived to be potentially disruptive (Laurier 2010), especially if a verbal discussion on the experience was taking place exactly during the experience itself. Paradoxically, even covert research, i.e. the placing of cameras without participants being aware of them during recordings—would have anyway not ensured objectivity, which is not easily reachable, and also not aimed at, through mobile video ethnography (Pink 2007a). In conclusion, it is increasingly accepted that, in "riding-along" techniques, the camera is best handled by the participants: the researcher, instead of *being* there, is somehow *seeing* there and *feeling* there (Spinney 2015).

The video has, therefore, evolved as a way in which researchers have retained and evoked the context and detail of the mobility practice, although they were not always accompanying participants. Nowadays it is believed that the use of portable devices in mobile video ethnography can somehow be a surrogate for direct participation because it allows for the recording of rich "audio-visual records of lived practice" (Büscher et al. 2011, p. 9), which are precious materials for collective reflection and eventually collaborative work after data collection. In other words, the idea of riding-along stands for the concept of "moving with" someone, and it becomes "a way of attuning the researcher to the mobile practice in question and in so doing, of facilitating cultural and social empathy" (Spinney 2015, p. 237). However, it should be noticed here that "seeing" is not the same as "knowing" the experience, and that the viewing of the clip by the researcher can only facilitate empathy, and will never correspond to the real life experience (Delaney 2016). In other words, it is believed that the use of mobile video technologies can facilitate empathy even when using indirect researcher participation in a journey, because multimedia can animate worlds and shed light on experiences that would be not accessible otherwise (Spinney 2015). However, there is no perfect correspondence between video recording and experience. Notwithstanding these issues, according to Büscher et al. (2011) mobile methods using video technologies have the advantage of creating a *double transparency* effect: through video recordings, they both offer a second-by-second (subjective) representation of mobility *on the move* and somehow provide documentary evidence of an innovative methodology of research, reporting its strengths and weaknesses. This re-calls the idea of self-reflection on visual ethnographic data introduced earlier in this chapter (Pink 2007a).

A second aspect linked to the non-realist nature of mobile video ethnography relates to the use of videos to stimulate recollection. Indeed, recorded videos can be a very helpful tool to recollect past events *in the now* (Spinney 2015), minimising the distortions related to the time-gap between event and its recollection. In addition, a recollection through a video might create new reductions and abstractions, especially if the video is edited, cut or viewed in slow motion. Once again, in mobile video ethnography video material is not recorded as a realistic representation of reality: subjectivity also pervades the recollection phases of research. This aspect was consciously taken into account when using video elicitation to measure the emotional reactions of participants (see later in this chapter: Sect. 3.4.5). A final remark on experience recollection through video material is needed to tackle those critiques asserting that mobile video ethnography catches mainly *glimpses* of movement (Brown and Spinney 2010), while it tends to overlook quiescent parts of the journey. This issue was problematized by David Bissel, who argued that memories of mobile journeys tend to privilege active moments towards quiescent ones, with the risk of leaving a record of only "action filled recollections" (Bissel 2010, p. 67). Knowing this aspect in advance has helped the analytical phase of this thesis to focus consciously on apparently "void" moments, on waiting times, on minutes or seconds where cyclists or motorcyclists stayed in silence, or stopped their journey. The recording of journey experiences second-by-second through a video allows the researcher to recall all such moments, and juxtapose them with more active ones, to stimulate self-reflection. As argued by Spinney (2015), the contemplative side of a journey can thereby become evident through mobile video ethnography, both by focussing on the verbal reports of participants, and on their visual attention (or conscious overlook) during recordings. Spinney's case of a cyclist especially selecting a cycle route without "'noisy' advertising among the main roads" (Spinney 2015, p. 238) is a good example of reflecting upon the voluntary "vacuum" that a travel journey might have in itself and has inspired this research.

3.4.1.5 Headcam Video Ethnography

In the light of the considerations above, it was decided that participants in this research would be unaccompanied while taking part in their mobile journeys and the "ride-along" method would be based on video recordings through action cameras. In the area of ethnographic mobile video recording, headcams have been widely used in recent years (Spinney 2011; Brown and Spinney 2010; Brown 2015, 2017; Brown et al. 2008; Delaney 2016) and it has been acknowledged how this practice enables researchers to "'go with' the subjects as they move, to follow the action, and go with the flow of micro and macro movements as they unfold" (Brown and Banks 2014, p. 99). It was also acknowledged that the presence of a camera somehow generates an impact on social relations, due to the awareness of being recorded (Delaney 2016). This happens particularly in walking experiences, where the use of headcams is rather uncommon, whereas in cycling or motorcycling it is more widespread. Notwithstanding the possible intrusive factor of the headcam, it is believed that for this study the distortion effect of wearing a camera is much lower than the effect of being interviewed by a "riding-along" researcher while travelling. Also the possibility of "acting" and not being authentic–developing "strategies of self-representation"–during the video is regarded as a minor issue, since it was acknowledged in previous studies that, especially in the case of technically challenging routes, participants tend to be "lost in their thoughts and practices" (Brown et al. 2008) and not engaged in acting unnaturally.

Among the relevant weaknesses of mobile video ethnography is the delivery of partial or generalised sensory and affect information, without quantifying emotional arousal and the corresponding external stimuli (Spinney 2015). Therefore, integrating bio-sensing technologies is a valid possibility to enrich the measurement and analysis of mobile experiences by integrating rich quantitative data. Bio-sensing is a way "to fortify go-along approaches by representing and geo-locating down to the second, pre-conscious intensities that have arisen through moving encounters with other materialities." (Spinney 2015, p. 240). Thus, mobile video ethnography "can provide insight into the quality of affect whilst bio-sensing can provide data on intensity/quantity" (ibidem). The use of bio-sensing combined with GPS information on the exact location of the participants was, therefore, used to combine "objective" data (biometrics and GPS position) with a "subjective story", producing a new kind of "psychogeography" (Nold 2009, p. 5). This call for an integration of bio-sensing in video ethnographic research illustrates how methods of data collection in ethnography are not inflexible: due to continuous self-reflection, a method can develop across time even during one research project, forming real "biographies of methods" (Pink

3.4 Mobile Video Ethnography: Ride-Alongs ... 95

and Leder Mackley 2012, p. 1). In this research, the integration of bio-sensing data was deemed as important to address the research questions and it was decided to collect these data through an add-on applicable on the headcam, which was capable of collecting biometric sources (heart rate), as well as movement-related information (GPS, altitude, speed).

In the light of the above, and in relation to the research questions and the theoretical framework presented earlier in this thesis, Phase II methods were decided upon: *unaccompanied riding-alongs using headcams in conjunction with bio-sensing* (GPS, heart rate and speed). There have been already other studies focussing on cycling experiences using headcam video ethnography in literature. However, the method implemented for this research provides a unique contribution to mobile methods in that it is integrating bio-sensing to enrich visual material, and in that it will ultimately compare these data on a cross-modal base among cyclists and motorcyclists.

3.4.2 Recruitment Strategy

A purposive sampling strategy was implemented, in order to ensure that the desired variety of respondents was involved to meet the research objectives. Purposive sampling (Robson 2002) allows to first identify the characteristics of the desired sample based on the research questions asked, and then recruit participants accordingly. Based on Robson (2002), purposive sampling occurs when "a sample is built up which enables the researcher to satisfy her specific needs in the project" (Robson 2002, p. 265).

Based on this sampling strategy, seven cyclists and seven motorcyclists, all visitors to the area, were recruited to take part to the research. The number of seven was chosen based on the close examination of previous mobile ethnographic studies (Delaney 2016; Spinney 2011; Brown 2015), which used respectively 14, 20 and 34 persons. The "minimum" number of 14 (7 + 7) valid journeys was reached, replicating the same design of Delaney (2016), although seven additional journeys were collected, that were not used due to the poor data quality. However, the number of 14 participants is offering a richer set of data per each unit analysed, because—compared to the work of Delaney (2016)–in this study the traditional ethnographic data are integrated with the novel bio-sensing data. The sample was collected in August and September 2016, selecting both high and shoulder season periods, as it will be explained based on the contextual description (see Sect. 4.2). Table 3.4 illustrates the details of the participants.

The fourteen visitors all started a trip including Sella Pass for recreational purposes, alone or in a group, and they were mostly selected from tourists overnighting in the valleys surrounding the case study area (Val Gardena, Val di Fassa, Val Badia and Valle di Fodom). A small number of day visitors (2 from each mode) were not overnighting on site. Motorcyclists were all riding their bike without passengers, except in one case, which was selected to explore possible features of verbal and non-verbal interactions while on the move. The choice was made to consciously

Table 3.4 List of participants (own elaboration)

ID	Pseudonym	Travel mode[a]	Visitor type[b]	Date	Place of residence	Frequency of riding	Age	Gender
1 M	Fabrizio	M	T	18.08.2016	Italy	1	<30	M
2 M	Lucio	M	T	18.08.2016	Italy	1	31–45	M
3 M	Christopher	M	T	23.08.2016	Italy	1	<30	M
4 M	Alois	M	T	24.08.2016	Germany	2	31–45	M
5 M	Juan	M	T	24.08.2016	Germany	2	31–45	M
6 M	Marco	M	S-D	11.09.2016	Italy	30	<30	M
7 M	Davide	M	S-D	11.09.2016	Italy	5	31–45	M
1 B	Carlo	B	S-D	24.08.2016	Italy	7	31–45	M
2 B	Corrado	B	S-D	24.08.2016	Italy	30	31–45	M
3 B	Peter	B	T	29.08.2016	Germany	1	<30	M
4 B	Elias	B	T	29.08.2016	Austria	1	46–60	M
5 B	Gabriel	B	T	06.09.2016	Brazil	2	31–45	M
6 B	Armando	B	T	06.09.2016	Brazil	2	31–45	M
7 B	Michael	B	T	09.09.2016	New Zealand	1	46–60	M

[a] M = motorcycle; B = road bicycle
[b] S-D = same-day visitor; T = tourist

select mostly people with little knowledge of the destination area, but also a small number of frequent visitors, to give the possibility to explore differences. Further sampling determinants were the frequency of riding activity along the pass and the patterns of destination exploration (base holiday trip, round trip, passing through), as well as the type of vehicle (only for motorcyclists). Most of the people in the sample were riding along the Sella Pass road for the first time (6); some others (4) had taken only one tour previous to the one analysed. Day visitors knew the area better, two of them having been there 5 or 7 times, two more than 30 times. This mix of visitors was deemed as crucial to allow an understanding of possibly different perceptions of the unique landscape of the Dolomites, which might evoke different feelings depending on travellers' familiarity with it.

Concerning mobility patterns, most of the cyclists were on base holiday trips, overnighting in one accommodation for more than one night and taking different tours during the same holiday. Motorcyclists were more frequently on round trips or passing through, and only in two cases were they doing base holiday trips. The type of motorbike was selected based on the following categories: naked bikes, cruisers, sport bikes and touring bikes (a naked bike is a standard bike, with an upright riding position; a cruiser has a reclining seating position, similar to a traditional Harley-Davidson bike; a sport bike is optimized for speed, acceleration, braking, and cornering on paved roads, typically at the expense of comfort; a touring bike offers better weather and wind protection, large-capacity fuel tanks for long ranges

3.4 Mobile Video Ethnography: Ride-Alongs ...

between fill-ups, and a more relaxed, upright seating position than sport bikes). The first three categories were covered in the sample, whereas touring bikers were not directly carrying a camera, but they were part of groups participating in the research. Therefore, their behaviour was also taken into account using the video ethnographic material.

Gender balance was very hard to ensure, since both motorcycling and road cycling communities are male dominated[1] and the few female riders the researcher met were accompanying persons or new riders and were not willing to carry a camera along the route, while sometimes pushing their husbands or partners to do so. Reflecting on these aspects might suggest that female cyclists might feel under pressure while climbing the challenging road of the pass—both physically and mentally—and therefore they might be less interested in carrying a camera. Overall, the collected video material retrospectively proved that female riders were a rare minority of the cyclists on the Sella Pass road and indirectly included one female rider in the research, being the accompanying wife of one participant. This case reveals interesting aspects in relation to the arousal of feelings that will be further explained in the results section (see Chaps. 4 and 5). Similarly to gender balance, age balance was also difficult to account for, since driving licences can be obtained up to 16 years for motorcyclists and the degree of fitness required to climb the mountain pass inevitably excluded most younger (<18) and elderly (65+) cyclists. The age category mostly involved was 30–45 years, although there were three visitors younger than 30 and one older than 46.

Participants were contacted both in specialized accommodation facilities (if tourists) or intercepted on the road. This second possibility was chosen in the case of same-day visitors and it was quite difficult to manage technically, especially since cyclists were not willing to stop and install the headcam while they were riding along the valley. Participants verbally accepted the recording of video material and shared their contact details to be addressed later on via email. On a later stage—when the video material was sent in combination with bio-sensing data, informed consent for data publication, based on the consent form in appendix (see Appendix) was given. Although acknowledging that informed consent should be collected in written form from the early stage of the research, this form of consent was preferred for two reasons: visual data recorded were related to the road and not encompassing participant's faces, ensuring thereby anonymity. Moreover, time constraints and complexities in managing the data collection procedure forced the researcher to agree with participants on a later written expression of their consent, which happened in all cases before starting the data analysis.

---

[1] According to the analyses collected in the EU project RIDERSCAN by Delhaye and Marot (2015), the population of female riders of moped and motorcycles ranges between 5% and 15% of the European population; according to Istat's survey "La pratica sportiva in Italia [The sport practice in Italy]" (https://www.istat.it/it/archivio/204663), the percentage of women older than 3 years practicing cycling sports in Italy amounted to 7.4% in 2015.

3.4.3 Data Collection, Research Design and Administration

The participants were selected based on their intention to climb the Sella Pass during their daily tour. The remaining part of the tour was asked for and taken into account to ensure that the wider context of the journey was captured, but the video recordings only rarely included riding journeys beyond the Sella Pass, which were outside the purpose of this analysis.

To facilitate the procedures of camera installation and to ensure its correct position and *mise-en-scene* (Rose 2012), the camera was installed by the researcher at the beginning of the climbing part of the pass (corresponding to the areas of Plan de Gralba or Pian Schiavaneis in Fig. 3.2, depending on participant's direction). At the beginning of the trip it was agreed with the participants to meet after the descent in a public restaurant, where a meeting was organised in a quiet corner to organise video elicitation and measure emotional responses through facial action coding (see Sect. 3.5.1.2). For this purpose, the video footage was easily uploaded from the camera to a laptop using an SD memory reader. At this point a questionnaire was also filled in by participants, as it will be explained later in this chapter (see Sect. 3.5.1.1).

Headcams installed were GoPro HERO4™ Silver Edition. They are quite small (58 × 41 × 30 mm) and light (89 g) and were chosen due to their high quality resolution (HD: 1280 × 720 240 fps) and relatively long battery autonomy (60–90 min recording with high resolution). As stated by Bédard (2015), they have the advantage of capturing deep-focus images and compensate for jarring movements, which

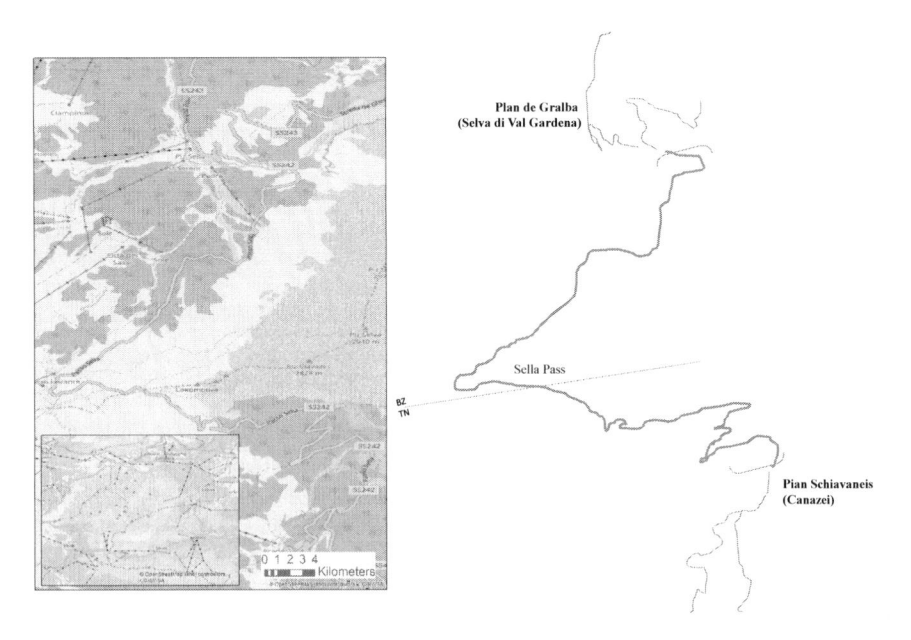

Fig. 3.2 Case study maps—Sella Pass and the Sellaronda tour (own elaboration)

3.4 Mobile Video Ethnography: Ride-Alongs ...

Fig. 3.3 Headcam positions on helmets (own elaboration)

is very important when the camera is mounted on travelers' bodies. Cameras were installed in order to ensure a first-person mode use, i.e. to guarantee a subjective point of view and evoke the process of identification of the video viewer with the traveller (see Fig. 3.3). One of the most common placements to facilitate the process of identification and immersion using the GoPro headcam is the one on the helmet (Bédard 2015). This process of identification and immersion happen because the gaze of the GoPro on the helmet is aligned with the gaze of the traveller (both having a centrifugal view) and because videos tend to replicate two main qualities of human experience: embodiment and intentionality (Schmidt and Thompson 2014). These features make it possible that the video recording somehow constitutes a first proxy of travellers' visual attention.

The alignment of camera and traveller gazes is possible by placing the headcam both on top and to the side of the helmet, corresponding approximately to the level of the mouth of the rider. The lateral position for motorcyclists was consciously preferred because it included a partial view of the left hand, which is normally used by motorcyclists to greet other motorcycles and thereby was an interesting object to observe during the journey. This position was unfortunately not acceptable for cyclists, because the weight of the camera would have made the helmet slope and the cyclist feel uncomfortable. In the light of the above, first-person, centrifugal gazes were selected for the *mise-en-scene*; it is acknowledged here that the type and position of the headcam to a certain extent influenced the framing of the video footage, but it is also accepted that—no matter how they are recorded–video data never correspond exactly to objective reality (Pink 2007a) and should be interpreted with this in mind.

When the choice of technical setting was made, more sophisticated tools such as eye tracking glasses were considered, but excluded for several reasons. Indeed, even if they would have been technically more suitable to track eye movement and visual attention (in addition to the same audio-visual material), the practicality of their

Fig. 3.4 Headcam and add-on used on riders' helmets (own elaboration)

use was not compatible with motorcyclists' and cyclists' equipment (e.g. helmet for motorcyclists, sunglasses for cyclists) and hardly compatible with bio-sensing while on the move. Moreover, both the practice of cycling and motorcycling could have made the glasses fall or be damaged, which might have compromised the entire data collection session. Go Pro Cameras, instead, are constructed to record the practice of extreme sports; they are more resistant and able to stabilize images in case of vibrations and high speed. Actually, they fell apart twice in the course of participants' journeys, but they continued working properly after these few accidents (and even those events were recorded).

Additionally to the headcam an add-on feature was provided—Get On Data Music-, which enabled the synchronisation of visual data with sensor data through the use of a mobile App (Fig. 3.4). Accordingly, a mobile phone and a heartbeat belt were provided to participants for enabling bio-sensing. The heartbeat belt measured heart rate and associated it to temporal and GPS information recorded by the camera and the mobile App. Additionally, through the mobile phone, it was possible to record speed and altitude instantly as the journey continued. It was found that the important add-on device for bio-sensing was powered by the battery of the Go Pro camera and this proved to be quite energy consuming. There were two cases (one on a bicycle, one on a motorbike) where the battery ran out before the journey came to an end. In both cases the riders had reached the peak of the pass and the visual data was analysed using its valid parts.

3.4.4 Data Analysis

The analysis strategy for Phase II involved several steps: visual content analysis (Rose 2012; Hanjalic 2004; Ying and Jay Kuo 2003) using NVivo Pro 11™, normalisation and visualisation of bio-sensing data through Microsoft Excel™ and their GIS mapping through ArcGis™. These analytical operations allowed the definition of personas (Cooper 1999), characterized through the integration of aggregated video

3.4 Mobile Video Ethnography: Ride-Alongs ...

clips, bio-sensing data and results from questionnaires and emotion measurement techniques (see Sects. 3.5.1.1 and 3.5.1.2).

Visual content analysis involved the simultaneous analysis of multiple cues (audio, visual, transcriptions), integrated in one same software project on NVivo Pro 11™. The steps to proceed were derived from (Hanjalic 2004):

- *parsing*, consisting of a temporal segmentation of the video data stream into three main moments: climb, pass area, descent;
- *video content indexing*, corresponding to the assignment of "chunks" of video to specific semantic categories, corresponding to codes;
- *video content representation*, with the aim to resume visual content and efficiently/effectively communicate its essence using video stills, clips and graphic representations of codes.

Clips are used to show particularly frequent or interesting coding categories and they are made available online, as well as presented in the paper through video stills, as suggested by Pink (2007a). Moreover, video clips contributed to a video representation of specific phenomena and to the archetypical description of personas (Cooper 1999). More detail about personas is given in Sect. 3.6.1.2. The representation of the coding categories was achieved through frequency tables in NVivo Pro 11™ software and bipartite network graphs built through the software Gephi. In network graphs, nodes correspond to both visitors and to coded categories of actions, whereas edges represent the frequency or duration of these categories of action in the individual video footage. An example of these graphs is, e.g. Fig. 4.10. The networked graph enables a fine grained representation of the thick grained analysis of single visitors, because it enlightens simultaneously the more relevant nodes of actions, in terms of duration or frequency, with a contemporary evaluation of single cases.

Sensor data were downloaded on a laptop using Get On Studio software—a software specific for the Add-on use–and they were matched to the visual data, enriching the video frame as illustrated in Fig. 3.5. Additionally, rough data connecting GPS, altitude, speed and BPM (heart rate) were analysed separately, involving the following steps: data cleaning, data normalisation, data graphical visualisation and data mapping. In data mapping, the correlation between speed and BPM was represented, to allow a georeferencing of specific moments. This might be interpreted as a first attempt to merge the "objective" biometric and GPS data with the more subjective, embodied experience of individuals, as the new kind of "psychogeography" and "emotional geography" proposed by Nold (2009, p. 5).

In conclusion, Table 3.5 summarizes the various data sources and how these worked to represent the different features of the journey experiences, producing several outputs, mainly persona descriptions, Gephi network graphs and GIS maps.

Fig. 3.5 Sensor data integration into the video footage (GPS track, speed, altitude, hearth rate) (own elaboration)

Table 3.5 Data sources, features of journey experiences and outputs (own elaboration)

	Features of journey experiences			
	Physical and kinaesthetic	Sensory	Social	Emotional
Video content analysis (video, audio, transcript)	√ (Infrastructure description, weather situation)	√ (Landscape, soundscape, description of actions, rhythm)	√ (Transcript, description of actions in video, sound)	√ (Transcript)
GPS data	√ (Altitude, steepness, georeferencing of data)			
BPM data	√ (In relation to steepness–effort)			√ (In relation to speed)
Speed data				√ (In relation to BPM)
Outputs	Diagrams, Gephi network graphs, GIS maps and personas			

3.4.5 Reflection on Mobile Video Ethnography, Ride-Alongs and Bio-Sensing

This section reflects upon mobile video ethnography and its novel implementation using bio-sensing as a supporting data source. Since the method is quite new, a self-reflection on its strengths and weaknesses is crucial before analyzing results and gives a prospective view of future implementations.

The first remark is that mobile video ethnography is a time and resource intensive approach, both for the researcher and for the participants. For the researcher, this approach requires extreme flexibility in adjusting multiple journey measurements in one day and accordingly in arranging possible meetings with visitors to first install and then collect back cameras, including also the post-trip video elicitation. The availability of only two action cameras and the initial difficulties in recruiting participants made it possible to record on average just two journeys per day, with the only exception of one day, where four recordings were made. This high investment of time relates to the concentration of departures in one typical daily hour (between 9 and 10 AM), which made it difficult to use the two cameras more than once each in one day, and to the difficulty of reprogramming meetings across days, due to visitors' short average length of stay. A second critical aspect that was noticed and partly resolved in the data collection process relates to travel direction: initially it was hypothesized that the travel direction for data collection would be from Plan de Gralba to Pian Schiavaneis. Nevertheless, especially for cyclists, this direction was quite uncomfortable, because the Sellaronda tour is most frequently performed counter clockwise, i.e. from Pian Schiavaneis to Plan de Gralba. The reasons for choosing the preferred direction were crucial for cyclists and related to the technical features of the road, particularly steepness and length of climbing versus descending parts of the tour. As a result, it was not always possible to get the journey experience data following the preferred direction. In order not to shape the already planned visitors' experiences according to the researchers' needs—a choice that might cause some distortion in the nature and intensity of the experience—journeys in both directions were recorded, according to the pre-existing tour plan of the participants. Only when participants were unsure about the direction they would follow along the Sellaronda tour, was the counterclockwise direction suggested. These considerations help reflect on the fact that the measurement of the experience in the field ended up highlighting the importance of apparently non-fundamental aspects of the journey, such as the direction in a circular tour. The importance of the direction for cyclists (and on the other hand the indifference of motorcyclists with regards to direction) turns out to be a partial result of the analysis, showing how different features of the infrastructural environment affect the journey experience.

A second critical aspect of mobile ethnography is related to the procedures of working with video technology, both in the data collection and analysis phase. Also this aspect was mentioned by Delaney (2016) in her work, and although the recording time was consciously reduced in this research, it remained a critical issue here. Technical challenges began with the consideration that the researcher was not familiar with the usage of headcams and add-ons in research and in real-life, therefore a considerable time-investment was made in understanding usability, settings, softwares and cleaning procedures to treat data before starting the empirical work. Still, one major problem in the data collection phase was that it was not possible to check the effective recording status of visual and sensor data on a real time basis. Therefore, during the whole unaccompanied journey (which lasted up to one hour) there was no possibility for the researcher and limited possibility for the participant to check for data quality. Moreover, even in the case of running data collection, heart frequency figures in some specific cases created some gaps in measurements, which were only visible when rough data was downloaded from the cloud memory of the software Get On Studio in a later phase. The non-specificity of the technological setting for research data collection was, therefore, a critical issue, which in some cases reduced data quality. On the other hand, technologies specifically designed for research purposes, such as eye tracking glasses, would have not been suitable for use outside the laboratory. This critical aspect illustrates that the technological equipment to conduct video ethnography in real worlds is still not advanced and needs further improvement to enable smoother data collection. Finally, data elaboration was a very delicate phase, because it needed major time investment in data cleaning and interpretation, related to the non-specificity of data generated by the Add-on tool. For example, the synchronization of rough bio-sensing data and videos was the result of a series of calculations and synchronization procedures when working with raw Excel data, whereas it was done automatically from the Get on Studio software when composing the enriched video clip illustrated in Fig. 3.5.

A last remark refers to the collection of visual documentary data related to the participants. There was perhaps not enough focus on gaining photographs of participants' bicycles/motorcycles, their technical equipment, and other physical aspects from a third-person perspective. Such data might have helped in the later definition of personas, even though punctual information such as vehicle (see above) type and demographic data was collected through an additional questionnaire (see Appendix). Additionally, video material recorded with a third-person perspective could have enriched the first-person mode of GoPro cameras, because this last perspective replicates only participants' gazes and does not represent them directly. This potential for additional visual information was unconsciously made clear by one participant that was by chance carrying his own GoPro cameras during the journey. To record the tour, he added two additional cams: one situated on the handlebars of the bicycle, allowing a third-person view of him while riding; the other under the seat of a friend riding with him, allowing a third person perspective from far away. Through the comparison of those perspectives, illustrated as an example in Fig. 3.6, it was interesting to notice the power of the *mise-en-scene* in influencing the richness of information collected and the amount of information missed by using just one camera.

Actions such as stand-up riding, pedalling, drinking, were not always evident with a first-person mode of recording, whereas they would have been unequivocal using a third-person mode. In conclusion, the triangulation of camera perspectives, although more intrusive and very expensive in terms of technical setting and time required for data collection and analysis, might represent an additional feature to consider for

Fig. 3.6 Triangulation of perspectives (own elaboration)

future research. This triangulation was partly achieved when multiple participants travelling together in a velo-formation—as a group of bikes sharing travel route and rhythm—were simultaneously recorded. Multiple perspectives on one shared journey were consciously pursued, to minimise the asymmetry of agency effect recalled by Brown and Banks (2014), which refers to the fact that the use of one single camera to describe collective journeys might convey very partial views of the journey itself, if it is a group tour.

3.5 Emotion Measurement: Self-reporting Techniques, Video Elicitation, and Facial Action Coding

3.5.1 Rationale

Emotions can be measured through self-report or observation techniques. Self-report techniques (Bagozzi et al. 1999; Isomursu et al. 2007; Lee et al. 2007) are normally appropriate when the subjectivity of feelings is investigated and the cognitive appraisal process is under examination. Conversely, observation techniques (Kim and Fesenmaier 2015) are suitable to monitor the physiological and expressive reactions to stimuli. Especially in cases of observation through facial action coding systems, categorical theories of emotion are applied to measure a set of basic feelings in a discrete way (Ekman et al. 2002). There is no best type of measurement strategy to use in applied research, because the emotional construct is ambiguous in its definition and especially because "experiential, physiological, and behavioural measures are all relevant to understanding emotion and cannot be assumed to be interchangeable" (Mauss and Robinson 2009, p. 209). Instead, the theoretical framework used and the type of emotional response investigated determine the preferred measurement technique for each case. This research goes for the application of categorical theories of emotions and triangulates comparable self-reporting and observation techniques: both rely on pre-defined emotions, although their categorization is not identical. Further details are provided below on self-reporting and observation techniques as well as on how they have been combined in this research.

3.5.1.1 Self-reporting Techniques

Self-reporting techniques essentially include ways of involving research participants in reporting on their own feelings. Possible data collection methods encompass questionnaires, focus groups, and diaries (Isomursu et al. 2007). Questionnaires for data collection might use not only verbal scales (protocols), but also non-verbal ones (pictograms), because emotions might be hard to verbalize (Desmet 2002). Two possible examples of self-reporting through pictograms are Self Assessment Manikin (SAM) (Lang 1980) and Emocards (Desmet et al. 2001). They are used in marketing research to explore consumption emotions or investigate reactions to advertising (Isomursu et al. 2007).[2]

Notwithstanding the strength of exploring the subjective nature of feelings, self-reported techniques have some weaknesses. For instance, they require a cognitive understanding of the emotion and its scale by the interviewees. Moreover, they require a self-judgment process, which might lead to some bias (Isomursu et al. 2007). Finally, they imply a post-consumption data collection, which is acknowledged to have a distortive effect (Kim and Fesenmaier 2015; Russell 2003). To (at least partly) overcome some of these critical issues, digital technologies have progressively offered some valuable instruments for researchers. Some examples are reviewed by Tähti and Arhippainen (2004), although many more are now available on the market. The 3E method, relying on free drawing feedbacks on digital interfaces (Tähti and Arhippainen 2004), helps overcome the cognition bias in predefined categories of emotions; the Mobile Feedback Application (Arhippainen et al. 2004) allows a real-time feedback through a questionnaire and helps avoiding biases related to post-experience reporting; the Experience Clip Method (Isomursu et al. 2004), relying on video observation of customers during experience valuation, is suitable to overcome self-judgment biases.

For this thesis, it was initially hypothesized to use a Mobile Feedback Application especially designed for ethnographic research of customers' journeys. However, during a first test it was acknowledged that the App was not suitable for analysing the dynamic aspects of mobility, because it mainly worked by hooking on to touchpoints, which in the case of Sella Pass might have been the starting and arrival points and the pass area, with almost no consideration of the riding part. Measuring emotions by hooking on to those few touchpoints would have been ineffective in grasping the feelings while on the route, contradicting the principles of mobile methods, which aimed to create a social science on the move.

---

[2]The SAM method uses a series of pictures of puppets "for measuring pleasure-displeasure, degree of emotional arousal and dominance-submissiveness" (Isomursu et al. (2007); Emocards are based on 16 cartoon faces which show eight distinct emotional responses Isomursu et al. (2007).

3.5 Emotion Measurement: Self-reporting ...

Table 3.6 Emotions measured, emojis and Likert-scales (own elaboration based on Ritchins 1997)

Emotions	Degree of involvement						When? (please describe)
	Intense/ high				Scarce/ low	No answer	
Optimism (optimistic, encouraged, hopeful)	O	O	O	O	O	O	
Happyness (happy, fulfilled)	O	O	O	O	O	O	
Peacefulness (calm, peaceful)	O	O	O	O	O	O	
Loneliness (lonely, homesick)	O	O	O	O	O	O	
Envy (envious, jealous)	O	O	O	O	O	O	
Shame (embarrassed, ashamed)	O	O	O	O	O	O	
Fear (scared, afraid, panicky)	O	O	O	O	O	O	
Sadness (depressed, sad, miserable)	O	O	O	O	O	O	
Worry (nervous, worried, tense)	O	O	O	O	O	O	
Discontent (unfulfilled)	O	O	O	O	O	O	
Anger (frustrated, angry, irritated)	O	O	O	O	O	O	

To overcome these difficulties in measuring emotion in real-time and on the move, it was decided to rely on video ethnographic methods and particularly on the relationships between the multiple cues of the action camera videos (visual data, dialogues) and the associated bio-sensing data (heart rate, speed) as a proxy for emotional content during the trip. In parallel, it was decided to integrate these data with a questionnaire for self-assessment of emotions as soon as the trip was finished. The questionnaire that was developed had the secondary advantage of collecting sociodemographic information, the motivation of the trip and several other relevant issues (see Appendix) that provided a more complete picture of the participant, minimising time investment and effort. The measurement of emotions in this questionnaire occurred according to the standard consumption scale developed by Richins (1997), using a 5-point Likert scale and representing the emotional states in words (including multiple synonyms in brackets) and by adding emojis (Arhippainen et al. 2004) to facilitate the familiarisation of participants with the written feelings. Emotions considered for analysis and their measurement scale are listed in Table 3.6. Besides the Likert-scale evaluation there was the possibility to write or describe moments when feelings were arising, to increase the richness of self-reported data. The questionnaire was available in 3 languages: Italian, German and English and it was filled in by participants themselves when debriefing after the recording of the journey.

3.5.1.2 Psychophysiological Observation Techniques

Similar to self-reporting techniques, observation techniques are methods for measuring emotional states (Kim and Fesenmaier 2015). However, they tend to quantitatively monitor the physiological/expressive nature of emotional reactions, and to rely on behavioural (facial expressions, speech, gestures) or neuro-physiological responses (skin conductance, eye tracking, bio-signals: pulse rate, blood pressure, brain activity) (Lohmeyer and Meboldt 2016). Psychophysiological measures have several advantages: they "(1) are close to mental and affective processes associated with consumer inquiry, (2) avoid concealment of true consumer reaction because they measure automatic processes without any manipulation; and (3) monitor the thoughts and feelings in real time when one is unaware, which cannot be retrieved, or which would become changed in subsequent verbal elicitation" (Babakhani et al. 2017, p. 959). The advantages of psychophysiological techniques rely also in the fact that they can trace the evolutionary process of emotional feelings. However, they often require specific know-how, ad hoc (and sometimes bulky) equipment, and a laboratory environment for experimental design; this leads to the paradox that the emotional reactions measured through observation techniques might be distorted by the measurement tools themselves, or by the non-natural context (Babakhani et al. 2017; Kim and Fesenmaier 2015).

In this dissertation it was decided to observe emotions partly in real time through the analysis of video recordings and bio-sensing data (see Sect. 3.4), and partly just after the journey had finished by monitoring second by second expressive participants' reactions when viewing their own video footage. The multiple video cues (above all, recorded gestures and transcription of dialogues) could capture in real time exclamations, comments, movements and emotionally charged descriptions of travelers' journeys, offering a first layer of observation for affect analysis. In addition, the bio-sensing data and particularly the heart rate and its relationship with speed were used as a further proxy for emotion, particularly referring to motorcyclists, since the heart frequency of cyclists was hardly influenced by the steepness of the route.

As a third source of measurement for emotional data, a combination of video elicitation and facial recognition systems was used. This took place just after the journey had finished, during a short stop at a restaurant or at a bike rental. Facial action coding systems were not applied directly on the move because, to analyse expressive reactions properly, they require some standard settings, such as full light and uncovered face, both of which would have not been possible during the journey. Therefore, to minimise biases in recalling the journey, the video footage was used as the material for video elicitation just a few minutes after the journey was finished, when the time gap between the lived experience and the remembered one was as short as possible.

Video elicitation is a method that entails the use of a video-recording to facilitate recall, reliving, and reflection on the recorded interaction by those involved (Henry and Fetters 2012). It was developed in the early 1980s by researchers who studied counsellor training (Kagan 1980; Erickson and Shultz 1982) to analyse counselling sessions. Later on it was used in the fields of knowledge engineering, interaction analysis, anthropology and other social science disciplines to recall interactional practices and discuss them in depth during elicitation interviews (Henry and Fetters 2012). Video elicitation works as a powerful tool also in visual ethnographic research to recall memories of past happenings and discuss them during qualitative interviews or collective views, minimising the biases related to a selective memory and at the same time creating new knowledge (Pink 2007a). In this dissertation, video elicitation was used as a tool to make participants recall the emotions lived a few minutes earlier, with the aim of simultaneously measuring their emotional reactions through facial action coding systems. Similar attempts to use videos as elicitation material in emotion research were made earlier using video elicitation in combination with electroencephalograms (EEG), (see e.g. Soleymani et al. 2012). The application of video elicitation in combination with facial action coding is very innovative in tourism and in mobilities research. In contrast to traditional self-reporting methods, it allows a second-by-second along with a mean or median analysis of facial reactions to visual contents. This recollection process happened on a second by second basis and just after the journey conclusion, recreating similar conditions to a real-time measurement, even if not being such.

Facial action coding systems were used in parallel to detect emotions evoked by the video footage and to label them, as well as to recognise their intensity on a second-by-second basis. SHORE™ is the software used for facial action coding. SHORE™ is the acronym for Sophisticated High-speed Object Recognition Engine (Wierzbicki et al. 2013; Kueblbeck and Ernst 2006) and is a fast, reliable and real-time capable software developed by the Fraunhofer Institute for Integrated Circuits in Erlangen, Germany (https://www.iis.fraunhofer.de/en/ff/sse/ils/tech/shore-facedetection.html). This software allows "recognition of human faces and in-depth analysis of facial expressions based on human muscular activity" using a standard camera (Wierzbicki et al. 2013, p. 60) through specific algorithms "from a large database of face images" (Wierzbicki et al. 2013, p. 61). The engine recognises the extent of four basic emotions (happiness, sadness, anger and surprise) with about 25 measures per second and it further detects gender and estimates the age of the participant. The highly sophisticated mathematical and computational features behind its activity, as well as the modular framework to detect and analyse facial expressions are beyond the explanation purposes of this methodological paragraph; further details and deeper insights are provided in (Ruf et al. 2011). What is relevant here is that the output of each measurement process is a CSV file, which encloses the "information about all annotated objects in the image" (Ruf et al. 2011, p. 240), including also multiple individuals, if they were contemporarily standing in front of the camera. The accuracy of SHORE^{TM} has been tested and has shown good results. The gender classification was checked twice and registered a recognition rate of 94.3 and 92.4%, whereas the happiness analyser had a recognition rate of 95.3% (Ruf et al. 2011). A further strength of SHORE^{TM} is the great richness of available features with minimal hardware requirements, which makes the software suitable for use outside as well as inside the laboratory.

3.5.2 Recruitment Strategy, Data Collection, Research Design and Administration

After the journey experience had finished, all participants that had carried the action camera along the journey were de-briefed in a restaurant or in a bike rental. Both places made a small and isolated room available, with good lighting and a quiet environment. This was the place where cyclists and motorcyclists, just a few minutes after they were finishing their journey–or at least their tour across the Passo Sella–responded to the self-report questionnaire and participated in the video elicitation combined with facial action coding. There was also no specified recruitment strategy, but rather all participants were invited to join the second session of measurements, based on a questionnaire and facial action coding.

After a short dialogue with the researcher and the recollection of action camera and sensors, participants were asked to have a look at (parts of) their video footage, while SHORE^{TM} was running in the background on the researchers' laptop. Since the journey lasted between 20 min for motorcyclists and 1 h for cyclists, it was not always possible to review the complete video footage. Therefore, it was decided to randomly select at least 2 min of the climbing part and 2 min of the descending part for each participant, with the possibility of showing more contents if the participant would tolerate a longer de-briefing time. This enabled the researcher to record each participant for at least 4 min of facial reactions to the visual content

3.5 Emotion Measurement: Self-reporting … 111

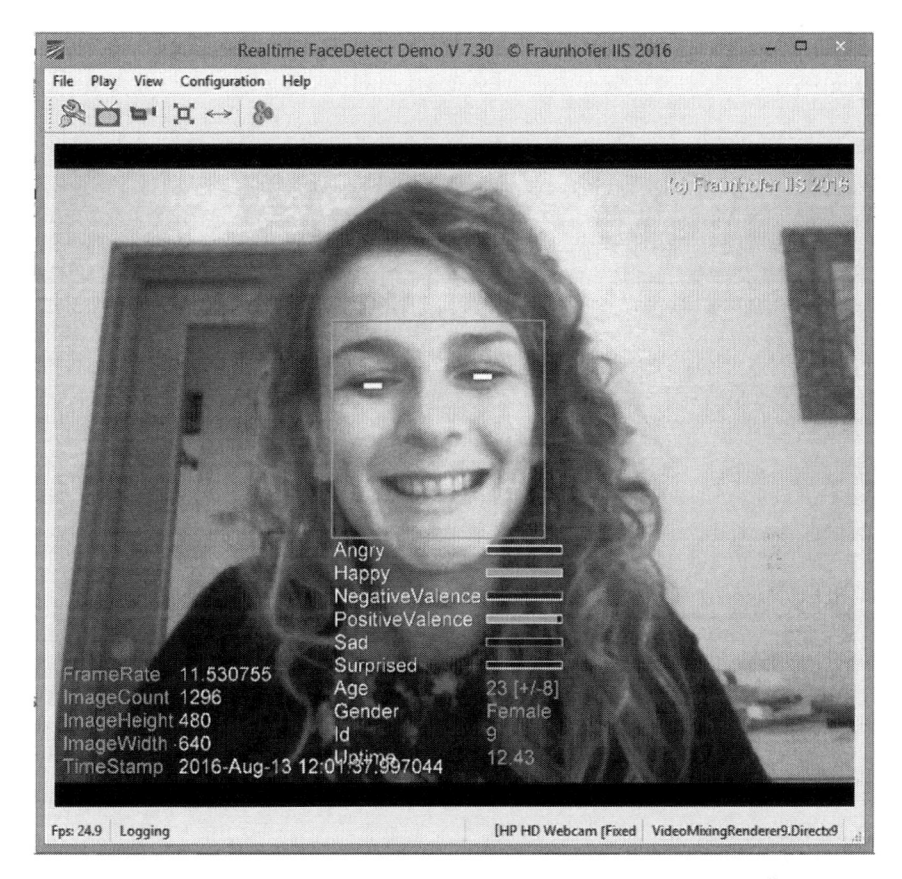

Fig. 3.7 SHORE™ interface (own elaboration)

of the journey experience and connect them to happenings in the video footage on a second-by-second basis. The synchronisation between the video footage and the SHORE™ measurement data was done manually, through simultaneously starting both programmes. Figure 3.7 shows the SHORE™ interface and output data.

After viewing the video footage and having facial reactions measured, participants filled in a questionnaire where they reported their feelings based on a standard scale (Richins 1997), and at the same time described the main happenings and the stimuli of these feelings in the form of written words or sentences (see Appendix 2 and Sect. 3.5.1.1). This written explanation helped triangulate information from facial action coding and at the same time facilitated the interpretation of self-reported categorical data.

The study of emotion-related proxies both during and after the consumption experience (heart rate and questionnaire), as well as the synchronization of the action camera video and the emotional response data recorded by SHORE™ enabled an exploratory picture of the emotional experiences on the move to be drawn. Moreover, questionnaires allowed a comparison between self-reporting and observation techniques of emotion measurement, assuming that they are more complementary than mutually exclusive methods for affect measurement.

3.5.3 Data Analysis

The analysis strategy for Phase III involved mainly descriptive statistics (frequencies and averages) and visual representations in the form of graphs. These data was initially analysed separately, to identify mean values for the expressed feelings per each participant. Then, self-report and observation methodologies were compared only on the individual level. Finally, emotional data—both the self-reported and observed–was related to video ethnographic material. The video footage was ultimately used to select those micro-events or longer activities imbued with a high emotional content. Based on these happenings and moments, clips were created to highlight emotionally charged aspects of the journey, which have then helped in the definition of personas (Cooper 1999) (see Chaps. 4 and 5). In this sense, sensory, self-report and observation techniques were converging in one big picture of emotional reactions to journey experiences. They were jointly defining the emotionally charged content of the journey, both in a positive and a negative sense. Moreover, the richness of the video footage as a source further enabled the description and understanding of objects, interactions or actions that worked as emotional stimuli for visitors.

3.5.4 Reflection on Emotion Measurement

Several reflections arise in relation to the self-reporting and observation techniques implemented in this dissertation to measure emotions. First, self-reporting and observation techniques were combined following the recommendation to use quantitative and qualitative data in an integrative rather than in a mutually exclusive way (Scuttari and Pechlaner 2017). This is rooted in the fact that it was found that objective measurement of physiological arousal through observation techniques helps with investigating how cognition works in the appraisal process and thereby in self-reporting. There is no perfect congruence between observed and self-reported responses (Kim and Fesenmaier 2015; Lee and Kyle 2012) because cognitive appraisal per se is relevant in emotional appraisal. What turned out to be clear after the measurements were made was that, although both self-reporting and observation techniques were equally important and complemented each other in understanding emotional arousal, the combination of quantitative and qualitative data collection and analysis appeared to be challenging in practice. Indeed, the classification by Richins (1997) on consumption emotions was partly different from that of basic emotions available in SHORE™, which made data comparisons appear difficult.

3.5 Emotion Measurement: Self-reporting … 113

Table 3.7 A comparison between self-report and observation-based categories of emotions (own elaboration)

		SHORE™			
		Happy	Angry	Sad	Surprised
Self-report questionnaire	Optimism				X (?)
	Happiness	X			
	Peacefulness				
	Loneliness				
	Envy				
	Shame				
	Fear				
	Sadness			X	
	Worry				
	Discontent				
	Anger		X		

Table 3.7 is a short representation of emotional categories in both scales and similar feelings are connected. While there are several emotions in the self-reporting scale that are not grasped by the facial action coding system of SHORE™, it is interesting to highlight how the "surprise" has no direct correspondence in the self-reporting scale. Since it has a positive valence in the software, it might be associated to optimism in the self reporting, nevertheless it is not perfectly equivalent.

Secondly, the decision to use observation techniques just after the end of the journey was very innovative, but at the same time it turned out to be somehow challenging for participants. Indeed, as explained in Henry and Fetters (2012), it is true that to conduct video elicitation properly it is important to minimise the elapsed time between video recordings and elicitation; however, in the specific case of cycling journeys, the collection of data just after the end of the journey was sometimes annoying, especially for tired cyclists. Therefore, the choice to conduct video elicitation and facial action coding just a few minutes after the trip, was successful from a methodological point of view, because participants had fresh memories of micro-events that happened during their trip; on the other hand and from a more practical perspective, it had the disadvantage of addressing participants during a very delicate moment: when they had already succeeded in their challenge and were resting and needing to relax—rather than recall the past journey. The novelty of the software used for facial recognition could partly mitigate this reticence to participate in the second part of data collection, because it made almost all participants curious and willing to test facial action coding.

Finally, a consideration should be expressed about the difference between living and recalling experiences. Indeed, the time gap between the moment where the journey was made and the one when it was recollected possibly made a difference in terms of attitude towards some actions. For example, the "pass challenge" might have evoked anxiety or even fear of failure during the climbing experience, but rather excitement when looking at the video footage and recalling the successful adventure. In this sense, a real-time measurement of physical reactions might have been more adequate to grasp emotions on a second-by-second basis, but—as was stated earlier in 3.3.5–it was almost impossible if considering the kinaesthetic aspects of cycling and motorcycling, the equipment of cyclists (e.g. sun glasses, helmets, etc.) and the high speed without a protection cabin. Once again, the combination of observation and self-report techniques, and the triangulation of multiple sources of evidence (e.g. heart rate during the journey, facial response after the journey and categorical as well as written self-reported responses) shows that it is crucial to gain a comprehensive overview of emotional arousal.

3.6 Integration of the Quantitative and Qualitative Results: Thick Description and Personas

3.6.1 Rationale

Mixed methods require time to systematically integrate quantitative and qualitative results, in order to produce a comprehensive conclusion of multiple sources of evidence. In this dissertation it was chosen to follow the principles of *thick description* (Geertz 1973) to holistically analyse travel journeys. Thick description enables the provision of details and micro-data on a second-by-second scale, contextualising them in the mobility space with its infrastructural and service features. Further, to filter out the essence of journey experiences in relation to mode, it was decided to work with the creation of *personas* (Cooper 1999), in order to provide simpler, archetypical features for bikers and motorcyclists, thus facilitating comparison.

3.6.1.1 Thick Description

Thick description is an approach to conducting anthropological research introduced by the philosopher Ryle (1971) and further conceptualized by the anthropologist Geertz (1973) in a dedicated essay. Geertz (1973) reflects on the complexities of doing ethnographic research and the need to always analyse the object of research in relation to its context, encompassing the aims of the actions taken and how these actions are understood by other individuals in the setting. According to Ryle, quoted by Geertz in his essay, one same physical action, such as the one of someone "rapidly raising and lowering their right eyelid" (p. 5) could indicate a nervous attitude, but also a wink to attract someone else's interest or even the imitation of someone else. Therefore, thick description suggests investigating not only *what* is happening, but also *why* and *for whom*. Thick description in this sense adopts more than a descriptive approach to objects and actions and aims to interpret them according to context and interactions. Recognising the complexities of understanding the world, (Geertz 1973) asserts that "doing ethnography is like trying to read (in the sense of 'construct a reading of') a manuscript–foreign, faded, full of ellipses, incoherencies, suspicious emendations, and tendentious commentaries–but written not in conventionalized graphs of sound but in transient examples of shaped behaviour" (p. 8).

Following the indications of Ryle and Geertz, thick description is used in this dissertation to construct a reading of the mobility space by different individuals and social groups, to understand their physical interactions with each other and with the environment, to understand social contacts and explore emotional and sensory worlds while on the move. Thick description enables, therefore, the introduction of an additional layer to the simple report of actions taken during the journey and the emotions measured. It enables the construction of a higher level of meaning for journey experiences, which, similarly to a system, is more than its constituent parts. Only based on this analysis is it then possible to crystallize personas.

3.6.1.2 Personas: A Description of a Descriptive Model

To grasp the essence of motorcyclists as riders and compare them to cyclists along pass roads, it was decided to define a first level of persona description, representing different types of visitors undertaking a journey along the Sella Pass. First conceptualised by Cooper (1999), personas are "fictitious characters, based on composite archetypes, and encapsulating 'behavioural data' gathered from ethnography and empirical analysis of actual users" (Idoughi et al. 2012, p. 288). The persona method was initially used in the context of IT system development, but it has since extended its application to product development, marketing, communication planning and service design (Nielsen 2013a).

Personas are normally "descriptive models of users" "captured in a narrative form" (Idoughi et al. 2012, p. 288), and they normally include some typical components of users, such as: photograph, identity, status, goals, knowledge and experience, tasks, relationships, psychological profile and needs, attitude and motivation, expectations, etc. (Idoughi et al. 2012; Courage and Baxter 2005). These components are by no means fixed and they work normally as flexible guidelines to create archetypical user profiles that assist service or experience design, as well as marketing choices. However, a persona is not the same as an archetype or person (Nielsen 2013a). In fact "[i]nstead of modelling only 'average' users, personas also take into account boundary cases as well as specific classes of users with special needs" (Idoughi et al. 2012, p. 288).

According to Nielsen (2013a), different approaches to personas design result in four different types of persona descriptions, that can be also combined together: the *goal-directed* personas, the *role-based* personas, the *engaging* personas and finally the *fictional* personas. All these, except for the fictional personas, are based on user research and data, but each of them focusses on different aspects of analysis. *Goal-directed* personas—based on the conceptualisation of Cooper (1999)—focus on the goals of the persona while using a product. *Role-based* personas—developed by Pruitt and Adlin (2006)—also describe user behaviour, but with a wider connection to quantitative and qualitative data and a more explicit focus on the contextual conditions, e.g. the role of the individual in one organisation or activity. The *engaging* perspective on personas embraces a broader understanding of the user, not only in his/her behaviour, but also in his/her attitudes, lifestyles, interests, needs, etc. This approach was developed by Nielsen (2013b) and it can definitely include roles and goals, but is more comprehensive by also addressing emotions, moods, etc. Finally, the *fictional* (or fiction-based) persona is not based on specific user data, but rather is used in the early stages of product and service design.

This dissertation follows the approach by Nielsen (2013b) and introduces engaging personas, based on the thick description of participant's journeys. Although personas descriptions might appear contradictory to thick descriptions, they are used in this dissertation as a complementary tool to abstract results from individuals and present common or contradictory features previously investigated in depth. This approach allows the construction of more "solid" personas, providing compact but deep and relevant information about physical, sensory, social and emotional aspects of journeys.

3.6.2 Data Integration and Administration

The integration of multiple sources of data is achieved through the use of NVivo Pro 11 ™ software, storing and administrating in one single project all visual, textual and numerical sources of evidence. This way of operating enables ensures the *construct validity* of the case study, because it enables the showing of a convergence of evidence in results based on data and methodological triangulation (Patton 1987). Additionally, the use of NVivo Pro 11™ software also increases the *reliability* of the case study, i.e. the possibility to replicate the case study following a transparent procedure. Cases (corresponding in this thesis to research participants) constitute the main anchoring point for all other data sources and they enable the connections between all other data

3.6 Integration of the Quantitative and Qualitative ...

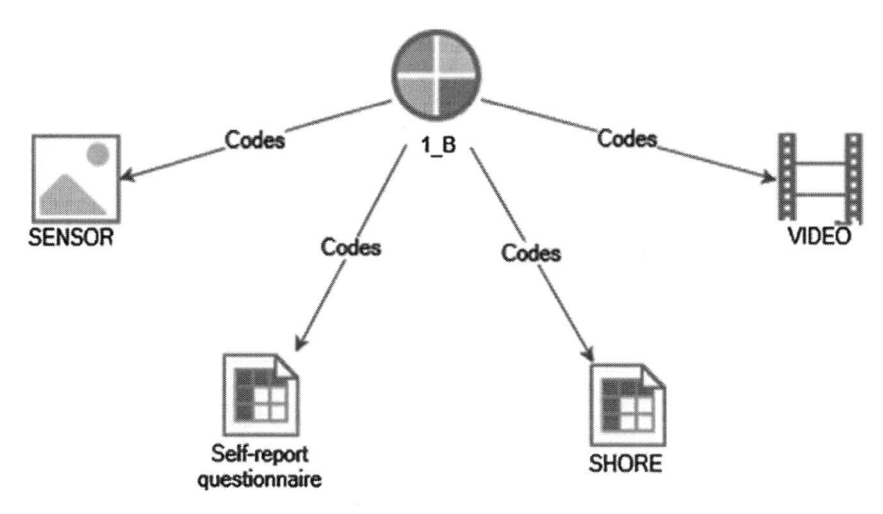

Fig. 3.8 Sources stored in NVivo Pro 11 ™ for one exemplary participant (own elaboration)

sets (questionnaires, sensor data, and facial action coding data). Figure 3.8 shows the multiple sources used for one single participant, and how the software allows for their integrated representation.

From a more technical point of view, NVivo Pro 11™ provides helpful tools to connect different data sources, from mind maps to graphs of coding categories (see Fig. 3.8). Nevertheless, the detail of these graphical representations is quite poor, since they do not allow the display of the intensity of the links among different coded categories. To overcome those difficulties, some aggregated visual representations of the thick journey description were developed using the open-source software Gephi, in forms of networks, where participants and type of actions were the nodes of the network, while frequencies or the duration of actions represented the nodes. This unique representation is proposed in Chap. 4 (Sects. 4.4 and 4.5).

Unique representations of emotional maps are also provided as a visual representation of thick description in Chap. 5, based on the suggestions of the book "Emotional Cartography—Technologies of the Self" by Nold (2009). This very experimental book is devoted to exploring possible visualizations of "people's intimate biometric data and emotions using technology" (p. 3). Nold (2009) presents possible solutions at the interface between art and geography to represent perceived spaces and merge them into a single (carto)graphical representation.

Finally, personas are created based on the evidence produced in thick description and presented according to some standard descriptors (photograph, identity, status, goals, means of transport, travel habits, psychological profile and needs, etc....), developed in relation to the questions in the questionnaire and the outcomes of thick description.

3.6.3 Reflection on the Integration of Quantitative and Qualitative Data

Integrating quantitative and qualitative data in this dissertation was very challenging. This was not only due to the multiple sources of evidence, but mainly because of the richness of video footages and their multiple cues. A major challenge was the synchronisation of different sources: sensor data were geo-referenced, but video data were time-based. The need to integrate the spatial and temporal perspective forced the development of innovative representations of results, using network analysis, video clips, and emotional maps. All these tools are in their exploratory stage, therefore it was sometimes very difficult to make decisions on how to best represent results. To give an example, actions coded in the video footage could be graphically represented according to their frequency or to their time duration. The choice of the one or the other representation had an influence on the possibility to highlight the power of routines in driving or, for example, the resting stops, which were typically few in number, but long lasting and charged in emotional content. Thereby, it is important to highlight that the researcher is aware that exploratory ways of integrating quantitative and qualitative results have some influences on results themselves. Therefore, where possible, it was decided to propose and compare alternative representations, to appreciate the most complete picture of results possible.

3.7 Chapter Summary

This chapter has described the theoretical perspective, the methodological strategy and the case study design used to assess journey experiences in mobility spaces. QUAL + QUAN mixed methods were implemented in a critical realist frame of thought, and research methods were related to corresponding research questions. Three phases of analysis were then described: *documentation and secondary data collection*, to frame the case study; *mobile video ethnography,* to grasp the essence of riding kinaesthetics, investigate social interactions and monitor biometric features; *emotion measurement techniques* based on self-reporting and observation, to explore the individual emotional value of mobility. The necessary integration between quantitative and qualitative data happens following the principle of thick description by investigating actions in relation to their context and motivations. Based on this in-depth analysis, personas are later designed to typify archetypical travellers.

The use of head cams in mobile video ethnography was combined with the innovative application of mobile methods of research—the ride-alongs (Büscher et al. 2011)—to provide documentary evidence of the whole journey on a second-by-second basis, even when the researcher could not individually accompany the participant along the route. Headcams were used with a first-person perspective, which facilitates the process of identification and immersion with the traveller (Bédard 2015), replicating the embodiment and intentionality of actions (Schmidt and Thompson 2014). This particular perspective also allowed the use of the video footage for video elicitation, with a parallel measurement of facial emotional responses of participants using the facial action coding system SHORE™. A questionnaire for self-reporting of emotions completed the data collection tool set and added important socio-demographic information. The actual data that were generated through this three-phased approach are presented in the following Chaps. 4 and 5 and discussed in Chap. 6.

References

Arhippainen L, Rantokko T, Tähti M (2004) Mobile feedback application for emotion and user experience collection. In: Proceedings of PROW 2004. Helsinki University Press, pp 77–81
Azienda "Musei provinciali" Touriseum–Museo Provinciale del Turismo, Merano (2017) Il turismo alla conquista dei passi alpini. Catalogo della mostra "Sui passi, pronti, via!" [Tourism winning Alpine passes. Catalogue of the exhibition "Ready, steady, pass!"], Merano
Babakhani N, Ritchie B, Dolnicar S (2017) Improving carbon offsetting appeals in online airplane ticket purchasing: testing new messages, and using new test methods. J Sustain Tour 25(7):955–969
Bagozzi RP, Gopinath M, Nyer P (1999) The Role of Emotion in Marketing. J Acad Mark Sci 27(2):184–206
Baxter P, Jack S (2008) Qualitative case study methodology: study design and implementation for novice researchers. Qual Rep 13(4):544–559
Bédard P (2015) Disembodied perspective: third-person images in GoPro videos. Alphaville J Film Screen Media 9 Summer 2015
Bhaskar R (2008) A realist theory of science. Routledge, London
Bissel D (2010) Narrating mobile methodologies: active and passive empiricisms. In: Fincham B, McGuinness M, Murray L (eds) Mobile methodologies. Palgrave Macmillan UK, London, pp 53–68
Braun V, Clarke V (2006) Using thematic analysis in psychology. Qualitative Research in Psychology 3(2):77–101
Brown K, Banks E (2014) Close encounters, using mobile video ethnography to understand human-animal relations. In: Bates C (ed) Video methods: social science research in motion. Routledge, London, pp 95–120
Brown K, Dilley R, Marshall K (2008) Using a head-mounted video camera to understand social worlds and experiences. Sociological Research 13(6):1–10
Brown K, Spinney J (2010) Catching a glimpse: the value of video in evoking, understanding and representing the practice of cycling. In: Fincham B, McGuinness M, Murray L (eds) Mobile methodologies. Palgrave Macmillan UK, London, pp 130–151
Brown KM (2015) Leave only footprints? How traces of movement shape the appropriation of space. Cult Geogr 22(4):659–687. https://doi.org/10.1177/1474474014558987
Brown KM (2017) The haptic pleasures of ground-feel: the role of textured terrain in motivating regular exercise. Health Place 46:307–314. https://doi.org/10.1016/j.healthplace.2016.08.012
Buscher M, Urry J (2009) Mobile methods and the empirical. Eur J Soc Theory 12(1):99–116. https://doi.org/10.1177/1368431008099642
Büscher M, Urry J, Witchger K (2011) Mobile methods. Routledge, London, New York
Cooper A (1999) The inmates are running the asylum. SAMS Publishing, Indianapolis, IN
Courage C, Baxter K (2005) Understanding your users: a practical guide to user requirements methods, tools, and techniques. Elsevier, San Francisco, CA
Cresswell T (2012) Mobilities II: still. Prog Hum Geogr 36(5):645–653

Creswell JW (2013) Research design: qualitative, quantitative, and mixed methods approaches. Sage, Thousand Oaks, Calif

Czarniawska-Joerges B (2007) Shadowing and other techniques for doing fieldwork in modern societies. Copenhagen Business School Press, Frederksberg, Denmark

Delaney H (2016) Walking and cycling interactions on shared-use paths. Doctorate thesis, University of the West of England

Delhaye A, Marot L (2015) The Motorcycling Community in Europe, Deliverable 9 of the EC/MOVE/C4 project RIDERSCAN

Della Lucia M, Franch M (2017) The effects of local context on World Heritage Site management: The Dolomites Natural World Heritage Site, Italy. J Sustain Tour 25(12):1756–1775. https://doi.org/10.1080/09669582.2017.1316727

DeLyser D, Sui D (2013) Crossing the qualitative–quantitative divide II inventive approaches to big data, mobile methods, and rhythmanalysis. Prog Hum Geogr 37(2):293–305. https://doi.org/10.1177/0309132512444063

Desmet P, Overbeeke K, Tax S (2001) Designing products with added emotional value: development and application of an approach for research through design. Design J 4(1):32–47. https://doi.org/10.2752/146069201789378496

Desmet P (2002) Designing emotions. Doctorate thesis, Delft University of Technology

Dinhopl A, Gretzel U (2016) Conceptualizing tourist videography. Inf Technol Tourism 15(4):395–410. https://doi.org/10.1007/s40558-015-0039-7

Ekman P, Friesen WV, Hager JC (2002) Facial action coding system. Manual and investigator's guide. Research Nexus, Salt Lake City, UT

Elmi M, Perlik M (2014) From tourism to multilocal residence? Revue de géographie alpine 102(3):1–10

Elmi M, Wagner M (2013) Turismo sostenibile nelle Dolomiti.: Una strategia per il Bene Patrimonio Mondiale UNESCO. [Sustainable tourism in the Dolomites. A strategy for the Natural World Heritage Site Dolomites UNESCO], Bolzano

Elmi M (2014) Turismo Sostenibile nelle Dolomiti, approfondimento dell'analisi. Questionario rivolto ai turisti nella stagione estiva 2013. [Sustainable tourism in the Dolomites. In-depth analysis. Questionnaire for tourists during the summer season 2013], Data available on demand, Bolzano

Erickson F, Shultz JJ (1982) The counselor as gatekeeper: social interaction in interviews. Academic Press, New York, NY

Fincham B, McGuinness M, Murray L (eds) (2010) Mobile methodologies. Palgrave Macmillan UK, London

Geertz C (1973) Thick description: toward an interpretive theory of culture. In: Geertz C (ed) The interpretation of cultures: selected essays. Basic Books, New York, pp 3–30

Glaser B, Strauss A (1967) The discovery of grounded theory: strategies for qualitative research. Aldine, Chicago

Greene JC (2007) Is mixed methods social inquiry a distinctive methodology? J Mix Methods Res 2(1):134–145

Hammersley M, Atkinson P (1995) Ethnography: principles in practice, 2nd ed. Routledge, London

Hanjalic A (2004) Content-based analysis of digital video. Springer, US, Boston

Henry SG, Fetters MD (2012) Video elicitation interviews: a qualitative research method for investigating physician-patient interactions. Ann Fam Med 10(2):118–125. https://doi.org/10.1370/afm.1339

Howes D (2005) Empire of the senses: the sensory culture reader. Berg, Oxford

Idoughi D, Seffah A, Kolski C (2012) Adding user experience into the interactive service design loop: a persona-based approach. Behav Inf Technol 31(3):287–303

Ingold T (2011) Worlds of sense and sensing the world: a response to Sarah Pink and David Howes. Soc Anthropol 19(3):313–317. https://doi.org/10.1111/j.1469-8676.2011.00163.x

Isomursu M, Kuutti K, Väinämö S (2004) Experience clip: method for user participation and evaluation of mobile concepts. In: Proceedings of the Participatory Design Conference, pp. 83–92

References

Isomursu M, Tähti M, Väinämö S, Kuutti K (2007) Experimental evaluation of five methods for collecting emotions in field settings with mobile applications. Int J Hum Comput Stud 65(4):404–418. https://doi.org/10.1016/j.ijhcs.2006.11.007

Johnson RB, Onwuegbuzie AJ, Turner LA (2007) Toward a definition of mixed methods research. J Mix Methods Res 1(2):112–133

Kagan N (1980) Influencing human interaction—eighteen years with IPR. In: Hess AK (ed) Psychotherapy supervision: theory, research, and practice. John Wiley & Sons Ltd., New York, NY, pp 262–283

Kim J, Fesenmaier DR (2015) Measuring emotions in real time: implications for tourism experience design. J Travel Res 54(4):419–429. https://doi.org/10.1177/0047287514550100

Kueblbeck C, Ernst A (2006) Face detection and tracking in video sequences using the modified census transformation. J Image Vis Comput 24(6):564–572

Lang PJ (1980) Behavioral treatment and bio-behavioral assessment: computer applications. In: Sidowski JB, Johnson JH, Williams TA (eds) Technology in mental health care delivery systems. Albex, Norwood, NJ, pp 119–139

Larsen J (2001) Tourism mobilities and the travel glance: experiences of being on the move. Scand J Hosp Tour 1(2):80–98. https://doi.org/10.1080/150222501317244010

Laurier E (2010) Being there/seeing there: recording and analysing life in the car. In: Fincham B, McGuinness M, Murray L (eds) Mobile methodologies. Palgrave Macmillan UK, London, pp 103–117

Lee J, Kyle GT (2012) Recollection consistency of festival consumption emotions. J Travel Res 51(2):178–190. https://doi.org/10.1177/0047287510394197

Lee N, Chamberlain L, Broderick AJ (2007) The application of physiological observation methods to emotion research. Qualitative Mrkt Res An Int J 10(2):199–216. https://doi.org/10.1108/13522750710740853

Lohmeyer Q, Meboldt M (2016) The integration of quantitative biometric measures and experimental design research. In: Cash P, Stanković T, Štorga M (eds) Experimental Design Research. Approaches, perspectives, applications. Springer International Publishing, pp 97–112

Lumsdon LM, McGrath P (2011) Developing a conceptual framework for slow travel: a grounded theory approach. J Sustain Tour 19(3):265–279. https://doi.org/10.1080/09669582.2010.519438

Mauss IB, Robinson MD (2009) Measures of emotion: a review. Cogn Emot 23(2):209–237. https://doi.org/10.1080/02699930802204677

Maxwell JA (2012) A realist approach for qualitative research. Sage, London

Micheletti C, Ponticelli L, Omizzolo A, Gianolla P (2015) Overall management strategy

Mokhtarian PL, Salomon I (2001) How derived is the demand for travel? Some conceptual and measurement considerations. Transp Res Part A Policy Pract 35(8):695–719. https://doi.org/10.1016/S0965-8564(00)00013-6

Muskat M, Muskat B, Zehrer A, Johns R (eds) (2013) Mobile ethnography as an emerging research method. British Academy of Management, UK

Nielsen L (2013a) Personas. In: Soegaard M, Dam RF (eds) The encyclopedia of human-computer interaction, 2nd edn. Aarhus, Denmark

Nielsen L (2013b) Personas–user focussed design. Springer, London

Nold C (ed) (2009) Emotional Cartography–Technologies of the Self. Creative Commons

Novoa A (2015) Mobile ethnography: emergence, techniques and its importance to geography. Hum Geographies J Stud Res Hum Geogr 9(1):97–107

Patton MQ (1987) How to use qualitative methods in evaluation. Sage, Newbury Park

Pechlaner H, Laesser C, Raich F, Bischof L (2004) Verkehrsentlastung Dolomitenpässe [Traffic calming in the Dolomites' passes]. Project report., Bolzano, data available on demand

Pink S (2007a) Doing visual ethnography. Sage, London

Pink S (2007b) Walking with video. Vis Stud 22(3):240–252

Pink S (2008) Mobilising visual ethnography: making routes, making place and making images. Forum Qualitative Sozialforschung/Forum: Qualitative Social Research 9(3)

Pink S, Leder Mackley K (2012) Video as a route to sensing invisible energy. Sociological Research Online. Retrieved August 18, 2018 from, http://www.socresonline.org.uk/17/1/3.html

Pörnbacher H (1995) Verkehrsbefragung im Dolomitengebiet [Traffic survey in the Dolomites area]. Project report., Bolzano, data available on demand

Pruitt J, Adlin T (2006) The persona lifecycle: keeping people in mind throughout product design (Interactive technologies). Morgan Kaufmann, San Francisco, CA

Richins ML (1997) Measuring emotions in the consumption experience. J Consum Res 24(2):127–146

Robson C (2002) Real world research. Blackwell Publishing, Oxford

Rose G (2012) Visual methodologies. An introduction to researching with visual materials. sage Publications Ltd, London

Ruf T, Ernst A, Küblbeck C (2011) Face detection with the sophisticated high-speed object recognition engine (SHORE). In: Heuberger A, Elst G, Hanke R (eds) Microelectronic systems. Circuits, systems and application. Springer, Berlin Heidelberg, New York, pp 237–246

Russell JA (2003) Core affect and the psychological construction of emotion. Psychol Rev 110(1):145–172. https://doi.org/10.1037/0033-295X.110.1.145

Ryle G (1971) The thinking of thoughts: What is "Le Penseur" doing? In: Ryle G (ed) Collected papers, vol. II: Collected essays 1929–1968. Hutchinson, London, pp 480–496

Savin Baden M, Howell Major C (2013) Qualitative research: the essential guide to theory and practice. Routledge, Abingdon

Schmidt B, Thompson B (2014) GoPro: professional guide to filmmaking. Peachpit Press, San Francisco

Scuttari A, Bassani R (2015) I passi dolomitici: Analisi del traffico e dei suoi impatti e proposta di misure di gestione. [Dolomites' passes. Traffic, its environmental impact and a proposal for traffic management measures]

Scuttari A, Della Lucia M, Martini U (2013) Integrated planning for sustainable tourism and mobility. A tourism traffic analysis in Italy's South Tyrol region. J Sustain Tour 21(4):614–637. https://doi.org/10.1080/09669582.2013.786083

Scuttari A, Della Lucia M (2015) Managing sustainable mobility in natural areas: the case of south tyrol (Italy). In: Orsi F (ed) Sustainable transportation in natural and protected areas. Routledge/Taylor & Francis Group; Earthscan from Routledge, London, New York, pp 99–114

Scuttari A, Della Lucia M (2016) Principi di management delle aree protette e patrimonio naturale. L'efficacia della gestione integrata e partecipata delle Dolomiti UNESCO [Management principles for protected and natural heritage areas. The effectiveness of integrated and participatory management of the Dolomites UNESCO WHS]. In: Valeri M, Pechlaner H, Gon M (eds) Innovazione, Sostenibilità, e Competitività. Teoria ed esperienze per la destinazione e l'azienda. Giappichelli, Torino, pp 113–124

Scuttari A, Marcher A, Vanzi G (2018) Dolomitesvives. Vivere un'esperienza naturale sulle Dolomiti. Monitoring qualitativo [#Dolomitesvives. Experiencing nature naturally in the Dolomites. Qualitative monitoring], Bolzano

Scuttari A, Orsi F, Bassani R (2019) Assessing the tourism-traffic paradox in mountain destinations. A stated preference survey on the dolomites' passes (Italy). J Sustain Tour 27(2):241–257. https://doi.org/10.1080/09669582.2018.1428336

Scuttari A, Pechlaner H (2017) Emotions in tourism: from consumer behavior to destination management. In: Fesenmaier DR, Xiang Z (eds) Design science in tourism: foundations of destination management. Springer, Cham, CH, pp 41–54

Sheller M, Urry J (2006) The new mobilities paradigm. Environ Plann A 38(2):207–226. https://doi.org/10.1068/a37268

Soleymani M, Pantic M, Pun T (2012) Multimodal Emotion Recognition in Response to Videos. IEEE Trans Affect Comput 3(2). https://doi.org/10.1109/t-affc.2011.37

Spinney J (2011) A chance to catch a breath: using mobile video ethnography in cycling research. Mobilities 6(2):161–182. https://doi.org/10.1080/17450101.2011.552771

Spinney J (2015) Close encounters? mobile methods, (post) phenomenology and affect. Cult Geogr 22(2):231–246. https://doi.org/10.1177/1474474014558988

Stickdorn M, Frischhut B, Schmid JS (2014) Mobile ethnography: A pioneering research approach for customer-centered destination management. Tour Anal 19(4):491–503. https://doi.org/10.3727/108354214X14090817031198

Stickdorn M, Grabmueller A, Zehrer A, Siller H (2010) Service DESIGN im Tourismus: Die Erfassung der touristischen Kontaktpunktkette durch Mobile Ethnographie [Service design in tourism: recording the chain of touchpoints through mobile ethnography]. In: Burgenlands F (ed) 4. Forschungsforum der österreichischen Fachhochschulen [4th Research Forum of the Austrian Universities of Applied Sciences]. FFH, Pinkafeld, Austria, pp 204–209

Stickdorn M, Zehrer A (2010) Mobile ethnography: How service design aids the tourism industry to cope with the behavioral change of social media. Touchpoint J Serv Des 2(1):82–85

Tähti M, Arhippainen L (2004) A proposal of collecting emotions and experiences. Interact Exp HCI 2:195–198

Thrift N (2008) Non-representational theory: space, politics, affect. Routledge, London

Trochim W (1989) Outcome pattern matching and program theory. Eval Program Plan 12:355–366

Wierzbicki RJ, Tschoeppe C, Ruf T, Garbas J (2013) EDIS–emotion-driven interactive systems. In: Proceedings of the 5th International Workshop on Semantic Ambient Media Experience (SAME). International SERIES on Information Systems and Management in Creative eMedia (CreMedia) vol 1, pp 59–68

Williams AM (2013) Mobilities and sustainable tourism: path-creating or path-dependent relationships? J Sustain Tour 21(4):511–531. https://doi.org/10.1080/09669582.2013.768252

Yin RK (2006) Case study research: design and methods, 3rd edn. Applied social research methods series, vol 5. Sage, Thousand Oaks, CA

Ying L, Jay Kuo C (2003) Video content analysis using multimodal information. For Movie Content Extraction, Indexing And Representation. Springer US, New York

Chapter 4
Results: Physical, Sensory, Social and Emotional Features of Journey Experiences

> *The great art of life is sensation, to feel that we exist, even in pain.*
> Lord Byron (1788–1824; 1813)

Abstract This chapter proposes a first set of aggregate results based on the empirical data collected. It analyses the infrastructure assets and the flow dynamics of the Sella Pass mobility space based on documentary material and secondary data; it studies the spatial and temporal features of fourteen journey experiences through video-ethnographic and bio-sensing data; finally it carefully describes the physical, social, sensory and emotional aspects of these experiences. Cycling and motorcycling journeys are finally classified as escapist (immersive and active) eudaimonic experiences.

4.1 Introduction

This chapter presents the empirical findings from the three phases of data collection and analysis outlined in the previous chapter: documentation and secondary data analysis, mobile video ethnography and emotion measurement. The chapter aims at addressing the first research question of this dissertation, i.e.:

- How to describe and how to measure the visitors' mobile journeys and their physical, sensory, emotional and social features in space and time?

In doing this, it also starts comparing the different travel modes, providing answers to the second research question, i.e.:

- How does travel mode—i.e. cycling vs. motorcycling—shape journey experiences?

Electronic supplementary material The online version of this chapter (https://doi.org/10.1007/978-3-030-17697-6_4) contains supplementary material.

© Springer Nature Switzerland AG 2019
A. Scuttari, *Cycling and Motorcycling Tourism*, Tourism, Hospitality & Event Management, https://doi.org/10.1007/978-3-030-17697-6_4

The findings are presented in three sections—corresponding to the three steps of the research design illustrated in Sect. 3.2.2—applying the approach of thick description, i.e. with particular attention to context and meanings of actions. To enable contextualisation, the *spatial fix* of the Sella Pass road is first described, based on secondary data and documentation material. Traffic flows and vehicle typologies are presented along with technical features of the road itself. Thereafter, space and time perspectives are used to divide the journey experiences into main spatial and temporal sections, which help to organise the data and facilitate comparison among users. Physical and social aspects of journey experiences are explored in one section, followed by a further section where sensory and emotional features are assessed, including the processes of negotiation of space.

In this chapter, data is mostly treated in an aggregate way, using descriptive statistics for quantitative data and coding categories for qualitative data, always making reference to all participants. Chapter 5 will then address selected individual journeys separately, in order to deepen the analysis, better integrate the data sources and, based on the convergence of evidence at the individual level, build personas and compare travel modes. Throughout the next chapters, respondents have been given an ID code, in order to keep their identity preserved (see Table 3.4).

4.2 Context Description: Features of the Transport System on the Sella Pass

4.2.1 The Sellaronda Road Transport System

The Sella Pass is crossed by the national road SS242, connecting Val Gardena Valley and Val di Fassa Valley (see Fig. 4.1), but it is part of a wider system of roads connecting four valleys across four passes, the Sellaronda transport system. Within this system, the connection between Val Gardena Valley and Val Badia Valley (see the link A-to-B) can take place through the Sella Pass or, alternatively, through a longer tour of three other passes (Gardena, Campolongo and Pordoi Pass). While the direct distance between A and B is about 10.9 km, the round trip along the other three passes is about 39 km long. The Sellaronda tour includes the complete round trip along the four passes, typically starting in Selva di Val Gardena and ending in S. Cristina Val Gardena, with a total length of around 58 km (see Fig. 4.2).

Figure 4.2 provides a more detailed overview of the altimetry of the Sella Pass road (between the two black lines) and the whole Sellaronda tour. Figure 4.2 shows that the area where data were collected for this dissertation (the Sella Pass road), includes one of the most challenging peaks (2.230 m a.s.l.), with a very steep climb over a short distance, particularly if starting from Selva di Val Gardena. It is important to note here that conventionally the tour is shown in *counter clockwise direction*, and with a Start in Val Gardena Valley. In practice the tour is made starting from all four valleys shown in Fig. 4.1 and in both directions, which might have a significant impact

4.2 Context Description: Features of the Transport System … 127

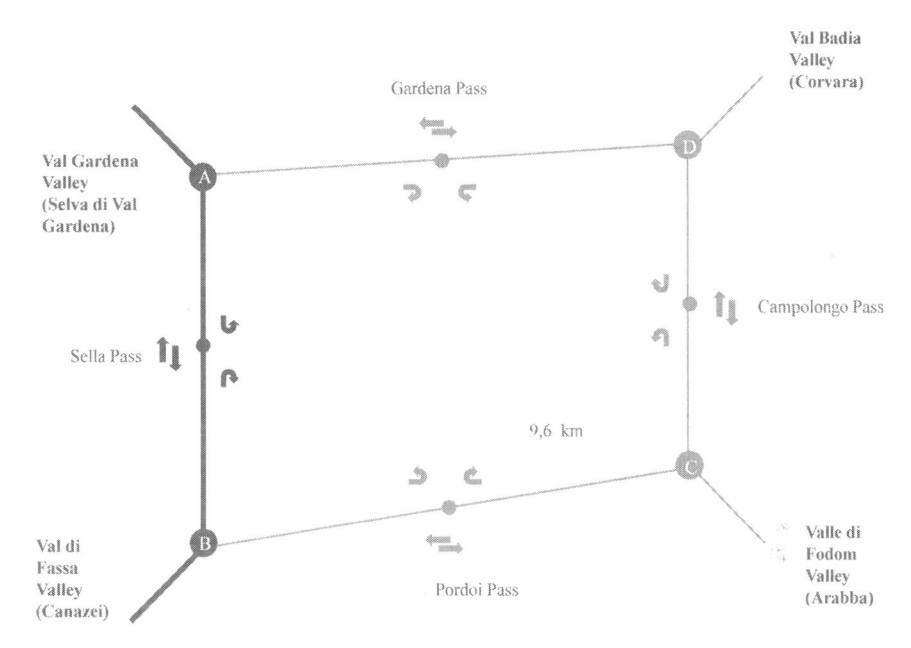

Fig. 4.1 Transport network of the Sella Pass and Sellaronda tour (own elaboration)

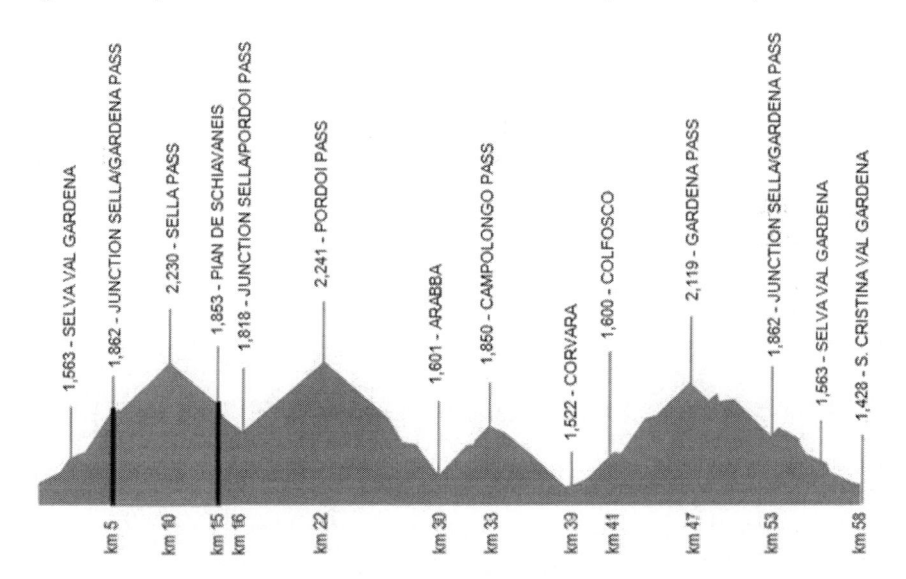

Fig. 4.2 Altimetry of the Sella Pass road (in between black vertical lines) and the Sellaronda tour (https://www.sellarondabikeday.com/it/tracciato.html, own elaboration)

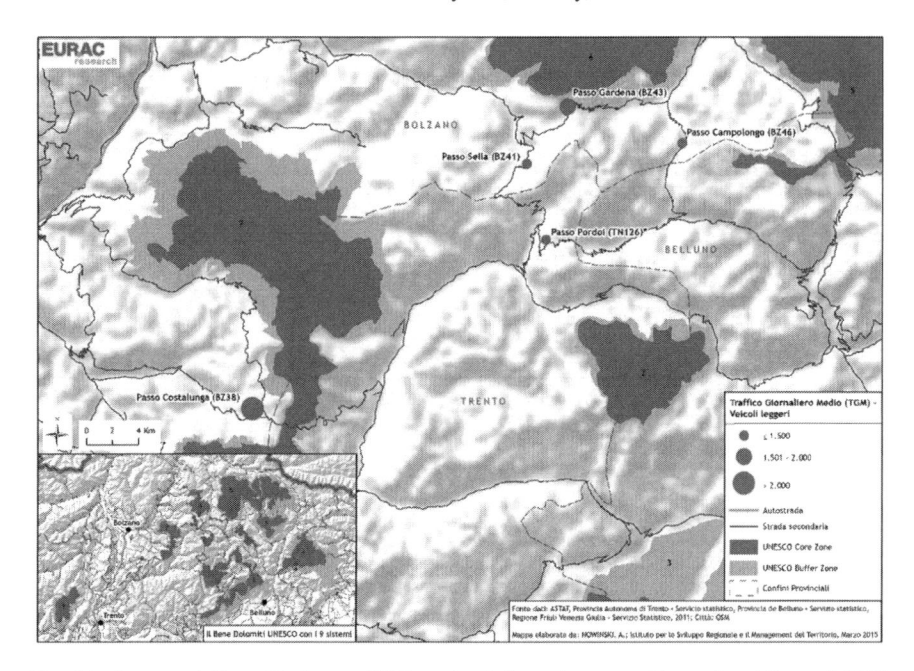

Fig. 4.3 Average daily traffic in year 2011 on the Sellaronda passes (Scuttari and Bassani 2015, p. 21)

on the perception of each pass, especially for cyclists. Considering the tour as it is represented in the Fig. 4.2 means having Sella Pass as a first challenge, because it is the first peak climbed along the round trip. Conversely, if the tour is made in counter clockwise direction or starting from other valleys, the Sella Pass would be just one of the passes climbed, or even the last challenge before the trip ends. Whichever route is taken, climbing to the summit of the pass from both valleys involves a very similar average steepness and length. Data analysis will take this aspect into account and it will highlight, per each participant and in aggregate ways, how the route was planned.

Several traffic counting stations monitor traffic along the Sellaronda route and one of them is located on the Sella Pass road, more precisely at the km 26.9 of the national road SS252. Figure 4.3 shows a map of this counting station (Passo Sella (BZ 41)) and shows also all the location of all other traffic counting stations on the Sellaronda tour. The proximity of the pass roads to the core and buffer zones of the Dolomites UNESCO WHS is reflected on the map in the short distance between the road and the darker areas, corresponding to core and buffer zones of the WHS. The circles in the map represent the intensity of average daily traffic. They show that Sella Pass, with 1,423 vehicles in transit on a daily average in 2016 (Provincial Institute of Statistics (ASTAT) of the Autonomous Province of Bolzano 2018), is significantly less congested than the near Gardena Pass (2,040 vehicles on daily average), although they are in the same road system.

4.2.2 The Sella Pass Road: Technical Features and Travel Demand

Focussing now only on the national road SS242, connecting Val Gardena Valley to Val di Fassa Valley across the Sella Pass, some additional features stand out that help contextualise journey experiences. According to technical data on road infrastructure made available by the provincial road office of the Autonomous Province of Bolzano, the road is between 5.60 and 6.00 m broad and the average steepness is around 7% (Provincial Road Office of the Autonomous Province of Bolzano, data available on demand).

Summer and winter traffic on Sella Pass is not equally distributed: 78% of traffic volumes happen in summer, only 22% in winter. Looking at absolute values of transit along the road (see Fig. 4.4) it becomes clear that the months from June to September are those when traffic volumes are more intense and motorbikes are increasing their absolute numbers. In the middle of August, around the Italian national holiday "Ferragosto", about 4,900 vehicles cross the pass area daily (Provincial Institute of Statistics (ASTAT) of the Autonomous Province of Bolzano 2018).

On average, motorcycles represent the 11% of daily traffic, but in the summer months (from May to October) they form 20% of daily traffic. In the period of data

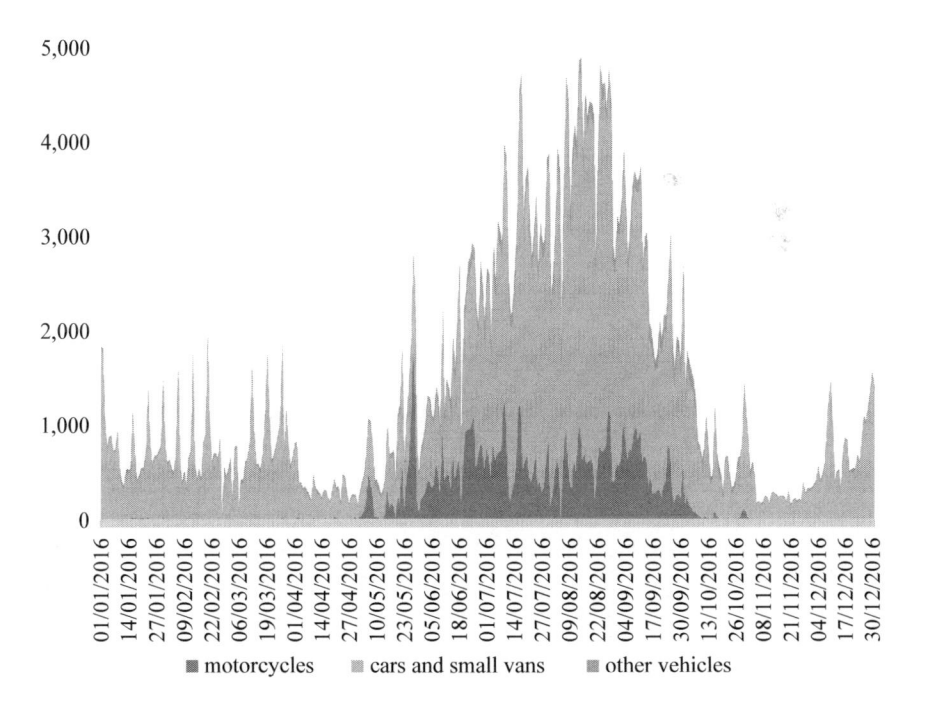

Fig. 4.4 Daily transits of cars and motorcycles on the Passo Sella road (2016) (ASTAT, 2018, own elaboration)

collection (August–September 2016) on average 589 motorcycles per day climbed to the top of the pass, with approximately 1,000 motorcycles on peak days.

Bicycles are not automatically counted by the counting stations, but a sample survey using radar technology conducted by the Autonomous Province of Trento in August of 2017 (Scuttari et al. 2018) reveals that on average 689 bicycles climb to the summit of the pass per day, of which on average 498 come from the Val di Fassa Valley (clockwise tour) and 191 from Val Gardena Valley (counterclockwise tour). This sample survey, done in 2017 and therefore later than the data collection phase of this dissertation, confirms that—although the official Sellaronda tour is organised by local tourism boards and guides in counterclockwise direction—the majority of pedal cyclists tends to prefer a clockwise tour. Unfortunately, this information was available only in 2017, so it could only confirm the difficulty in recruiting cyclist doing the counterclockwise tour, but it could not influence the research design.

From this first analysis it is clear that even though traffic on Sella Pass is not high on average, volumes are highly concentrated in summer season, which is likely to cause congestion in a relatively narrow road. Moreover, it shows that there are on average around 700 motorcyclists per day, and about 600 daily pedal cyclists. They both represent a minority compared to cars, but they travel along the road to take a tour, rather than to reach the pass, a feature that makes them similar and offers fertile ground to explore the experiential features of travel.

The relationship between traffic and tourism flows becomes clearer if looking at official data on monthly arrivals of visitors in Val Gardena and Val di Fassa Valleys, which are distributed very similarly by time period to traffic flows in the summer season (see Fig. 4.5).[1] A study of vehicle license plates by the Road Office of the bordering Province of Trento (Provincial Road Office of the Autonomous Province of Trento, data available on demand) confirms that there is a direct relationship between tourism and traffic in summer. 80% of vehicles travelling along the Sella Pass road in summer are not attributable to the vehicles from the nearby provinces of Bolzano, Trento and Belluno, and, therefore, are likely to belong to tourists. Sella Pass appears therefore to be a unique setting to analyse tourist mobility and to explore the intrinsic value of travel.

A final remark might be helpful to understand tourist travel patterns along the pass. A previous study by Eurac Research (Scuttari and Bassani 2015) revealed that the Sella Pass is very attractive due to its multiple functions for tourists. Firstly, the Sella Pass is a *departure point* for several hiking tours on the surrounding mountain peaks. It is a hub for hikers of several different levels of expertise. *Secondly*, it is also a unique attraction point for families to have lunch while admiring the Dolomites, since there are some restaurants and huts in the close proximity to the road with spectacular views. *Thirdly*, it is an *intermediate stop* for long or short breaks while travelling from Val Gardena to Val di Fassa Valleys or vice versa. The visits to the pass—with a stop of more than 30 min at the summit of the pass—account for around 45% of traffic on an average daily basis, while transit to reach further destinations

---

[1] In the winter seasons tourism flows are much higher than traffic on the passes, because tourists visit Sella Pass and make the Sellaronda tour by skiing.

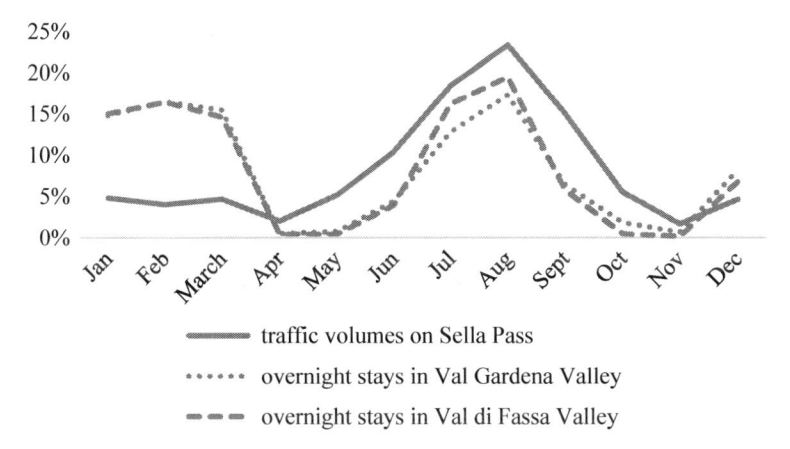

Fig. 4.5 Monthly % distribution of traffic volumes and of overnight stays (Provincial Institute of Statistics of the Autonomous Province of Bolzano; Provincial Institute of Statistics of the Autonomous Province of Trento 2018) (own elaboration)

accounts for the remaining 65% of daily traffic volumes in summer (Scuttari et al. 2018). During a sample survey on the pass it was noted that about 16% of the visitors were planning to complete the Sellaronda tour and these were mostly cyclists and motorcyclists (Scuttari and Bassani 2015).

The research design was planned in the light of all the above mentioned features and more recent data were continuously collected also during the data elaboration process, to enable and support interpretation. Data was collected on travel journeys during the month of August as well as in early September, when, with a high or medium intensity of traffic, vehicles were more likely to transport tourists. This had also the advantage of taking a picture of crowded days, where interactions among different road users might show up in a more evident and frequent way. It was also chosen to imagine a tour where the pass was not the ending point of the journey, since cyclists and motorcyclists were likely to make a tour and visit more than one pass in the same day.

4.2.3 Key Findings

The Sellaronda transport system, with its four passes, four valleys and 58 km of mountainous roads is a unique space to study tourist mobility. In the summer season, 80% of vehicles crossing the pass road are related to tourism and there is an evident relationship between the monthly distribution of overnight visits and traffic flows. Sella Pass is a unique setting in this transport system, because it works both as a tourist attraction in which to stop, and as a strategic hub from which to start daily hiking tours in the surrounding Dolomites. Moreover, it is also a place for road users, especially motorcyclists and cyclists taking a longer tour, typically the Sellaronda tour. While on daily average 1,423 vehicles crossed the pass in 2016, in summer there are daily peaks of traffic with more than 4,000 vehicles per day, a level of usage which is causing congestion and multiple interactions among different road users. In August, about 700 motorcycles and 600 bicycles per day climb to the summit of the pass and then continue their experiential journey to the valley or to the next pass. This phenomenon is the object of the analysis of the dissertation.

4.3 Journey Experience Description: Space, Time and Speed

Before describing individual types of actions, interactions, sensations and emotions during journeys it is important to define *a temporal segmentation of the video data stream* (Hanjalic 2004). Later, in the next Sects. 4.4 and 4.5, video content indexing will help illustrate physical, social, sensory and emotional features of journeys, representing them through network graphs or video clips.

4.3.1 Sella Pass Mobility Space and Its Temporal Sections

Three main dimensions of the Sella Pass mobility space were reflected in three types of experience along the journey: climbing to the summit of the pass, crossing the watershed, and descending. These temporal sections were created after viewing video content and conducting a first screening of bio sensing data, because it became clear that these three temporal sections had very different characteristics, as it will be explained later on. Moreover, these three dimensions could be associated with specific road sections, thanks to the quite regular altimetry of the road (see Fig. 4.2), having a one continuous climb, a peak and a descent. As explained in Sect. 4.2.2, depending on the direction of the tour (clockwise or counterclockwise), the climb can become a descent for some tourists and vice versa. Whichever, the altimetry of the road (see Fig. 4.2), showing a symmetrical pattern between climb and descent, allows the creation of a correspondence between experience dimensions and road sections. Thereby, it was decided to use geographical features of the road to create the segmentation of the video footage, which facilitated also comparison among different videos. Temporal section cuts correspond therefore to physical features on the road (e.g. junctions, traffic signals indicating the start of the pass area) (see Fig. 4.6).

In dividing the journeys into three main temporal and geographical segmentations, interesting relationships between geographical space and experience space stand out. On the one hand, the experience of climbing can occur in different settings; on the other hand, the same geographical setting (e.g. the section from Plan De Gralba in Val Gardena Valley to the beginning of Pass area) might be the physical stage for

4.3 Journey Experience Description: Space, Time and Speed   133

Counterclockwise tour   Clockwise tour

Plan de Gralba (Val Gardena Valley)

Plan de Gralba (Selva)

Plan de Gralba (Val Gardena Valley)

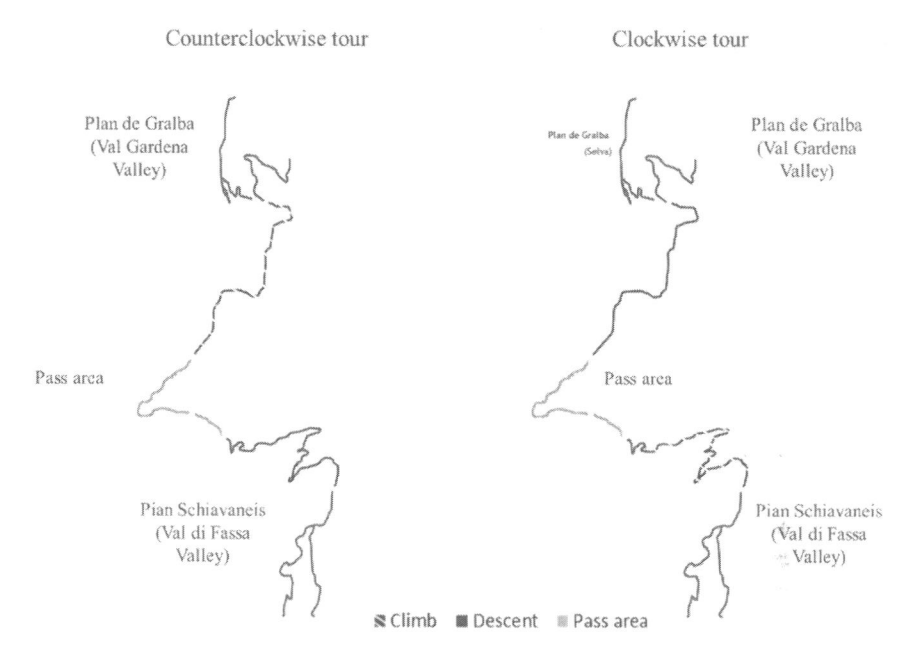

Pass area

Pass area

Pian Schiavaneis (Val di Fassa Valley)

Pian Schiavaneis (Val di Fassa Valley)

Climb   ■ Descent   ■ Pass area

Fig. 4.6 Temporal sections and geographical dimensions of the Sella Pass mobility space (own elaboration)

climbing or descending. This has several implications: from a physical perspective, participants taking the tour in different directions have travelled on different lanes of the same road and have interacted with different pavement conditions, curves, climbs as well as different landscape views; from a psychological perspective they possibly have different attitudes towards the mobility space they are crossing, depending on the fact that they are climbing to the summit of the pass or descending to the valley.

Based on these considerations it becomes clear that both a geographical and an experiential grid stand out to describe journey experiences. Both will be taken into account in the next sections.

4.3.2 *Journey Duration: Time and Speed*

A second aspect crucial to understanding journey experiences along the mobility space of Sella Pass is journey duration. Journey duration in the 14 journeys examined was between 12:51 and 57:26 min. The longest journey was a clockwise Sellaronda tour of an Austrian tourist (participant 4B) travelling in a velo-formation with a guide and two other cyclists. The main reason for the length of the tour was the bad weather, which forced cyclists to stop firstly on top of the pass and later on in the descent, to put on waterproof clothes and wait until riding was safe. The shortest journey was made by a motorcyclist in September (participant 6M), with smooth traffic conditions due to shoulder season and cloudy weather.

Below is a bar chart (see Fig. 4.7) that shows journey duration per participant and on average. On average, motorcyclists were far quicker than cyclists only in climbing the pass. The climbing part for cyclists lasted about 25:27 min, while for motorcyclists about 04:02. The difference in time between the two groups is more than 20 min for this section. The time spent in the pass summit area lasts almost twice so much for cyclists as for motorcyclists. On average, cyclists spent 11:34 min in crossing the pass area, whereas motorcyclists about 6:55 min. Only one motorcyclist (participant 3 M) stopped for about half an hour to take some pictures, make a walk and carefully study the mountain peaks while on the summit of the pass. He was riding a naked bike, but he was accompanied by a passionate motorcycling tourer, who enjoyed taking pictures in the summit area of the pass and discovering mountain peaks through the support of a map. Cyclists typically stopped for a few minutes and took some quick pictures in the proximity of the road sign indicating the peak of the pass and often commented that they wanted to keep warm and go on pedalling.

A last remark worth mentioning regards the variability of travel time: for motorcyclists, the variability between participants is quite small: 6 out of 7 participants take between 13 and 14 min to climb to the summit of the pass and descend. The only exceptional case was the already mentioned case 3M, spending about half an hour in the pass area and therefore making a journey of 41 min. Conversely, cyclists show a high variability in time spent climbing to the summit of the pass, depending on their fitness, the number of stops and the travel direction. Indeed, it took them between 15:31 min (7B—counterclockwise tour) and 31:11 min (1B—clockwise tour) to reach the pass area. Cyclists doing the tour clockwise (1B to 5B) spent more time in climbing to the summit compared to those doing the tour counterclockwise (6B and 7B).

Based on this evidence, journey duration turned out to be linked basically to three types of factors: *individual behaviour* (speed, direction, number and duration of stops), *mode* (bicycle or motorbike), and *contextual conditions* (weather conditions, steepness, traffic congestion).

A further perspective when analysing journey experiences in relation to travel time is *speed*. Speed is analysed comparing individual participants, modes and temporal sections of the journey. On average, motorcyclists in the sample are faster, tend to live the journey as an uninterrupted flow and—thanks to the motorization of the vehicle—accelerate and decelerate suddenly and frequently. Conversely, cyclists are slower—at least in climbing—, tend to stop more than once and have a constant speed in climbing and smoother accelerations and decelerations in descending. Figure 4.7 reports the average speed of participants while climbing, crossing the pass and descending. On average, cyclists climb the pass at an average speed of 10 km/h, while motorcyclists achieve an average speed of 50 km/h. In the pass area motorcyclists tend on average to reduce their speed to 37 km/h, while cyclists tend to increase their speed to 17 km/h. This different pattern in speed reduction vs. increase in the pass area might have an impact on the emotional perception of participants towards the pass, as will be explored later on (see Sect. 4.5). Depending on the direction taken

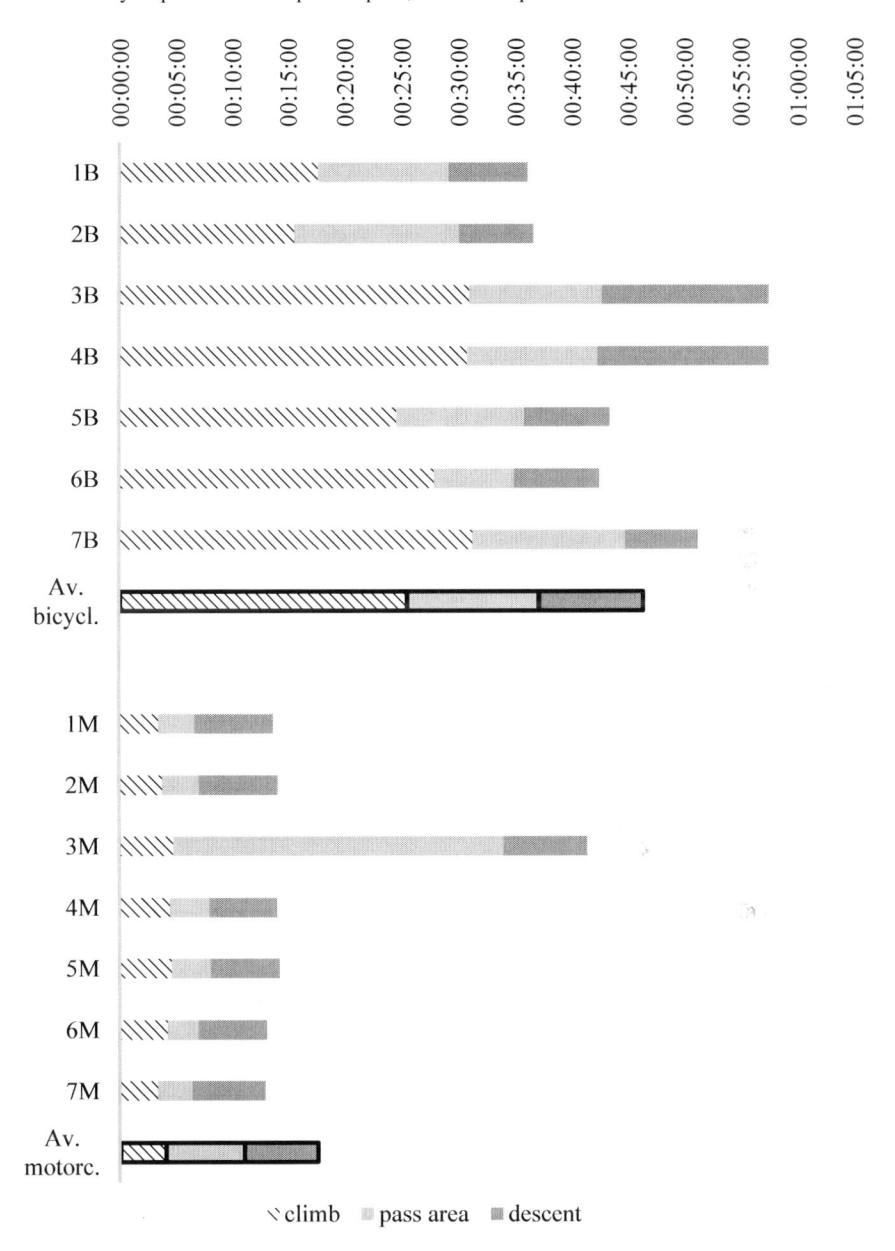

4.3 Journey Experience Description: Space, Time and Speed

Fig. 4.7 Travel time of bicycle and motorcycle journeys per geographical section (own elaboration)

Table 4.1 Maximum speed per participant (own elaboration)

	Maximum speed in climbing (km/h)	Maximum speed in pass summit area (km/h)	Maximum speed in descending (km/h)
1B	17	31	61
2B*			
3B	17	43	42
4B**	13	42	
5B	16	53	60
6B**	21	28	
7B**	15		52
1M	94	68	69
2M	81	69	72
3M	104	78	65
4M	95	76	62
5M	92	69	84
6M	109	75	102
7M	99	93	97

*Missing bio-sensing data for the participant;
**Missing bio-sensing data in one section

for the tour, the pass area is crossed on a slight rise or slope. Therefore, cyclists tend to be quicker in the pass area if moving clockwise than counterclockwise. Finally, the descent is the section where cyclists and motorcyclists reveal similar patterns. On average, the speed of cyclists is 38 km/h, while motorcyclists travel only a few km/h faster (42). Also this pattern needs further interpretation in Sect. 4.3, because similarities in average speed and travel time might suggest similarities in sensations and emotions.

Besides average speed, peaks in speed also reveal interesting aspects of the journey. Table 4.1 shows that motorcyclists are faster in the ascending phase, reaching peaks of more than 100 km/h, where the speed limit is 60 km/h. In the descending section, they tend to be slightly slower, and there is considerable variability in maximum speed among the participants. This might suggest that not all motorcyclists trust themselves to accelerate in descending to the valley as they did in climbing to the summit of the pass, probably because of a higher perceived risk, or a greater difficulty in overtaking while descending. As far as cyclists are concerned, the ascending part of the journey almost never reaches 20 km/h, whereas the descending part is quite fast and has peaks in speed of around 60 km/h, especially for the more expert cyclists.

Speeds defines—together with stops—the rhythm of the journey. To start understanding rhythmical patterns of the journey, the evaluation of stops—defined as moments with speed equal to zero—offers interesting insights. Stops in this

4.3 Journey Experience Description: Space, Time and Speed

Table 4.2 Number and duration of stops per participant and on average (own elaboration)

	Number of stops	Total duration of stops
1B	1	00:00:44
2B*	5	00:03:01
3B	7	00:10:18
4B**	5	00:10:03
5B	10	00:11:27
6B**	4	00:03:16
7B**	6	00:16:32
Av. bicycl.	5	00:07:54
1M	1	00:00:52
2M	2	00:01:37
3M	3	00:25:02
4M	1	00:01:22
5M	2	00:04:07
6M	3	00:02:31
7M	1	00:01:16
Av. Motorc.	2	00:05:15

*Missing bio-sensing data for the participant
**Missing bio-sensing data in one section

dissertation correspond to moments of video footage where the bio-sensing tools are turned on and the participants can move, but they are not in motion, for several reasons.

Table 4.2 shows that cyclists participating in the research stopped a couple of times during their journey (on average 5 times), typically to rest, drink or to take some pictures of the pass. Another reason for them to stop is to wait for their travelling companions, since velo-formations often dissolve due to different rhythms while climbing to the summit. In this sense, stops often represent "waiting times" or ways to compensate for different fitness levels between cyclists. Indirectly, these kind of stops are also the expression of a desire to unite in the journey, to share the experience as much as possible, even if pedalling with different rhythms. Although frequent, cyclists' stops in this sample are short, because—as mentioned above—the Sellaronda tour is a challenging tour and 50 km of hilly roads need to be covered in a few hours, keeping the body always warm.

Compared to cyclists, motorcyclists in the sample stopped fewer times, and typically not in the pass area. They tended to wait for their travelling companions at the beginning of the journey to start together, and then wait for them again at the end of the journey. However, for motorcyclists it was easier to proceed in a velo-formation until the end of the journey, especially because riding rhythm was not dependent on their fitness, but rather on their riding skills, which could not cause significant differences in travel time within a distance of 10 km.

Fig. 4.8 Average speed in bicycle and motorcycle journeys (own elaboration)

- Average speed in climbing
- Average speed in pass area
- Average speed in descending

*Missing bio-sensing data for the participant
**Missing bio-sensing data in one section

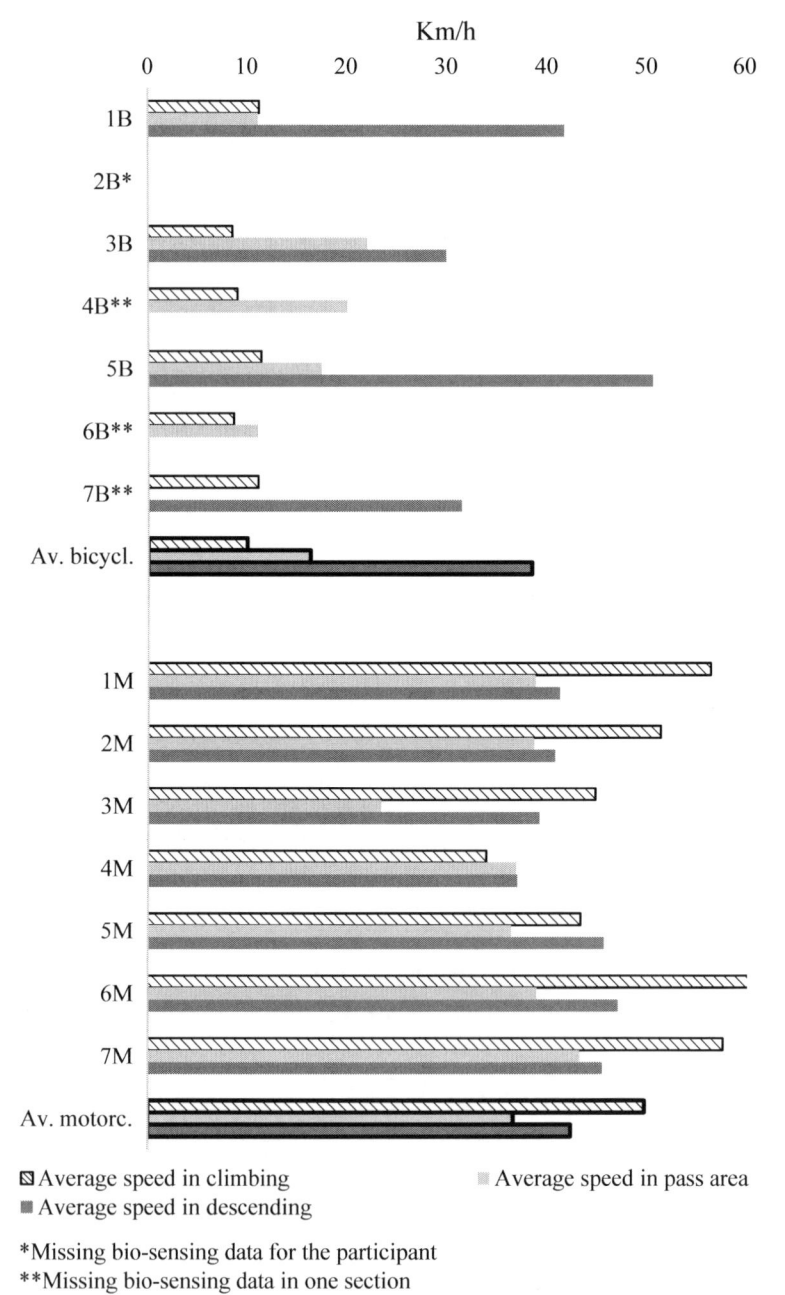

4.3.3 Key Findings

Section 4.3 provided a temporal segmentation of the video data stream into basic units of meaning: climbing to the summit of the pass, crossing the watershed in the pass area, descending to the valley. These units correspond to the experiences of participants, but do not always correspond to the same road segments; they depend on the direction of the tour. Furthermore, even if there are slight differences in journey duration and speed patterns along the pass area according to direction, the most evident differences are between cyclists and motorcyclists (Fig. 4.8). This relates particularly to the climbing part of the journey, because this is normally the quickest and fastest for motorcyclists, and the slowest and longest for cyclists. The pass summit area is a space where cyclists start to increase their speed, but also a point where they stop and rest or wait for their travel companions, while for motorcyclists it is a space where the riding is slower, but stops are more rarely made. Only one of the participants riding a naked motorbike with a friend riding a tourer had a longer stop within the pass area to take some pictures of the landscape, but all other riders made a trip without stops across the pass. The descending part to the valley below is the moment where motorcyclists' and cyclists' experiences tend to become similar from the point of view of speed and journey duration. Particularly for cyclists, this is the road section where they reach—and sometimes exceed—the speed limits, just like the motorcyclists. Physical, sensory, social and emotional features related to speed, space and time follow in the coming sections.

4.4 Journey Experience Description: Physical and Social Features

This section discusses the physical and social features of journey experiences. The description is based on indexing the video footage through video content analysis (see Sect. 3.4.4) and the content of the transcribed dialogues. In the following subsections, results are presented using NVivo Pro 11™ frequency tables, which show the frequency counts of coding categories, but also using bipartite network graphs calculated with Gephi software, that relate coding categories to related participants. Finally, some relevant coding categories—corresponding to specific actions—are further analysed in depth through edited clips. The interpretation of their possible meanings is given with reference to context and to the multiple data sources collected, following the principles of thick description (Geertz 1973).

4.4.1 Physical Features: Primary and Secondary Tasks Besides Driving

Using the expression "physical features of the journey", the aim is to understand the variety and frequency of actions made by the individuals while climbing to the summit of the pass, crossing the watershed and descending. These actions refer both to primary tasks—related to the riding activity—and secondary tasks—referring to any other activity, undertaken while driving in a dual-task condition, or during a stop.

Figure 4.9 illustrates all coded actions, divided into primary and secondary tasks. Among the primary tasks, the *riding actions* are divided into several sub-categories. The most frequent are: *"solo riding"*, when participants and their vehicles move on a clear road, without interactions with other vehicles; and *"queue riding"*, when participants and their vehicles are moving in line and are forced to change their travel rhythm because of other road users. These two actions reflect the juxtaposition between travelling in a continuous flow, and adjusting the travel rhythm to other users, interacting with them.

As it is shown in the network graph (see Fig. 4.10), most of the time during the journey is spent riding on a clear road, especially for cyclists, and less time is spent in a line. The amount of time spent in a line—even if short—interrupts the travel rhythm and causes different actions to happen. For example, when in a line, motorcyclists tend to perform secondary tasks, such as checking the camera position, the helmet etc.

Cyclists need to keep the equilibrium, without detaching their shoes from the clip-in pedals. In the section dedicated to emotional features of journey experience (see Sect. 4.5.2), the interruption of riding flow is further analysed, studying the emotional reactions of participants. Figure 4.7 also highlights features related to single journeys, such as taking pictures for participants 7B and 3M, or kinaesthetic actions for participant 5B.

4.4.1.1 The Kinaesthetic of Riding

The kinaesthetic of riding reflects different possible conditions of stability when controlling the vehicle with one hand or even without hands. These positions often occur in safe situations, when controlling the vehicle is not a priority for the rider: in relaxed moments, on straight road and often in dual-task conditions. Tasks performed while riding with one hand for motorcyclists are mainly greeting and setting the helmet (opening/closing the visor of the helmet) or, as already mentioned, checking the position of the headcam. Cyclists ride with one hand mostly while climbing onto the peak of the pass, and they use the time to drink or adjust the position of the headcam, as well. Only one professional cyclist (5B) repeatedly performed secondary tasks in a routine while riding with one hand: he monitored the route and the performance on a GPS tool and continuously took pictures while on the move.

4.4 Journey Experience Description: Physical and Social Features

Nodes

Name	Sources	References
LEV 1 - PHYSICAL	16	717
1a Driving tasks	16	589
queue_riding	14	106
kinaesthetics	7	41
accident	1	2
camera fall	1	2
equilibrium	1	1
interaction infr.	4	4
no-hand riding	1	1
no-pedalling	1	4
one-hand riding	5	29
parking	10	12
preparation	13	17
solo riding	16	344
standing riding	5	9
stop	16	51
waiting time	12	19
travelling back	3	3
walking	3	6
1b Secondary tasks	15	128
Actions	10	46
dress waterproof	2	3
drink	1	3
helmet setting	3	7
map check	2	2
motorbike setting	4	10
picking water	1	1
taking pictures	6	20
Technology	14	82
camera setting	14	46
play with camera	2	2
smartphone use	2	8
technology setting	3	26

Fig. 4.9 Nodes coding physical features of journey experiences, including categories and sub-categories, sources and coding references (own elaboration through NVivo Pro 11^{TM} software)

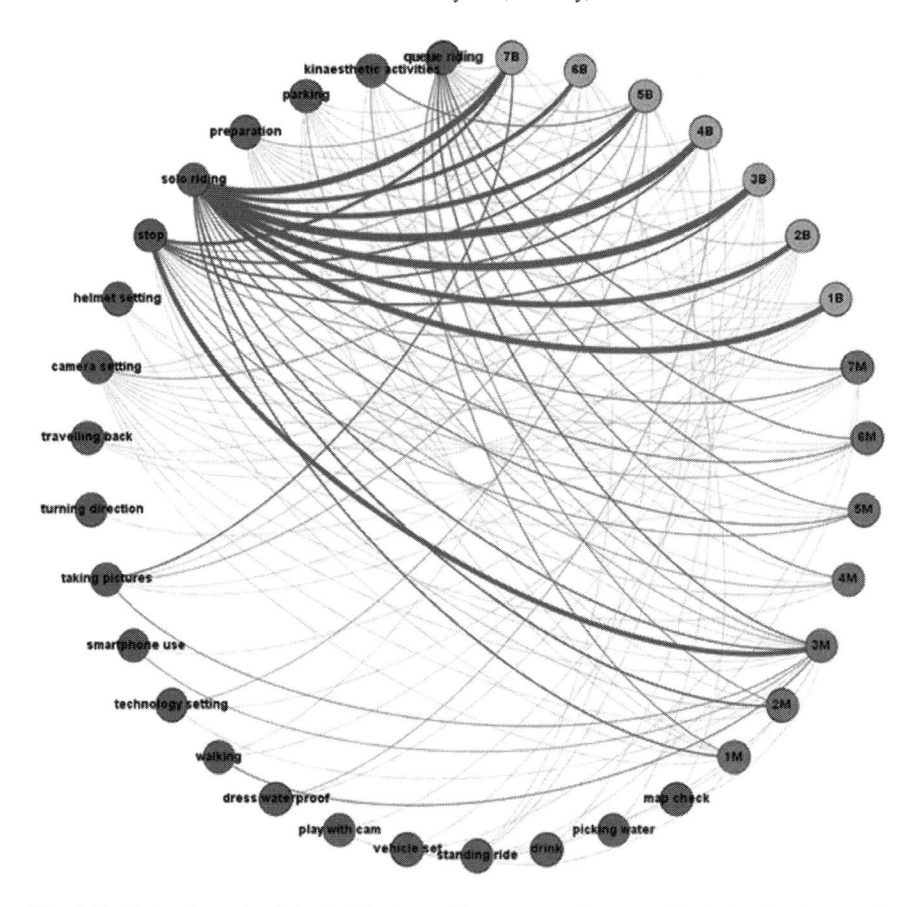

Fig. 4.10 Network graph of physical features of journey experiences and their duration in seconds per participant (own elaboration through Gephi software)

A deeper insight into the unique features of this journey experience is given in the next chapter (see Sect. 5.3.2).

4.4.1.2 Picture Shooting and Technology Setting

Secondary tasks were also performed when cyclists and motorcyclists stopped. These secondary tasks were often, but not always, related to tourism and to the need for a better understanding of the space beyond the road. For example, one motorcyclist, the one travelling with the tourer biker, had a close look at his travel map while in the pass area and tried to interpret the mountain peaks surrounding him. And both, cyclists and motorcyclists, took several pictures. Often, these were taken on the peak of the pass, especially by the road sign for the Sella Pass or by the sign for the Val Gardena Valley (see Fig. 4.11 and the corresponding Video ESM_1). As the

4.4 Journey Experience Description: Physical and Social Features

Fig. 4.11 Video stills of moments when participants took pictures by the road sign of Sella Pass (own elaboration)

visual sources show, both places seemed to work as a tourist attraction, not only for participants, but also for other cyclists and motorcyclists on their way to the pass. One of the pictures below is taken from a repeat visitor, who reported that he had made the tour for more than 30 times and, notwithstanding this, he explained to his travel companion that he wanted to take a picture of the sign, as if it could be a proof of his journey. Among the non-touristic secondary actions are also preparatory actions before travel. Setting the vehicle, turning it on, putting on gloves or dressing up are the most common. Weather conditions also influences behaviour: during two simultaneous journeys, the rain forced cyclists to stop and put on waterproof clothes, while drying off their bicycles and seats.

Technology worked as an interesting mediator when participants were looking for a better understanding of the journey. Both smartphones and GPS devices worked as sources for the interpretation of space, in terms of route, steepness (and therefore upcoming challenges), but also as opportunities to read the landscape. Especially for cyclists, GPS devices were used to foresee upcoming climbs and plan the effort and the travel time necessary accordingly. They helped keeping the flow, i.e. the balance between perceived challenges and available skills. This layer of journey reading is fascinating, because technology shapes cyclists' behaviour while on the move, motivating them to succeed in the challenge and regulating their rhythm.

4.4.2 Social Features: Overtaking, Velo-Formations, Verbal and Non-verbal Interactions

The expression "social features of the journey" refers to the variety of interactions among participants, with the researcher, with travel companions or with other people or animals along their way. Similarly to the physical tasks, social interactions are examined separately according to their relatedness to the riding activity—primary tasks—or their independence of riding—secondary tasks.

Primary tasks refer to interactions of vehicles as they have been described in the theoretical Sect. 2.2.2 based on Jensen (2010). These driving tasks negotiate the existing road space among different road users to enable mobility: overtaking, being overtaken, frontal meetings with other vehicles or more rarely negotiation of parking space or unintentional changes of lane—mainly due to a distraction. Figure 4.12 presents two forms of overtaking: the active "overtaking" and the passive "being overtaken". The first refers to motorcyclists or cyclists passing other vehicles (bicycles, buses, cars, motorcycles, pedestrians, vans or campervans) and also includes "overtaking trials"; the second refers to motorcyclists or cyclists being passed by other vehicles (bicycles, cars, motorcycles, buses, vans and campervans). The frequency of these active and passive actions seems to be related to both the speed of motorcyclists and cyclists and the number of vehicles on the road per each category.

Secondary tasks relate to interactions happening besides riding the bycicle or motorcycle and they have different aims than the mobility of these vehicles. Examples of secondary tasks are greetings, other gestures, dialogues, etc. Sometimes it is very difficult to distinguish between primary and secondary tasks from the communication perspective, because the interaction at mobility level is happening together with the interaction at personal level. Therefore, some ambiguous coding categories were attributed to primary or secondary tasks based on their contextual use. For example, turn signals and horns can be used as a primary task to negotiate the mobility space (e.g. to ensure safe overtaking), but also to communicate non-verbally messages that are not directly related to mobility (e.g. to say hello). Based on the contextual use of horns and turn signals, that were both used to support overtaking procedures in almost all cases, it was decided to attribute them to the primary group of activities. A similar ambiguity works for the attribution of the category of velo-formations. As stated in Sect. 2.2.2.4, cyclists are mobile in a group and this causes several interactions among people sharing one collective journey. In the sample, all participants except for one cyclist were travelling at least as a couple or in group, which caused very interesting dynamics along the road. Interactions due to velo-formations are hardly attributable to a primary (driving) or secondary (non-driving) task, because they actually include both. Nevertheless, velo-formations were discovered to be moments where the journey experience is shared on a personal level, through a shared rhythm of driving and through verbal and non-verbal interaction. In the video footage it was clear that the non-driving component of this interaction was very important, especially for cyclists. Therefore it was decided to treat velo-formations as secondary

4.4 Journey Experience Description: Physical and Social Features

Name	Sources	References
LEV 2 - SOCIAL	16	1173
2a Driving tasks	16	852
negotiation of space	16	852
being overtaken	12	462
BO_Bike	6	11
BO_bus	6	12
BO_Car	10	199
BO_Motorbike	11	113
BO_Van or campervan	7	18
frontal meeting	8	8
horn	5	10
lane_change	4	7
negotiation of parking space	1	2
orthogonal meeting	1	1
overtaking	16	359
O_Bike	14	67
O_bus	8	12
O_Car	14	68
O_Motorbike	9	20
O_Pedestrians	10	40
O_Van or campervan	7	12
Overtaking_trial	1	1
turn signal	3	3
2b Secondary tasks	16	321
Non-verbal interaction	16	84
gestures	3	4
greetings	9	31
other mode	2	3
meeting animals	3	5
pointing to something	9	11
velo-formation	14	33
Verbal_interaction	16	237
ask for picture	1	1
dialogue between cyclists	9	106
dialogue between motorcyclist	5	29
dialogue with other people	4	6
dialogue with passenger	0	0
dialogue with researcher	13	26
exclamation	10	27

Fig. 4.12 Nodes coding social features of journey experiences, including categories and sub-categories, sources and coding references (own elaboration through NVivo Pro 11T^{M} software)

tasks, i.e. forms of interactions that enrich (and do not only enable) the mobility of participants.

Figure 4.13 illustrates the time spent in doing the main activities expressed in the coding categories of Fig. 4.12. Links express the number of seconds spent doing a task and data is not weighted, to show the absolute differences in time spent on different tasks according to mode and participant. Several interesting features stand out. Firstly, the amount of time spent in a velo-formation for all participants is quite high. Cyclists spend about 14 min (843 s) on average in a velo-formation, while motorcyclists about 5 min (307 s) on average. For both, this amounts to approximately one third of the journey time. Secondly, it stands out how important the dialogue is for cyclists. Finally, from the comparison between Figs. 4.12 and 4.13 it becomes clear that overtaking—both active and passive—is a frequent, but quick action, because there are high numbers of coding references, but few seconds spent doing this activity.

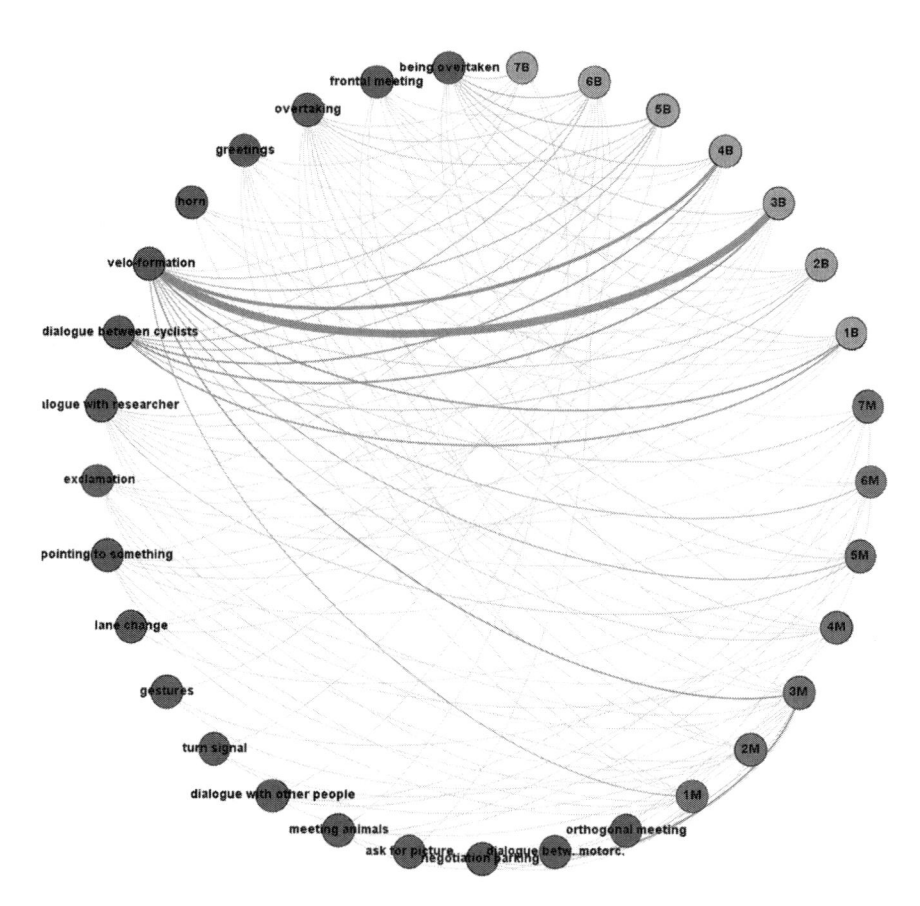

Fig. 4.13 Network graph of social features of journey experiences and their duration in seconds per participant (own elaboration through Gephi software)

4.4 Journey Experience Description: Physical and Social Features   147

Cyclists spend on average about two minutes (144 s) in passing or being passed by other vehicles, motorcyclists spend less than one minute (54 s).

Besides investigating frequencies of coding categories, a deep analysis of the video footage can help to show the relationship social features and geographical space. Below is a more detailed presentation of these results, which contextualizes micro-actions into the mobility space.

4.4.2.1 Active and Passive Overtaking

Notwithstanding the short duration—or possibly due to the short duration—the analysis of passive and active overtaking dynamics shows interesting features. Figure 4.14 presents the frequency of coding references related to active and passive overtaking, per each participant and on average. The left side of the figure shows that there is a strong difference between motorcyclists and cyclists in passive overtaking. Cyclists are passed on average around fifty (48) times during one journey, and mainly by cars and motorcycles. Motorcyclists are passed on average only twice, and mostly by motorcyclists. On the other hand, motorcyclists are very active in overtaking themselves, with passing other vehicles on average 16 times in one journey. Cyclists are more passive, but, contrary to what might be thought, they can also pass motorized vehicles while descending. This happens on average three times in the whole journey. Thereby, results show that motorcyclists tend to be very active in negotiation space through overtaking, while cyclists tend to be more passive. Nevertheless, in occasional cases their roles can be similar. Finally, cars tend to be the vehicles that mostly interact with both motorcyclists and cyclists, because—as it was shown in Fig. 4.4—they represent the majority of vehicles on the Sella Pass road.

Overtaking—a typical and recurring habit for motorcyclists in the ascending and descending phase of the journey—follows an interruption of riding flow due to some time spent in line, while it precedes a high acceleration and a moment of solo riding. Overtaking for cyclists follows a similar pattern, but happens only in the descending part of the journey, because, as it was seen in Sect. 4.3.2, there they tend to be as fast as motorised vehicles. Overtaking of busses, vans and campervans happens quite rarely, but it has different dynamics compared to the interaction among cars, bicycles and motorcycles. This is linked to the dimension of the vehicle, offering lower visibility and less room to overtake, especially in curvy segments of the road. Interacting with buses in Sella Pass road seems to be very annoying for both motorcyclists and cyclists and they frequently complain through exclamations, imprecations and using the horn to keep safe.

Figure 4.15 (and the corresponding Video ESM_2, with multiple examples of motorcyclists and cyclists) shows problematic interaction with buses, the dynamics of overtaking and the difficulties in dealing with room on the road and visibility. In the example of Fig. 4.15, the interaction with the bus in the pass area started much earlier than the overtaking took place. Firstly, cyclists stopped because several cars were in line after the bus, then they overtook the cars and finally, after staying in line for some seconds, they finally overtook the bus. While the overtaking per se lasted

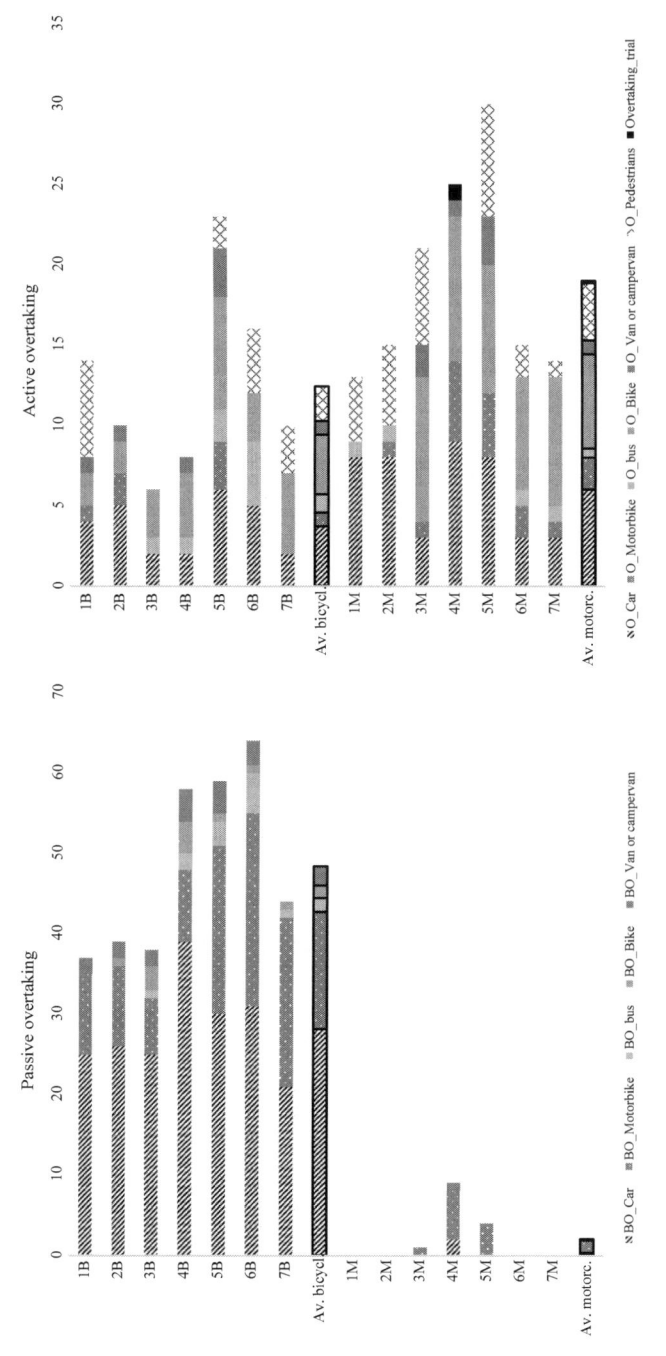

Fig. 4.14 Number of active and passive overtaking actions per participant and on average (own elaboration)

Fig. 4.15 Video stills of the dynamics of bicycles overtaking buses (own elaboration)

only four seconds, cyclists had to wait for the right moment to overtake for about 1:40 min, adapting their descending rhythm to that of the bus.

Contrary to what happens with buses, the interaction between motorcyclists and cyclists appears to be very smooth: they can both keep their own rhythm of flow, their speed and trajectory, as if they were on two parallel tracks of the same road. This relates to the notion of personal and use space mentioned in Sect. 2.2.2, according to which the space negotiations depends both on the dimension of the person and vehicle, and the space necessary to drive. Nevertheless, it is stated in the video footage that motorcyclists' sound works as a disturbing factor for cyclists, as it will be discussed in the coming section on sensory features (see Sect. 4.5).

4.4.2.2 Velo-Formations and Dialogues

Not only overtaking dynamics, but also velo-formations deserve a qualitative in-depth analysis, because they reveal interesting social features of journey experiences. Configurations of velo-formations are diverse but share some similar characteristics.

The start of the journey was typically made together by all group members and everyone waited for their companions to be ready to start. After a few curves, and usually after some minutes spent travelling on a parallel track and talking, cyclists tended to separate according to their personal travelling rhythm, expression of their individual degree of fitness, as is theorized by Oldenburg (2015). In one case, thanks to the availability of technological settings that enabled a pre-vision of the climbing effort, participants agreed on the person that would lead the group until a certain point, as it is stated in this excerpt of dialogue between participant 6B and 5B:

5B: Administra esta subida! São 5 quilômetros
 [Keep control of this rise! It is 5 km long]
6B: Mas antes temos subido quanto? A terceira foi quanto?
 [How much did we climb to the peak of the pass previously]
5B: 9
 [9 km]
6B: Pois é! Metade eu faço, tranquilo!
 [OK! I will lead the half of it!]

Technology worked in this case as a source of information and therefore as a portable support to organise the challenge and to distribute tasks and efforts among different travellers during the climb.

When they reached the watershed, and very often when they reached the Pass Sella sign, cyclists tended to wait for the companions, and—after a few pictures—start the descent, again in a velo-formation.

Another function of the velo-formation of cyclists is that of allowing verbal interaction, one of the most important secondary tasks for cyclists. Verbal interactions are often short dialogues related to the journey itself, to athletic performance in the ride or to the route. One interesting example about the route is reported below:

4B: Ja, da müssen wir rauf!
 [Yes, we have to climb to that peak!]
3B: Da rauf wollen wir?
 [To that peak? Really?]
4B: Ja. Oder vielleicht fahren wir darunter vorbei
 [Yes. Or maybe we travel over there.]
3B: Warst du öfters schon oben?
 [Have you ever been up there?]
4B: Ja, damals bin ich von der anderen Seite gekommen
 [Yes. But the other time I was coming from the opposite direction]

Participants 3B and 4B were travelling with a travel guide and they did not know the route exactly. They were pointing to the Dolomites' peaks and thinking that their journey had to reach one of those peaks, which was not the case in reality. This happened notwithstanding the fact that one of the cyclists had already covered the route in the opposite direction. Conversely to what happened to cyclists 5B and 6B, participants 3B and 4B seem not to be familiar with the mobility space surrounding them, which creates uncertainty in the physical effort to climb to the peak of the

4.4 Journey Experience Description: Physical and Social Features

pass as well. Participant 3B and 4B not only ignored the real pattern of the road, but they also did not know each other, because they were participating in a guided tour organised by their hotel. Therefore, they used the moments of velo-formation to get to know each other, to talk about their country of origin as well as to comment on other cycling tours made during their holiday. Similarly, in the group of 1B and 2B travel companions used their time to discuss heroic experiences of climbers they knew on the peaks surrounding them (Torri del Sella) as well as commenting on winter training possibilities to stay fit for the season. They also commented on the research they were participating in, by highlighting the importance of dialogue in the cyclists' journey, which gives a meta-value to the following excerpt of dialogue:

1B:	Volevo dirle—mi sono dimenticato—che alla fine il ciclista interagisce
	[I wanted to tell her—then I forgot—that the cyclists do interact]
Travel companion:	In che senso?
	[What do you mean?]
1B:	Lei dice 'gruppi che non interagiscono'; sai motociclisti… il motociclista no non parla. Ma i ciclisti sono in gruppo
	[She says 'groups that do not interact', you know, motorcyclists… motorcyclists, they don't speak. But cyclists, they are in a group]
Travel companion:	Beh ma a suo modo anche i motociclisti
	[Well, motorcyclists as well, in their own way]

Cyclist 5B took also the chance to comment on the journey for the researcher. While he was using Portuguese to interact with his travel companions, he repeatedly talked in English to the camera, commenting on the journey experience and explaining in words what he was undergoing:

5B: Boa, agora sí! *[Perfect! Now it's fine!]* I had a problem with my helmet, but now it's ok!

Motorcyclists interacted differently in velo-formations and talked only when they stopped. Due to the noise of the engine and the presence of the helmet, as well as the higher speed, verbal interactions are hardly possible on the move without an intercom and never happened in the video footage, neither between motorcyclists on two vehicles, nor in the case a passenger was carried. For motorcyclists the velo-formation seems to be kept united by the leader of the group, who is often repeatedly checking for the presence of the travelling companion(s) in the rear-view mirror. Velo-formations of motorcyclists are typically interrupted because of different patterns of overtaking cars. Sometimes motorcyclists in groups show different attitudes to taking the risk of overtaking and this creates a gap between the rider leading the group and the one following. Anyway, if the velo-formation of motorcyclists is interrupted, it often gets rebuilt without stops, in a play of accelerations and decelerations of the two or more travel companions, as if there were a rubber band connecting the two vehicles.

4.4.2.3 Greetings

Besides primary driving tasks and dialogues, several secondary tasks involve interaction among travellers. One important element is greetings. Greetings happen between motorcyclists and between cyclists, but motorcyclists use gestures to express greetings, while cyclists usually talk. Motorcyclists use their left hand to say hello to other motorcyclists coming in the opposite direction, while cyclists use verbal expression and say hello to cyclists they overtake. Fascinating interaction dynamics show up when analysing greetings in the video footage.

All greetings happen on straight parts of the road, when concentration on riding control is less pervasive and there is greater attention to the surrounding environment. For cyclists, greetings tend to happen when they are climbing to the peak of the pass, while they never happened in the video footage when descending to the valley. The interesting phenomenon about greetings is to understand who participants did *not* say hallo to and explore the reasons why. Indeed, motorcyclists do not say hello to other road users, while cyclists do it with pedestrians. This seems to suggest that motorcyclists use the greetings to honour a closed community of travellers: themselves. In one extreme case, the community addressed was even smaller: participant number 4M—riding a chopper—only considered motorcyclists with chopper bikes for greetings, and ignored those riding naked, touring or sport bikes. Greetings seem to work as identity markers, and multiple identities are reflected in the different behaviours of participants.

4.4.2.4 Gestures and Signals

Among other non-verbal interactions, the use of horn and turn signals stand out to communicate travel intentions. Motorcyclists also often use gestures to share decisions about the journey, e.g. whether to stop or continue riding, whether to let the travel companion go first or not. Finally, gestures are used to identify something happening in the background landscape, or to celebrate the climb (see Fig. 4.16 and the corresponding Video ESM_3). For example, to the left side of Fig. 4.16, participant 1B was pointing to a climber on the rocks the mountains, participant 7 M was pointing to a roe deer crossing the road in front of him, participant 3B was (wrongly) hypothesising the location of the Sella Pass. To the right of Fig. 4.16, participants 3B, 4B and 5B were enjoying the moment of reaching the top of the pass. More about visual attention and moments dedicated to the perception of landscape is explained in Sect. 4.5.1, focussing on sensory elements.

4.4 Journey Experience Description: Physical and Social Features

Fig. 4.16 Video stills of non-verbal language to point to landscape features (left) and celebrate the climb (right) (own elaboration)

4.4.3 Key Findings

Section 4.4 has introduced two dimensions of analysing travel experiences on the Sella Pass road: the physical/kinaesthetic dimension and the social dimension. These were described through coding categories corresponding to actions, described through frequencies, network and bar graphs and video clips or stills. Both physical and social dimensions of travel journey included actions classifiable into main tasks and secondary tasks. Main tasks relate to driving, focussing on the control of the vehicle in different conditions, secondary tasks refer to other activities, including those related to tourism. Among the main tasks, it was noted that there were two ways of conducting the vehicles: in line, i.e. adapting one's travel rhythm to the one of the vehicles preceding, or solo, i.e. determining the own rhythm and proceeding in a flow. A middle ground between the two was identified in the velo-formations, where moments of individual riding flow were combined with moments of waiting time or deceleration, in order to ensure the compactness of the travelling group. Secondary tasks were identified both from the physical point of view and from the social point of view. Taking pictures, drinking, dressing for rainy weather were among the individual tasks, while dialogues, gestures, and dynamics of greeting other vehicles or travellers were among the social ones. Secondary tasks seemed to happen when the riding concentration could be lower, e.g. on straight parts of the road and or on road segments where the speed had to be reduced. Concerning the social features, a remarkable aspect was the use of the camera as a tool to record an inter-temporal dialogue with the researcher, and to comment on a meta-level about the characteristics of the own journeys.

4.5 Journey Experience Description: Sensory and Emotional Features

Building on the previous sections, the sensory and emotional features of journey experiences are illustrated here. These features are partly described using video footage and its content analysis, including textual statements on sensations; partly they result from the analysis of the self-report questionnaires. Data generated with facial action coding systems is not used for this section, because it refers to portions of the video footage and is not accurately presentable at an aggregated level. It will be used to process a comparison between self-report and observation techniques on an individual level in Chap. 5.

4.5.1 Sensory Features: Travel Glance, Sound and Silence

Sensory features relating to the travel journeys were self-reported by participants and observed in the video footage. These multiple sources of evidence were often used to integrate one another, i.e. often self-reported answers helped to recollect and reinforce sensing moments in the clips. Of course, the video footage had the limit of capturing and recording only audio-visual perceptions, and, therefore, only two of the five senses were coded into categories, as will be explained later. Moreover, the video material helped in partly understanding the embodiment of experiences, for example recording cornering and banking, as well as vibrations, and wind, within the audio cue.

Contrary to other sections, this section does not start with the analysis of video content indexing. It first describes self-reported sensory perceptions—a more comprehensive source of evidence—and then links them back to the embodied experiences of driving recorded by the video footage—with audio and visual perceptions only. Self-reported data offers a first overview on sensory involvement, including sight, hearing, touch, taste and smell. Figure 4.17 shows the individual scores of sensory involvement per participant and the averages for each means of transport. The scores used in the questionnaire followed a 5-point Likert scale and ranged

4.5 Journey Experience Description: Sensory and Emotional Features

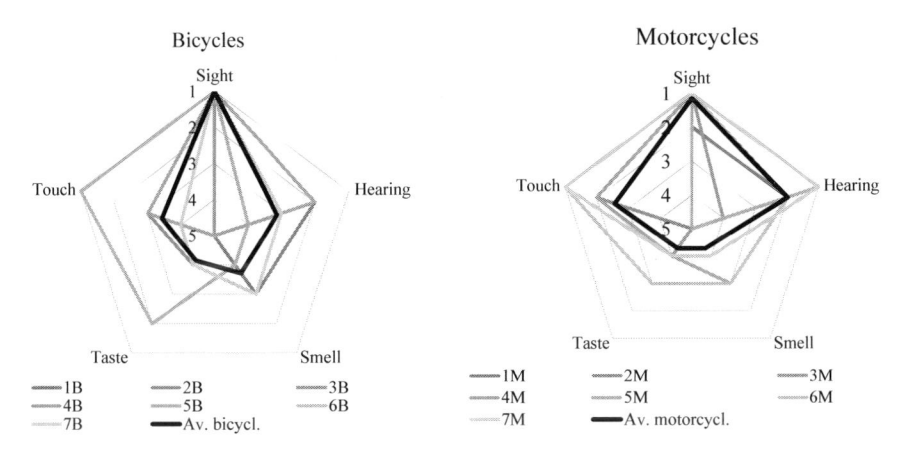

Fig. 4.17 Self-reported scores on the involvement of the five senses during the journey per participant and on average (1 = highly involved; 5 = slightly involved) (own elaboration)

from 1 (high involvement) to 5 (minor involvement). As found in the existing literature, sight is a predominant sense during journey experiences, both for cyclists and motorcyclists. Only one participant gave a score of 2 to sight, all others reported 1, the maximum involvement possible. Among the moments when sight was mostly elicited, motorcyclists reported the moments when they could ride alone in an open road or when they could have a look at other motorcycles, whereas cyclists reported moments when they could admire mountain peaks, green fields, valleys, mountain passes.

Hearing and touch appear to be the second and third mostly involved sense. For motorcyclists, hearing was perceived as always elicited during the whole journey, probably because they were listening to the sound of their bike's engine. Conversely, cyclists reported different kinds of stimuli: the sound of silence and the regular rhythm of their breath; birds and the sound of a small river; cow bells; dialogues among cyclists; and finally the sound of other motorised vehicles. It is important to note that these stimuli were reported from four different cyclists and none of them repeated a stimulus mentioned by another. This difference in the variety and the rhythm of hearing stimuli relates probably to the different mode used—motorcycles are noisy vehicles, bicycles are silent vehicles—but also to the duration of the journey experience. Motorcyclists' soundscapes were controlled by the motorcycles' engines, whereas cyclists' soundscapes were dominated by nature, other vehicles and—eventually—their own rhythm of breath. Touch was associated with the kinaesthetic of riding a bicycle or a motorbike, especially when in the descending phase, but it was not described in detail by participants. This might be related to the fact that while they were actually gripping the handle bar, they were all wearing gloves, which might have reduced the sensitivity of their hands. Concerning smell, motorcyclists could not report particular moments when they were smelling positive or negative fragrances, while once again cyclists reported a variety of both pleasant

Nodes		
Name	Sources	References
LEV 3 - SENSORY	16	559
Rythm Sound	2	6
birds	1	1
Visual attention	16	553
animals look	2	3
backward look	15	155
bike look	4	36
cyclist look	5	61
dashboard check	8	58
landscape look	16	191
mirroring oneself	1	1
pedestrians look	1	2
signs look	2	6
sky look	2	2
vehicle look	13	37

Fig. 4.18 Nodes coding sensory features of journey experiences, including categories and subcategories, sources and coding references (own elaboration through NVivo Pro 11^{TM} software)

and unpleasant smells (e.g. flowers and nature, but also traffic related gasses). Finally, taste was not rewarded as an important source of sensations, apart from one cyclist (2B), who was drinking energy drinks while climbing to the peak of the pass and a second cyclist (5B) who reported he was feeling "the taste of blood" because he had a small accident while descending.

The video footage is a helpful source for analysing the sense of sight in a deeper detail. Figure 4.18 shows the coding categories (nodes) used to describe sight and hearing in the video footage. As already stated in the methodology chapter, the interpretation of visual attention through headcam data needs to be done very carefully, because there is no exact information about what exact object eyes are gazing at. But, the fact that—in absence of stimuli—riders tended to look in front of them without moving their head, facilitated the detection of changes in visual attention and the possibility to hypothesise on possible attractions for their gaze.

Among the most frequent and common actions made by cyclists and motorcyclists while in motion were the travel glance towards the landscape and the repeated checking of the situation behind them (see Fig. 4.18, nodes "landscape look" and "backward look"). Both actions deserve a better analysis, because they reveal interesting features of journey experiences on the Sella Pass.

4.5 Journey Experience Description: Sensory and Emotional Features 157

4.5.1.1 The Riders' Glance

The analysis of participants' glances towards the landscape shows that the main attractions are the "Sassolungo Group", a massif whose bare rocks represent one of the icons of the Sella Pass, or the "Sella Group", the massif around which the tour is made. Typically, if doing the route in the counterclockwise direction, the main attraction was the Sassolungo Massif, whereas in case of a clockwise tour, the panoramic views were more diverse, but often focussed on the Sella massif, as well. This seems to be related to the fact that, especially cyclists, look at landscape when they climb to the top of the pass and do less so when they descend. The frequency and duration of gazes towards the Sassolungo Group is different across modes and individuals. Figure 4.19—and the corresponding video footage attached to this thesis ESM_4 and ESM_5—show some of the moments where cyclists and motorcyclists were looking at landscape. Interestingly, the comparison of multiple participants in the two route directions reveals that there are some specific places (e.g. the place illustrated from multiple views in Fig. 4.19 and in Videos ESM_4 and ESM_5) where almost all participants looked at the "Sassolungo Group", as if it were an irresistible point of interest (a sort of touchpoint) gazed at while on the move.

These are places where the road was straight, and often there are trees that—while the vehicle is moving—uncovered marvellous views, as if they were curtains in a theatre. Typically, cyclists tend to look at these objects and panoramic views for a longer time during the climb, because their low speed permits the distraction of their gaze. Among them, there is a range of different attitudes towards the landscape, probably also reflecting the predominance of varying interests in the place or in their athletic performance. For example, cyclist 7B stops several times during the climb and takes multiple pictures of the landscape; 5B and his travel companion 4B seem to be more focussed on their athletic performance and they avoid stops until they reach the top of the pass; they then spend several minutes taking pictures of themselves with the astonishing background landscape of the Dolomites. It is interesting to note that 7B takes pictures of the landscape that do not include him or his bike, whereas 5B and 4B carry their bikes on their back to take pictures of themselves in the green grasses of the pass area, with astonishing views but—more importantly—with the sign of the pass below them. It seems that in the first case there is a deeper interest in nature and its configuration around the pass, whereas in the second case the picture works mainly as evidence that the summit was reached.

Compared to cyclists, motorcyclists tend to look towards the surrounding landscape in quick and repeated movements, as if they were attracted by landscape beauty, but could not detach their gaze from the road for safety reasons. They can distract themselves from their main task of riding the bike mainly on straight parts of the road; otherwise they keep focussed on the highway. If looking at Fig. 4.20, this difference between cyclists and motorcyclists in spending their journey time by looking at landscapes is reflected in the different thickness of the linkages between participants and the corresponding node (landscape look). The only exception is the participant 3M, because he stopped a long time on the pass summit area and spent a time by looking at landscapes which was comparable to the cyclists. Nevertheless, this gaze

Fig. 4.19 Video stills of moments when participants looked at the Sassolungo group massif (own elaboration)

was different from that of cyclists, because it was related to steadiness and not to mobility.

Some interesting findings help to explain the backward looks of cyclists and motorcyclists. The aim of both cyclists and motorcyclists when they turn their heads is to check for the position of their travel companion. Cyclists turn their head and often unconsciously move towards the centre of their lane, potentially creating dangerous dynamics in the interaction with other vehicles. Motorcyclists check the rear-view mirror, especially after having passed other vehicles or having overcome obstacles along the road. The explanation for backward looks seems to also be determined by

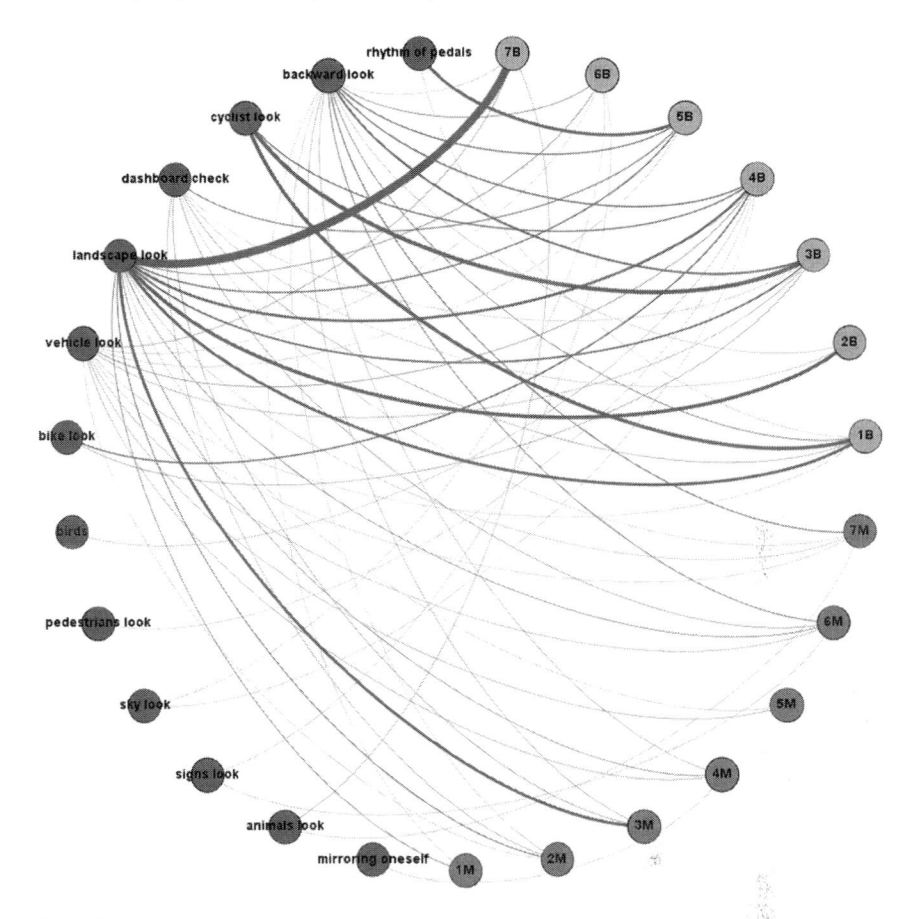

4.5 Journey Experience Description: Sensory and Emotional Features 159

Fig. 4.20 Network graph of sensory features of journey experiences and their duration in seconds per participant (own elaboration)

the need for *control over the travel companion's journey*, not only over the individual one.

Apart from mountain massifs, travel companions and other vehicles, other objects of interest for participants were animals met along the road or in the pass area, as well as participants' own vehicles or travel companions. Concerning vehicles, motorbike dashboards were looked at routinely, probably to check and control speed. Similarly, cyclists repeatedly looked at GPS tools on their bikes, to check data on speed, route direction and steepness. Both types of actions express a certain desire to keep *control of the journey*, to monitor speed, route and performance. Travel companions were looked at during dialogues along the road and this happened mainly amongst cyclists (see Fig. 4.20).

Although different in their duration, moments of visual attention seem to be quite similar among participants and modes. Be it for *interest*—in mountains, motorcycles, or animals—for the *need for control*—of speed, track or steepness—or for *interactions*—with vehicles or travel companions—the video footages show that the journey experience is characterised by a primary visual attention to the road and multiple secondary, quick and repeated, moments of attention towards other objects. This happens in a flow between concentration and distraction, where the higher the speed, the shorter the possibility to divert the gaze.

4.5.1.2 Rhythm and Sound

Apart from visual aspects of the journey, rhythmical aspects related to sound can be also detected in the video cue. NVivo Pro 11™ allows for the visualisation of the audio wave, which is available for each participant in the coding scheme of each video. Similar patterns are visible among different participants riding a bicycle, with a very silent journey when climbing to the peak of the pass and a louder journey when descending. Also motorcycling soundscapes are very similar, although the intensity of the sound depends substantially by the type of motorcycle used. A more accurate visualization of sound patterns of an exemplary cyclist and motorcyclist (see Fig. 4.21, created through the software Sonic Visualizer) helps to better understand the rhythmical patterns of the journey experience.

Cyclists' experiences are bipartite. The climb is a multi-sensuous, poly-rhythmic experience. Iso-rhythmic (repetitive) patterns are mostly related to pedalling, and they intersect with arhythmic (irregular) patterns, mostly deriving from motorized vehicles overtaking cyclists. Figure 4.21 visually shows this twofold pattern, illustrating how the cyclists' experience is made predominantly in a quiet environment, but small peaks in sound are interrupting this silence. But what are these sounds? The regular rhythm of pedals, which is often perceivable in the form of a soft, pulsing beat in the silence, is sometimes accompanied by a movement of the head, so that it also translates into a visible waving of frames in the video footage. On top of this regular pattern, the irregular, arhythmical, interaction with other vehicles translates into the sound of cars, motorcycles or buses coming closer, sometimes tooting their horn at cyclists, and finally passing them. A third level regards occasional sounds from nature, for example cow bells or birds, which enable a layer of interaction with the surrounding environment. Cyclists' descent is a very different sound experience. It is dominated by the arrhythmic pattern of the sound of wind, which is directly related to the increase and decrease in speed, reflecting in turn the shape of the road. Namely, it seems that the sound of the descent traces back the shape of the road, with its curves and straight parts, expressing different acceleration and deceleration patterns.

Motorcyclists' sound data show an even more marked arhythmical pattern, related mostly to the sound of the motorcycle, which is prominent and somehow hiding all other sounds during the whole journey. Only in a few cases was it possible to hear the sound of the preceding motorbike, in a sort of duo. The sound produced by motorcyclists is irregular, because it results from the interaction between the motorcycle, the road (e.g. its curves, gradients etc.) and other road users—in an unpredictable repetition of accelerations and decelerations, moments of solo riding

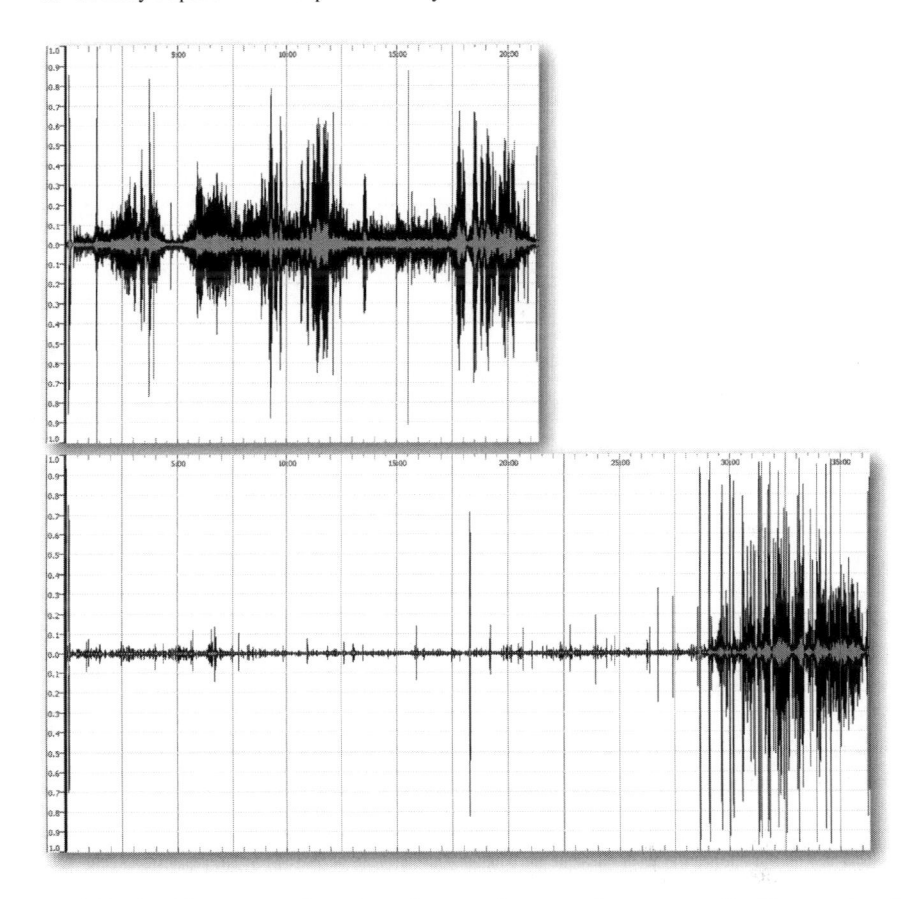

4.5 Journey Experience Description: Sensory and Emotional Features

Fig. 4.21 Graphic representation of soundscapes of an exemplary motorcyclist (first wave) and cyclist (second wave) (own elaboration through the software Sonic Visualizer)

and of riding in line. Both motorcyclists and cyclists perceive the sound of wind when speed is increasing, i.e. in case of acceleration. It is interesting to note that the pass area (corresponding in Fig. 4.21 to the minutes around min. 15:00 of the first wave) is the most quiet moment of the motorcyclist's journey, because the speed is lower and the congestion is higher. As it will be seen in the next section (Sect. 4.3.2), these are the moments where motorcyclists are more nervous or angry.

In sum, it seems that cyclists are (almost) silent road users, that listen to a *symphony* of multiple sources of sound—regular and irregular—, whereas motorcyclists are loud road users—that play their own—irregular—*solo* engine performance. Namely, motorcyclists play the road music, whereas cyclists silently listen to the symphony of road and nature happening together.

4.5.1.3 Embodiment

Apart from sight and sound, a third aspect worth analysing is embodiment. One of the possible indicators of embodied effort during the journey is the analysis of the heart rate. A micro-analysis of how heart rate develops along the journey on a second-by-second scale is made in the next chapter, while average heart rate values are presented here in the three main temporal dimensions of the journey. Figure 4.22 illustrates that the greatest differences in heart rate between the climb, the pass area and the descent relate to cyclists. Reaching the peak of the mountain on a bicycle requires substantial muscular effort, reflected in the high heart rate (on average, 154 BPM). The pass area is the area where the heart rate begins to descend (130 BPM), because of the reduced effort and the frequent stops. The descending phase is the one with least physical effort, which translates for cyclists into a lower heart rate (113).

Comparing the previously presented Fig. 4.8 on average speed in each temporal dimension, it seems that for cyclists speed and hearth rate are inversely proportional, probably because low speed is related to a higher physical effort—and therefore a higher BPM. For motorcyclists, it seems that they are directly proportional, because high speed might be related to a parallel emotional arousal, as analysed in the coming section and, in more detail, in Chap. 5.

4.5.2 Emotional Features: The Thrill of Speed, the Worry to Stay in Line

Emotional features, self-reported by participants using the scale by Richins (1997) and a 5-point Likert scale, reveal overall positive valence of emotion during journey experiences. Happiness, optimism and peacefulness are intense feelings for both cyclists and motorcyclists, with average scores between 1 and 2 and detailed descriptions of stimuli. Negative valenced feelings are rarely described and less intense, showing average scores between 4 and 5. Figure 4.23 reports individual (in grey) and average (in black) scores of emotional arousal, based on the self-reporting by participants. On average, happiness is the most intense feeling for both cyclists and motorcyclists, followed by optimism and peacefulness. Among the negative feelings, fear and anger are the most intense, both for cyclists and motorcyclists. Loneliness is slightly present in cyclists, with direct reference to the romantic landscape. Worry is present in motorcyclists with respect to pavement conditions and the risky behaviour of travel companions.

Assessing participants individually it becomes clear that some of them show particular emotional patterns. For instance, cyclist 5B and motorcyclist 5M report different patterns for negative valenced feelings. 5B, travelling with his wife and having had an accident during the journey, reported feelings of fear (for the accident) and worry (for the difficulties his wife might have in descending the pass). Motorcyclist 5M also revealed peculiar patterns with regard to envy (related to other

4.5 Journey Experience Description: Sensory and Emotional Features 163

▨ Average BPM climbing   ▨ Average BPM pass area   ■ Average BPM descending

*Missing bio-sensing data for the participant
**Missing bio-sensing data in one section

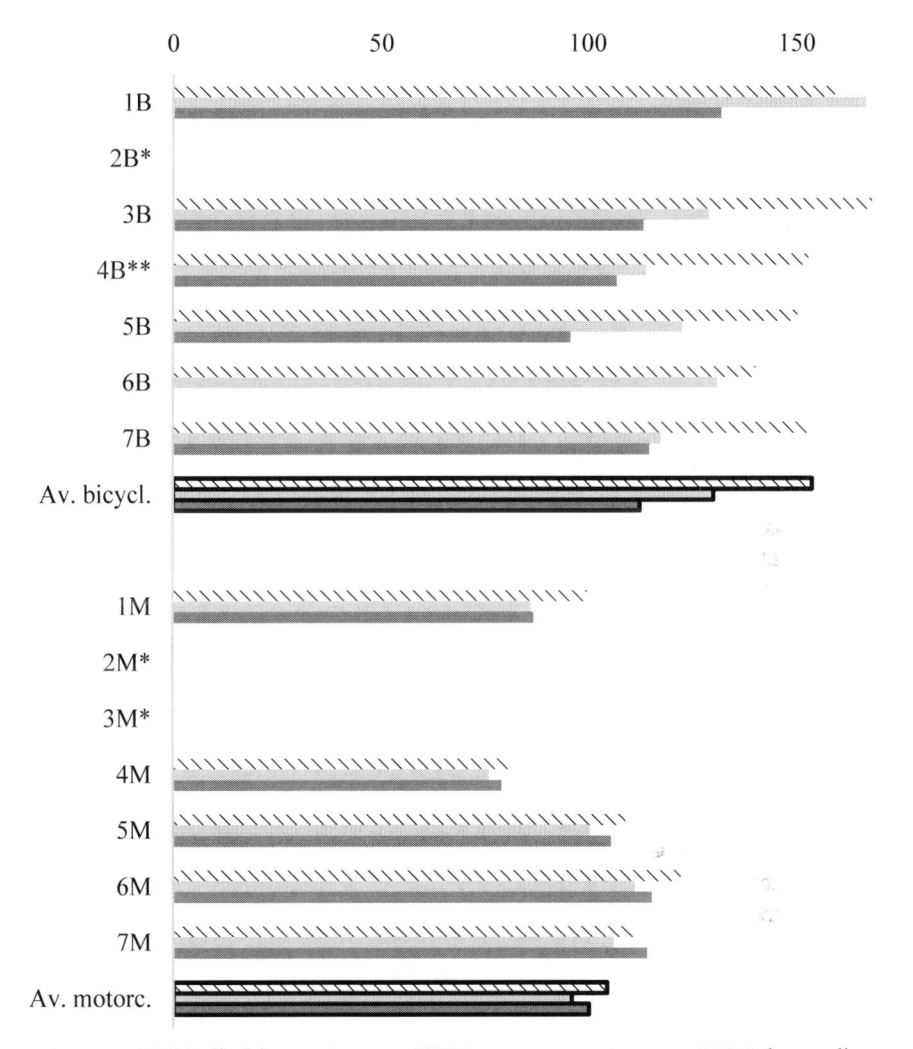

Fig. 4.22 Average BPM of bicycle and motorcycle participants per journey section (own elaboration)

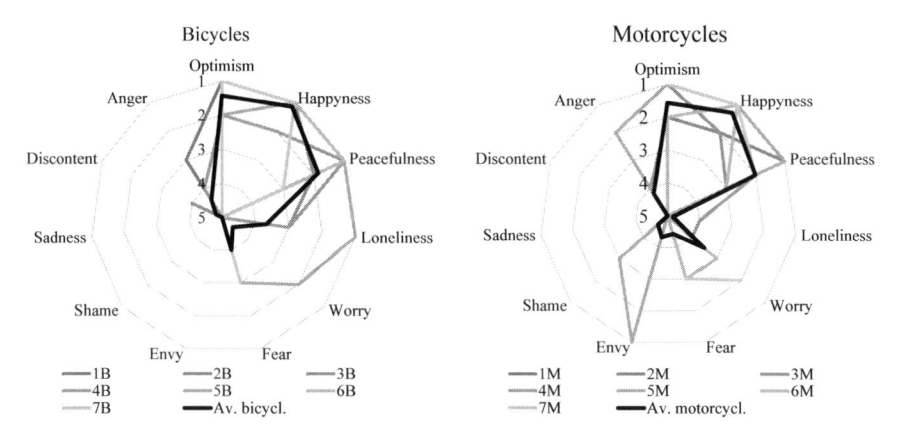

Fig. 4.23 Self-reported scores on the emotional arousal during the journey per participant and on average (1 = highly involved; 5 = slightly involved) (own elaboration)

motorcycles), shame (related to slowness in curves) and anger (related to traffic and other road users). Tables 4.3 and 4.4 provide useful help to understand Fig. 4.23, in that they report in words the stimuli of the most intensely perceived emotions. Below are descriptions of the most important positive-valenced emotions (optimism, happiness, peacefulness) and the most important negative feelings (fear, anger, worry and discontent) accounting for both types of travellers.

Optimism seems to be a pervasive and long-lasting feeling, with three participants reporting that it was perceived all along the tour (1M, 4M, 1B) and three of them—all cyclists—associating it with the beginning of the journey (2B, 3B, 6B). Some participants associated this feeling also to single moments or events. These were related to the road infrastructure and the landscape for motorcyclists—the clear road (7M), the landscape (6M), the great curves (5M)—and mostly related to the individual fitness or performance for cyclists—awareness of riding abilities (2B), body responding well (5B), achievement of the summit of the pass (7B).

Happiness, similarly to optimism, is perceived both as a long-lasting feeling, and a precise reaction to single stimuli. Participants 2M, 4M, 1B, 2B reported a generalised feeling of happiness associated to the whole tour; 5M, 6M, 3B and 5B related happiness to the landscape, with particular mention of the rocks (the Dolomites); 1M and 7M, both motorcyclists, associated happiness to speed and banking; 2B, 3B, 6B, all cyclists, related happiness to the achievement of the goal of reaching the pass. Descending was a reason for happiness for the cyclists 7B, and partly for 2B, but not for motorcyclists. Based on this evidence, it seems that common stimuli for happiness are related mostly to the destination environment, whereas driving activities make fun for motorcyclists and athletic challenges do the same for cyclists.

Peacefulness is associated mostly to villages, valleys and natural landscapes (1M, 7M, 3B, 5B, 7B), but also to the action of riding a motorcycle in safe conditions (2M,

4.5 Journey Experience Description: Sensory and Emotional Features

Table 4.3 Intensity and stimuli of most intense feeling of motorcyclists (average score < 5; with 1 = highly involved; 5 = slightly involved) (own elaboration)

	Optimism		Happiness		Peacefulness		Fear		Worry		Anger	
	Score	Moment	Score	Moment	Score	Moment	Score	Moment	Score	Moment	Score	Moment
1M	2	During the whole journey	1	In the moments of clear road and quick curves	2	Around the village centre	5		3	When my travel companion was making a rash overtake	5	
2M	2	I hope to repeat the tour	2	I am happy that I did this tour	1	Riding a motorcycle makes me relax	5		5		5	
3M	1	Because I was aware of my riding capacities	2	Because of the quantity of numerous motorcycles along the road	3	Because of the pavement	5					
4M	2	Always	1	Always	2	Always	5		4		4	Other means of transport (cars)

(continued)

Table 4.3 (continued)

	Optimism		Happiness		Peacefulness		Fear		Worry		Anger	
	Score	Moment	Score	Moment	Score	Moment	Score	Moment	Score	Moment	Score	Moment
5M	1	Great curves	1	Marvellous landscape	1	Riding = peacefulness	5	No reason why	4	Traffic was very intense	2	When other means of transport were too slow on the road
6M	2	When I look at the landscape	1	When I see the mountains	3	When I was in the pass summit area	3	In curves during the descending part, when the road was wet	3	In curves, while descending, with wet road surfaces	5	
7M	1	Clear road	1	In curves/when banking	2	The stillness you perceive when you look at mountains	3	When descending, because of the damp pavement due to rain	2	On bumpy pavement on the pass summit area		
Av. Motorcycle	2		1		2		4		4		4	

4.5 Journey Experience Description: Sensory and Emotional Features 167

Table 4.4 Intensity and stimuli of most intense feeling of cyclists (average score < 5; with 1 = highly involved; 5 = slightly involved) (own elaboration)

	Optimism		Happiness		Peacefulness		Loneliness		Fear		Discontent		Anger	
	Score	Moment	Score	Moment	Score	Moment	Score	Moment	Score	Moment	Score	Moment	Score	Moment
1B	1	From the start to the end. A good emotional attitude on the bike is essential as much as the training. Negative thoughts (when they occur) make me go back home	1	As said earlier: it is a very hard effort, without any real or concrete reason. If one does not feel happy in doing it, it turns out to be very difficult	2	In moments of low traffic, when the bike seems to proceed alone along the street because the body can cope perfectly with the needs. In those moments one reaches a different way of thinking and elaborating thoughts	5		3	Due to congestion. Cars were too close, risk evaluation was not always perfect	5		3	Feeling related to rudeness on the road: horn blowing, cars that overtake very close to cyclists, motorcycles running at 10,000 rpm with the associated racket

(continued)

Table 4.4 (continued)

	Optimism		Happiness		Peacefulness		Loneliness		Fear		Discontent		Anger	
	Score	Moment	Score	Moment	Score	Moment	Score	Moment	Score	Moment	Score	Moment	Score	Moment
2B	1	During the climb, I was aware of my riding capacities. More than optimism, I had positive sensations related to an overall feeling of well-being related to the place and the effort	1	Similar to previous answer, I had this sensation during the whole tour, including the descent, because I had met the first of the four objectives of the day	3	Peacefulness can be felt more in day trips to the countryside. I was calm from the emotional point of view, but the prevailing emotions were others		I never felt this emotion	5	A little bit of fear when descending is always good! It makes you be more prudent!				

(continued)

4.5 Journey Experience Description: Sensory and Emotional Features 169

Table 4.4 (continued)

	Optimism		Happiness		Peacefulness		Loneliness		Fear		Discontent		Anger	
	Score	Moment	Score	Moment	Score	Moment	Score	Moment	Score	Moment	Score	Moment	Score	Moment
3B	2	When I started the tour	1	When I crossed the watershed, landscape	2	Stillness in the nature	3	Loneliness for the mountain landscapes, which we do not have at home	5		4	I had some problems with my knee	5	
4B	2		2		1		3		4		5		4	
5B	2	When I felt my body was responding very well	1	Every time I saw a mountain rock facing me	1	When I saw the cows in the road	1	Mountains	3	When the camera fell and I almost fell, too	5	Nope		Never
6B	1	Beginning of the tour	1	Reaching the peaks and end of the tour	1	Lunch time, end of the tour	5		5		5		5	

(continued)

Table 4.4 (continued)

	Optimism		Happiness		Peacefulness		Loneliness		Fear		Discontent		Anger	
	Score	Moment	Score	Moment	Score	Moment	Score	Moment	Score	Moment	Score	Moment	Score	Moment
7B	1	Cresting the passes	1	Descending	3	Valleys	5		3	Couple of tight corners going a little too fast	5		5	
Av. Bicycle	1		1		2		4		4		4		4	

4.5 Journey Experience Description: Sensory and Emotional Features   171

3M, 5M) and to the flow of riding a bike in low traffic conditions (1B). The end of the cycling tour is also associated with a sense of peacefulness (6B).

Loneliness is a feeling mostly perceived and described by cyclists (3B, 5B). It is related to landscape and particularly to the emotions that mountains can evoke. Loneliness results from the comparison between the landscape of one's country of origin and the one seen in Sella Pass. Indeed, 3B and 5B were from Germany and Brazil, both places where, quite often, flatland prevails over mountainous areas.

Fear was a slightly perceived feeling both for cyclists and motorcyclists. Motorcyclists (6M and 7M) reported to feel fear in the descending part of the journey, particularly when the road was wet. Cyclists also reported to have felt fear during the descent, when the speed was high and, therefore, there was more perceived risk of a fall (2B, 7B). One of them (2B) even reported that fear is a (sort of) positive feeling in the cycling journey, because it can protect the rider from taking risky actions during the descent. Finally, fear was associated also with specific dangerous conditions, such as the moment when 5B had an accident and the camera fell down, or when 1B was overtaken by cars that did not keep a safe distance.

Discontent was felt only by one cyclist (3B), because he had pain in one knee while making the tour, whereas *worry* was a more common feeling for motorcyclists, mostly related to the intensity of traffic and risky interactions with other traffic (1M, 5M), wet road surface conditions (6M, 7M).

Finally, *anger* was felt both by cyclists and motorcyclists in relation to other road users. Motorcyclists 4M and 5M reported this feeling in relation to other vehicles (especially cars or slow vehicles), whereas cyclist 1B felt angry when other road users behaved rudely, e.g. overtaking him without keeping a safe distance, making too much noise. Anger seems therefore to be a reaction to the limitation of one's freedom of riding, which is perceived due to differences in speed, as well as travel rhythm and sound. Hence, some interactions are perceived as unpleasant, intrusive, risky or simply annoying because they interfere with the participants' personal or use space.

4.5.3 Key Findings

Concerning sensory involvement during the journey, the five senses, the heart rate and the associated rhythmical patterns of the journey were analysed. A major result from the five senses analysis is that sight and hearings are the predominant sensory aspects. They both relate to the main task of driving, but also to secondary tasks. Cyclists tend to be more sensitive to audio-visual stimuli coming from the natural context or secondary tasks, whereas motorcyclists use their senses mostly in relation to motorcycling activity. For example, both motorcyclists and cyclists gaze at the two main massifs around the Sella Pass (Sassolungo Massif and Sella Massif), but motorcyclists dedicate shorter and more repeated glances at mountains than cyclists do. Moreover, motorcyclists are those tending to have a look at other motorcycles, whereas cyclists rarely look at other cyclists to stare at their bikes—they tend to look at them for other reasons, for instance to talk. A common aspect in visual attention is the importance of travel companions. Both cyclists and motorcyclists repeatedly check for the position and the safe condition of their travel companions, both by using rear-view mirrors or turning to look back. This type of visual attention confirms—adding to what has been previously said about velo-formations—that the group of travellers is a very important unit for both cyclists and motorcyclists.

For motorcyclists, hearing perceptions are constantly activated by the sound of their own vehicle's engine, whereas cyclists perceive a variety of different sounds, including the sound of nature (e.g. birds). This greater variety of stimuli perceived by cyclists is evident also for smell, since cyclists perceive different perfumes and odours, e.g. flowers and nature, (but also traffic related gases), while motorcyclists do not report any particular perfume.

Hearing and visual attention both contribute to designing the rhythmical pattern of the journey, that results in *polyrhythmic* patterns for cyclists—because it includes multiple different stimuli, each one having its own rhythmical pattern—and *arhythmical* patterns (irregular) for motorcyclists, because it follows the patterns of the road and the riding behaviour of the rider, with more limited influences by other rhythms, e.g. slow vehicles.

The analysis of average heart rate scores during the trip is a proxy of the embodied effort and, possibly, also of emotional arousal during parts of the journey. Average scores confirm that the climb is the hardest part of the journey for cyclists, as heart rate is inversely proportional to speed. For motorcyclists there are almost no differences in heart rate between climb and descent. The pass summit area is for both types of road users a moment of reduced heart beat intensity.

Interestingly, while analysing the emotional aspects of the journey it becomes clear that the moments where higher physical effort is demanded are not necessarily those where negative feelings are experienced. Indeed, happiness and optimism are feelings that some cyclists have associated with the beginning of the tour, when they started to climb the pass. Conversely, negative valenced feelings, such as fear, were related to moments where the physical effort was less prominent, particularly in the faster descending part. Weather and infrastructure conditions seem to affect the perception of risk, translated into worry or fear, whereas beautiful landscapes, in particular mountains, evoke optimism, happiness and—sometimes—even loneliness. Finally, anger seems a feeling perceived in relation to encounters with some other road users, particularly in cases of their rude or disrespectful behaviour.

4.6 Journey Experience Description: The Overall Picture

As explained in the theoretical background (see Sect. 2.3), (tourist) experiences are classifiable according to several theoretical frameworks. To classify journey experiences of motorcyclists and cyclists on the Sella Pass, three seminal contributions to the taxonomy of tourist experience will be used. The orchestra model by Pearce (2011), Pearce and Zare (2017) enables the description of tourist experiences as pivotal

4.6 Journey Experience Description: The Overall Picture

constructs based on multiple sensory, affective, cognitive, behavioural and social components. Pine and Gilmore's matrix (1999) classify experiences according to the level of *participation* and the degree of *connection* into four realms: e*ntertainment experiences, educational experiences, escapist experiences, aesthetic experiences.* Finally, the dichotomy between *hedonic* or *eudaimonic*, experiences introduced by Knobloch et al. (2016) attributes an affective component to the experience, depending on its ability to generate immediate wellbeing, or rather, delayed positive effects connected, for instance, to the achievement of specific goals. These three theoretical perspectives as well as the associated layers of interpretation and levels of customer engagement helped classify cycling and motorcycling experiences in relation to the context they were performed in. Table 4.5 reports the dimensions of the orchestra model (Pearce 2011; Pearce and Zare 2017) and highlights the features specific to cycling and motorcycling.

Several features stand out that are common between the two types of experiences, such as the predominance of sight and hearing as sensory components, the dominance of positive feelings lasting over the whole journey and the perception of negative feelings as less intense and punctual, the presence of routines for the cognitive appraisal of the journey, the prevalence of primary (driving) tasks over secondary (non-driving) tasks, especially in case of high speed, finally the importance of velo-formations. On the other hand, some specific characteristics stand out that differ among cyclists and motorcyclists. For instance, concerning sensory perceptions, cyclists appear to be more immersed and sensitive to the sounds and smells of the environment, while motorcyclists are more bound to the sound and smell of their bikes. Cyclists report sometimes a feeling of loneliness towards the mountainous landscape, whereas motorcyclists do not. Cyclists—particularly while climbing—tend to express an intention to understand the surrounding area below the road, for instance talking about hiking routes, mountain peaks, or huts. Motorcyclists are less inclined to do so, or at least they cannot share these kinds of thoughts, apart from the moments when they stop and can talk. Indeed, the interactions of motorcyclists are necessarily non-verbal, because of the helmets, the speed and the bikes' sounds, while for cyclists the dialogue is a very important secondary task, especially during the climb. A last difference regards the active role of motorcyclists in the interaction with road vehicles, related to their speed and acceleration, and the passive role of cyclists, at least in the climbing part of the journey.

In the light of the above, given the active physical engagement in riding and the intense interaction with road (and partly landscape) features, the cycling and motorcycling results are both attributable to escapist experiences, as they are theorized by Pine and Gilmore (1999). As shown in Fig. 4.24, cyclists seem to undergo a higher physical effort and experience a wider immersion in the mobility space. It seems that, due to the lower speed and the longer time of the journey, they can imaginatively access a wider space that goes far beyond the road and includes the natural environment. On the other hand, motorcyclists seem to practice a more *focussed* escapist experience, within a narrower mobility space, and which is limited by the road boundaries and the individually bike produced sound and smell.

Table 4.5 Journey experience description according to Pearce's orchestra model (own elaboration)

	Cycling	Motorcycling
Sensory component	Sight and hearing as prominent senses, smell and taste (rarely) mentioned	Sight and hearing as prominent senses
	Embodiment (physical effort in climbing)	Embodiment (banking)
	Rhythm: polyrhythmic experience	Rhythm: arhythmical experience
	Generally, stimuli from the surrounding environment	Generally, stimuli from the motorcycle
Affective component	Optimism, happiness, peacefulness as pervasive and long-lasting positive feelings	Optimism, happiness, peacefulness as pervasive and long-lasting positive feelings
	Loneliness, anger, fear, discontent as punctual and less intense negative feelings	Fear, worry, anger as punctual and less intense negative feelings
	Stimuli: riding actions, speed, landscape and weather conditions, infrastructure, interactions with other vehicles	Stimuli: riding actions, speed, landscape and weather conditions, infrastructure, interactions with other vehicles
Cognitive component	Routine performance checks	Routine performance checks
	Understanding the activity space below the road (huts, hiking tours, mountain peaks)	Focus on driving activities, other cognitive aspects are difficult to grasp
	Self-reflection on the cycling experience	
Behavioural component	Secondary tasks > primary tasks in climbing	Primary tasks >> secondary tasks during the whole journey
	Primary tasks >> secondary tasks in descending	
Relationships component	Importance of velo-formations	Importance of velo-formations
	Verbal interactions with cyclists and pedestrians (greetings)	Verbal interactions almost absent
	Non-verbal interactions to celebrate the climb (gestures)	Non-verbal interactions with motorcyclists only (greetings)
	Passive road user in climbing, active road user in descending	Always active road user

Moreover, considering the above mentioned dichotomy between hedonia and eudaimonia in tourist experiences Knobloch et al. (2016), it can be argued that both cycling and motorcycling *are* eudaimonic experiences, because they generate both positive and negative feelings during the experience consumption, and the sensation of well-being seems to occur more intensely when the goal is reached—in form of a sense of achievement-, rather than during the drive. Indeed, both do require a certain amount of risk taking, effort and fatigue and include both the perception of fear and

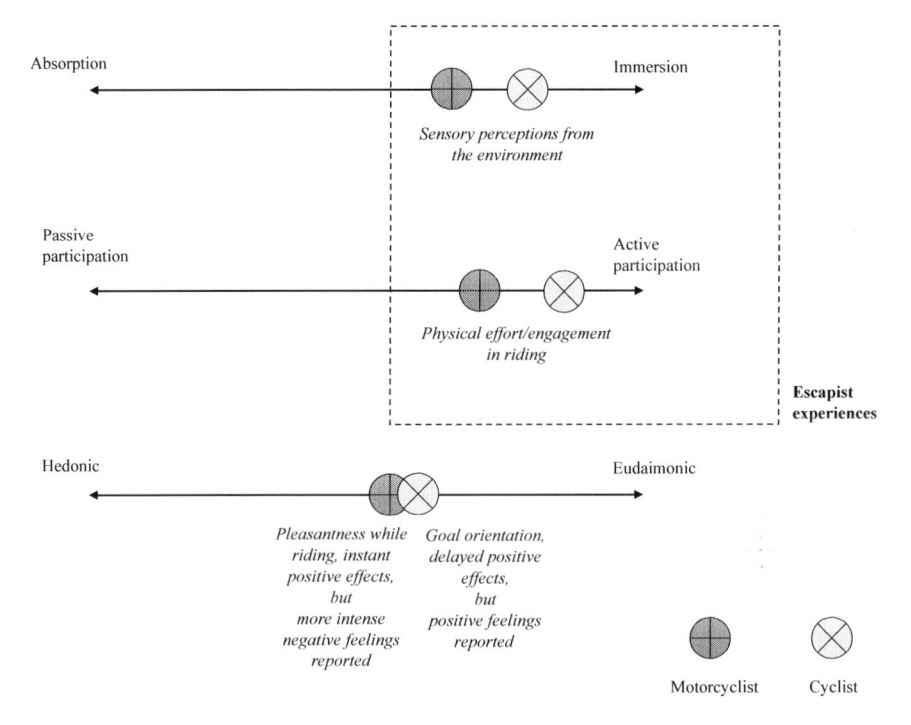

4.6 Journey Experience Description: The Overall Picture

Fig. 4.24 Classification of motorcycling and cycling experience according to the four realms of experience and the hedonia—eudaimonia continuum (own elaboration)

worry as recurring feelings along the trip. If comparing the two experiences, motorcycling experiences seem to appear less eudaimonic than cycling experiences, because of the lower physical effort and the lack of intention to reach a precise goal (e.g. the peak of the pass, a certain degree of fitness, etc.). Nevertheless, the scores of self-reported emotions highlighted slightly higher negative and lower positive feelings of motorcyclists if compared to cyclists. In other words, although in motorcycling the value of the delayed positive effects of making the tour is less prominent than it is in cycling, the challenge of riding seems to provoke more positive feelings to cyclists than to motorcyclists. Still it is true that risk taking while overtaking and driving in unsafe weather conditions is perceived as a source of anxiety, which seems in turn not to affect the overall wellbeing of the rider in the journey.

4.7 Chapter Summary

This chapter has offered a first set of results based on the empirical data treated in aggregated form. It has reported on and discussed the infrastructure and the flow dynamics of the Sella Pass mobility space based on documentary material and secondary data; it has analysed the spatial and temporal features of fourteen journeys across the mobility space through video-ethnographic and bio-sensing data; finally it has described in detail the physical, social, sensory and emotional aspects of these experiences.

By doing this, it has enabled a comparison between the cycling and motorcycling experiences through the orchestra model by Pearce (2011), Pearce and Zare (2017), it has allowed a classification of these experiences according to the four realms by Pine and Gilmore (1999), and it has investigated their emotional value according to the dichotomy between hedonia and eudaimonia by Knobloch et al. (2016). Based on empirical evidence, cycling and motorcycling experiences are classified as *escapist experiences*, but the mobility space they refer to seems to be broader for cyclists and narrower for motorcyclists, who are more focussed onto the features of the road than those of the surrounding space. Finally, cycling experiences appear slightly more *eudaimonic* than motorcycling ones, because of the physical effort of performing them, as well as the goal orientation and the delayed positive effects in terms of fitness and goal achievement. Nevertheless, they also have some hedonic and aesthetic connotation, particularly in the moments when, during the climb, cyclists seem to compensate for the fatigue by gazing at the marvellous landscape.

References

Geertz C (1973) Thick description: toward an interpretive theory of culture. In: Geertz C (ed) The interpretation of cultures: selected essays. Basic Books, New York, pp 3–30
Hanjalic A (2004) Content-based analysis of digital video. Kluwer Academic Publishers; Wiley, Boston, [Lieu de publication inconnu]
Jensen OB (2010) Negotiation in motion: unpacking a geography of mobility. Space Cult 13:389–402. https://doi.org/10.1177/1206331210374149
Knobloch U, Robertson K, Aitken R (2016) Experience, emotion, and eudaimonia: a consideration of tourist experiences and well-being. J Travel Res 56:651–662. https://doi.org/10.1177/0047287516650937
Oldenburg von T (2015) Representing bicycle-based interaction an interaction design exploration into bicycling research, Malmö University
Pearce PL (2011) Tourist behaviour and the contemporary world. Channel View, Bristol
Pearce PL, Zare S (2017) The orchestra model as the basis for teaching tourism experience design. J Hosp Tour Manag 30:55–64. https://doi.org/10.1016/j.jhtm.2017.01.004
Pine BJ, Gilmore JH (1999) The experience economy, Updated ed. Harvard Business Review Press, Boston, Mass
Provincial Institute of Statistics (ASTAT) of the Autonomous Province of Bolzano (2018) Dataset on traffic flows. http://astat.provincia.bz.it/it/banche-dati-comunali.asp. Accessed 28 April 2018
Provincial Institute of Statistics of the Autonomous Province of Trento (2018) Dataset on tourism flows. http://www.statweb.provincia.tn.it/movturistico/index.html. Accessed 28 April 2018
Richins ML (1997) Measuring emotions in the consumption experience. J Consum Res 24:127–146
Scuttari A, Bassani R (2015) I passi dolomitici: Analisi del traffico e dei suoi impatti e proposta di misure di gestione. [Dolomites' passes. Traffic, its environmental impact and a proposal for traffic management measures]. http://www.dolomitiunesco.info/attivita/i-passi-dolomitici-pubblicato-lo-studio-eurac-commissionato-dalla-fondazione/. Accessed 18 August 2018

References

Scuttari A, Marcher A, Vanzi G (2018) #Dolomitesvives. Vivere un'esperienza naturale sulle Dolomiti. Monitoring qualitativo [#Dolomitesvives. Experiencing nature naturally in the Dolomites. Qualitative monitoring]. http://www.eurac.edu/it/research/Publications/Pages/publicationdetails.aspx?pubId=0103724&pubType=E. Accessed 18 August 2018

Chapter 5
Results: Selected Individual Journey Experiences

> *A journey is a person in itself; no two are alike. And all plans, safeguards, policies and coercion are fruitless. We find after years of struggle that we do not take a trip; a trip takes us.*
> John Steinbeck (1902–1968; 1961)

Abstract This chapter proposes a second-by-second analysis of individual journey experiences. The physical, sensory, social and emotional features of two motorcyclists' and three cyclists' journeys are presented, with the aim at identifying commonalities and differences, and to reflect upon the connections between the tangible and intangible elements of tourist travel. Journey experiences are confirmed to be eudaimonic, emotionally rich escapist experiences, where individuals, modes and contextual conditions are combined to form a unique and composite space-time mix. Based on the evidence collected, the personas methodology helps to transform the thick descriptions at individual level into fictitious characters—the personas—to enable future tourism and transport planning.

5.1 Introduction

This chapter presents a thick description of selected individual journey experiences, both motorcycling and cycling ones. Through an analytical and systematic process of disaggregation of journey features and related data, the chapter adds a deeper level of second-by-second analysis of individuals in mobility space, which differs from the aggregated mean-based level presented in Chap. 4. Based on the assumption that experiences and emotions are profoundly subjective, time- and space-specific, the study of single individuals in precise contextual (traffic and weather) conditions helps to generate convergence of evidence based on linking multiple data sources of one

---

Electronic supplementary material The online version of this chapter (https://doi.org/10.1007/978-3-030-17697-6_5) contains supplementary material.

participant—rather than comparing the same data source for multiple participants, as it was done in Chap. 4.

Both the aggregate data analysed in Chap. 4 and the individual data analysed in this chapter help to highlight aspects of tourist experiences on site and derive evidence-based policies to improve those experiences. A first step towards the crystallization of knowledge for these policy purposes happens in this chapter with the generative process of persona design. The creation of personas enables the definition of specific mobility and activity patterns for cyclists and motorcyclists that translate into specific infrastructural and service requirements, and thereby help in developing strategies and actions in destination marketing and management.

In the light of the above, the chapter ultimately aims at further expanding—through individual perspectives—on the first and second research questions (and sub-questions) of the dissertation, i.e.:

How to describe and how to measure the visitors' mobile journey experiences and their physical, sensory, emotional and social features in space and time?

How does travel mode—i.e. cycling vs. motorcycling—shape journey experiences?

Further, it uses the multiple sources of evidence at individual and aggregate level—respectively derived from this and the previous chapter—to design personas, addressing the third research question of the dissertation, i.e.:

How to develop personas to address motorcyclists and cyclists in mobility spaces?

The definition of personas allows a discussion, in the next chapter, of policy implications—planning, marketing, and management consequences—of the analytical work developed in this dissertation.

It should be noted here that the analysis of individual data was conducted for each of the fourteen participants and it was a precondition for the aggregate analysis of Chap. 4. Nevertheless, individual journey experiences are not presented here for each of the fourteen participants at this granular level, because more of the same homogeneous data was highlighted during the analytical phase. The selection of six individuals and their presentation within this chapter followed four criteria: (i) the *avoidance of redundancy* in results; (ii) the *inclusion of both overnight tourists and day visitors*; (iii) *the inclusion of both first-time and repeat visitors*; (iv) the *data quality*, in particular the complete coverage of the video ethnographic material along the journey and the accuracy and continuity of sensor monitoring. The application of these criteria allowed the selection and individual description of two out of seven motorcyclists and three out of seven cyclists.

The findings in this chapter are presented in three sections. The first section describes two individual motorcycling experiences; the second section adds three cycling experiences; finally, the third section designs four personas, based on the mode used (motorcycle versus bicycle) and the attitude towards the journey (performance versus leisure). In this chapter, ID codes of individual travellers have been replaced with fictitious names, to make the description of individuals and personas appear more personal.

5.2 Motorcyclists Second-by-Second

Individual journey experiences are presented through an analytical and systematical process of disaggregation. Firstly, the rider's and motorcyclist's characteristics are highlighted; then journey features are presented to contextualise the trip; finally the multiple sources of data—video footage, sensor data, emotional data—are presented and compared.

5.2.1 Juan and the Custom Cruiser

Juan (participant 5M) is a German tourist in his forties, born in Spain but living in Germany. He declared to be on tour on the Dolomites' roads to admire the landscape, to drive on spectacular roads, to practice motorcycling using his motorcycle, and finally to "have fun". He was riding a Harley Davidson Breakout bike model—a very common custom cruiser—and associated the idea of riding a motorcycle with "great tours, relaxation, and regeneration with friends". He was spending a one week holiday (20-28.08.16) with his friends in Arabba, a small village between Passo Pordoi and Passo Campolongo, in the Fodom Valley. He travelled along the Sella Pass Road only once before participating in the data collection.

Juan's journey started from Plan de Gralba on August 24th 2016 around 10 a.m. (09:59) and lasted about 15 min (00:14:53), proceeding in counter-clockwise direction. That day the weather was sunny and the temperature in Selva di Val Gardena was between 9.3 and 22.7 °C (Provincial office of the Autonomous Province of Bolzano—Meteorological service, data available here: http://meteo.provincia.bz.it/dati-storici.asp). The recorded video footage is longer than the effective journey (00:19:06), because Juan did not stop the recording after having reached the end point of the journey (Pian Schiavaneis). He made the journey in a velo-formation with his travel companion and friend—the German Alois—who also participated in the data collection. On average, Juan was travelling at 43 km/h in the climbing phase of the journey, 36 km/h in the pass summit area and 46 km/h in the descending part. His highest speed was 92 km/h in the climbing phase.

Figure 5.1, representing the coding scheme of Juan's video footage with the coding categories presented in Chap. 4, reveals interesting patterns. Overall, physical features are more important than sensory and social features, because the primary task of riding is prevailing on secondary tasks or perceptual reactions from the external world. Social interactions are very few and they happen through a few gestures and greetings (to chopper bikers only), as well as dialogues after the end of the journey. Concerning processes of negotiation of space, a first remarkable difference between the left hand of Fig. 5.1 (the climb) and the right hand of the figure (the descent) is the intensity of the overtaking manoeuvres.

Active and passive overtaking takes place more often in the climbing part than in the descending part, whereas the second part of the journey is characterized by longer

182   5 Results: Selected Individual Journey Experiences

Fig. 5.1 Juan's coding scheme of the video footage (own elaboration)

5.2 Motorcyclists Second-by-Second

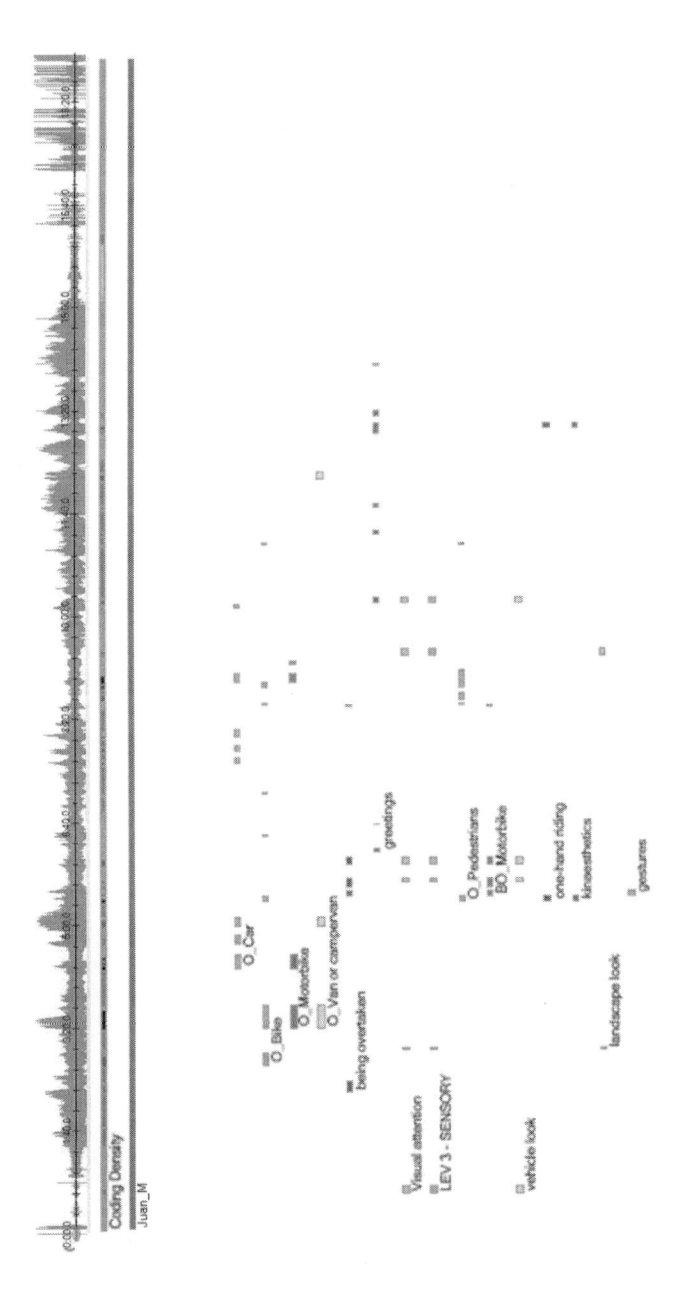

Fig. 5.1 (continued)

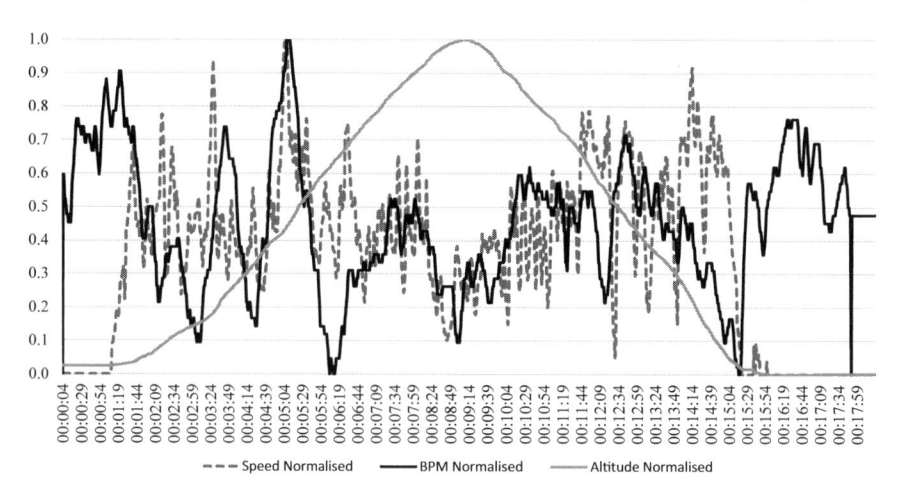

Fig. 5.2 Juan's sensor data: heart rate, speed and altitude (normalised values) (own elaboration)

moments of "solo riding". Recalling the hourly distribution of traffic in the official statistics (Scuttari and Bassani 2015), it is possible to explain this phenomenon because of the congestion in the climbing part of the pass around 10am, a time when hikers and other pass visitors tend to reach the pass summit area. On the other hand, the descending part of the pass is not congested at this time of the day, allowing motorcyclists some moments of solo ride. Based on this evidence, one could hypothesise that Juan would have been quicker in the descending part with a clear road, than in the climbing one with a congested road, but—as it was mentioned earlier in this section—this was not the case. In fact, despite the clearer road, both the average and the maximum speed in descending (46 and 84) were lower than those in climbing (respectively 43 and 92 km/h). This pattern, confirmed by additional cases in Chap. 4, might suggest several implications. For instance, the lower speed in descent despite a clear road suggests that, while descending, Juan is more prudent in the ride, which might be associated with a higher technical difficulty of the ride—due to the steepness of the road. On the other hand, this pattern also explains why the problem of the noise of motorcycles, which is in turn directly connected to speed and acceleration patterns (Scuttari and Bassani 2015), is more evident in the climbing part of the journey, than in the descending one. All these possible interpretations, if confirmed by additional cases, might have very concrete policy implications, concerning—for instance—the positioning of speed checks in the future.

To compare speed patterns in the climbing and descending phase of the journey, Fig. 5.2 illustrates second-by-second speed data in relation to altitude and heart rate. The figure reveals that the climbing phase of the journey was characterised by a higher variability in speed, with multiple high peaks. Cross-checking these moments with the events depicted in Fig. 5.2 shows that these peaks correspond to moments of overtaking.

5.2 Motorcyclists Second-by-Second

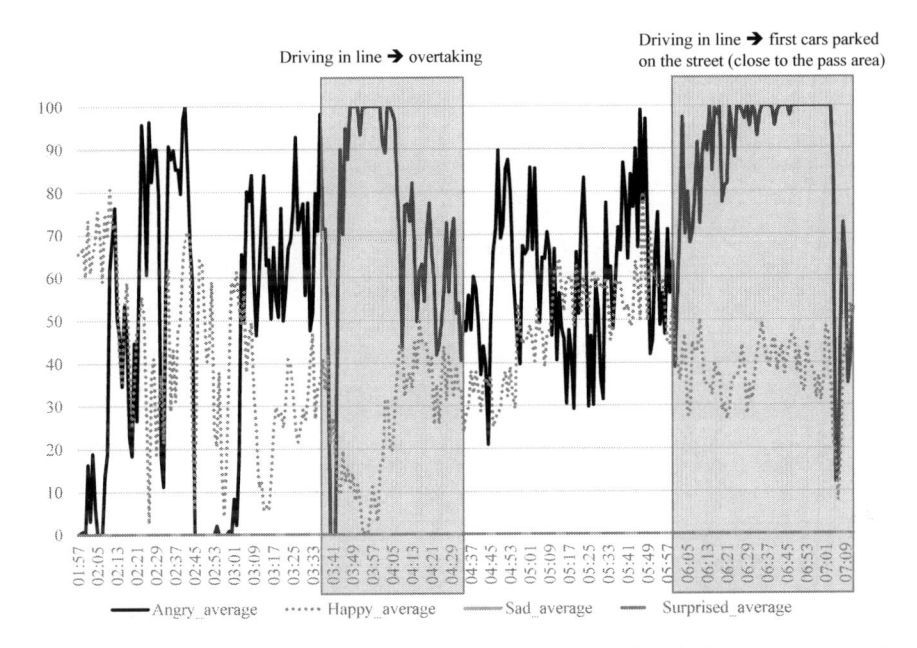

Fig. 5.3 Juan's emotion data based on facial action coding (own elaboration)

A second comment on Fig. 5.2 is related to the relationship between peaks in speed and peaks in heart rate. In particular, between minutes 04:54-05:16 of the journey, Juan reached the highest speed and heart frequency of the whole journey. In the video footage this moment corresponds to when he was first in line and then overtook a car and a van (see also Fig. 5.1), which made him probably experience a certain degree of excitement. It is also remarkable to note that the peaks in speed and heart rate also correspond to peaks in sound produced by motorcyclists (see the waveform on top of Fig. 5.1).

This hypothesis seems to be supported by the data gathered with the facial action coding system, according to which, in the time frame indicated, the score of happiness increased and the score of anger decreased, as shown in Fig. 5.3, in the first grey box. In the geographical representation of the mobility space, this moment corresponded to the first long straight section of road, resulting in a black line in the map of Fig. 5.4.

An additional point emerges from the analysis of video and sensor data within the pass summit area. If looking at the coding categories, the pass area is experienced between minutes 05:40 and 09:11. This is a temporal framework where speed is not particularly high, Juan is experiencing passive overtaking by a couple of motorcycles and the flow of riding is interrupted by other vehicles. This phenomenon seems to cause negative feelings to Juan, who is increasing his "anger" score when reviewing the moments of riding in line. Indeed, in the self-report questionnaire, Juan reported feeling worried when there was too much traffic and angry when he had to interact

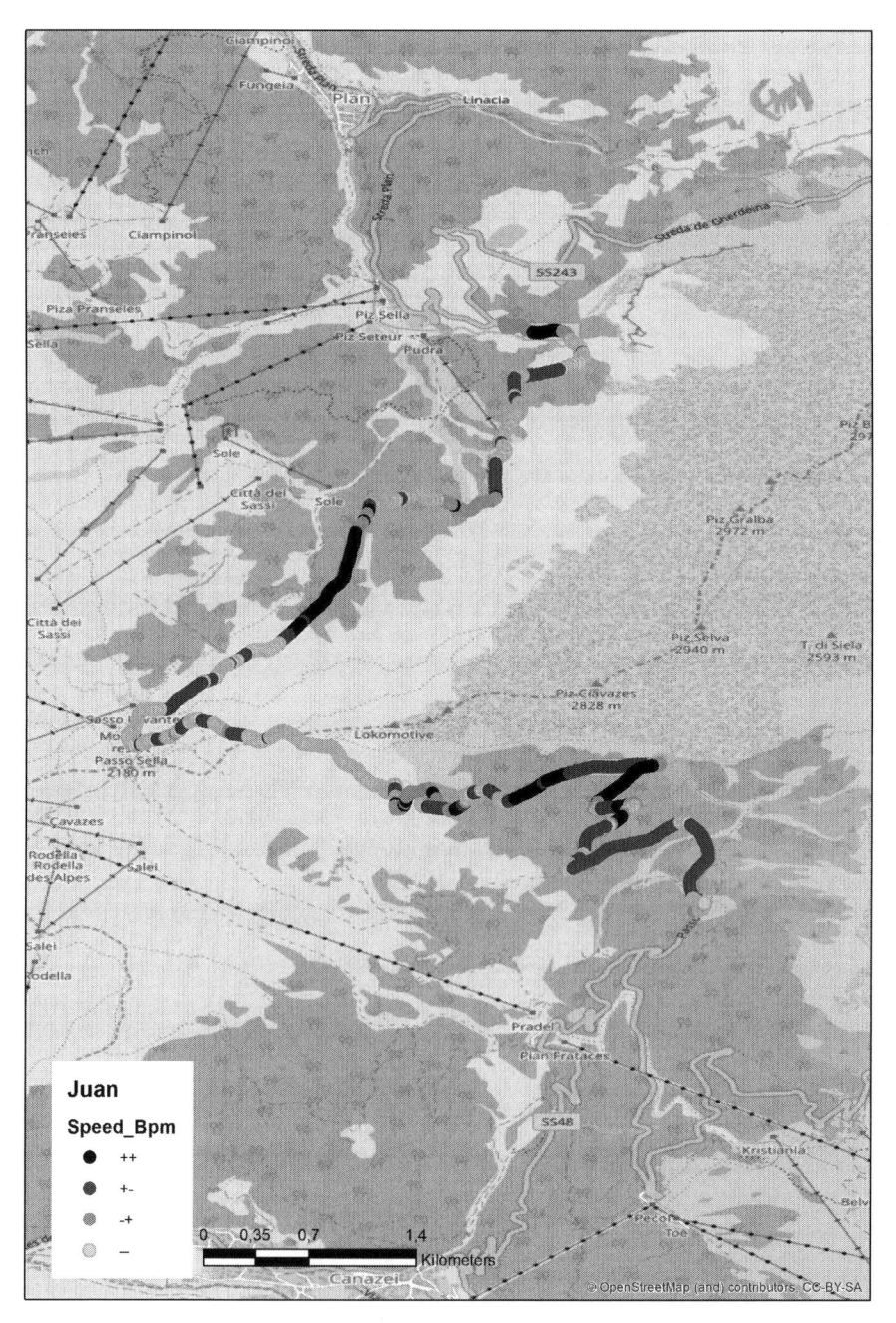

Fig. 5.4 Geo-referenced maps of Juan's sensor data: heath rate and speed (normalised values) (own elaboration)

with slower vehicles. The emotional reactions in the self-report questionnaire and in the revealed facial response seem to correspond (see Fig. 5.3).

The geographical representation of the mobility space on a map, including the representation of the journey experience through the sensory data collected, helps contextualise the actions and feelings in relation to the infrastructural features of the road. Figure 5.4 maps the relationship between heart rate and speed, based on four possible combination of the two. These result from the comparison of the normalised (0–1) values analysed in Fig. 5.1. The light grey colour in the map stands for low (<0.5) values of both heart rate and speed; the middle grey colours stand for a combination of high and low values—respectively the first stands for low speed (<0.5) and high heart rate (>0.5), second stands for high speed (>0.5) and low heart rate (<0.5); finally, the black colour stands for both high speed and high heart rate (both >0.5).

Based on this scale, the map shows that the pass area, corresponding to the central section of the journey, is characterised by the light grey colour, whereas the climbing and descent parts are darker. Straight roads tend to be lighter than curving sections of the road, unless there is a reduction in speed and heart rate linked to congestion—which turned out to be very irritating for Juan. Generally, sharp bends are either light or middle grey, reflecting the fact that curves are always taken at lower speed, but the degree of heart rate increase varies, probably reflecting different conditions, and the attitude and feelings of the rider. Juan's video footage, as well as the empirical data collected, analysed and geo-referenced from the self-reporting, bio-sensing and facial action coding techniques seems to suggest some preliminary findings that are in line with the aggregate data of Chap. 4. Climbing and overcoming obstacles on the way are both exciting for motorcyclists, while standing in line and proceeding slowly without the chance to escape is an irritating part of the journey. It seems, therefore, that traffic is perceived as an ambivalent factor for the journey experience, being a positive challenge as soon as there are possibilities to overtake slow vehicles and manage accelerations and decelerations, but also an irritating disturbance, when congestion is so great that no overtaking can take place and standing in line is the only solution. This ambiguous valence of traffic for motorcycling seems to depend on the possibility to manage the own personal and use space on the road, as well as the individual rhythm. This issue will be further explored in the individual journeys analysed below.

5.2.2 Marco and the Naked Bike

Marco (participant 6M) is an Italian day visitor in his thirties, starting his trip from the surroundings of Bolzano/Bozen, around 45 km from Selva di Val Gardena. He reported that he decided to take the Sellaronda tour to admire the landscape, to ride on spectacular roads, and to show his girlfriend the mountains he loves. He was riding a Yamaha MT09—a common naked bike—and linked the idea of riding a motorcycle to a sense of "freedom". He had been over thirty times on the Sella Pass road and he knew the road quite well.

Marco's journey started on September 11th 2016 at 12:53 from Selva di Val Gardena—and reached Plan de Gralba around 8:30 min after the start, to take the Sellaronda tour in counter-clockwise direction. That day the weather was cloudy, the road was wet and the temperature in Selva di Val Gardena was between 8.7 and 18.6 °C (Provincial office of the Autonomous Province of Bolzano—Meteorological service, data available here: http://meteo.provincia.bz.it/dati-storici.asp). He made the journey with his girlfriend on board and in a velo-formation with two travel companions and friends, (and one of those was also participating in the data collection).

On average, Marco travelled at 61 km/h in the climbing phase of the journey (around 20 km/h quicker than Juan), 39 km/h in the pass summit area and 47 km/h in the descending part (similarly to Juan). His highest speed was 109 km/h in the climbing phase, but also in the descending phase the peaks in speed were higher than 100 km/h. On average and in terms of maximum speed, he was the quickest motorcyclist in the climbing and descending phases, although the only one carrying a passenger on the motorcycle.

Similarly to Juan, the recorded video footage of Marco is longer than the journey considered here for the purpose of the analysis (22:02 versus 12:59 min), mainly because the camera also recorded the trip between Selva di Val Gardena and Plan de Gralba, before climbing the pass. Despite this additional data, the results are presented here in relation to the section between Plan de Gralba and Pian Schiavaneis in order to guarantee coherence and comparability with the data from the other participants.

Figure 5.5 visually describes Marco's entire journey in its duration and soundscape, reporting the content analysis for the section of road between Plan de Gralba and Pian Schiavaneis—i.e. up to minute 08:30. Overall it can be seen that, similarly to Juan's video footage, the climbing section of the journey is the richest in interactions, with a greater number of overtakings than the descending phase. Nevertheless, conversely to what happened in Juan's journey, for Marco the road was less congested during the climb than during the descent.

This could be partly explained because Marco was riding on a cloudy September day at the beginning of the shoulder season, in dry road conditions, with far less traffic on the road than in August (see Fig. 4.4) and at a different time of the day (1 pm). By midday visitors have already reached the peak of the pass and vehicles are mostly in the parking slots of the area, with few on the road. Indeed, the road during the climbing part of Marco's journey was quite clear, allowing him to ride for a long time in solitude and easily overtake slower vehicles. Similarly to Juan, few secondary tasks characterise the journey of Marco, who was mostly concentrated on riding activities. During the climbing part of the journey Marco was leading a velo-formation with his two travel companions. During the descent, he was initially riding in line for a while, but then managed to overtake and ride solo again. Figure 5.5 reveals the routines he repeats to control his own trip and to ensure the closeness of the velo-formation itself. To be sure that the group was compact, he repeatedly—almost compulsively—checked the rear-view mirror to make sure that his travel companions

5.2 Motorcyclists Second-by-Second

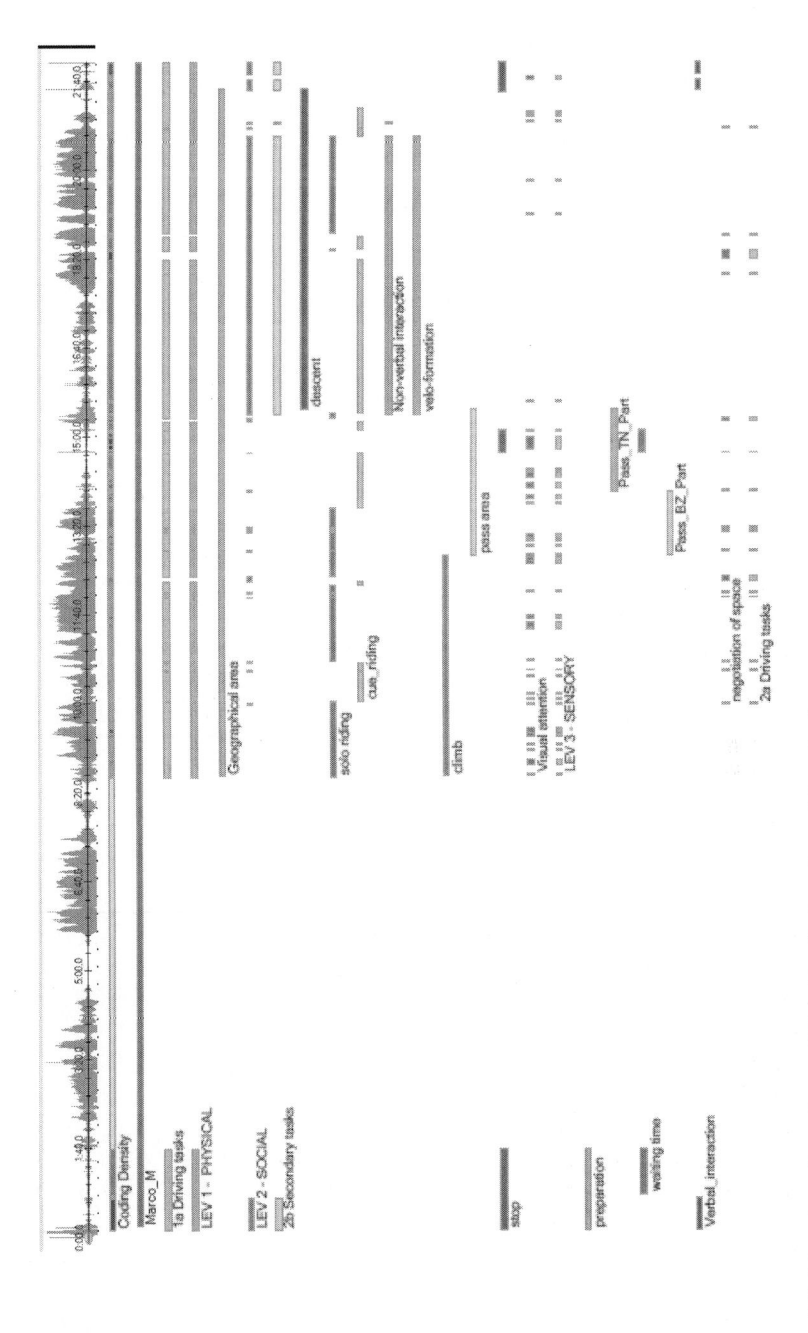

Fig. 5.5 Marco's coding scheme of the video footage (own elaboration)

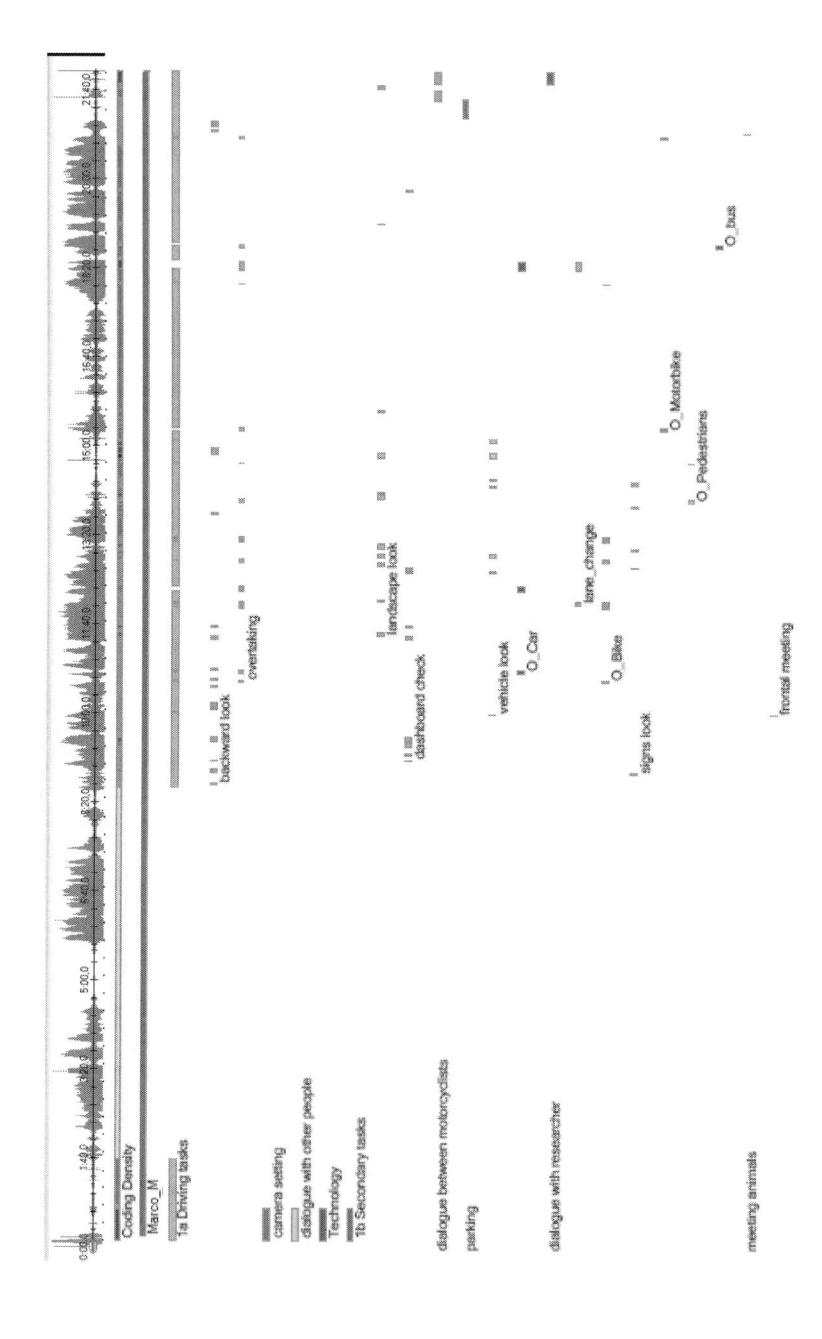

Fig. 5.5 (continued)

5.2 Motorcyclists Second-by-Second

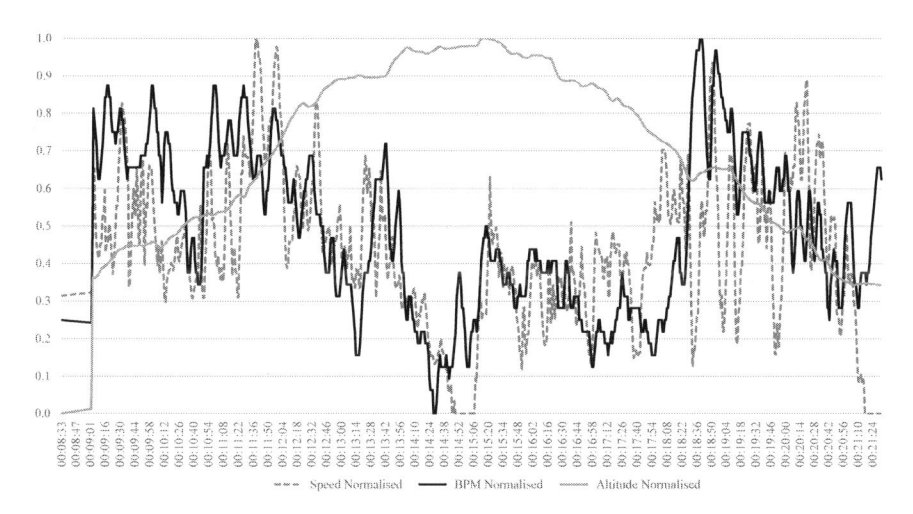

Fig. 5.6 Figure 5.1 Marco's sensor data: heath rate, speed and altitude (normalised values) (own elaboration)

are following him within a short distance after he overtakes. At the same time, he controlled his speed by repeatedly checking the dashboard.

Marco is also visually interested in landscapes. In the self-report questionnaire he declared that "mountains" are both the reason why he is travelling and a source of optimism and happiness. Notwithstanding the fact that he has taken the Sellaronda tour more than 30 times, he keeps looking at the landscape, particularly in the climbing part of the journey, and he also looks at road signs, although he should know the way to go. Concerning interactions, he had no verbal interaction with the passenger—his partner—and greetings were not traceable, because the only possible positioning of the camera on his helmet was unfortunately too high to include the handlebars and the hands.

The analysis of sensor data (Fig. 5.6) reveals similar patterns to Juan's data, with higher peaks in speed in the climbing part of the journey, and particularly on the straight road before entering the pass area. As seen in Juan's sensor data, the pass summit area is characterised by lower speed and lower heart rates. Similarities are also evident in the direct relationship between speed and heart rate; there seems to be a direct correlation.

Notwithstanding these similarities, some differences to Juan's journey stand out. For instance, differently to Juan, Marco's heart rate reached its peak during the descent (and not the climbing) phase, in particular while overtaking two cars at once, on a bumpy and narrow section of road. The video stills reported in Fig. 5.7 (as well as the Video ESM_6) show these dynamics between the overtaking action and the later increase in heart rate before a sharp bend. Marco's heart rate reached almost 130 bpm after the overtaking manoeuvre, reflecting some kind of emotional alteration in the body. In the questionnaire he reported to have felt "worry" and "fear" while negotiating bends on wet roads while descending. This general remark might refer

Fig. 5.7 Video stills of moments of overtaking while descending on the motorcycle: a peak in hearth rate (own elaboration)

to the bend of the video clip, although it is impossible to link it to a precise moment during the descent. What is interesting to note is that there seems to be no direct correspondence between the feelings reported on the questionnaire by Marco and the ones revealed by the facial action coding system (see Fig. 5.8).

For instance, if looking at the descent, starting around minute 15 (and more precisely at 15:23 according to the geographical video sections), it seems that the time of riding in line caused some peaks of sadness, which are not reported in the questionnaire explicitly. On the other hand, the moment of overtaking (around minute 18) causes a peak in happiness on the video, whereas it was reported in the questionnaire to evoke worry and fear during the trip. Finally, the moments of landscape observation, associated with "happiness" and "optimism" in the questionnaire seem to be linked to sadness according to the facial action coding data. This inverse relationship between positive- and negative-valenced feelings reported during the trip or revealed after the trip opens up new reflections on the emotional value of mobility in tourism. It seems to suggest that risky actions taken while travelling—although

5.2 Motorcyclists Second-by-Second

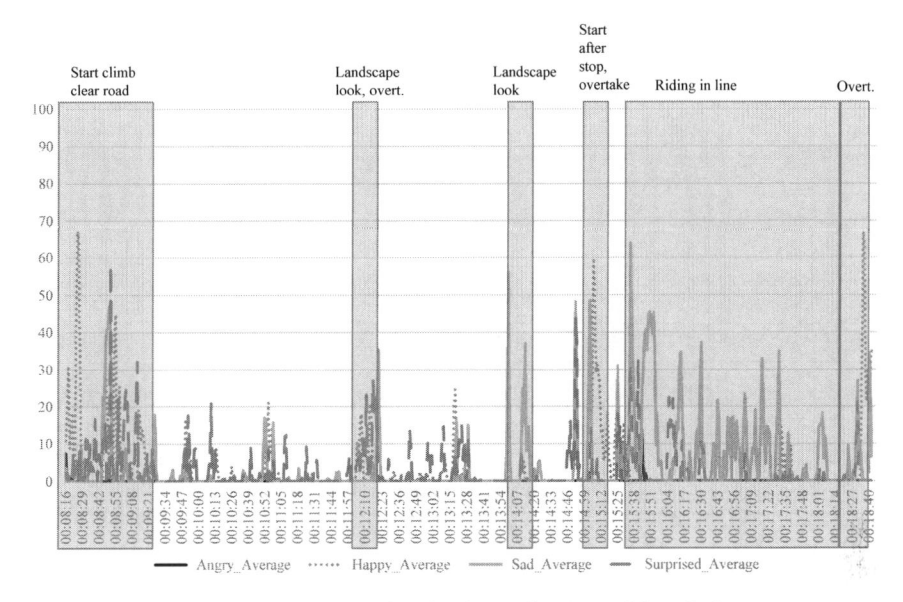

Fig. 5.8 Marco's emotion data based on facial action coding (own elaboration)

provoking negative feelings at the moment of performing them—generate positive feelings when they are recalled. Conversely, more passive contemplative actions—in this case the vision of marvellous landscapes—can turn into negative feelings when they are recalled, probably due to a sense of loneliness towards the past.

Figure 5.9 contextualises physical, sensory, social and emotional features of Marco's journey in the mobility space. Mapping the relationship between heart frequency and speed, it shows very similar features to the map of Juan's journey in Fig. 5.4. The predominance of black and light grey colours is recurring, and it seems to suggest that heart frequency and speed are connected by a direct relationship at least on the straight and clear parts of the road. During Marco's journey, when the road is straight, speed and heart rate are high if the road is clear, but they are both low if the road is congested. It seems, therefore, that speed was acting as a mediator of emotional arousal along straight roads. The dynamics related to curves are different. Curves are almost always associated with a lower speed, but still to a high—sometimes even increasing—heart frequency. This aspect seems to match with the feelings of "worry" and "fear" reported in Marco's questionnaire in relation to curves. In this case it is not speed, but rather the technical challenge of banking on a curving road and carrying a passenger that might make emotion arise. In Marco's case it seems that this feeling of worry and fear turned into happiness when reviewing the video, i.e. after the challenge was overcome.

Marco's video footage, together with the empirical evidence collected and analysed above, confirmed the power of speed in provoking emotional arousal in motorcyclists, as well as the positive emotional reactions after overcoming "obstacles"

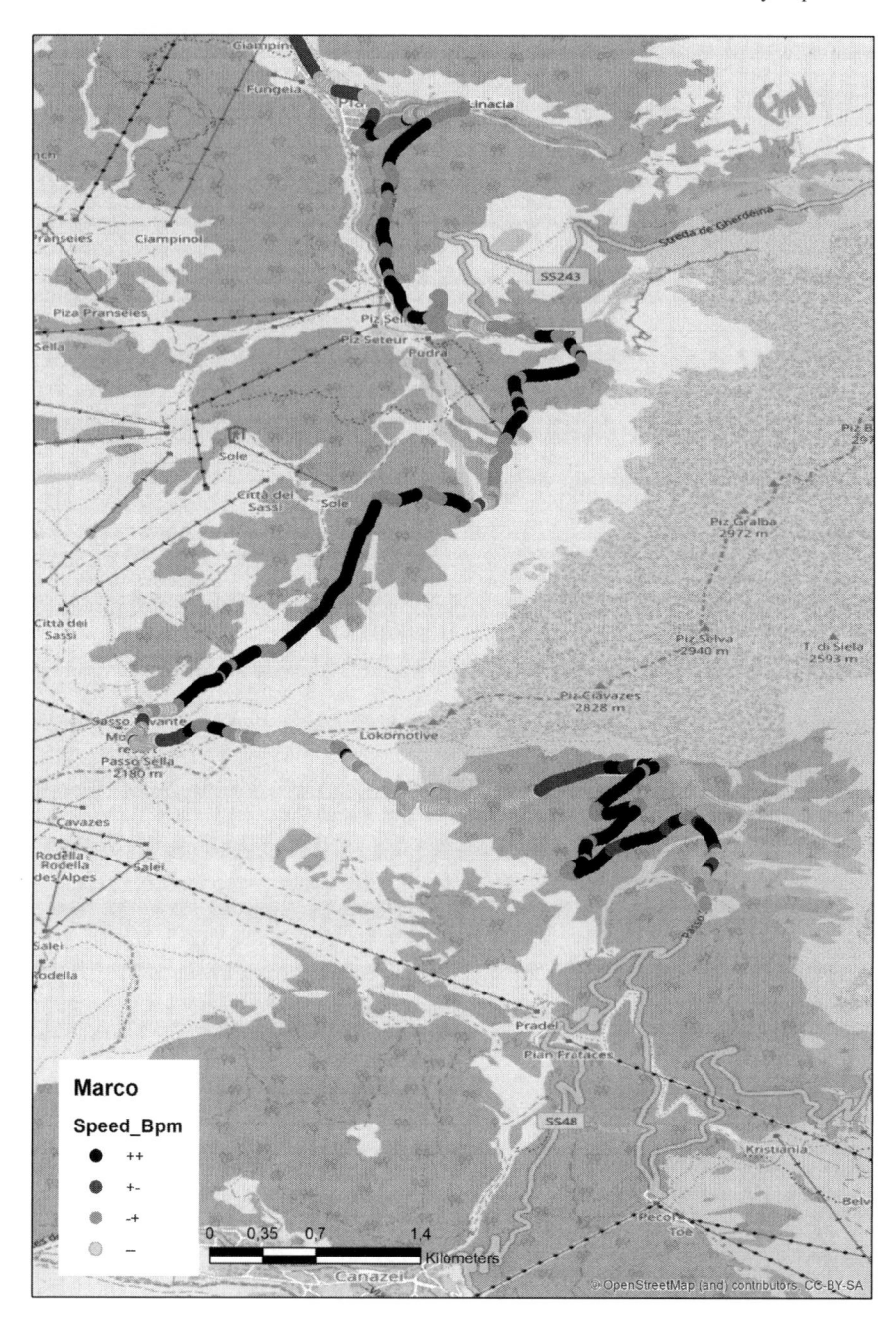

Fig. 5.9 Geo-referenced maps of Marco's sensor data: heart rate and speed (normalised values) (own elaboration)

through overtaking. Marco seemed to be less irritated by traffic than Juan, and was reporting sadness instead of anger when riding in line. An additional aspect added through this analysis is the power of the road's varying alignments to stimulate feelings, e.g. through sharp bends. A last remark refers to the sometimes inverse relationship between feelings during and after the experience: fear and worry turn into happiness after the riding challenge is overcome, whereas happiness turns into sadness once the marvellous landscapes are left behind. More thoughts about the development of feelings across time will follow in the coming sections about cyclists.

5.2.3 Key Findings

The second-by second analysis of two motorcycling experiences, Juan's and Marco's journey, revealed several additional results when compared to the overall description of journeys. Comparing codes of climbs and descents it became clear that the climbing part is the richest in interactions, the one in which speed is higher and accelerations are more sudden in moments of overtaking. These changes in speed are both exciting—when the obstacle is behind the motorcyclist, but also annoying—when the narrow road prevents motorcyclists from overtaking. This is the contradiction of riding in traffic. The descents are slower in speed, but they can cause emotional arousal, as well, especially when overtaking and reaching higher speeds before braking and banking.

Speed, speed variations and the overcoming of obstacles seem to work as stimuli to emotional arousal, together with landscape beauty. Nevertheless, the type of feeling perceived during or after the journey with reference to these stimuli is different. Worry and fear are felt when overtaking in risky conditions, but they turn into happiness when looking at the video footage. Optimism and happiness are felt when looking at landscape, but they can turn into sadness when the journey is over. These changes of positive-feelings into negative-valenced ones and vice versa reveals that the time perspective is fundamental to address feelings, which are subjective, contextualised and embodied reactions to the external world.

5.3 Cyclists Second-by-Second

Cyclists' journeys are described following the same scheme as motorcyclists' tours. However, the number of individual journeys described is three and not two, because, besides the same-day visit and the tour with friends, a guided tour was also recorded. The presence of a guide created interesting dynamics of interaction that are explained in the following section.

5.3.1 Peter and the Guided Tour

Peter (participant 3B) is a young German cyclist in his thirties, starting his trip from Badia/Abtei, a small village in Val Badia valley—between Gardena Pass and Pordoi Pass. He was having a long cycling holiday lasting from August 20th to September 3rd 2016 and taking several base holiday trips, mostly led by a cycling guide. He was overnighting in a specialised hotel that offered this kind of service and had taken several tours in the surrounding valleys and areas before participating in the research. He reported that he decided to take the Sellaronda tour to enjoy the landscape, to pedal on spectacular roads, and to use his bike, a "2danger" road bike. He associated the idea of cycling with "freedom", "ambition" and "sport experience". He also reported that his ultimate goal for the holiday was to reach the summit of the Stelvio Pass/Stilfserjoch, a very steep and panoramic pass, with a difference in height of more than 1,800 m along 25 km.

Peter's recorded journey started on August 29th at 12:15, nevertheless he had started the Sellaronda tour about one and a half hour earlier, climbing to the top of Passo Campolongo and Pordoi first. He was taking the Sellaronda tour in the clockwise direction and therefore the Sella Pass was the third pass he was aiming to reach that day. He was pedalling in a velo-formation with three other cyclists, of which one was the travel guide, and another was an Austrian tourist—Elias—who was also participating in the research. The weather was cloudy: the temperature in Selva di Val Gardena was between 9.3 and 22.7 °C (Provincial office of the Autonomous Province of Bolzano—Meteorological service, data available here: http://meteo.provincia.bz.it/dati-storici.asp). When Peter reached the summit of the pass, he stopped for around 10 min and decided to turn off the headcam, indirectly suggesting how—in his interpretation—the stop should have not been considered as part of the cycling experience. The same was done on the headcam of the travel companion, so that it was impossible to reconstruct which kind of activities were done in the pass summit area. After they started the tour again, when Peter turned on the camera, the weather was very cloudy and it started to rain. This was the moment when the cyclists stopped for the second time and put on waterproof clothes, to protect themselves. This part of the journey was recorded and contained interesting dialogues. The total journey from Pian Schiavaneis to Plan de Gralba lasted about 00:51:19 min (00:33:36 for the first video footage and 00:17:43 for the second), of which about 8 min were spent waiting for the rain to stop.

Concerning speed patterns, as it was described in Sect. 4.3.2, cyclists were far slower in the climbing section of the tour than motorcyclists. On average, Peter was climbing to the top of the pass at 9 km/h, crossing the pass summit area at 22 km/h, and descending at 30 km/h. His peak in speed was in the pass summit area, when he reached 43 km/h (minute 4:27 of the second video). This was a moment of solo riding after he managed to overtake a bus (see Fig. 5.11) and before he had to slow down due to the rain. It should be noticed here that the bad weather, and particularly the rain, had an impact on speed in the journey, as the travel guide recommended

5.3 Cyclists Second-by-Second

in the footage to slow down and keep distance from other vehicles, because braking was becoming dangerous.

Figures 5.10 and 5.11 visually describe the two video footages recorded by Peter. The first includes the climb from Pian Schiavaneis to the pass summit area, the second includes the crossing of the pass summit area and the descent, including the stop when it was raining.

From a first look it stands out that the climbing part of the journey is more silent than the descending part (see waveforms of Figs. 5.10 and 5.11) and denser with interactions among road users. Conversely to what happens for motorcyclists, in this case cyclists are experiencing multiple passive overtaking in the climbing section of the journey, both by cars and by bicycles, and they are very much interacting verbally. With respect to this, a verbal interaction with Peter and his travel companion Elias stresses how disturbing the noise of motorcycles can be for cyclists during passive overtaking:

[14:18–14:36]

Elias   Ach das tut weh!
       [Ouch, this hurts!]
Peter   Man muss schon auf die Quälerei stehen!
       [You have to love this cruelty!]
Elias   Und wir hören es ja nicht so.
       [And we don't hear it that much.]

Interestingly, when the travel companion is complaining about motorcyclists, Peter uses an oxymoron to explain the attitude of cyclists towards motorcycling traffic. With the sentence "You have to love this cruelty!" he is suggesting that cyclists are disturbed by motorcycles' noise, but on the other hand they calmly accept this noise as part of their experience, probably with a similar attitude as the one towards physical effort as part of the journey. Therefore, individual data seem to support the hypothesis (see Sect. 4.6) that the cycling experience is a eudaimonic experience, where not only physical effort, but also interaction with other vehicles represent the negative elements one has to suffer to reach the goal, i.e. the summit of the pass. The dialogue among Peter and Elias during the climb stresses another aspect connected to eudaimonia in cycling: the attitude towards risk. This issue is discussed by Peter and Elias a few seconds later, when they talk about cyclists' accidents.

[15:17–16:33]

Peter: So ging es auch am Samstag hoch?
       [Did you also have a similar climb on Saturday?]
Elias: Nochmal steiler.
       [Even steeper]
Peter: Wart ihr zu zweit, du und der Andy?
       [Was it the two of you climbing, you and Andy?]
Elias: Ja, genau. Wir haben zwei Unfälle gesehen.
       [Yes, of course. We saw two accidents]

Peter: Ja, hatte er schon erzählt. Hat es am Samstag geregnet?
[Yes, he told me. Did it rain on Saturday?]
Elias: Nein, am Samstag war es schön. Die Straße war perfekt, aber viele überschätzen sich einfach. Dann passieren die Unfälle.
[No, we had good weather. The road was perfect, but many people overestimate themselves. And then accidents occur]
Peter: Gerade was die Abfahrten angeht. Man kommt oben an und fährt direkt herunter, die Konzentration ist auch nicht da.
[Particularly during descents. You reach the summit and then ride directly towards the valley, without having any concentration]
Elias: Ja, und die Motorradfahrer..
[Yes, and the motorcyclists...]
Peter: Ja, die sowieso. Die fahren in den Kurven rein...
[Oh, yes, of course. They take the curves so harshly...]

Risk taking is rewarded as a dangerous attitude during this conversation, especially when cyclists overestimate their abilities. This can lead to accidents, particularly during the descent, when more concentration is needed, despite the exhaustion of the climb. Motorcyclists seem to increase risk perception due to their trajectory in the curves and their speed. They seem to work as an additional element of disturbance, which can lead to distraction and accidents. These statements are also indirectly suggesting the technical challenges of descents, and explain one of the possible reasons for cyclists to stop at the summit of the pass: to freshen up and regain their concentration.

Comparing Fig. 5.10 with Fig. 5.11 it becomes clear that the descent is indeed a more focussed activity, where driving tasks prevail over secondary tasks and dialogue is hardly possible, with the exception of the moments of stop. Indeed, after minute 12:15 in Fig. 5.11 almost nothing happened, apart from riding the bicycle with a high concentration on the road conditions and on the travel companions (through backward looks).

Figure 5.12 illustrates the dynamics of heart rate, speed and altitude for Peter. The relationship between speed and heart rate for the cyclists is different to that of the motorcyclists (see Figs. 5.2 and 5.6). It seems that in the climbing section of the pass there is an inverse relationship between heart frequency and speed, due to the increasing steepness and the related raised physical effort. During the descent, the relationship is again inverse, but with higher speeds and lower heart rates. When Peter stopped (corresponding to the dashed grey line equal to zero), the heart rate is slightly lower, and it rises again when he starts descending in the wet road conditions.

The constant and inverse relationship between speed and heart rate is also evident on the map (Fig. 5.13). Middle gray lines correspond to moments when the heart frequency is low and the speed is high, during the descent, whereas orange lines refer to the climb, when low speed is associated with high heart rate. What is interesting to note is that among the few light grey areas are the places where cyclists stopped, with low (or no) speed and low heart rate values. Overall, the map as well as the sensor data seem to show how cyclists 'experience is a bipartite experience, com-

5.3 Cyclists Second-by-Second   199

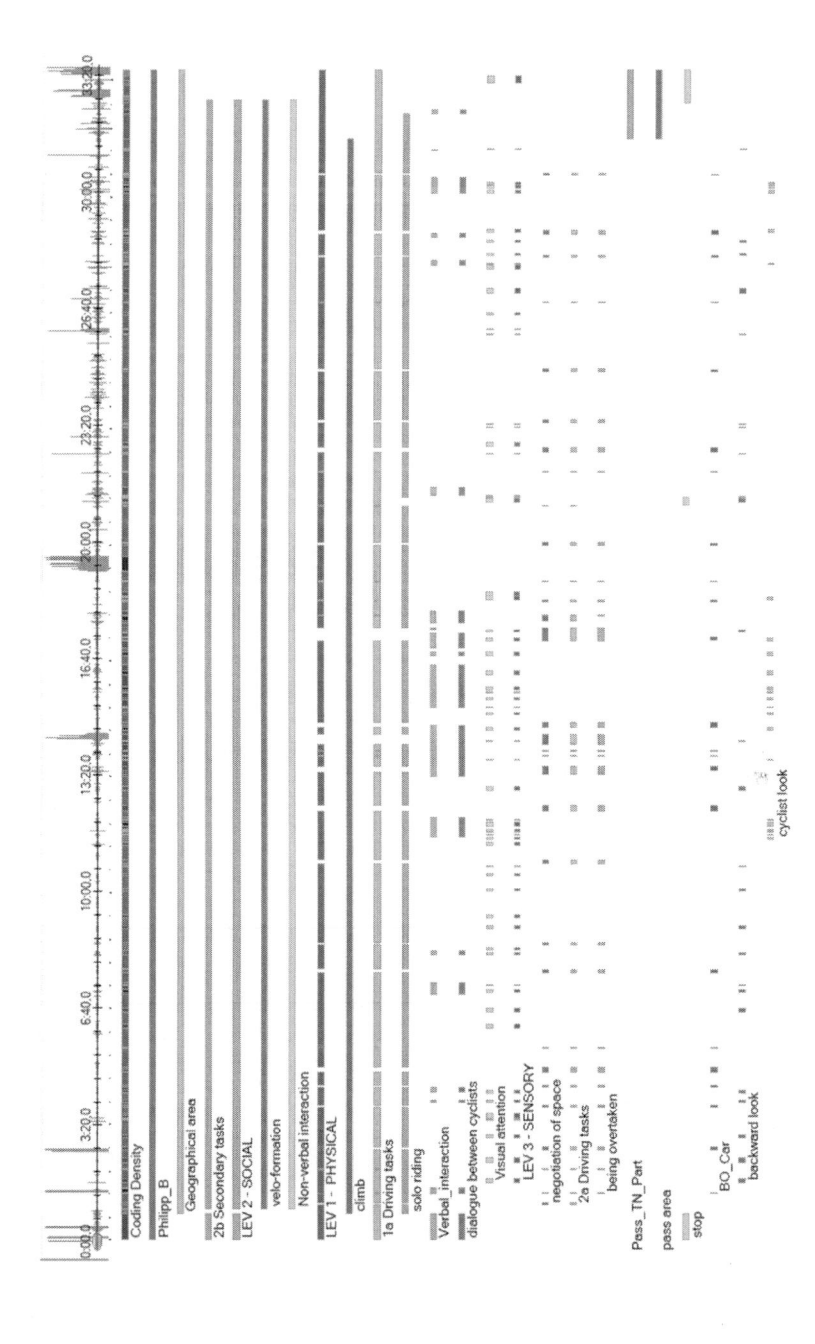

Fig. 5.10 Peter's coding scheme of the video footage (climbing section) (own elaboration)

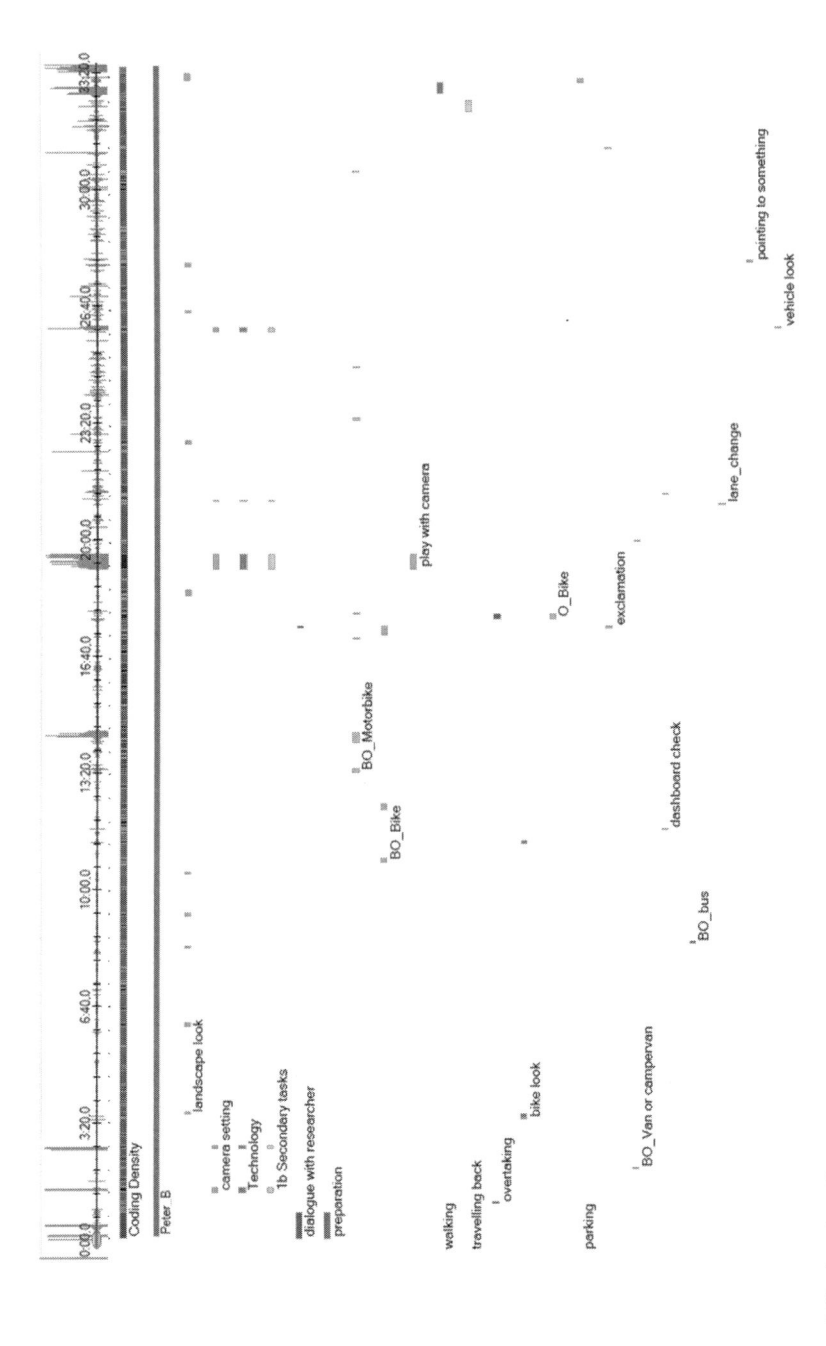

200   5 Results: Selected Individual Journey Experiences

Fig. 5.10 (continued)

5.3 Cyclists Second-by-Second 201

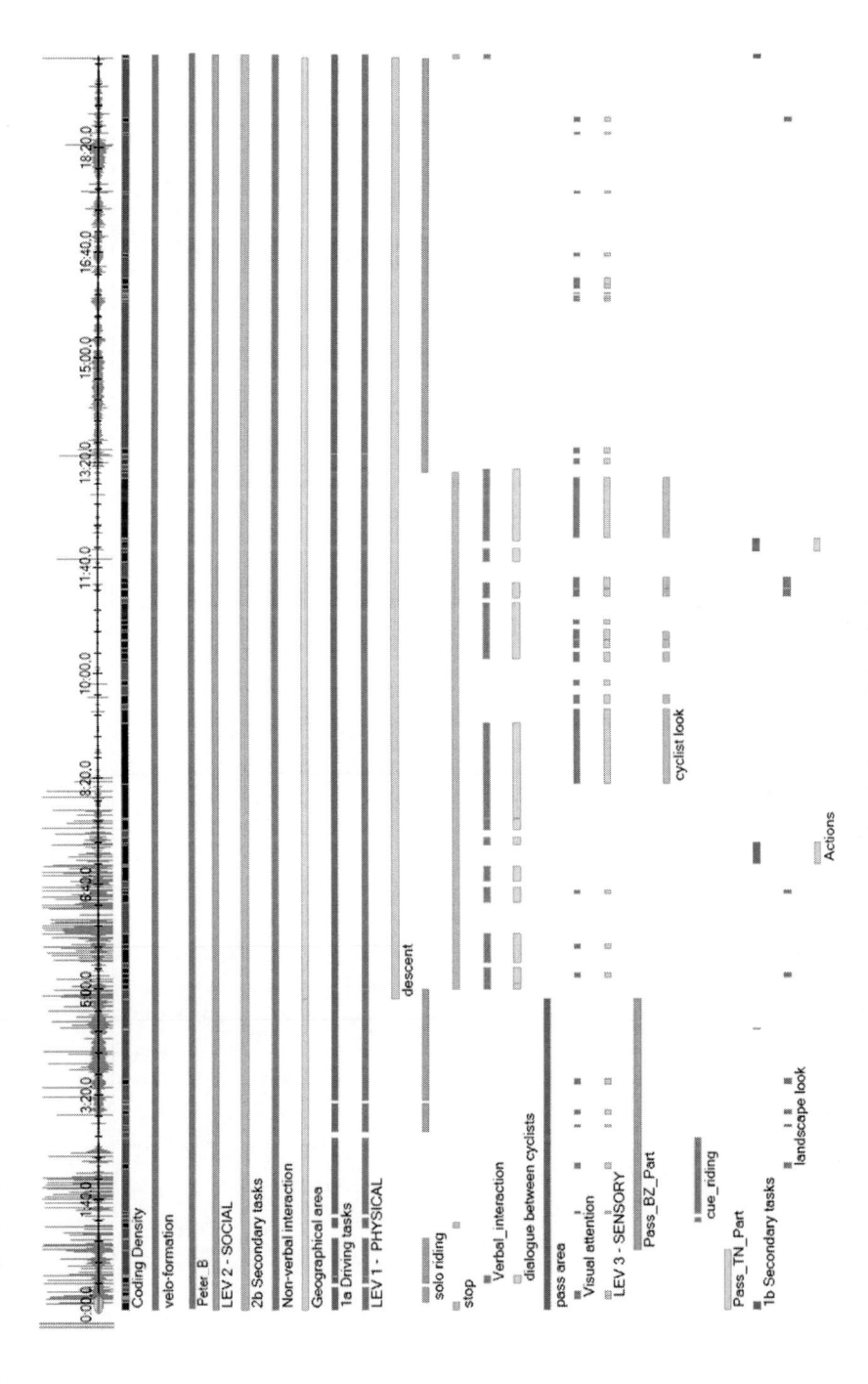

Fig. 5.11 Peter's coding scheme of the video footage (descent section) (own elaboration)

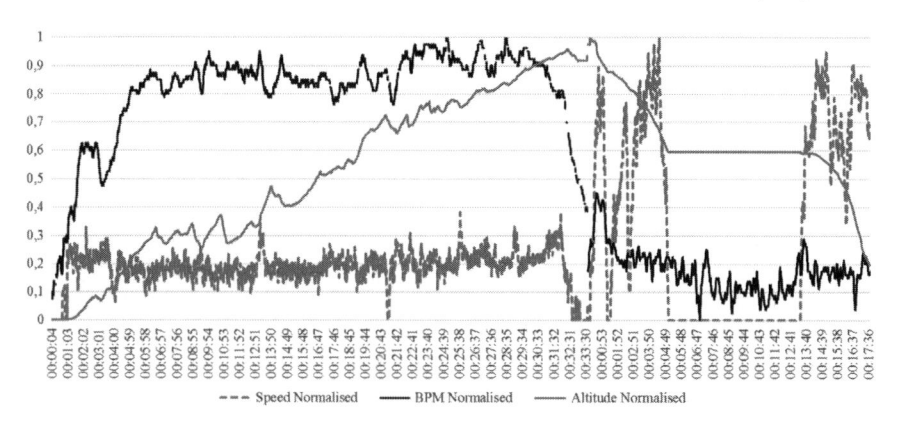

Fig. 5.12 Peter's sensor data: heath rate, speed and altitude (normalised values) (own elaboration)

posed of the climb and the descent. These two sub-units of experience have different characteristics and therefore have different effects on cyclists' bodies and minds.

Notwithstanding this bipartition, it seems that—for Peter—the video elicitation could evoke only sad reactions, which were indeed linked to a mostly neutral (and tired) facial expression after the trip was concluded.

As it can be seen in Fig. 5.14, very small peaks of happiness were registered in moments where the landscape was gazed at in the video footage. Some moments, particularly the moment of riding in line after a bus seemed to provoke higher levels of sadness in the cyclist, and a decrease in his ratings when overtaking (see Figs. 5.10 and 5.11). Notwithstanding this monocategorical type of emotional reaction detected through facial action coding systems, the reported emotions were more diverse for Peter. Table 4.4 reports the stated emotions and reveals that, although being one of the few cyclists reporting to have felt loneliness and discontent (due to a knee problem), Peter was also feeling happiness and optimism, respectively when he crossed the watershed and when he started the trip. Similarly to Marco, it seems that comparing stated and revealed emotions, the moment of arousal of a feeling is matching, but the type of feeling is different. One interpretation might be that, due to the physical knee problem, reported in the questionnaire, as well as the rainy weather and the wet travel conditions, cyclists reached the end of the tour with far less enthusiasm than at the start. This might have led to the predominance of negative-valenced feelings, and particularly sadness, when reviewing the video footage. The comparison of this experience with another detailed individual experience will further enlighten cyclists' features in the following sections.

5.3 Cyclists Second-by-Second

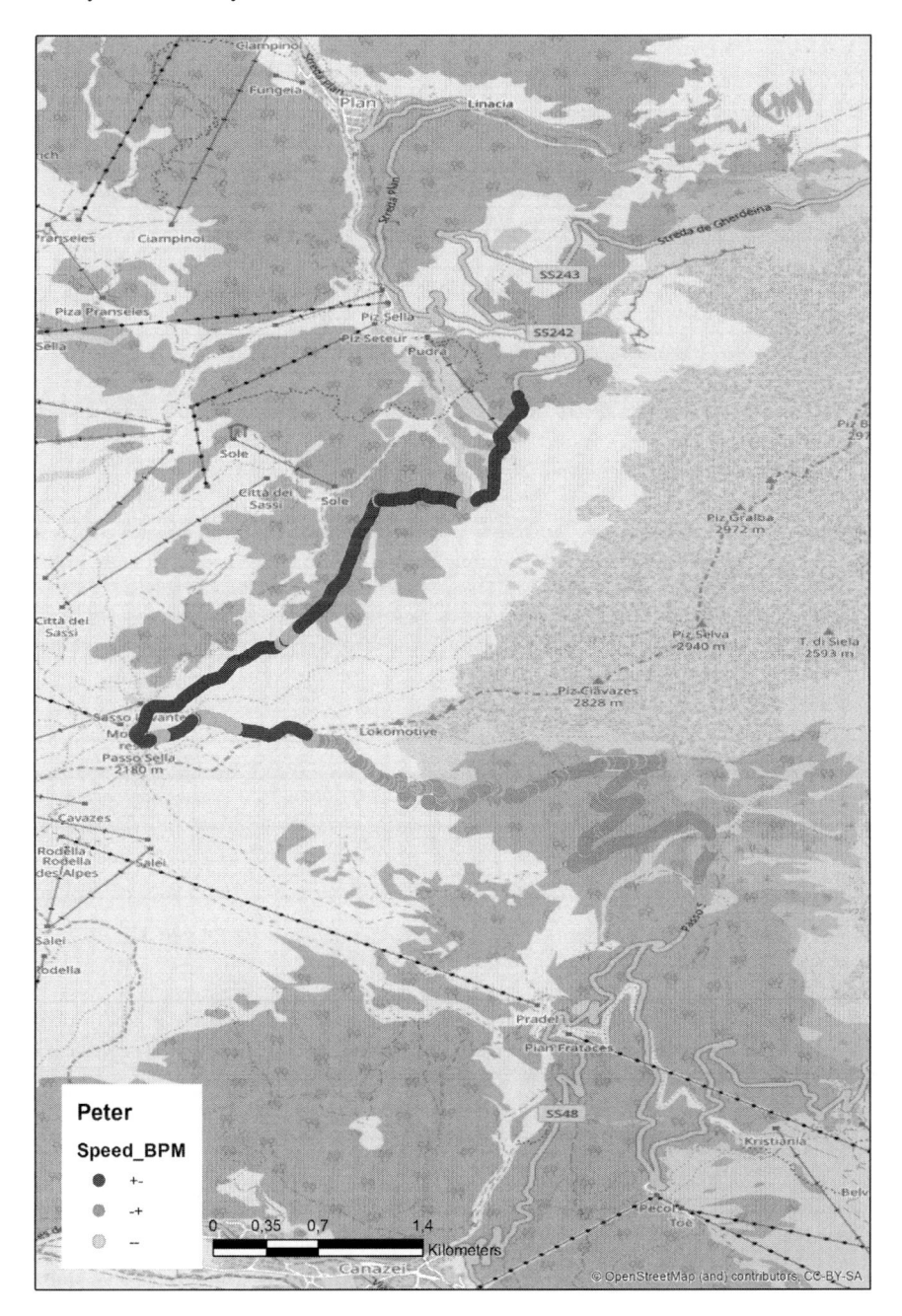

Fig. 5.13 Geo-referenced maps of Peter's sensor data: heath rate and speed (normalised values) (own elaboration)

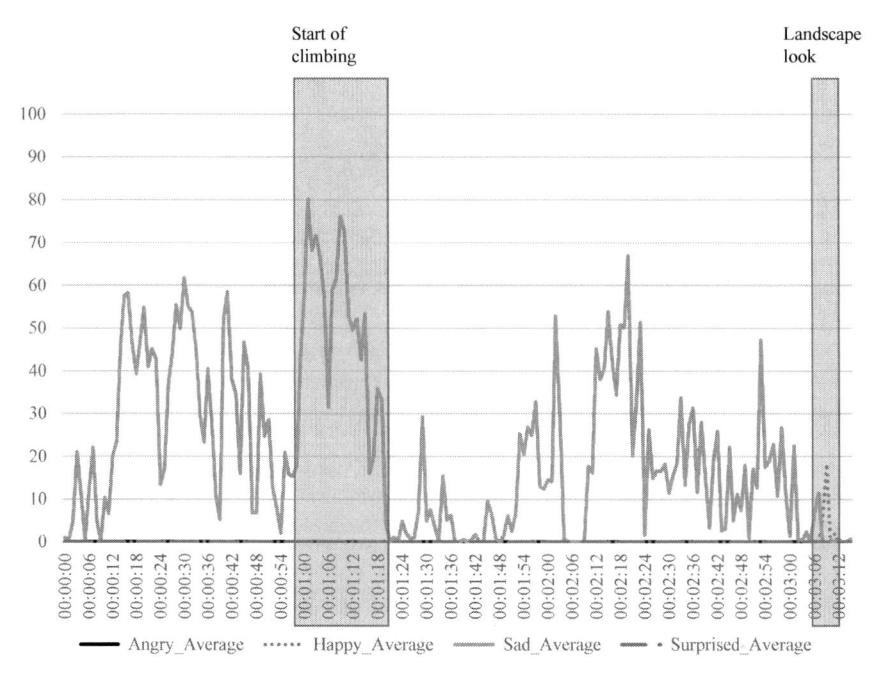

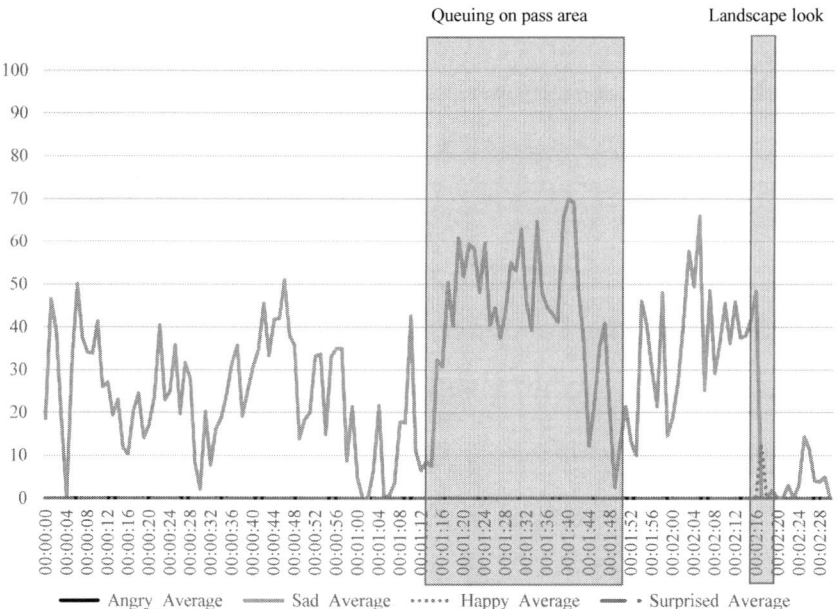

Fig. 5.14 Peter's emotion data based on facial action coding (first and second video) (own elaboration)

5.3.2 Gabriel and the Sport Performance

Gabriel (participant 5B) is a Brazilian athlete in his forties, starting the Sellaronda trip from Selva di Val Gardena, with his wife and a Spanish friend on September 6th 2016. He is taking the tour in counter clockwise direction and therefore the Sella Pass is for him the last pass climbed of the four belonging to the tour. He is spending a four-day holiday in Selva di Val Gardena (from September 3rd to 6th). The day of the tour is his last day and he declared in the questionnaire to have covered the mountainbike Sellaronda tour on off-road trails in the previous days, because he is a professional mountainbiker. The bike he was using was a Bianchi bike and he rented it in a shop in Selva di Val Gardena, because he was not carrying the own bike for logistical reasons. Similarly to Peter, he reported that he decided to take the Sellaronda tour to enjoy the landscape and to pedal on spectacular roads. He associated the idea of cycling on paved roads with his desire to use a road bike, being himself a mountainbiker.

Gabriel's recorded journey started at 14:50 at Pian Schiavaneis, but he started the Sellaronda tour about two hours later, climbing to the top of Passo Gardena, Campolongo and Pordoi first and—according to what he reported—stopping for a while to have lunch. The total journey from Pian Schiavaneis to Plan de Gralba lasted about 51:07 min, but the effective time of the journey was 44:50 min.

The weather was sunny on that day: the temperature in Selva di Val Gardena was between 5.4 and 15.1 °C (Provincial office of the Autonomous Province of Bolzano—Meteorological service, data available here: http://meteo.provincia.bz.it/dati-storici.asp). The relatively low temperature was clearly perceived by this group of cyclists, who discussed feeling cold along the journey. Gabriel's wife even broke the velo-formation and started the trip before headcams were installed because she was feeling too cold and was not willing to stop pedalling.

Gabriel collected additional material during the tour about himself and the other participants, because he was carrying two additional cameras. One was positioned on the handlebars of the bicycle, and could monitor his face and his movements in a third-person perspective. A second headcam was located at the back of his friend's saddle, so that many pictures were taken from multiple perspectives during his journey. Although not covering the whole journey, these additional perspectives have provided additional understanding of some of the features of the journey and have uncovered strengths and weaknesses of the selected method (Fig. 5.15). For instance, at the moment when Gabriel was overtaking his travel companion, the camera on the saddle recorded the feeling of pleasure on his face while overtaking, whereas the two cameras on the heads of the other participants could register their heart rate and speed, related to that single moment. These kind of analyses are beyond the scope of this dissertation, for which one main point of view was selected to describe the journey, but they suggest innovative ways of analysing interactions, including a comparison of sensor data for more than one participant. The analysis is enlightening how different individuals can feel differently in the same time-space context. Further, the camera located on the handlebar offered additional layers for the interpretation

Fig. 5.15 Comparison of three perspectives of Gabriel's journey (own elaboration)

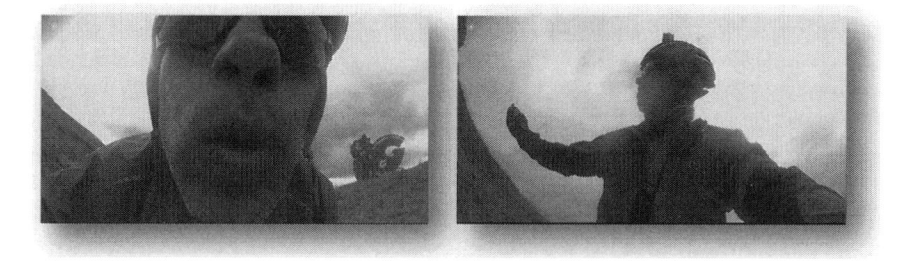

Fig. 5.16 Video stills of special moments grasped through the handlebar camera (own elaboration)

of Gabriel's behaviour. For instance, it could be detected more clearly when head movements were related to landscape viewing; it could be recorded when he was taking selfies while riding (see Fig. 5.16 and the corresponding Video ESM_7), it could be detected when he was feeling strong fatigue, when he was sweating, when he was smiling or even when he was so euphoric when he reached the pass summit area, that he kissed the camera and shouted "Grazie Italia! [Thank you Italy!]", while indicating the beautiful view on the Sassolungo mountain group (see Video ESM_7). This last exclamation—if viewed from the traditional headcam view—seemed to be directed to a pedestrian who was walking along the road. In reality, the handlebar perspective showed that it was directed to the camera. Ultimately, through the handlebar perspective it was also possible to get an impression of the feeling of temperature, due to the repeated actions of opening and closing the jacket—which were not visible using the headcam standard perspective.

5.3 Cyclists Second-by-Second 207

Besides these methodologically relevant self-reflections on camera perspectives, interesting features also stand out in the content analysis of the main video footage of the journey along with sensor data. Concerning speed patterns, Gabriel was among the quickest cyclists in climbing to the top of the pass, pedalling with an average speed of 11 km/h, and the quickest both in the pass area and in the descent (17 km/h and 51 km/h on average). His peak in speed was at minute 38:59, when he reached 60 km/h—the road's speed limit—while descending and following the speed patterns of a public bus travelling in front of him. The increase in speed is visible in Fig. 5.17 if looking at the sound wave, visually reproducing the sound of the wind. A few seconds after that, Gabriel was forced to stop because, due to the high speed, the camera on the handlebar was falling apart and he almost fell, too.

A closer look at Fig. 5.17 reveals a repetition of patterns already detected in Peter's video footage, but at the same time highlights additional features specific to Gabriel. As already discussed, the climbing section of the journey shows a greater richness in secondary tasks, whereas the descent is focussed almost solely on driving tasks. Active overtaking happens rarely and while descending, whereas passive overtaking is frequent while climbing. The difference in speed between climbing and descending is also visible in the difference in sound, reproduced on the waveform at the top of the figure. Routines of backward looks are repeated to check the status of the velo-formation and to make sure that travel companions are travelling safely.

What is particular to Gabriel is the routine related to technology setting. In fact, he was repeatedly checking for route progress and steepness, saying out loud the length of the climb and the kms left to reach the top of the pass. He was also using technology to lead the dynamics of the velo-formation: he was agreeing with his travel companion to let him lead the first part of the journey, while himself leading the second part of it. The partition of the climb into two main parts was possible thanks to the real time monitoring of the progress made on the road, as well as the difficulties in terms of steepness. Technology worked as a mediator for the perception of the travel space and the administration of physical effort, as well as the interaction dynamics within the group.

Additionally, Gabriel was very communicative about his own journey experience and he was the only participant to start an inter-temporal conversation with the researcher during the journey. This strange monologue was easily detectable due to a change in language—he spoke Portuguese with his travel companions and switched to English when establishing contact with the researcher, as already mentioned in Sect. 4.4.2.2. The object of discussion was the setting of the helmet, the difficulties of climbing, the happiness when reaching the pass summit area, and finally the dynamics of the accident he experienced. It seemed that Gabriel was trying to increase the researcher's understandings and participation in the journey through verbal explanation. While on top of the pass, Gabriel stopped several times to take pictures in the pass area. Although most of the pictures were taken on a hill just off the road, Gabriel (and his two travel companions) brought their bikes with themselves, to include them into the picture frame as if they were important elements of the journey.

Figure 5.18 (visually very similar to Peter's Fig. 5.12) shows the relationship between speed, altitude and heart rate. Unfortunately, the sensor for the heart rate

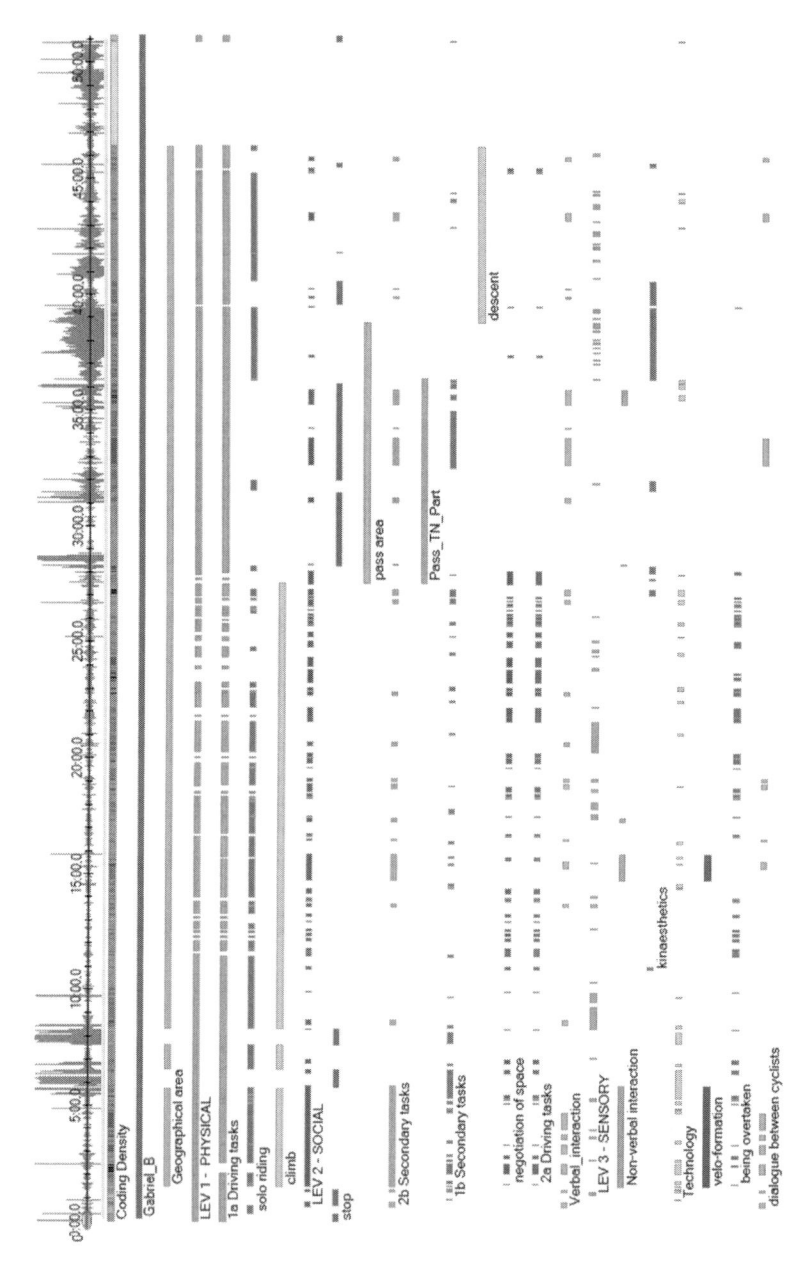

Fig. 5.17 Gabriel's Coding Scheme of the video footage (own elaboration)

5.3 Cyclists Second-by-Second

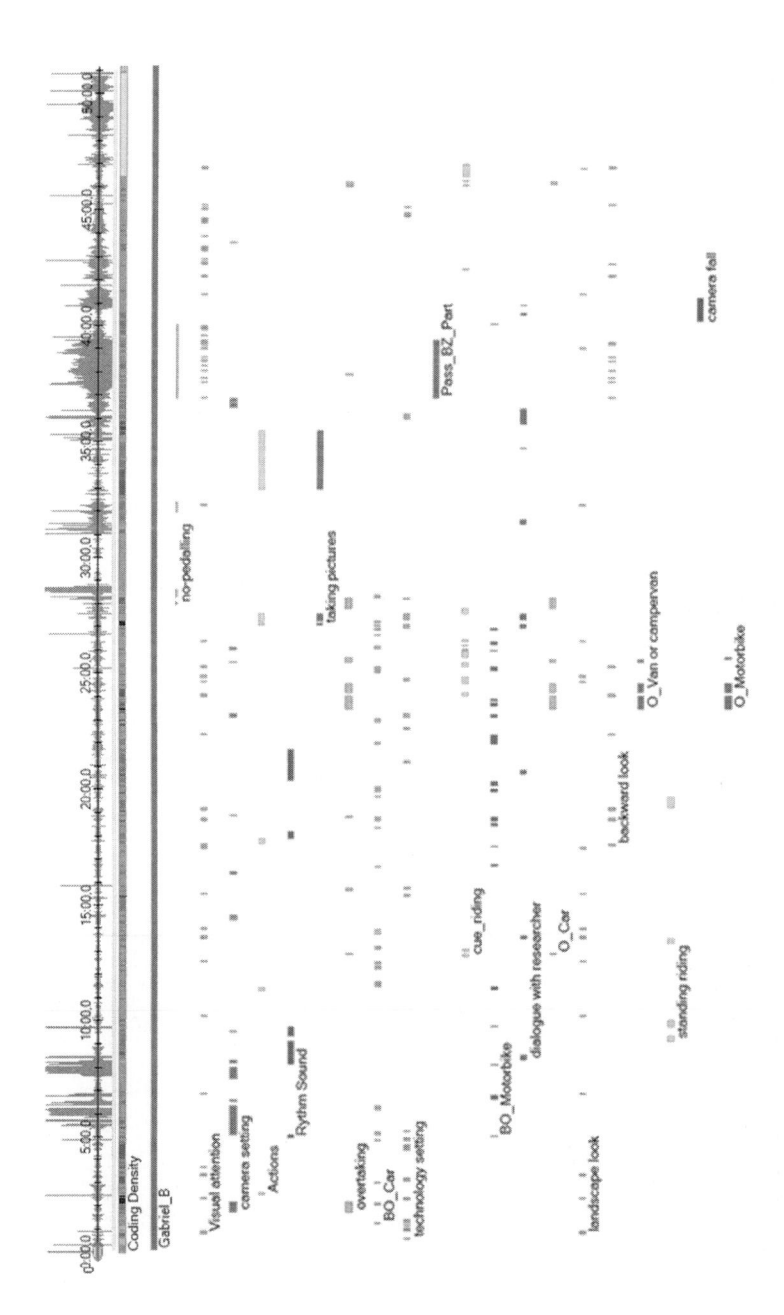

Fig. 5.17 (continued)

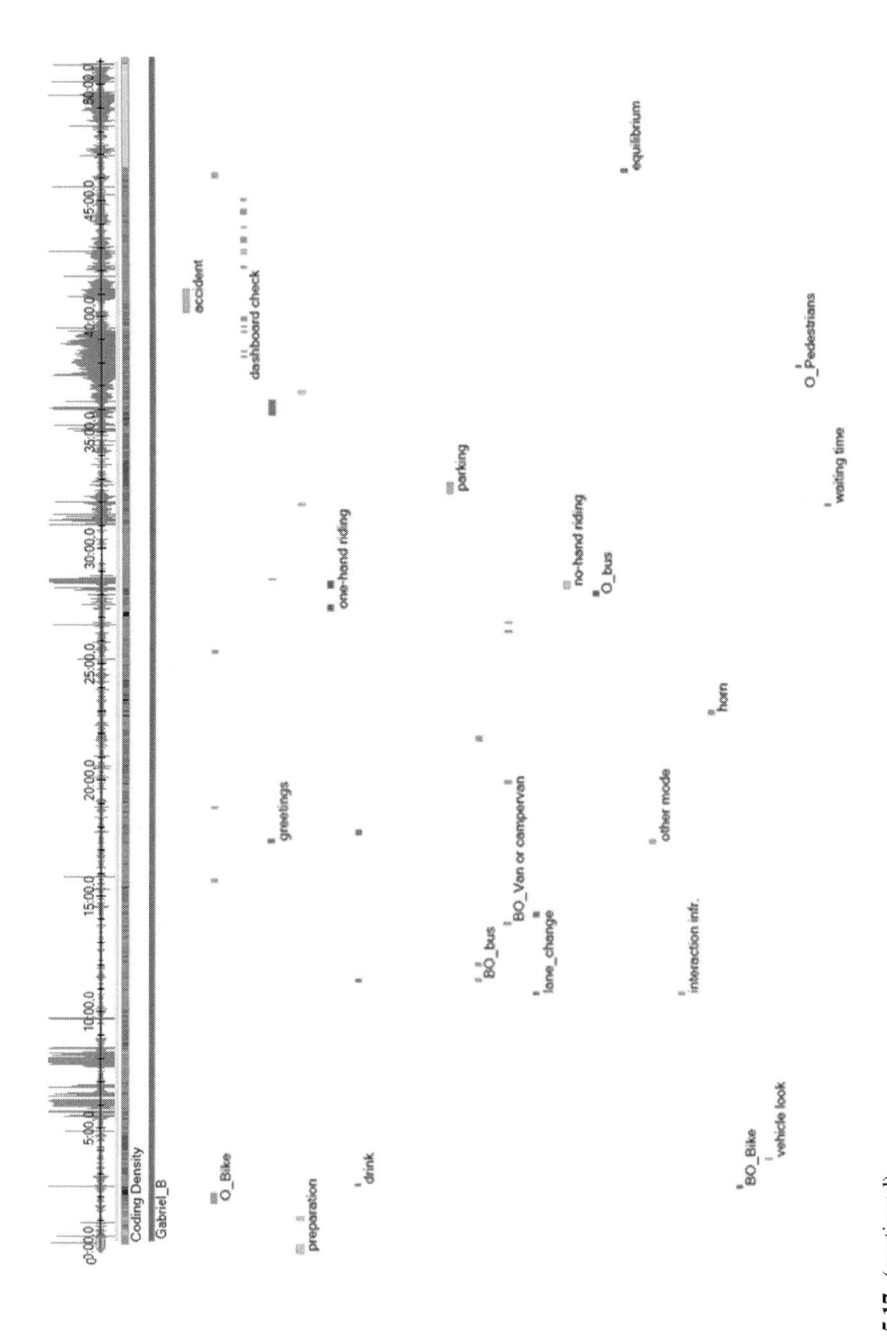

210 5 Results: Selected Individual Journey Experiences

Fig. 5.17 (continued)

5.3 Cyclists Second-by-Second

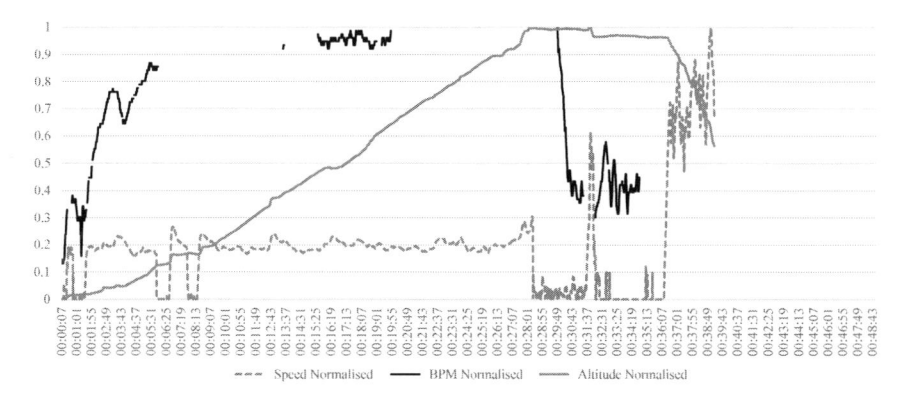

Fig. 5.18 Gabriel's sensor data: heart rate, speed and altitude (normalised values) (own elaboration)

did not work properly during the whole journey, but the comparison of the visible patterns with the ones in Fig. 5.12 shows interesting features.

The climbing section of the journey lasted about 28 min for both cyclists, and the relationship between heart rate and speed appears very similar. In the pass summit area there is a decrease in both heart rate and speed, because Gabriel—just like Peter—stopped for a while. The limited availability of heart rate data (Fig. 5.18) affected the results represented in the map (Fig. 5.19), where it was only possible to confirm the inverse relationship between speed and heart rate in the climbing section. This is one of the reasons for the inclusion of one additional individual case for cyclists, which could better illustrate sensor patterns (Fig. 5.22).

Notwithstanding the gaps in sensor data, Gabriel also represents a very interesting case for emotional data based on facial action coding (Fig. 5.20).

Minute 02:11-14 refers to one of the many "setting moments" of Gabriel's journey. It is a moment when Gabriel is first following his travel companion (peak in anger around 02:05-02:11), then he is noticing that his companion's camera is not in the correct position to frame the road and the landscape properly, therefore he is adjusting its position (02:11-17) and this causes a peak in surprise and a lower peak in happiness, finally Gabriel overtakes his companion and starts to set his own cameras. In this setting procedure, he is unconsciously occupying the left hand side of the road by changing the lane he is riding in, which probably causes him a sense of anger—maybe shame—during the video elicitation (minutes 02:32-41). A second interesting moment is shown in Fig. 5.20, i.e. when (around minutes 03:38-44) Gabriel admires the landscape around him. At a first glance, it could seem straightforward to interpret that that landscape's beauty is surprising him. Nevertheless, when listening to the audio recordings and looking at the dialogue transcriptions, it becomes clear that the reason for the emotional reaction might more likely be Gabriel's ironic answer to his friend, commenting on the temperature:

Armando: E você está com frio ou está bem?
  [Are you cold or are you ok?]

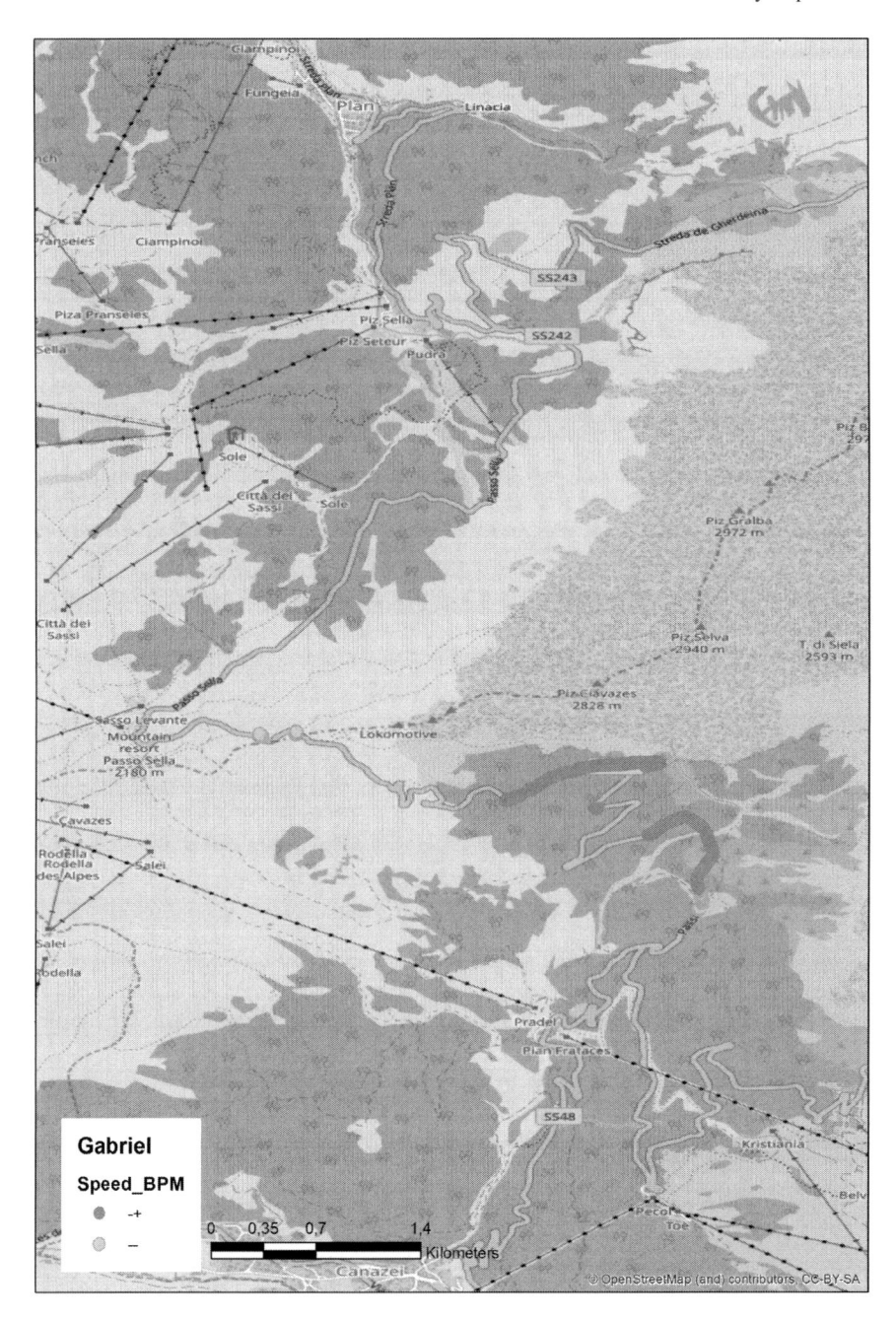

Fig. 5.19 Geo-referenced maps of Gabriel's sensor data: heath rate and speed (normalised values) (own elaboration)

5.3 Cyclists Second-by-Second

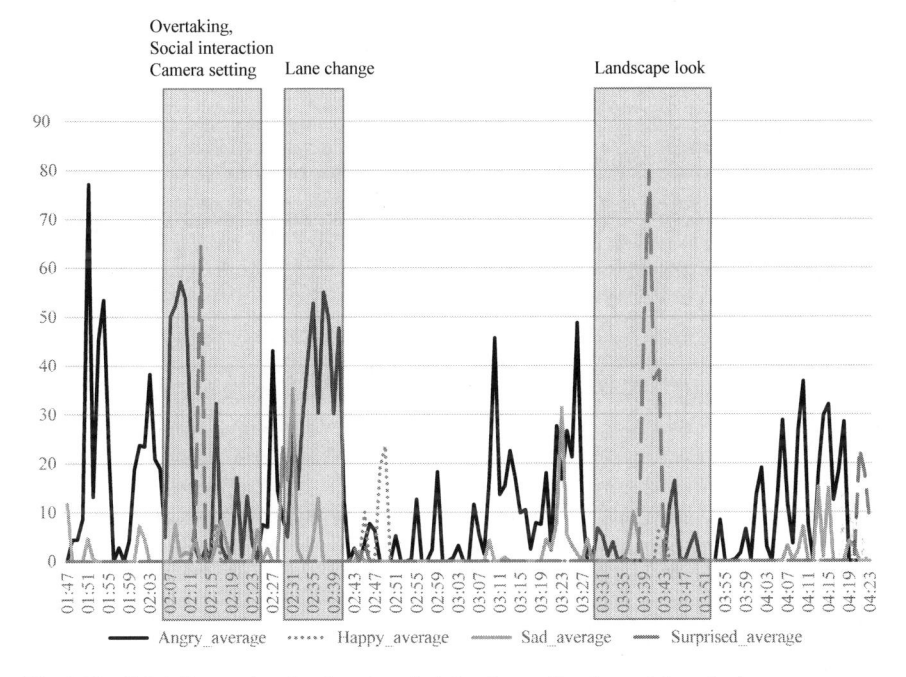

Fig. 5.20 Gabriel's emotion data based on facial action coding (own elaboration)

Gabriel: *Não com frio, só com um pau.*
              [No, I'm not. I am just like a stick]

This interaction is just an example of how based on the (even unfavourable) contextual conditions, interactions among travellers might evoke (even positive) emotional reactions, in this case represented by the joke between the two cyclists.

If comparing these revealed feelings with the ones reported in the questionnaire, almost no match can be found. Indeed, Gabriel reported that he was not feeling anger at all—whereas in the facial action coding data it is the prevailing feeling—and that he was mostly feeling positive emotions, such as optimism when the body was responding well to the challenges of the climb, happiness every time he saw a rock, loneliness related to mountains, and peacefulness associated to cows seen along the tour. The only negative feeling he reported was fear, when he had the small accident in the moment of descending. However, this incongruence must not be taken as valid for the whole video footage, because Gabriel—just as the other participants—was looking only at a short part of the video he collected, a part in which probably the emotions felt while climbing did not correspond to those felt by recalling the experience just after it was made.

5.3.3 Carlo and the Same-Day Tour

Carlo (participant 1B) is a South Tyrolean same-day visitor in his forties, making the Sellaronda tour on August 24th—the same day as Juan's tour –with two friends. Although they are all from Bolzano, the capital city of South Tyrol, Carlo and one of his friends started the cycling journey together in Ortisei (a small village at the beginning of Val Gardena Valley, 10 km away from Plan de Gralba) and planned to get back there after concluding the tour. The third friend, Corrado, was more fit and started the tour in Bolzano, covering additional 45 km to reach Val Gardena valley. They were travelling in counter clockwise direction—and they were the only ones doing so in the sample. This means that the Sella Pass was the first pass they were climbing, therefore—compared to the other cyclists—they were fresher in the climbing phase. Carlo was riding his own bike, a Rosa Avant, and linked the idea of cycling with "Physical effort, silence, time not to think: possibility not to think about anything, because thoughts find their own way". The reasons for taking the tour were to enjoy the landscape, to cycle on spectacular roads and to train. He had made the tour seven times already in the past.

Carlo's video footage was recorded with a start in Plan de Gralba at 12:12, where the headcams were installed and the recordings started. It finished in Pian Schiavaneis after 36:18 min, with a very short stop along the way. The questionnaire and the video elicitation part was done after the end of the tour, because cyclists did not want to stop in Pian Schiavaneis for a longer time. They simply took off the headcam there, but then continued the tour towards Pordoi, Campolongo and the Gardena pass, because it was already almost 1 PM and they feared that they might not to finish the tour in a reasonable time. The weather was sunny on that day and—as already mentioned—the temperatures were quite high compared to other days (9.3–22.7 °C) (Provincial office of the Autonomous Province of Bolzano—Meteorological service, data available here: http://meteo.provincia.bz.it/dati-storici.asp).

Carlo's journey is interesting for several reasons. First of all, to introduce the perspective of a same-day visitor and compare his physical, sensory, social and emotional patterns with those of a tourist. Secondly, to understand physical and biosensing features in the case of a counter clockwise tour, which implies climbing the Sella Pass on the same lane that motorcyclists did and also as the first pass of the journey. Thirdly, to compare two types of visits on the Sella Pass happening on the same (crowded) day—August 24th—, but with two different means of transport– the bicycle for Carlo and the motorcycle for Juan.

Carlo was the quickest cyclist in covering the distance between Plan de Gralba and Pian Schiavaneis, both because he never stopped and because his speed in climbing was high, similar to that of Gabriel (11 km/h in climbing and in the pass area). The speed in descending was slower (42 km/h compared to the 51 of Gabriel). He was also the cyclist with the highest peak in speed in the descending part of the journey, reaching 61 km/h—which is below the road's speed limit. This can be noticed also looking at the soundwave in Fig. 5.21, where the difference between the silence in

5.3 Cyclists Second-by-Second

climbing and the noise of wind in descending is very evident. The peak in speed happened at minute 32:27, after actively overtaking two cars.

When comparing the journeys of Juan and Carlo it becomes clear that—although in the climbing phase Carlo is obviously spending more time because he cannot rely on a mechanical engine, during the descent the difference in average speed between the cyclist and the motorcyclist is only 4 km/h. Once again, data suggest that with the same infrastructure and in similar weather and traffic conditions during the same day, cycling and motorcycling experiences are very similar in the descending part of the journey. Data show also that Carlo and his friend Corrado—taking the tour counter clockwise, were faster than other cyclists, both because their pedalling rhythm was good in climbing, and because they were stopping for less than one minute on top of the pass, just time to take a quick picture of the pass sign.

Figure 5.21 illustrates the coding scheme for the journey of Carlo in detail. Some patterns already mentioned in the previous two individuals will not be described in detail again. Among these, the dissolution of the velo-formation after the start of the climb, the passive overtaking happening mostly in the climbing section of the road and the active role of overtaking in the descending phase.

One interesting aspect of this journey is the visual attention and the interpretation of the landscape surrounding the pass within the dialogues between cyclists. In fact, notwithstanding the relatively considerable amount of traffic on the road, Carlo and his travel companions managed to talk quite a lot during the climb and in their dialogues it was evident that they knew the area and they could recognise landscape features. They even talked about one via ferrata (hiking route with cables) starting in the surroundings of the road and they could recognise a mountain hut by name in the landscape. Looking at mountain features, both routes and huts, they started to talk about dangerous adventures that their friends or acquaintances had while climbing in mountainous areas, in a sort of legendary tale of epic adventures. It is important to notice here that there seems to be an increased deepness in the perception and interpretation of the landscape, if comparing the dialogues of Carlo and his travel companions and the ones of Peter in the previous section. It is also interesting to notice that—to be able to dialogue while pedalling—cyclists tend to ride side by side and turn their head to get eye contact. This is on the one hand facilitating conversation, but on the other hand is causing more difficulties when negotiating space with other vehicles. Indeed, sometimes vehicles used the horn before they overtook them (e.g. minute 03:38). These observations at micro-scale can be helpful both for tourism marketing purposes and for infrastructure planning. Indeed, on the Sella Pass road—at the opposite side of the pass—a specific lane for cyclists was introduced, to ensure safe climbing. Both increasing the width of this lane where it is possible and—eventually—some additional information on landscapes and views might be an additional enrichment for cyclists.

Figure 5.22 illustrates the sensor data for Carlo. Comparing these data with the ones of Peter (Fig. 5.12) and Gabriel (Fig. 5.18) it becomes clear that, from a sensory perspective, the patterns are very similar. Additionally, it seems to be confirmed that in the climbing phase of the journey heart rate is inversely proportional to speed, whereas in the descent, it can be correlated, especially in specific moments when

Fig. 5.21 Carlo's coding scheme of the video footage (own elaboration)

5.3 Cyclists Second-by-Second

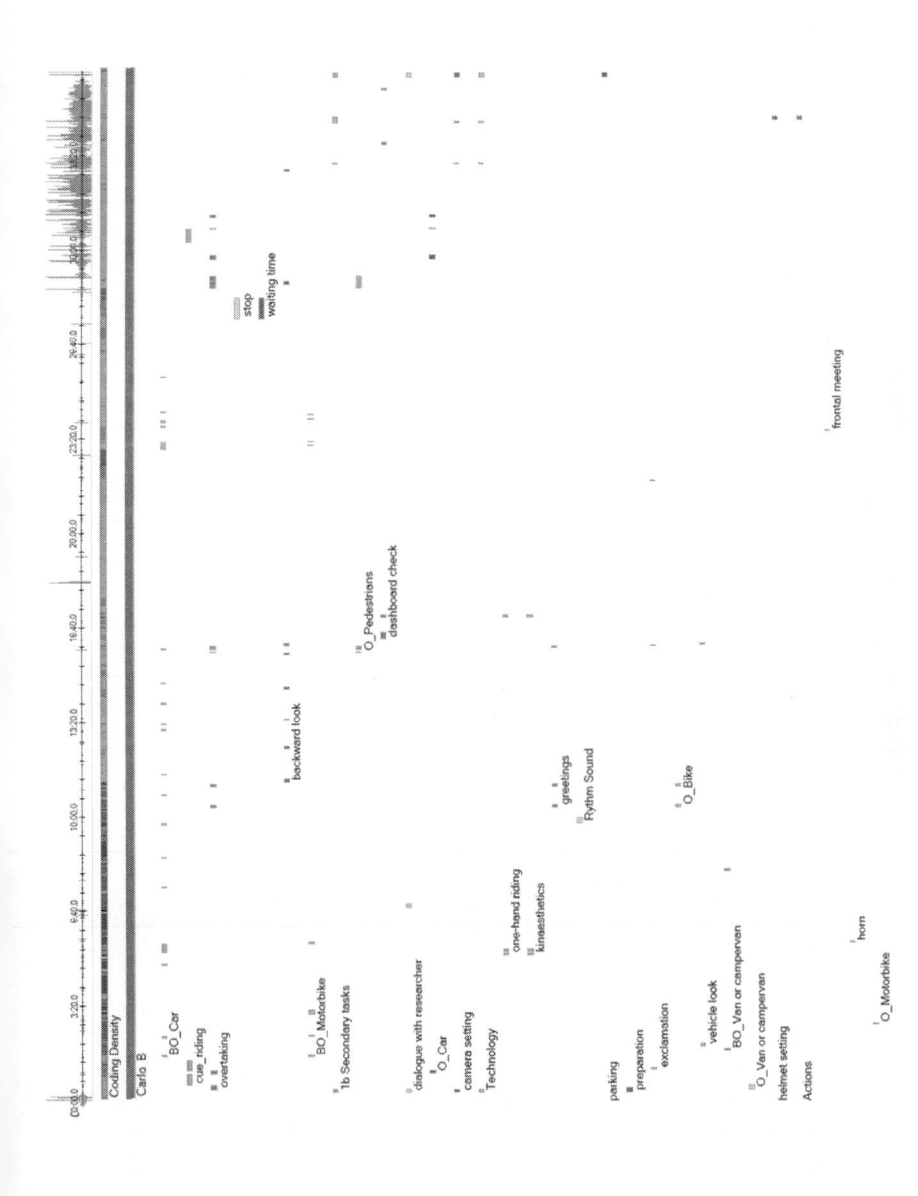

Fig. 5.21 (continued)

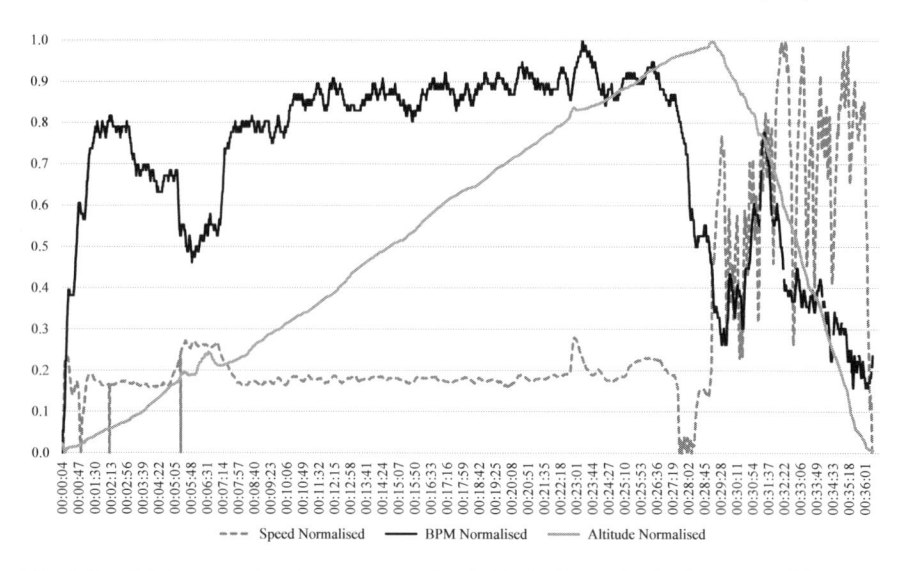

Fig. 5.22 Carlo's sensor data: heart rate, speed and altitude (normalised values) (own elaboration)

Fig. 5.23 Video stills of moments of overtaking while descending on the bicycle: a peak in hearth rate (own elaboration)

risky tasks are performed (e.g. Fig. 5.21, min 29:40–31:17 and Fig. 5.23). Figure 5.23 illustrates exactly the moment when the peak in speed and in heart beat is reached. It corresponds to the moment when Carlo interacted with a car and, after some trials, managed to overtake it, reaching speeds around 60 km/h.

5.3 Cyclists Second-by-Second 219

The map (Fig. 5.24) illustrates the relationship between speed and heart rate in space. The numerous similarities with the map of Peter (Fig. 5.13, where the colours are inverted due to the opposite direction of the tour) confirm that the climbing part is characterised by an inverse relationship between heart rate and speed. Concerning the descending part of the journey, moments of high speed and low heart rate prevail, but there are some moments when both indicators are very high. These are often moments when risky actions are taken.

The black portion of the map (corresponding to minutes 30:51-32:12 and also to the video stills of Fig. 5.23 and the Video ESM_8) show exactly one of those moments and corresponds with the time frame when Carlo was overtaking several cars. This suggests that moments of active overtaking can be as exciting for cyclists as they are for motorcyclists, especially when riding in good weather conditions. On the other hand, the maps also shows some light grey parts of the road. These correspond to curves, particularly during the descent. Curves are moments where the speed is reduced and—probably—there is no particular effort in pedalling and no stimulus for emotional arousal, so that the heart rate is also below average.

Carlo's emotion data based on facial action coding show the already mentioned emotional value of social interaction while cycling together on the pass road. Indeed, Carlo and his two friends are continuously talking and joking while they are climbing. They recall the adventurous tours of the days before, they talk about the effects of the heartbeat belt on their physical conditions, in term of mental pressure towards performance, and finally Carlo tells a story about a friend. This is a story of an accident happened while climbing on the Sella Towers, a mountain peak that is very close to where they are pedalling. When Carlo says that his friend was hardly injured, but survived, the peak in sadness is visible on the emotion features (see Fig. 5.25). In between, the gaze of Carlo is distorted by the transit of a vintage car, which probably determines a peak in happiness close to the sad peak. Overall, this data shows the importance of social interactions among cyclists, especially while there are climbing, and recalls what Carlo deliberately says during the climb, criticizing the researcher's identification of cycling as an individually-based activity (see Sect. 4.4.2.2) *"Lei dice 'gruppi che non interagiscono'; sai motociclisti... il motociclista no non parla. Ma i ciclisti sono in gruppo [She says 'groups that do not interact', you know, motorcyclists... motorcyclists, they don't speak. But cyclists, they are in a group]"*.

5.3.4 Key Findings

Adding on the second-by second analysis of two motorcycling experiences, the detailed study of cyclists' experiences enriches the overall picture of journey experiences on the Sella Pass. Similarly to motorcyclists, cyclists also seem to dedicate more time and effort to secondary tasks when they are climbing, than when they are descending, but they establish a deeper relationship with the landscape than motorcyclists do. Indeed, the long duration of their climbing experience compared to that of motorcyclists makes them appreciate additional details of the surrounding panorama.

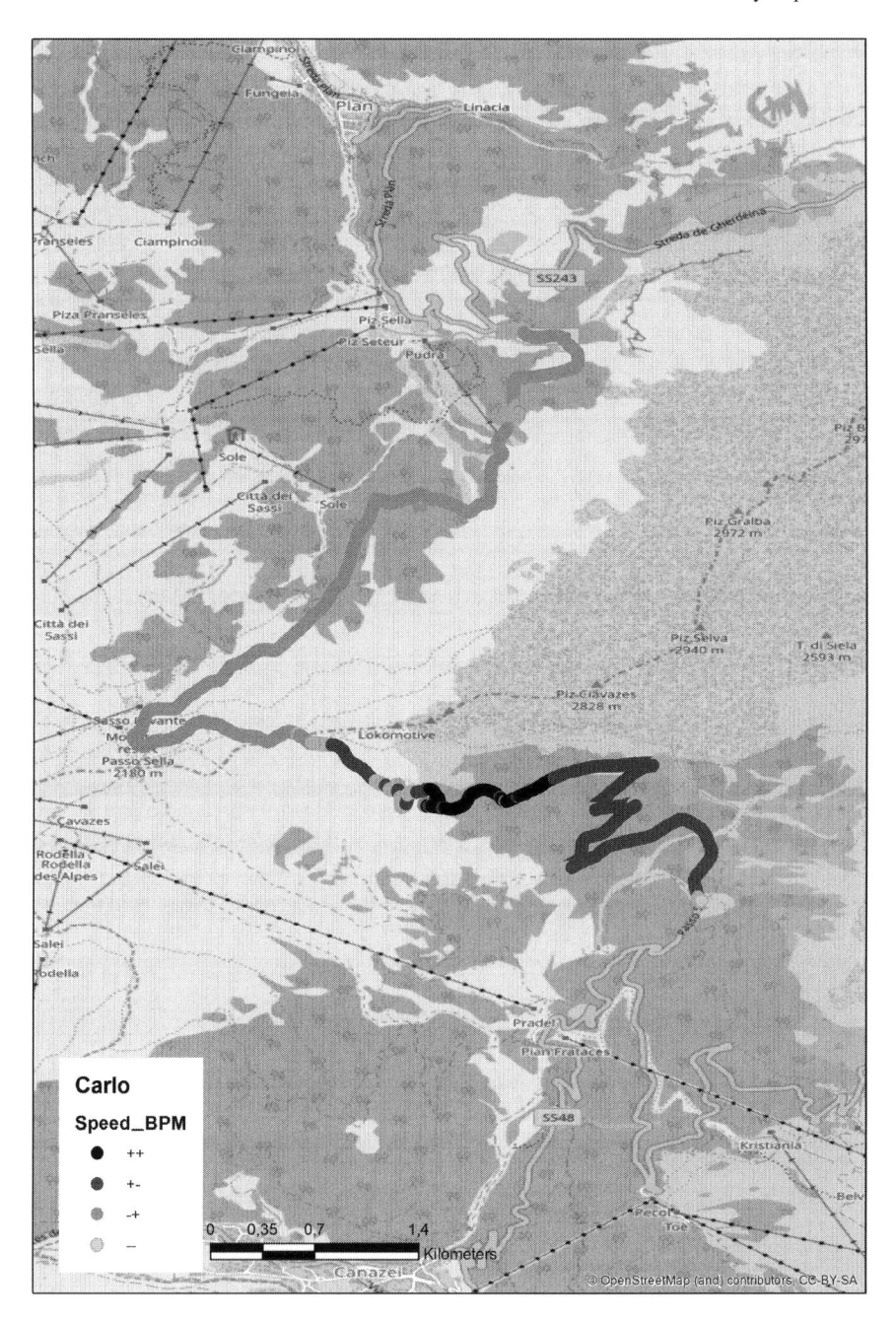

Fig. 5.24 Geo-referenced maps of Carlo's sensor data: heart rate and speed (normalised values) (own elaboration)

5.3 Cyclists Second-by-Second

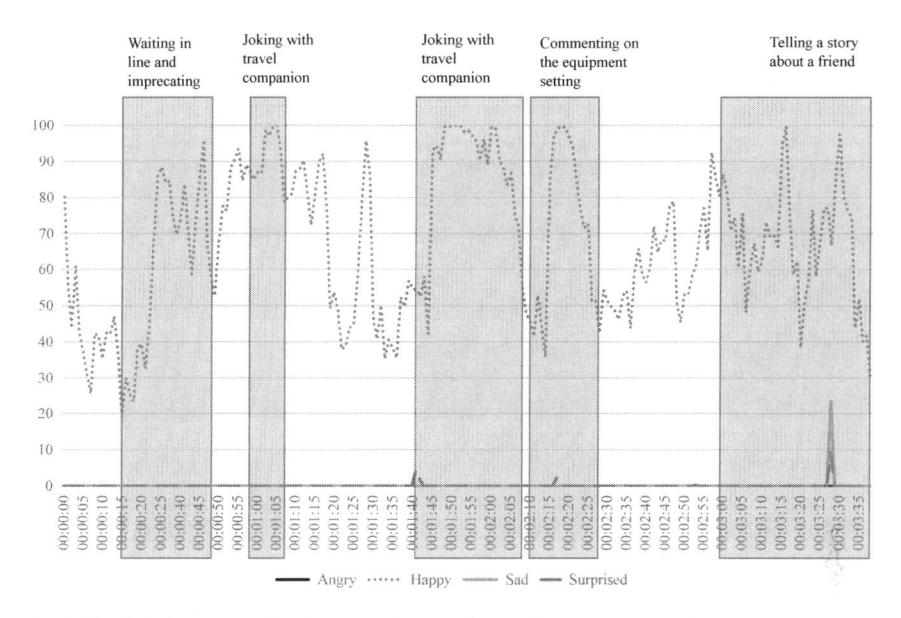

Fig. 5.25 Carlo's emotion data based on facial action coding (own elaboration)

For instance, they are able to detect routes, to identify huts, to see hikers on trails, whereas motorcyclists just give a quick glance to the most spectacular massifs. Speed seems therefore to affect the sharpness of perceptions and also the cognitive attention dedicated to understand the surrounding environment. In a similar pattern to motorcyclists, but with a reduced frequency, speed, and particularly speed variations seem also to work as stimuli to emotional arousal for cyclists, who experience active overtaking fewer times, but feel excited.

A second aspect to consider in the experience of cyclists is the importance of achieving the pass summit area, relaxing and taking pictures to remember—or to show—that the challenge was met. In two cases the temporal distinction between the climb and the descent was so strongly perceived by the cyclists that they decided to turn off the headcam once they reached the summit area, and turn it on again when starting the descent. Also those cyclists that have climbed to the top of the pass several times, and even same-day visitors, take the time to shoot a picture. Some of them include themselves and their bicycle in the picture, other just photograph the sign for the pass, to show that they have been there (again).

Finally, the thick description of the journey by Peter, Gabriel and Carlo helped understanding the importance of contextual conditions and individual attitudes along the ride. Indeed, on the one hand weather played a fundamental role in Peter's journey because it changed the rhythm of the trip, both with respect to stops and to speed while riding. On the other hand, technology played a fundamental role in Gabriel's journey, where the additional information on steepness, length and performance facilitated the management of the individual route, but also the organisation of the velo-formation. Finally, for Carlo, the social interaction with travel companions and the way he joked with his friends contributed to the overall positive attitude and happy feelings towards the journey (as well as its recollection).

The findings for the five selected individual experiences are very rich and they can be very useful for both road management and tourism niche-marketing for cyclists and motorcycles. Of course, speed and overtaking are issues to be kept under control—rather than incentivized—and they need to be subject to safety and security regulations. In this sense, knowing the exact positions of the road where speed limits are exceeded, where cyclists are afraid, or want to stop to take pictures, helps infrastructure managers to operate very precise controls, with the aim to avoid accidents, reduce noise and improve the tourist experience. Specific infrastructure changes, such as dedicated lanes, information panels or signs, if tailored to the needs of cyclists and adjusted to the needs of other road users, can increase the experience value for cyclists and therefore work not only as safety tools, but also as marketing instruments for the destinations. The landscape has been proved to have an important power, especially for cyclists. Knowing the places where mountain massifs are gazed at might help provide dynamic information while on the move, increasing thereby the awareness of the cyclists and motorcyclists that would otherwise not leave the road to immerse themselves in the natural environment. To facilitate the link between micro-data on experiences and strategies for destination management and marketing, the next section will focus on personas as tools to design customer types.

5.4 Personas Description: An Engaging Perspective on Cyclists and Motorcyclists

Based on the methodological features of personas presented above (see Sect. 3.6.1.2), an *engaging* perspective on personas description is implemented here. Personas are therefore designed based on the quantitative and qualitative data collected so far, the goal of the travellers are taken into account, as well as their role in the mobility space. The generative process of personas description should therefore not be interpreted as a synthesis of the already mentioned features of travellers into one stereotyped person, but rather as a realistic description of new characters, resulting from the composition of different features.

5.4.1 Hypotheses for Personas Description

According to Nielsen (2013), during a first phase of analysis, data are collected and certain hypotheses are formulated based on user data, that will then help to describe personas. This first part of the process can happen through affinity diagrams, empathy maps or other tools. In the case of this dissertation, both sample-based and individual-

5.4 Personas Description: An Engaging Perspective on Cyclists and Motorcyclists

based descriptions have helped to highlight affinities among users. Based on these results, and particularly on the overall picture presented in Sect. 4.6 and the selected individual experiences presented in Sects. 5.2 and 5.3, the following hypotheses are formulated:

- Journey experiences on cycles and motorcycles are immersive experiences: The (natural) environment plays an important role to motivate trips, and the sensory perceptions, especially vision and hearing, are very important along the journey;
  - Immersion happens at different levels according to mode and the related speed patterns— motorcyclists are immersed in the road space, whereas cyclists seem to be immersed in a wider nature-based space;
- Journey experiences on cycles and motorcycles are active experiences: physical effort and emotional engagement are key parts of the journey, be it with or without an engine;
  - speed, time and heart rate patterns are different across modes, but very similar within modes;
  - speed, partly depending on the technical features of the engine, the attitude of the traveller, and the interactions with other users, defines the rhythms of the journey;
- Journey experiences on cycles and motorcycles are composite experiences: they can be parsed into three main sections (climbing, crossing the pass summit area, and descending) and they can be described as made up of primary (driving) tasks and secondary (non driving) tasks;
  - Cyclists' experience are bipartite: the climb is a long and slow journey, where the senses perceive the surrounding environment, whereas the descent is a quick, focused journey, where the road attracts the attention of the traveler;
  - Actions happen on different *layers*, with secondary tasks—including tourism-related tasks—taking place only when primary tasks are not all-absorbing;
  - The type and duration of secondary tasks differs according to mode, due to the mediating role of speed;
- Journey experiences on cycles and motorcycles are eudaimonic experiences: long-term wellbeing counts more than immediate benefits while riding on top of a mountain pass;
  - *Happiness* while riding seems to be greater for motorcyclists than for cyclists, who—at least during the climbing section of the journey—are motivated by the goal of reaching the summit of the pass;
- Journey experiences are emotionally rich experiences, during which individual challenges, risk-taking actions and changes in speed provoke emotional arousal;

- Positive-valenced emotions prevail during the journey and after it, although the contingency of emotion measurement and the subjectivity of feelings can produce contrasting results.

- Journey experiences can be performance-oriented or leisure oriented: technical abilities in riding or physical fitness for cycling can (but need not) play a role for some users along the route;
  - Performance-oriented journey experiences are those focused on speed patterns, where technical and technological tools can help to plan, organize and control the journey;
  - Leisure-oriented journey experiences are focused on contextual condition, such as the dialogues with travel companions or the aesthetic contemplation of the landscape;

- Journey experiences are embedded: the contextual conditions, such as the design of road space, the panoramic views, the traffic conditions and the weather conditions affect the experience itself;
  - The same experience on the same road with similar weather condition and vehicles seem very similar, but with different vehicles or weather conditions they seem far different.

Based on this hypotheses, mode and attitude towards speed seem to be the factors that mostly differentiate the type of journey experiences people undergo.

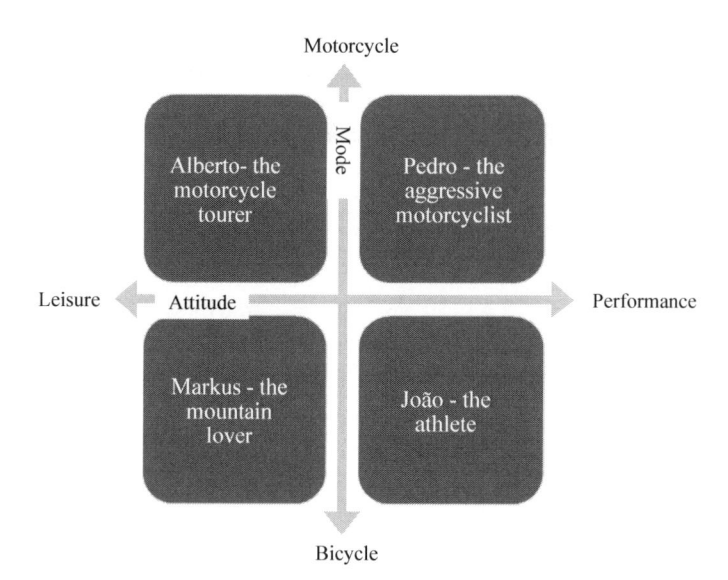

Fig. 5.26 Matrix of differentiating factors for personas description (own elaboration)

5.4 Personas Description: An Engaging Perspective on Cyclists and Motorcyclists 225

Therefore, the personas description will be based on the matrix in Fig. 5.26, combining modes and attitudes to create four personas—two motorcyclists and two cyclists. Hereafter, these four fictious characters—the personas—are described according to the features suggested in Nielsen (2013).

5.4.2 The Motorcycle Tourer: Alberto

Background. Alberto is a 37 year-old man, he lives in Tourin (Italy) and loves motorcycle touring. He is single and works as researcher and travels a lot for international conferences and meetings, but when he is not on the road for work, he enjoys riding his KTM 1290 Super Adventure S on panoramic roads (Fig. 5.27).

Activities, goals and motivations. When Alberto was young, he used to take motorcycling tours with his father, and enjoyed his time on the road, singing aloud in his helmet and looking at green and peaceful landscapes. When he was 18, he got his driving licence and since then, he never stopped motorcycling. Motorcycling for him means freedom, it means seeing and understanding different places, enjoying curving roads and panoramic views, stopping to talk to people, in whatever language he might (or might not) know. He normally travels with a friend, but he also loves to plan

Fig. 5.27 The motorcycle tourer: Alberto (own elaboration)

and to take some tours by himself, without any restrictions. He normally plans his tour in advance, books the overnights day-by-day and avoids stress while travelling. He is well equipped with light luggage and GPS devices, but also traditional maps, just in case he runs out of battery. His tours are driven by curiosity and a certain wish to challenge himself to cover long distances and see diverse roads. However, he loves to stop and take pictures of the marvellous landscapes he sees along the way. In the past, he made a Tour of more than 1,000 km across the Alpine bow. It was the richest experience he had ever had (Fig. 5.28).

The Sellaronda tour. During the last tour in September 2016, his final destination were the Dolomites. He reached the area after a 2-day tour in the Swiss Alps, and accessed South Tyrol through the Stelvio Pass, a spectacular road on the western side of the province. He slept one night in Selva di Val Gardena and took the chance to make the Sellaronda tour, before travelling to Cortina, the "Queen of the Dolomites". He was very excited because, although he knew the Alpine region quite well, he had never visited the Dolomites before. His reflex camera and his action cam could get the most exciting landscapes and rides of the tour, to show them to his friends once back.

When he rides his motorbike on Alpine panoramic roads he loves starting early in the morning, because there is no traffic congestion, and so did he when he made the Sellaronda tour. When he reached the summit of the Sella Pass he stopped for about

Fig. 5.28 The aggressive motorcyclist: Pedro (pixabay/Uwe-Georg)

40 min to enjoy the astonishing landscapes and have a fresh drink. He loved riding in a steady flow, with few interruptions and fluid banking, but of course overtaking was exciting on that road, as well. While riding, he had an immense sense of tranquillity and peacefulness, and felt as if he was having a dialogue with the shapes of the road, particularly in the climbing part of the journey, when the asphalt was new and there was no congestion, probably also due to the cloudy weather and the time of the day. In a conversation with a hotel entrepreneur, he heard that in some summer months the road was very congested. He would definitely accept policies to reduce traffic on the road, and is in favour of tolls and road restrictions to mitigate traffic impacts on the environment. He is a well organised and adaptive traveller: he would make it anyway.

5.4.3 The Aggressive Motorcyclist: Pedro

Background. Pedro is a 48-year old Spanish man living in Munich (Germany) (Fig. 5.28). He is married and has two children, but once a year he needs a short break with his friends and his motorbike to escape to the daily stress of being a lorry driver. He is riding a Harley Davidson Breakout and has a group of about 15 friends who share the same passion for custom cruiser bikes. This is his second family.

Activities, goals and motivations. When he goes on motorbike holidays, Pedro and his friends carry their bikes on a trailer as far as the hotel where they are staying, because they are not willing to make long circular tours. The motorcycles are not designed for touring. They stay around four to five days in a hotel and day by day they decide what tours to make, based on the advice they receive in the hotel. They want to enjoy their time on holiday, therefore they tend to start not earlier than 10 AM, after having a good breakfast. The main motivation for the tour is sharing their escapist experience with friends, making something exceptional, possibly in beautiful landscapes. Sometimes, Pedro thinks that there must be some vanity in his attitude towards motorcycling, especially when he feels satisfied when people look at him riding his Harley. He sometimes even feels envious when he encounters other chopper bikers with beautiful custom bikes. Pedro also pays attention to the way he is dressed: he uses a half helmet and a leather waistcoat. It is a sort of uniform for him, to be part of the family. When interacting with other vehicles, he tends to be quite aggressive. He gets annoyed if other vehicles are slow, or if some cyclist is not keeping to the right of the road. When he travels on his bike, he only greets chopper bikers, because he feels he has nothing to share with other types of bikers.

The Sellaronda tour. Pedro made the Sellaronda tour in August 2016, after a few days of holidays in the Dolomites area. He enjoyed the curves, but was annoyed by the amount of traffic he found on the road. Overtaking was difficult and cyclists were everywhere. He could not stand it. He was particularly annoyed that he could not overtake very often, and he felt he was not riding fast enough, especially in some of the curves. But, it was very relaxing to enjoy the fresh air while travelling with bare arms and the Harley leather gilet.

When he is on vacation with his friends, Pedro likes to ride in a group, and then to comment on the motorbikes seen during the trip once he is back at the hotel. Very often, after the tour, Pedro likes to drink a beer and relax while looking at the wonderful panoramic views, but sometimes he also takes the chance to enjoy the hotel's wellness centre. He needs to calm down before travelling back to his daily life.

5.4.4 The Mountain Lover: Markus

Background. Markus is a 42-year old cyclist living in the city of Bolzano and working as a public employee in the local public administration (Fig. 5.29). His partner, Giulia, is working abroad, so that he can dedicate a lot of free time to cycling during the week.

Activities, goals and motivations. In summer, when he finishes working he usually takes a tour with his Pinarello road bike to switch himself off from work. He starts training in April on the local cycling routes and the more he gets fit, the greater his circular daily tours. It is a matter of challenging his individual skills on the toughest climbs in his region, while at the same time letting his thoughts flow freely in a kind of mental relaxation. It is also a matter of adventure seeking, silence and at the same time, fun. Markus loves mountains and when he cycles on a climb he feels he is part

Fig. 5.29 The mountain lover: Markus (pixabay/Ben_Kerckx)

of the landscape, immersed in the beauty of his homeland. Markus normally cycles with a friend, Andreas, who is less fit than him, but performance is not their main concern when they tour. Climbing a pass together is a great experience, because a shared goal—when achieved—is a great pleasure. Markus and Andreas often take pictures of the passes they climb, mostly when they reach the summit of the pass and stop for a while at the road sign. They have a collection of pictures of pass signs and they add them to a shared album on social media.

The Sellaronda tour. When they started the Sellaronda tour, (it was a cloudy day in August 2016, in Bolzano), they had both taken a day off work to make the experience. Markus had already made the tour with his bike, but Andreas knew the road only from previous visits by car. This is the reason why Andreas was not self-confident enough to reach the Val Gardena Valley on his bike. It seemed to him that the journey was too challenging and the weather too uncertain, so that he decided to reach Selva di Val Gardena by car to wait for Markus there. When they met, Andreas was fresh and Markus was already quite tired, so that their travel rhythm was similar and they could climb the Sella pass side by side for a while. While they were climbing, they discussed friends that they have in common, the hiking tours they did or wanted to do in summer and the huts they went to. They also stopped to take some pictures from a few panoramic points along the road. After a few kilometres, Markus had a more intense pedalling rhythm and dissolved the velo-formation, cycling solo for a while. He enjoyed the silence, the views on the Sassolungo massif and the rhythm of his own pedals and breathing. He reached the summit of the pass earlier than Andreas, so that he could take a quick picture of the pass sign and get off the bike for a while. When he was waiting for Andreas, he was very surprised to see a goat walking in the pass summit area and he took some pictures of it. As soon as Andreas arrived, they both started the descent, because they were afraid that they might not be able to cover all the four passes and get back in time. The descent was very exciting. Not only was it quick, but the view was astonishing. Anyway, soon after they started, they were too focussed on the road to detach their gaze and enjoy the view. They were quite quick, and they overtook a couple of cars while descending, which made them feel the adrenalin of speed. Unfortunately it then started to rain and they were forced to slow down and put on waterproof clothing. The descent was very dangerous. However, it then stopped raining and they could reach Bolzano by car in the evening. They were tired, but very proud of themselves.

5.4.5 The Athlete: João

Background. João is a 34-year old professional mountainbiker from Brazil used to tough training and exciting routes (Fig. 5.30). He is travelling around the world to join mountainbike competitions and his wife—Gabriela—often follows him.

Activities, goals and motivations. João is obsessed by performance, he is used to being very competitive and—even in his leisure time—when he makes a road cycling tour he wants to measure every detail of it. He has a set of devices to monitor

Fig. 5.30 The athlete: João (own elaboration)

performance: two headcams, one GPS tool, one smartwatch and he always downloads the technical features of the route he wants to cover, to be able to ration his energy during the climbs. When he does road cycling tours, he often makes the experience with his wife and with a friend, in a sort of group formation that he—as the only athlete—is leading. Based on the technical features of the road, the steepness and the length of the climb, he decides to lead the group himself or to let his travel companions start, in order to achieve the best results for the group as a whole. João is very ambitious and somehow conceited. When he cycles on a climb, he is focussed on high-level performance. He tries to avoid distractions and be focussed on his muscular activity; sometimes he is so proud of his adventure, that he takes a selfie of himself with his smartwatch. All the pictures and videos that he records with his multiple devices are stored and shared to prove his performance. He is extremely excited by performing well, being fast and overtaking others, because this proves that he is fit and competitive.

The Sellaronda tour. João was doing the Sellaronda tour with his wife Gabriela and his friend Antonio by the beginning of September 2016 in changeable weather conditions. There were a few vehicles on the road, which made him feel safe while cycling and free to use the road space as he liked. The temperature was quite low and João was not used to European climate, so that he was feeling quite cold. But the further he climbed the passes, the more he was enjoying the fresh and pure air of the

Dolomites. He started the tour from Selva di Val Gardena and—after climbing Passo Gardena, Passo Campolongo and Passo Pordoi, he reached the Passo Sella—his last challenge of the day—at around 3 pm. Gabriela was quite cold and João was worried for her, because she had got too light clothes and not enough water to face the last climb. But he believed in her: she had always been too proud to give up. His friend Antonio was also very tired, but was more used to take cycling tours and less sensitive to temperature. He decided to lead the group for about the half of the climb, so that in the last half of the climb João could take the lead for the final rush. At the end of the day, as João was explaining to his friend during the climb, cycling performance is a group work and you must take care of your travel companions. During the four climbs, João was repeatedly calculating his partial and overall performance in terms of speed, kilometres covered and steepness. He was feeling very satisfied of the performance, and felt just as if the body could go on cycling alone, following a sort of natural beat: the rhythm of his pedals. He was only annoyed when he encountered those big and polluting buses, which were interrupting his flow and creating long queues of cars and motorcycles. The last desire he had during the climb was to be enough quick in the descending part, so that he could establish the record of the tour. And he did: he was quicker than 60 km/h—below the road speed limit—and risked to break one of his devices, the headcam. Anyway, before descending, he needed to stop on the pass summit area and take a couple of funny pictures with Gabriela and his friend Antonio. Of course, in those pictures some important objects could not miss: the wonderful landscape, the sign of the pass and the real protagonist of the tour: the bycicle. The great feat they all made was only possible due to the Bianchi bike and this is the reason why it should deserve a prominent position in the souvenir photos to take back home.

5.4.6 Key Findings

Journey experiences on the Sella Pass are *immersive* and *active* experiences, enabling to *escape* from the ordinary life and establish a link with the road and the natural landscapes. Their rhythm is regulated mainly through *speed* and its variations, which mostly depend on the *vehicle used*, on the *individual attitude*, and the other *vehicles encountered*, in turn affecting the emotions felt. Journey experiences are also *eudaimonic* experiences, because the long-term wellbeing generated through them counts often more than the contingent pleasure to ride. This is particularly true for cyclists, who are motivated by the goal to reach the pass summit area, whereas motorcyclists seem to be more motivated by the hedonic purpose of riding. No matter which of the two, journey experiences are *emotionally rich*, and they are mostly positive valenced, notwithstanding the physical effort to accomplish them. From the individual perspective of users, journey experiences are *composite* experiences: they are based on different layers of actions, where the main task of riding is always present, while all other tasks happen in multi-tasking or when vehicles stop. Depending on the individual attitudes, they might also be *performance-* or *leisure-oriented*, both in case of cycling and motorcycling. From a spatial perspective, journey experience are *embedded* experiences, because they are related to the contextual conditions, such as space, time, weather and interactions. These contextual factors seems to affect the emotions felt significantly.

Based on these general hypotheses on travel experiences, four main personas can be designed that embody different attitudes and speed patterns. Since, as mentioned above, speed patterns are related to modal choice, the first differentiating variable is the transport mode. The second differentiating variable, which was visible in both cyclists and motorcyclists, is the attitude towards speed and performance. Therefore, four personas stand out from the analysis: Alberto—the motorcycle tourer; Pedro—the aggressive motorcyclist; Markus—the mountain lover; and João, the athlete. These personas are composite characters based on the features explored in user data collection and represent new— although fictitious—characters to support future policy making, both in the tourism and the transport sector.

5.5 Chapter Summary

This chapter has integrated the previous results presented in Chap. 4 by proposing a micro-analysis of individual second-by-second experiences. It has disaggregated and precisely described the components of journey experiences in the way they occur at individual level; it has presented two cases of motorcyclists and three cases of cyclists that participated in the data collection, highlighting how similar, but also how different experiences in the same space can be. Finally, it has used the personas methodology to transform the thick descriptions at individual level into fictitious characters—the personas—to enable future tourism and transport planning.

Journey experiences are found to be *eudaimonic, emotionally rich escapist experiences*, where individuals, modes and *contextual conditions* are combined to form a unique and *composite* space-time based mix. Speed acceleration and deceleration patterns—together with individual attitudes for leisure or sport—are the most important differentiating factors among participants. They were the criteria to design four personas: the motorcycle tourer (Alberto), the aggressive motorcyclist (Pedro), the mountain lover (Markus) and the athlete (João). These were based on user data at macro and micro level, but were described in narrative form, to facilitate the audience's engagement with the user profile.

Besides presenting individuals, the chapter also presents new possibilities for data-visualisation. For instance, the second-by-second coding stripes resulting from the video parsing and indexing represent a very innovative perspective to analyse an experience, encompassing time, sound and actions. Maps of sensory data are also innovative ways to present emotional engagement in tourism and mobility, and they offer the geographical perspective needed to implement precise policies. A self-reflection about the methods, the data visualisation techniques as well as their limitations will follow in the next chapter.

References

Nielsen L (2013) Personas—user focussed design. Springer, London

Scuttari A, Bassani R (2015) I passi dolomitici: Analisi del traffico e dei suoi impatti e proposta di misure di gestione. [Dolomites' passes. Traffic, its environmental impact and a proposal for traffic management measures]. http://www.dolomitiunesco.info/attivita/i-passi-dolomitici-pubblicato-lo-studio-eurac-commissionato-dalla-fondazione/. Accessed 18 Aug 2018

Chapter 6
Discussion and Conclusion

> *Keep Ithaca always in your mind.*
> *Arriving there is what you are destined for.*
> *But do not hurry the journey at all.*
> *Better if it lasts for years,*
> *so you are old by the time you reach the island,*
> *wealthy with all you have gained on the way,*
> *not expecting Ithaca to make you rich. […]*
> *Ithaca gave you the marvellous journey.*
> *Without her you would not have set out.*
> *She has nothing left to give you now.*
> Konstantinos P. Kavafis (1863–1933; 1911)

Abstract This chapter summarizes the key findings of the dissertation and illustrates its theoretical as well as methodological and managerial contributions. From the theoretical point of view, journey experiences are ultimately interpreted as performances on the move, mobility spaces as their stages. Interactions among infrastructures and individuals are deeply mediated by speed, in turn depending on individual attitude of riders, travel modes and contextual conditions. The strong linkage between individuals and modes enables the theorisation of the notion of *human-vehicle hybrids*, which needs further study in future research. Methodological contributions relate to the measurement of journey experiences in a real-life environment, as well as to the innovative visual representation of empirical results from multiple sources. Managerial implications in terms of tourism product development, road planning and sustainable mobility are valuable for future destination development. Finally, limitations related to the work are discussed and used as opportunities and leverages to improve future research.

6.1 Introduction

The dissertation goals, introduced in Chap. 1 of this work, can be summarised as follows: (a) to fill the knowledge gap on tourist mobility and mobility spaces; (b) to analytically and systematically describe journey experiences in mobility spaces; (c) to explore mobile methods to measure journey experiences using visual, sensory and self-reported data; (d) to design personas of motorcyclists and cyclists to refine and improve traffic management measures encompassing a user-based approach. Overall, to provide new knowledge about the travel segment of the tourism experience, and, of great importance, to find and test new research methodology to explore these areas. This chapter highlights how this goals are met through the dissertation results and identifies limitations and challenges for future research.

6.2 Key Findings

This section summarizes the key findings of the dissertation project, relating them to the dissertation goals and specific aims. The dissertation has explored tourist mobility and mobility spaces through the single and exploratory case study of Passo Sella, Italy, a multi-use pass close to the Dolomites UNESCO WHS, which has high intensity tourist flows and is experiencing a transition towards more sustainable transport solutions.

Through the aggregated and second-by-second analysis of 14 mobile journey experiences—7 cyclists and 7 motorcyclists—the dissertation has developed an innovative methodology to record, describe and analyse actions and interactions occurring in the mobility space of the pass. It has defined a temporal segmentation of the journeys into basic units of meaning: climbing to the summit of the pass, crossing the watershed in the pass area, descending to the valley.

Further, it has identified primary and secondary tasks undertaken by tourists while on the journey, both in a physical sense and using interaction dynamics. For instance, the main tasks relate to driving—in line, solo or in a velo-formation-, while the secondary tasks refer to settings—technology setting, dashboard checks, etc. Secondary tasks were more frequent and lasted longer when riding concentration was lower, e.g. on straight parts of the road or when speed was reduced. Social tasks—both primary and secondary—happened through verbal interactions and non-verbal interactions, as well as through the negotiation of space. These relational dynamics indirectly show more hidden social aspects of mobility, such as: power relations among vehicles, related to the dimension, speed or noise of vehicles, but also the individual needs for personal and use space along the way; group dynamics across users, related to practices of greetings and arranging collective actions and velo-formations on the route.

Ultimately, this dissertation has also investigated the sensory involvement during journey experiences, i.e. the five senses involvement, the heart rate patterns and the rhythmical patterns along the way. A major result from the five senses analysis is that sight and hearing are the predominant sensory aspects for all travellers. They both relate to the main task of driving, and also to secondary tasks, especially for cyclists. A common aspect among cyclists and motorcyclists involving sight is the importance of controlling the own journey and assisting the journey of travel companions. Both cyclists and motorcyclists repeatedly check for the position and the safe condition of their travel companions, be it by using rear-view mirrors or turning to look back. This

6.2 Key Findings

type of visual attention together with the verbal and non-verbal interactions along the way show again how important the group can be for these types of individual travellers. With regard to hearing, motorcyclists can be defined as noise producers who listen to the music of their own engine, whereas cyclists are rather similar to spectators, because their engine is silent and they are more open to the external environment around them, including both the sound of nature and the (possibly disturbing) noise of other vehicles. Hearing and visual attention both contribute to designing the rhythmical patterns of the journey, that results in *polyrhythmic* patterns for cyclists—because they include multiple different stimuli, each one having its own rhythmical pattern—and *arhythmical* patterns (irregular) for motorcyclists, because they follow the patterns of the road and the riding behaviour of the rider, with the influence of other road users' rhythms along the way.

The analysis of average heart rate scores and their temporal development across the journey is a proxy for the dynamics of physical effort and (partially) emotional arousal. In fact, an inverse relationship between speed and heart rate during cyclists' climbs stands for a significant muscular effort, which makes the heart rate increase while their speed decreases. Nevertheless, this relationship can change when descending, because there the emotional arousal related to the thrill of speed can make heart frequency and speed rise together. Concerning motorcycle journeys, it seems that the relationship is always positive, given the limited and constant physical effort in motorcycling. While analysing the self-reported and observed emotional aspects of the journey it becomes clear that the moments where higher physical effort is demanded—those where the heart rate is high—are not necessarily those where negative feelings are experienced. Indeed, happiness and optimism are feelings that some cyclists have associated with the beginning of the tour, when they started to climb the pass. Conversely, negative valenced feelings, such as fear, were related to moments where the physical effort was less prominent and the risk related to driving was higher, particularly in the faster descending part. Therefore, according to the self-reported data, the moment where a rise in heart frequency was registered could both stand for excitement or worry, not always depending on physical effort. Finally, weather and infrastructure conditions, as well as vehicle interactions, seem to affect tourists' perceptions of risk. The emotional reaction to risk taking is interesting to observe across time. Indeed, when participants reported their emotions in cases of dangerous overtaking manoeuvres they were reporting that they felt fear, but when reviewing the video footage they experienced excitement. Similarly, beautiful landscapes, in particular mountains, evoked optimism when they surrounded the participant along the journey, but can evoked loneliness when the journey was finished. Finally, anger seems to be a feeling perceived in relation to other road users, particularly in cases of rude or disrespectful behaviour or by great discrepancies in travel patterns and rhythms (e.g. interaction of cyclists/motorcyclists with big and slow busses).

Based on the key findings mentioned above, some concluding remarks stand out. They are explained in the following subsections, with the purpose of reflecting on the key findings and opening up the contributions of the dissertation project to theory development, methodological innovation and management strategies on tourist mobility.

6.2.1 Speed and Its Variation as the Main Mediator for Actions and Perceptions

In the existing literature on slow travel, slowness (as opposite to speed) was rewarded as a main mediator for tourist experience (Dickinson and Lumsdon 2010). In their view, slow equates to quality time and quality experience (p. 4), as well as positive emotions (p. 139). And the lower the speed, the more intense the experience. In contradiction to this assumption is the desire for, and thrill of, speed (Germann Molz 2009), according to which travellers seek fast journeys and benefit from them, not only from a utilitarian point of view by reaching the destination earlier, but also from a non-utilitarian point of view, being "thrilled" by high speeds.

This dissertation reflects upon these contrasting hypotheses and deepens the analysis of the relationship between speed, experience and emotional arousal. It can be argued based on the selected data that speed depends at least on four factors: the engine power (mechanical or human); road features (steepness, curvature, surface and weather conditions); the rider's behaviour (inclined to or adverse to speed), and finally on other vehicles' actions (with their engines, shapes and drivers). The interaction between rider, engine, other road users and roads produces a certain speed during a certain journey, as well as the possibility or ability to increase and decrease speed across time.

In turn, speed plays a crucial mediating role in the overall journey experience: it regulates individual non-driving actions, it shapes vehicle interactions and it changes perceptions along the way. In case of active drivers, results show that speed influences the amount and the duration of non-driving tasks performed along the journey. Based on sensor data, these tasks are inversely proportional to speed. Moreover, an increased speed seems to reduce the ability to perceive the space around the driver, making that driver become focussed only on the road features, instead of the overall landscape and contextual aspects of the journey. Increasing speed seems to reduce mobility space. Conversely, it also seems that the lower the speed, the broader the space for visual attention and the capacity to grasp details of the landscape, the sounds and the smells around the route covered. Moreover, differences in speeds among road users—both in average terms or in terms of different acceleration patterns—determine variances in travel rhythms, which can in turn cause dynamics of space negotiation (e.g. overtaking, being overtaken, riding in line, etc.) and differences in travel time. Ultimately, but not less importantly, speed variations affect emotional states: they can cause excitement, when an overtaking operation is taking place, but also worry if the perceived control of the vehicle is reduced. Usually, speed variations seem to evoke positive feelings when they are recalled in a post-experience context.

6.2.2 Contextual Conditions, Velo-Formations and Encounters as Crucial Experience Aspects

Contextual conditions such as road infrastructure, road size and design, traffic congestion, weather, temperature, encounters with vehicles, animals or people, have an impact on the perceived experience. These features of the destination, including also other tourists on the move, deeply interact with the individual, and co-create the unique essence of the journey.

To understand this consideration, it might be very interesting to think of the analysed journey experiences and change these features one by one. For instance, the Sella Pass road without sharp curves or with a reduced difference in height between valley floor and summit, would imply diverse speed patterns, increased possibilities for overtaking and thereby changing speed and emotional patterns for travellers. This type of interaction between road space, speed and individuals is particularly perceivable when looking at the travel maps (see, e.g. Figs. 5.4, 5.9, 5.13, 5.19, 5.24) and comparing their colours on linear or curving sections of the road. Therefore, according to the survey results, it seems that the shape of the infrastructure can affect the physical and emotional features of the journey, because infrastructure—together with travel mode and individual behaviour—shapes the rhythm of the journey.

On the other hand, it has been noticed by comparing individual journeys through the video material that the same road crossed during high or shoulder season produces different speed patterns and dynamics of space negotiation among travellers. This can be clearly seen by comparing the interactions of Juan—travelling on August 24th (see Fig. 5.1)—with those of Marco—travelling on September 11th (see Fig. 5.5). The figures show that Juan was mostly climbing the pass with others in line, whereas Marco was riding solo, with different emotional perceptions as a consequence. Similarly to seasonal patterns, weather conditions might also affect congestion in that they encourage a higher number of daily trips if the day is sunny—possibly increasing the number of vehicles around the area and causing more congestion—but on the other hand they imply a decrease in journey speed when it rains, especially for bicycles and motorcycles, as it was seen in the experiences of Peter (see Sect. 5.3.1) and Marco (Sect. 5.2.2). The same patterns are true for the perception of temperature. Cyclists and motorcyclists are particularly exposed to these contextual conditions, because—being in the open air and without a cabin—they are more sensitive and more affected by environmental changes.

Finally, *encounters* with vehicles, animals or people are essential elements of the journey, because they make the experience appear even more unique. The same works for velo-formations, which appear as invisible and plastic vehicles of a variable dimension, made up of many single units linked by the desire to travel as a group. These type of encounters and relationships happen often casually and can represent a positive surprise for travellers. For instance, the encounter with a goat in the pass summit area during the journey of Michael, or the crossing of a deer in the journey of Marco were unique events that no other journey could register in the video footage. Even encounters with other vehicles caused visual interest and emotional arousal, for example in the case of Juan watching other motorcycles along the road. Interactions with other vehicles were also showing power relations in the video footage. For instance, bulky busses were an obstacle for cyclists and motorcyclists (see Sect. 4.4.2), because they prevented them from maintaining their travel rhythm in the journey. On the other hand, the sense of community and the desire to travel as a group worked as a motivator to reach the summit of the pass for cyclists, notwithstanding their differences in fitness and rhythm.

These considerations help recall and enrich the notion of the tourist transport system presented above (see Sect. 2.2.1.3), which is definitely more complex than its constitutional parts—infrastructure, operational services, and travel demand (Mills and Andrey 2002; Rodrigue et al. 2006). Particularly, this dissertation enlarges our understanding of travel demand, which is not simply made up of individuals and their behavioural choices, but is rather based on a set of social practices embedded in space, time and communities. Therefore, to use a metaphor, the transport system does not only allow a *dialogue* between its physical infrastructures and the travel demand through service provision; it rather offers a setting—or to say it in Pine and Gilmore's terms (1999), a *stage*—for an animated discussion between the destination, its constituent attractions and all the individuals (and animals) in that mobility space in a precise time-frame. The mobility space *is* the lived destination. How it is lived depends on multiple factors, but travel *mode* and individual *attitude* are among the most relevant ones. In particular, demand attitudes are as much worth considering as behavioural choices and detailed market information is crucial to design accurate traffic management policies.

6.2.3 Individual Attitudes and Behaviours as Ways to (Re-)Construct Space

If the setting—the stage- is crucial to the experience, the individual is as equally important as the stage. Individual tourists behave in transport systems according to their attitudes and to the technical possibilities enabled by their mode. Their attitude, role and motivation to climb to the top of the pass can be different, and also their behaviour, particularly when it comes to stops and interaction with the landscape or with other vehicles.

Attitudes towards the journey can change the emotional value of the experience. For instance, *tolerance* towards other road users was different among participants. Motorcycles were perceived as disturbing elements by both pedal cyclist Peter and by his travel companion Elias, but—when hearing a loud motorcycle along the way—the first says *"Man muss schon auf die Quälerei stehen! [You have to love this cruelty!]"*, while the second is annoyed and simply complains *"Ach das tut weh! [Ouch, this hurts!]"*. Similar dynamics of rejection were occurring also in the case of motorcyclists, especially when Juan was complaining and feeling angry about encountering too much congestion on the road. *Irony* can also work as a mediator towards a negative emotional reaction during the journey. One example is Gabriel, when he jokes about the fact that he is freezing and transforms a sensation of discomfort into a funny moment for himself and his travel companion.

These examples clearly show how the same actions can provoke different reactions from individuals, with possible consequences for the entire mobility space. For instance, the dynamics of rejection could encourage the selection of a different road to climb for the coming tour, based on the presence/absence of motorcycles. And this could cause—on a later stage—dynamics of adverse selection of users on panoramic roads.

The system logic traditionally used in literature to approach tourist transport seems thereby coherent with the empirical evidence standing out from the dissertation, and it is at the same time enriched by adding details on individuals, their attitudes, motivations, roles and behaviours on the road. In other words, results suggest that all layers of the journey experience—the physical, the social, the sensory and the emotional—have the potential to affect the mobility space and the transport system within a destination and should be taken into account when designing tourism transport policies.

6.2.4 Generalisability of Findings

The findings can provide insightful knowledge for current and future infrastructure planning, as well as for the marketing and management of tourism and transport. As stated in the methodology chapter when presenting case study research (see Sect. 3.2.3), the generalizability of findings beyond the specific case study is not straightforward for single case studies, although it is pursued by making reference to pre-existing theoretical frameworks, with the aim of broadening them. The main theories that support the case study propositions and that were enriched by the research results are: the compositional features of journey experiences found by Delaney (2016) the non-utilitarian nature of travel theorized by Mokhtarian and Salomon (2001); the mediation effect of slow versus fast and motorised versus non-motorized travel modes introduced by Larsen (2001). Findings, as they were presented above, have related to those theoretical frameworks by:

- illustrating the power of speed and its variation as a mediator for individual actions and perceptions,
- analyzing the emotional features related to single (driving and non-driving) actions along the way, as well as
- studying the compositional feature of journey experience in relation to individuals, context, time and space.

This transparent research procedure enables analytical generalization (Yin 2006), thereby ascribing the particular set of results of this dissertation to a more general theory. Notwithstanding this, it is acknowledged here that journey experiences are very place-specific and, therefore, the future replication of the study in other situations might provide stronger support for the theories, thanks to the accumulation of knowledge across different case studies. In fact, the Sella Pass road has some specific local features that can limit the generalisability of findings. For instance, one of the main local factors is the presence of a circular tour of four passes and the presence of a World Heritage Site in the surrounding area. This affects the mix of vehicles and of journey purposes along the Sella Pass road. On the other hand, other aspects of the Sella Pass are common to many other Alpine passes: the climbing and descending patterns, the presence of a sign on top of the pass, the multi-functionality of the pass as a place, the narrow and curvy road and the presence of multiple road users, including cars, bicycles, motorcycles and buses.

Finally, it can be argued that the research findings will prove insightful for other pass roads in the Alpine area, which are interested by intense tourism flows and located in particularly sensitive areas. They can be helpful for the design of traffic management measures on the multiple passes of the Dolomites area (Passo Campolongo, Gardena, and Pordoi), but also to design effective development and tourism marketing policies along other surrounding passes (Passo Costalunga, Passo Stelvio). Additionally, when considering the wider implications of this research, the findings could be tested in different types of roads using the innovative methodology applied on the Sella Pass, to consider and compare other dynamics of interaction, speed and biometric patterns among users. This dissertation consciously analysed multiple individuals in one mobility space. The future consideration of one (or more) individual in multiple different mobility spaces could be crucial to increase the external validity of the research.

6.3 Theoretical Contribution

The main theoretical contribution of this dissertation is to add to our current knowledge and critically reflect upon the construct of mobility spaces, using journey experiences as insights to understand the role of mobility as part of tourism. Three main theoretical contributions emerge from the results previously summarised: a deeper description of the components of a journey experience; a conceptualisation of the notion of mobility space, which includes infrastructures, interactions and individuals; finally, the interpretation of motorcyclists and cyclists as human-vehicle hybrids, i.e. individuals non-detachable from their vehicles.

6.3.1 *Journey Experiences: Performances on the Move*

Journey experiences on panoramic mountain pass roads, interpreted through the lenses of mobilities and experience research, are *moving performances*. While on the move, primary tasks related to driving activities are performed in multi-tasking

6.3 Theoretical Contribution

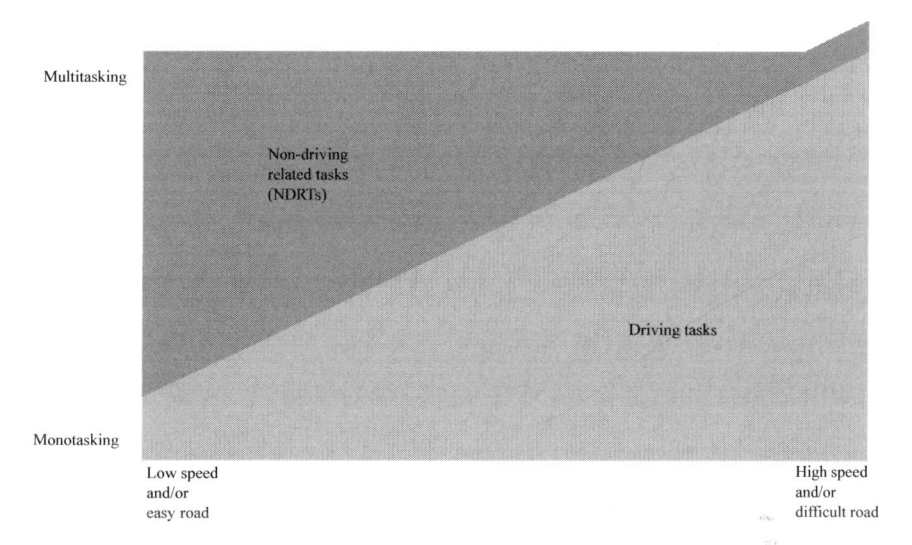

Fig. 6.1 Driving and non-driving related tasks on the move (own elaboration)

with secondary tasks, related to non-driving (and possibly touristic) activities. The more driving is demanding attention to cyclists and motorcyclists, the more they perform routines to keep control of the vehicle and the less attention is dedicated to non-driving tasks. Conversely, when the technical difficulty of riding is low (e.g. in straight parts of the road), or when speed is low (e.g. when the steepness is high for cyclists), more attention is dedicated to the environment, to socialisation and to activities other than keeping control of the vehicle. Figure 6.1 is an attempt to visualise this relationship between road difficulty, speed and number of tasks executed while riding.

Sensory perceptions follow the same pattern of driving and non-driving tasks. As it was mentioned in Chap. 4, the visual analysis showed that participants tend to look at the landscape and perceive external stimuli in the moments when they can detach their eyes from the road. Conversely, when they are concentrated on the driving activity, they tend to prioritize sensory perceptions related to themselves or other vehicles along the road. However, it was noticed that in case there is a very attractive touchpoint along the road (e.g. the "Sassolungo massif"), tourists tend to gaze at it notwithstanding the speed, the road difficulty, the traffic and other contextual conditions, e.g. the weather. Their gazes turn into short and frequent glimpses and sometimes they turn into stops, to take a picture of the touchpoint itself. In these stops induced by landscape beauty, the passive contemplation gains more importance than the active performance. In sum, journey experiences *are* escapist experiences according to Pine and Gilmore's matrix (1999, See Fig. 2.3), because of the *immersion* in the road/in nature and to the *active ride* of travellers. However, sometimes they are blurred with and enriched by moments of contemplation, when the speed is typically reduced or equal to zero and the landscape is particularly eye-catching. Although every performance on the move is unique, several common features stand out. The eudaimonic nature of the climbing experience for cyclist and the more hedonic ride for motorcyclists is found both in individual and aggregated data. This means that cyclists' experience is bipartite (climb vs. descent), whereas motorcyclists' experience is quite continuous, although some minor features are different comparing climbs and descents. The *emotional richness* is a second common feature in journey experiences. Stimuli for emotional arousal are both related to the active ride and performance, but also to moments of space negotiation with other road users, and to landscape contemplation. Therefore, both driving and non-driving tasks are provoking emotions, and these emotions are overall positive. Risk taking while driving is one of the few actions that evokes negative valenced feelings, but these feelings turn into excitement and happiness, once the challenge is overcome. In conclusion, it can be stated that journey experiences are experiences where an individual performance takes place on a specific road, and the road is felt and lived in its unique features, according to mode, speed and individual attitudes. The way the space around the road is perceived is related to multiple factors, as it will be explained in the next section.

6.3.2 The Mobility Space: A Moving Stage

The mobility space was previously defined (see Sect. 2.5.2) as space for travel opportunities and experiences (Canzler and Knie 2002), which relies on existing infrastructures and transportation networks and modes (Lew and McKercher 2006). Evidence collected in this dissertation supported the idea by Pechlaner et al. (2009) that the mobility space is not only related to infrastructure. Rather, it embraces both resources and (driving and non-driving) activities, as well as context-related experiences. The space results in the mediation of individuals' actions, perceptions and interactions while on the move in a specific space-time context. These actions, perceptions and interactions were uncovered before starting this dissertation journey. Thanks to the application of mobile video ethnography in combination with self-reporting and observation techniques for emotion measurement on the move, the mobility space is not a blank space any more. It is a space framed in its boundaries by infrastructure and by perceptions, which are in turn mediated through speed, contextual conditions and social interactions. Some of these constituent elements of the mobility space could be found in the previous literature, but their importance and their contribution to physical, social, sensory and emotional features of journey experiences were still uncovered.

One main aspect learned through this dissertation regards the *similarities in speed, time and sensory patterns* among individuals in a given mobility space. This means that, once the resource and the activity space is given (Pechlaner et al. 2012) and once the travel mode is chosen, some features of the experience seem to be fixed, with relatively low variability ranges. However, data variability seemed to increase when the contextual conditions such as seasonal or daily changes of traffic, weather or

6.3 Theoretical Contribution

temperature affected individual behaviour. This seems to confirm the results obtained by Pechlaner et al. (2012) according to which the satisfaction with the resource space affects the satisfaction with the tourist experience. However, it also highlight how much contextual conditions can mediate the interactions between resource, activity and experience.

Possibly, the pattern of regularity among participants data is facilitated by the *segregation* of the segment of road analysed, which does not enable the making of route choices—there are no alternative crossings—nor does it allow tourist to penetrate into the surrounding natural environment. Tourists are confined to the limits of a pre-defined road path (Edwards and Griffin 2013) and therefore their experiences might be more similar than in other contexts. Notwithstanding this aspect, it should be noticed that in a given setting with limited behavioural choices, experience spaces remain unique. Their uniqueness seems to be generated by the contextual and the relational features of the journey, and by individual (emotional) reactions to them. For instance, the relationship between *speed, happiness and experience* can be further explored through the revealed results. In the previous literature, these three aspects of journeys were connected under the concept of the attractive power of distance (Ram et al. 2013), which makes longer and faster journeys desirable; nevertheless, the single stimuli able to arouse happiness in travellers on the move were not clear. Based on the results of this dissertation, it is possible to hypothesize that speed variations (particularly in overtaking manoeuvres) are the most important stimuli that cause emotional arousal in the participants, both cyclists and motorcyclists. It can also be argued that the "thrill of speed" does not necessarily correspond to a positive-valenced feeling for all participants. Often the sensation is of worry or fear during the journey, but it sometimes turns into happiness in a post-consumption context. At the same time landscape also seems to evoke emotional reactions, but speed tends to reduce the time exposure to landscape—and thereby the sense of happiness and optimism associated to landscape views. What was only partly confirmed by dissertation results is that *aesthetics* (i.e. an aesthetically pleasing activity space) might work as a mediator of speed (Drottenborg 1999). Thus, there was only one case of a cyclist and one case of a motorcyclist who stopped their journeys along the road to take pictures of marvellous panorama views. All other stops seemed organised to rest or to take a souvenir photo that proved the achievement of the climbing goal. In this sense, it could be argued that aesthetics can (but need not) work as a mediator of speed along travel journeys. Conversely, it seemed that framework conditions such as weather or processes of space negotiation were more crucial in determining changes in speed. Indeed, it seems that the mobility space works as a moving stage for interaction processes (*performances*) among human-vehicle hybrids "made up and constructed by both the immaterial and the material" (Delaney 2016, p. 34), which in turn shape the space.

6.3.3 Human-Vehicle Hybrids: Mobile Co-creators of the Mobility Space

A further aspect of the mobility space the dissertation has contributed to regards *the role of transport mode*, and particularly the effects of human-vehicle hybrids on journey experience and—as a consequence—on the perception of space. Based on the results it seems that the presence of the a motor-based engine in the vehicle can contribute to shaping the perception of objective infrastructural features of the road—e.g. steepness and distances—and, as a consequence, that it can change the perception of the temporal units of the experience and introduce moments of pause between climb and descent. This assumption is motivated by the fact that the bipartition of the journey into climb and descent seems much more evident for cyclists, than for motorcyclists. In fact, having a "human-powered engine" means individually facing completely different efforts in the climbing phase, than in the descending phase. In other words, it seems that the road is perceived as flatter for motorcyclists, than for cyclists. Cyclists have a sharper perception of the peak of the pass. And it could be interpreted that the human-powered engine of the cyclists needs to get "fuel" on top of the pass to recover from the effort and regain the concentration for the descent, whereas motorcyclists do not necessarily need this recovery time. The embeddedness of the power engine in the vehicle or "in the traveller" has therefore evident impacts on behaviour and needs during the journey and also on travel rhythm and space perception. Indeed, it can be noticed based on mode that the human powered engine tends to provoke regular rhythmical patterns (at least while climbing), whereas the fuel engine—independently of the steepness—enables patterns of sharper acceleration, allowing arhythmical patterns and sharp effects on soundscapes and sensory perceptions. *Technology* is a third element in between the human-vehicle hybrids, that mainly enables individuals to control their journeys, as well as the journey of travel companions, through an augmented knowledge of the road's features and thereby an increased control on mobility. Travel control happens through routines (e.g. backward looks, dashboard looks) and it might be that—as suggested in the literature—it can help reduce travel stress (Evans and Carrère 1991). In fact, worry was a sentiment that very rarely came out in the self-statements of participants. Finally, as stated by Buscher and Urry (2009, p. 102) "There are various assemblages of humans, objects, technologies and scripts that contingently produce durability and stability of mobility. [...] Such hybrid assemblages roam countrysides and cities, remaking landscapes and townscapes as they move".

In the future, the technology of automation in vehicles might change the balance between driving and non-driving related tasks (Naujoks et al. 2018), opening up for new types of human-vehicle hybrids, especially for motorized vehicles. Having this technological change in mind, it might be possible that non-driving (and possibly even tourism-related) tasks increase their importance in journey experiences, with vehicles taking care of most driving tasks and activating takeover requests in case of risky situations. Notwithstanding these disruptive changes in the transport industry, it is reasonable to think that those transport modes where driving tasks are performed

6.3 Theoretical Contribution

"for the fun of it", like, e.g. motorcycling or cycling, will not work as pioneer markets for this change. Nevertheless, technological innovation—e.g., e-bikes or automatic motorcycles.

6.4 Methodological Contribution

The methodological contribution of the dissertation consists of an increased knowledge about how to measure customer experiences, particularly on the move. The use of mobilities geography and transport geography as co-existing frameworks to understand journey experiences and the implementation of mobile mixed methods based on both psychophysiology and mobile video ethnography, enabled improved data collection and analysis on journey experiences, providing real-time and second-by-second data of different kinds, that were all synchronised and jointly analysed to create more precise, informed and innovative policies at destination level. These place-specific insights have the power to offer evidences that help rethink marketing, road safety and signing policies of a space (Edwards and Griffin 2013), based on consumer behaviour and social practices.

6.4.1 Mobile Mixed Methods in Real-Life Environmental Setting

The use of mixed methods (see Sect. 3.2.2), with a combination of traditional (and somehow simplistic) questionnaires for self-statements and more innovative (and sometimes bulky) technological tools for psychophysiological monitoring helped to enrich the traditional knowledge about customer journeys and add relevant details to known processes in customer experience. For instance, mixed methods enabled the analysis and quantification of (both in frequency and duration) the phenomenon of active and passive overtaking, its spatial consequences, its soundscape and—ultimately—its emotional valence for travellers. Therefore, the methodological innovation relies not only in the use of innovative methods (headcams with sensors, facial action coding systems), but also in their *combination* and *synchronisation*, in order to investigate the convergence of different sources of evidence.

A second innovative aspect in the methodology was the implementation of the above mentioned mixed methods in a *real-life environment setting*, while previous research was focussing mainly on a laboratory environment (Babakhani et al. 2017). The use of field data—which was somehow fundamental to investigate the relationship between mobility and space—required a considerable effort in terms of flexibility, but at the same time strict rules to ensure (at least partial) comparability of cases. One example was the necessity to partially rethink minimalistic aspects of the research design once faced with real tourists making real journey experiences.

This was the case when it turned out that—although the official Sellaronda tour was proposed to tourists in a counter clockwise direction—the majority of them took the tour clockwise. Minimal adjustments to the research design were fundamental in that case, because the availability of previous knowledge on the journey experience was not enough to plan the data collection in every detail. It is recommended for future research that—prior to the data collection phase—qualitative primary data is collected on journeys, in order to set adequate technological tools and research designs that fit the user's needs and behaviours.

Finally, a third methodological contribution regards the combination of a descriptive approach, based on the principles of thick description (Geertz 1973), with a user focussed design approach, based on the definition of personas (Nielsen 2013b). The power of deep contextual analysis is thereby combined with the power of narrative explanation, in order to maximise the contribution to improve aspects of future experiences.

In the coming section a deeper reflection is provided on the mobile video ethnographic method and on the emotion measurement method.

6.4.2 Measuring (Mis)Understandable Experience Worlds: New Insights for Experience Research

The use of mobile video ethnography and bio-sensing by handing action cameras to tourists (the ride-along method) enabled the gathering of an incredibly rich description of the journey experience (Fig. 6.2). It highlighted the great importance of space and time perspectives, as guiding variables to understand a journey. Moreover, it allowed the possibility of locating and recording actions and micro-actions in space and time, to understand the sequence of events characterising one experience, and not only its components. This meant that the use of the video stream helped understand processes, besides describing actions. Among the processes having the most relevant role in the journey experiences are velo-formations: groups of cyclists (or motorcyclists) travelling together and trying to adjust their rhythms in order to stay together during the journey, as if they were imaginary united vehicles. This phenomenon expresses the strong sense of community that cyclists (and motorcyclists) have and the importance of sharing experiences in unique moments with travel companions. Other important passive and active overtaking procedures were found to be associated with peaks in speed and emotional arousal, as well as peaks in sound—the engine for motorcyclists, the wind for cyclists.

The use of a first-person perspective on the headcam, the recording of audio cues and the transcription of dialogues enabled an increase of the embodiment effect for the researcher, which in turn improved the understanding of the mobile worlds of participants. Indeed, they often explain in words or through gestures the way they are experiencing space, the efforts they are facing and the emotions they perceive. Nevertheless, a deeper and critical reflection on the method highlights that this possibility

6.4 Methodological Contribution

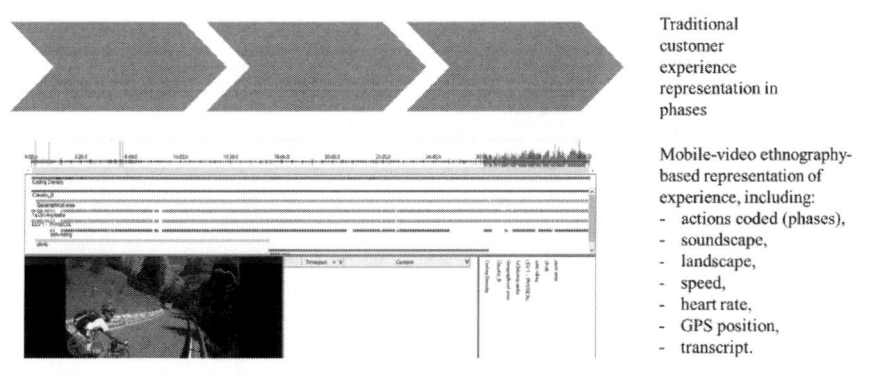

Fig. 6.2 Mobile video ethnography and bio-sensing as tools to enrich experience measurement (own elaboration)

of immersion into the cyclists' and motorcyclists' worlds can be tricky and can also cause misunderstandings: the first-person perspective enables an insight into what the traveller sees, but actually it omits what the traveller *is* and only partially shows what the traveller *does*. This partial view can sometimes produce false interpretations of actions, as explained by the example of Gabriel in Sect. 5.3.1. Therefore, future research should consider multiple perspectives of video recordings on one participant, which would help triangulate views and sharpen the interpretation of actions and processes.

6.4.3 Network Graphs as Tools to Represent Individuals and Journey Features Across Time

In Chap. 4, network graphs have been used to represent the physical, sensory, social and emotional features of journey experiences. These representations are quite innovative and very rich, because they can reproduce subjects, actions and their time duration at a glance (Fig. 6.3). This representation was not available in NvivoPro 11™ software, but it was possible to create network graphs using Gephi software, with a relatively short set of intermediate steps of data cleaning and preparation. NvivoPro 11™ enables the use of queries about coding categories and subjects (cases), and generates pivot tables representing frequency or durations of the categories for each subject. This type of analysis enabled the understanding of travel rhythms, because it helped identify short and frequent actions (routines), as well as long-lasting, but infrequent happenings (happenings). In the dissertation it was decided to highlight the simple duration of each coded action, but there is uncovered potential for future analysis. For instance, the combined analysis of data on frequency, duration and place of non-driving actions can show the moments and the time budgets for each single activity. In turn, such precise information can support policy decisions, such

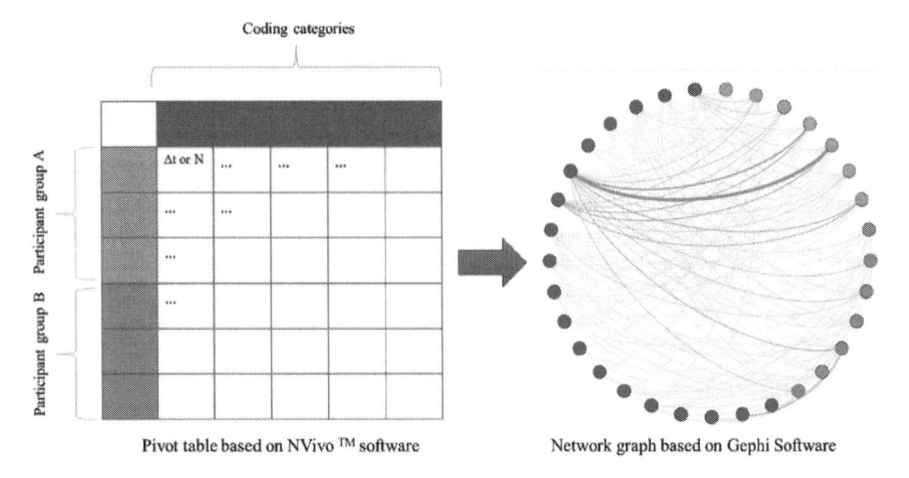

Fig. 6.3 Pivot tables and network graphs (own elaboration)

as—for instance—where to place areas for stopping and parking along the road. On the other hand, the visualisation of NVivo Pro 11™ generated data as network graphs suggests future possibilities for software developers to work on data visualization and valorisation.

6.4.4 From Customer Experience Analysis to Mobility Space Design: The Use of Personas

The application of the personas method in the context of mobilities geography is a third novel methodological aspect of this dissertation. Traditionally, transport demand is studied through transport geography perspectives, that tend to analyse demand as an aggregate (e.g. through O/D matrices) or as a segmented market, without really pursuing a user-centred approach to understand and describe travellers. This dissertation overcomes this traditional way of analysing travel demand, by adding data-driven personas as tools to understand how users decide their final modal choice. Personas enable an understanding (and not only the description) of the user, since they assess their motivations, and the roles and behaviours of individuals with respect to a specific aspect of concern (Nielsen 2013a). The narrative form of description that personas enable can evoke a higher level of empathy, although it is still based on user data. Indeed, the transformation of multiple collected data into a few users is a powerful tool that increases the usability of results in terms of policy and service design. This happens because, similarly to a benefit segmentation assessment (Palacio 1997), it develops "the relationships between site characteristics and benefits expected from a recreational engagement" (p. 236) with respect to a specific service or experience and, therefore, it offers new layers for the interpretation of behavioural change (or resistance to change).

Finally, personas enable users to perform a paradigm shift in travel demand assessment: from a pattern- or mode-based analysis of travel demand, based on traditional O/D matrixes or segmentation patterns, towards an experience-based understanding of users. This paradigm shift helps overcome the normative descriptions of road users based on modal choice and travel pattern, thus enabling a better understanding of demand. Motorcyclists, and cyclists travelling for leisure purposes are not all the same. Among them, there are different niches that can be selected and targeted through specific strategies for niche marketing.

6.5 Managerial Contribution

The managerial contribution of this dissertation consists in an improved understanding of motorcyclists and cyclists in Alpine mobility spaces—and particularly on mountain passes-, in order to refine and improve traffic management measures, which in turn are linked to destination and road management. Results are organised by different outputs—network graphs on physical, social, sensory and emotional feature of journeys, visual representation of processes along journey experiences through encoded videos, finally patterns for sensor data and sensory maps. Each of those outputs offers extensive insights for destination management, road management and traffic management. Ultimately, these data are precious because they help understand how to valorise the mobility space of the destination (i.e. how to shape infrastructure and enrich mobile tourism products), while at the same time preserving safety on the roads and possibly increasing sustainable behaviour.

6.5.1 Cycling and Motorcycling: Mobile Tourism Products to be Enhanced

As far as *destination management* is concerned, the understanding of the linkage between user experiences and mobility space helps identify the appropriateness or need for various product development strategies. For instance, the need and habit of cyclists to stop on top of the pass area to have a rest seems not supported by an adequate set of services for the cyclists, both in infrastructure and in catering facilities. Bicycle racks, fountains with fresh water, sport menus, and other target-specific services might help improve the experience on the pass. A second important aspect, i.e. the importance of velo-formations and dialogues in cycling, could envisage opportunities for a better valorisation of activities on the move, at least in the climbing phase of the journey. For instance, regular tours led by local athletes could not only lead and motivate the velo-formation, but also provide cyclists from far away with novel information on the destination and the landscape, while climbing to the top of the pass. Technology could also help in increasing the information exchange on the destination while travelling, e.g. through augmented reality (AR) tools. AR Apps offer new ways to observe objects, and could be used—maybe through voice messages—to interpret the landscape and mountain peaks around the route in order to facilitate and broaden the immersion process, thereby enriching travel experiences. This aspect of recreational engagement on the move is particularly valuable for cyclists, since motorcyclists are less immersed in the landscape and their distraction might be dangerous for road safety.

A third relevant aspect was the role of accompanying persons, often women and sometimes having different travel rhythms to many men. This aspect relates to the limited participation of women in cycling and motorcycling and is reflected in results surrounding the dissolution of the velo-formation due to different degrees of fitness. To facilitate the access of women into cycling, e-road bikes might be an interesting product to rent at destination level. Indeed, the market penetration of road e-bikes in the road cycle market is less than the one of e-mountain bikes, because they are completely changing the relationship to climbs, but still there are several products on the market that could be tested, particularly for leisure-oriented users similar to "the mountain lover" persona (see Sect. 5.4.3). Of course, such initiatives would not be attractive only for mountain lovers or accompanying persons, but also to new users, as well as to former users that have encountered physical difficulties when climbing passes due to age or disabilities. Electric mobility could also be interesting to test for motorcycle tourers, who were more prone to enjoy the natural environment and had quieter vehicles. These users might be fascinated by new e-based technologies, but on the other hand their trips should be well organised, because they would normally travel with their own bike and on linear patterns. Circular patterns to test e-motorbikes could be opportunities to increase the awareness of noise disturbance and speed limits, as well as designing more immersive experience through additional tourist information while touring. Attempts could also be made with motorcyclists to persuade them to leave the road and explore the landscape in a more profound way. There might be travellers that would enjoy a short and simple itinerary on foot in the pass area. Again, this kind of experience would only be possible if the equipment for cycling and motorcycling—as well as the vehicles themselves—could be storable in secure lockers in the pass area.

Finally, the place where the sign of the pass is placed was perceived by many as an attraction. Valorising this attraction might enrich the moment of picture shooting by providing additional information on the Dolomites, on the mountain peaks and on the UNESCO WHS. Also in this case, augmented reality features could support the interpretation of the pass area, without disturbing the visitors' travel patterns and the landscape views.

6.5.2 Road Planning Based on Micro-Data: An Opportunity for Road Safety

As far as road management is concerned, major insights are provided by GPS based sensor data on speed, which could create a fundamental shift in demand measurement techniques: from traffic counting on site to journey monitoring on the move. In fact, instead of traffic counting stations, offering merely quantitative data based on transits at one specific point of the road—the one where the automatic counting station is installed-, the dissertation has monitored journeys along a wider itinerary, integrating quantitative and qualitative approaches to understand interaction experiences. In fact, the second-by-second georeferenced information on journeys allows the analysis of the road as a continuum—a sort of stage, where interactions among vehicles are performed—and identify processes in space and time, in relationship to road infrastructure and to users. The data-driven representation of maps on individual speed patterns can work as a diagnostic tool (Edwards and Griffin 2013) to discover areas of the road where speed is regularly above limits and eventually provide precious information on how to adjust traffic control systems and infrastructure to seek to guarantee road safety.

The videos collected also show the road condition in general and surface conditions in particular, as well as details of dangerous interactions between vehicles and road at some places. Although the sample is not very big, this kind of information might help road planners to identify possible improvements in terms of road width, safety fences, parking areas, bus stop locations, cycle lanes, etc. Despite the limited use of collected data for road managerial purpose in this dissertation, some critical aspects regarding the pass areas were mentioned, e.g. the difficult interaction between cyclists/motorcyclists and buses, as well as the dangerous dynamics of side-by side riding of cyclists. These critical aspects could be tackled, for instance, through the provision of a public transport service based on smaller vehicles, or through the definition—where possible—of a bicycle lane in the climbing part of the road. All these and similar improvements on road safety would in turn affect the emotional perception of the journey, probably increasing its pleasure and safety.

6.5.3 Transition Management Towards Sustainable Mobility: Evidence-Based Policies and Niche Marketing

According to the existing literature, a transition towards more sustainable forms of mobility can happen by applying leverages both on transport demand and on the system of service provision (Hall 2013). The system of service provision refers to the governance system of the destination (Scuttari et al. 2016), which is usually able to design and implement a balanced mix of carrot and stick management measures (Cullinane and Cullinane 1999; Holding 2001; Scuttari and Della Lucia 2015) to facilitate behavioural change in tourists. *Carrot* measures—incentives to use sustainable forms of transport—include, for example, enhanced public transport services, low-impact mobility device rental, mobility cards, etc.; *stick* measures refer, for example, to traffic restrictions, access tolls and parking fees. To be effective, both types of measures rely on background knowledge about road users and their mobility patterns, which may be available for residents, but is often not given in case of tourists. Therefore, a deeper knowledge of tourist user types and route patterns is very important to design evidence-based and tailor-made traffic management measures on site, that take into account different modes, types of users and specific needs. For instance, the knowledge about vehicle interactions and space negotiation among different vehicles on the road investigated in this dissertation should be taken into account when policy makers plan to enhance public transport services, because the increased bus service should achieve a modal shift towards public transport, but at the same time it should not disturb cycling along the road. In the case of Sella Pass, one possible solution to increase public transport without affecting the cycling experience could be to use smaller busses that enable easier interactions with other vehicles. A second example of evidence-based traffic management policies refers to stick measures, and particularly to access tolls, which are designed to discourage the use of private means of transport, but could be worth paying to get exciting travel experiences and special routes, putting a price tag on the journey experience value. Particularly in the case of an attractive route for motorcycle tours, such as the Sella Pass panoramic road implementation of a toll could have the tricky effect of encouraging more riders, because the road might become less congested and the riding experience therefore better. Therefore, without the definition of specific restrictions for motorcycles, the application of a toll might have the negative side-effect of increasing motorcycle visits and noise significantly, which in turn might disturb pedal cyclists on their way to the pass. These two examples represent only a few of the possible applications of the knowledge produced in the thesis to a policy design and better management of the transition towards sustainable forms of transport.

A second way to facilitate the transition consists of actions directly targeted to road users, e.g. niche marketing to promote sustainable forms of tourism on the move or nudging strategies to foster behavioural change (Hall 2013). Niche marketing is based on market information, but important market insights critical for journey experience development on specific travel modes are still lacking at destination level. The market knowledge produced in this dissertation and the development of two personas for each means of transport are crucial elements in developing a better understanding of the cycling and motorcycling tourist types and encouraging users towards more sustainable practices. For instance, the valorisation of pass roads (and particularly climbs) for cyclists is a very recent idea, which is only at its very early stages in tourism marketing. The Trentino province—one of the two provinces sharing the Sella Pass road—is pioneering the promotion of 23 provincial climbs in a dedicated webpage on the provincial tourism board (https://www.visittrentino.info/it/articoli/outdoor-estate/ciclismo-grandi-salite), but the effective content of this marketing material is still quite poor. Besides the description of the technical features of the climb there are few pictures of the road, many of which do not illustrate the experience value of the climb and its emotional power for cyclists. On the other hand, other media such as travel blogs by web writers or journalists (e.g. http://ladradibiciclette.it/le-grandi-salite-in-bicicletta/) do grasp the individual and emotional value of cycling on passes, involving readers in mythical stories about their passion to cycle. Product and marketing managers in tourism destinations could take advantage of the market insights provided in this thesis to develop more attractive marketing content—in form of journey experiences—that are able to evoke the eudaimonic nature of cycling, its challenges and goals. In this sense, the direct involvement of (professional) cyclists and/or bloggers in the promotion of legendary climbs could help to improve the content quality and its engaging potential. Of course, niche marketing could be used also for other categories of road users, not only to attract them, but also to sensitize them to codes of conduct that respects other road users, e.g. marketing campaigns directed at more "aggressive" motorcyclists in order to decrease their speeds and noise.

Besides carrot and sticks measures, and niche marketing policies, nudging emerges as an alternative strategy to facilitate behavioural change leading to sustainable mobility behaviour. Thaler and Sunstein (2008) pioneered this concept in their ground breaking 2008 book, *"Nudge: Improving Decisions About Health, Wealth, and Happiness"*. Nudging focuses on the intelligent design of an "architecture of choices" that facilitates a change in behaviour, without restricting individual choices and by strategically using cognitive biases (Hall 2013). In the case of noisy motorcyclists, nudging strategies could work to raise awareness on noise problems related to motorcycling and encourage the use of electric engines to ride on the pass road as innovative substitutes for fossil fuel engines. Nudging could be used by offering electric motorcycle rental services at destinations, in accommodation facilities or at the bottom of pass roads, addressing the target of motorcycle tourers and facilitating the choice of a new travel experience. Of course, these initiatives should be designed according to the needs of the users and the thesis provides important market knowledge to define tailor-made products. In the case of linear tours and overnights in different accommodations, they could offer the possibility of picking up the bike at one point and dropping it off at another point after few days; they should provide well-designed and precise information about these opportunities, maybe combined with a meal in a restaurant or a visit to a village. The knowledge produced in the thesis could also help in the design of the tour, because it helps identify the important features of the journey from consumers' perspective (e.g. the presence of a group, the interaction with landscapes, the selection of places where to stop, etc.). An additional nudging strategy could consist in organising a one day or weekend festival to celebrate the route experience with sustainable means of transport, bringing in celebrity riders or cyclists on electric motor bikes, stage heritage pedal bike or heritage bus rides etc.

All these strategies and measures could work as tools to re-define the identity of the road (Delaney 2016), by blending its utility function with its recreational (and therefore non-utilitarian) function. Such a re-definition should encourage those users and experiences that encourage safe and positive interactions among users on the road, minimising negative impacts on other users. Some initiatives have been already implemented, e.g. the #Dolomitesvives project, consisting in a road closure for fuel-based transport on Sella pass on Wednesday of July and August in 2017, combined with a series of initiatives to promote sustainable mobility on the pass road. Nevertheless, these initiatives are in a pioneering phase and need experience and market knowledge to gain transformative power on tourism destinations.

6.6 Limitations

There are several limitations in this dissertation, which mostly refer to the empirical part of the research. They should be interpreted as a sign of the methodological innovativeness of the data collection method, which was tested for the first time in this project. Therefore, on the one hand, the limitations listed in this section might have somehow affected the descriptive findings on physical, sensory, social and emotional features of journey experiences. On the other hand and despite these limitations, the findings uncover many methodological possibilities to measure those customer experiences, providing enlightening suggestions for improvements in future research.

The method of ride-alongs lacked application in tourism and had been deemed to be integrated with bio-sensing data to become more effective (Spinney 2015). This dissertation applied ride-alongs to tourism-related journeys and integrated bio-sensing data, recognising—for the first time—the difficulties and challenges associated with multiple cues of micro-data collected on the move: sensor setting and data quality control, as well as synchronisation with multiple sources of evidence. Overall, the method proved to be effective, but labour-intensive and the number of journeys that could be gathered was limited by the number of headcams and add-on devices available, as well as by the overall research (monetary and timely) budget. Moreover, the attitude towards action cameras and the habit to use them was found to affect the willingness to participate in video ethnographical research, possibly determining some distortion in the recruitment procedure. Finally, video material was deemed as very useful to describe reality, but it was found that it was weak in presenting an understanding of the cognitive interpretation of the real. In the coming sections, these aspects are addressed in a deeper detail.

6.6.1 Sensor Setting, Data Quality Control, and Synchronisation

The conduct of the research in a real-life environment and the involvement of real tourists was definitely a strength of this research, but caused several limitations in the data collection process. A first aspect regarded the setting of sensors and cameras and their control over the journey. In fact, the setting was done according to a checklist by the researcher, but—even if cameras and sensors were working perfectly at the start—once the cyclists or motorcyclists started their journey, the researcher lost

6.6 Limitations

control over the settings and the proper work of the sensors. Indeed, the devices chosen for this research lacked the possibility to have remote control by the researcher during data collection; therefore the data quality could be checked only too late, when the journey was over. This meant significant extra-work, because seven journeys additional to the fourteen analysed could not be used due to the lack of sensor data or very poor quality data. For some participants sensors only worked intermittently, collecting lower quality, but still usable, data. The difficulties in sensor data collection was related both to the real-life environment on the move (e.g. vibrations, speed, sweating, etc.), that created non-optimal conditions to collect primary data, but also linked to technological aspects, such as the proper synchronisation of the add-on device with the corresponding mobile phone. With regard to this last aspect, in the test phase of the research it was planned to hand out only the action camera and add-ons to participants, while using their mobile phone to synchronise video and sensor data through a dedicated App. Nevertheless, after a few trials it became clear that participants neither had the time nor the patience to download an App and synchronise devices, although the whole procedure lasted only a few seconds. Moreover, the use of participants' mobile phones made the overall setting dependent on their phone's setting, possibly affecting data collection standards. Therefore, it was decided that the whole setting process, including the dedicated mobile phones, had to be completed in advance to ensure a smooth preparation procedure and good data quality. It was therefore decided to buy two mobile phones—each associated to one action camera and add-on—that were handled out as a package to participants.

A second aspect regards the synchronisation of video and sensor data with post-experience measurement of emotions through observation techniques. This synchronisation happened manually at the moment when video elicitation and facial action coding was performed, because there was no technological device available to automatically couple the video footage of the journey with the SHORE™ facial action coding data. Such synchronisation, which was manually done based on a third video recording of both the video footage during video elicitation and the participants' faces, was a delicate operation and the risk of lack precision in synchronising facial reactions with video happenings was always present. This is the reason why the second-by-second analysis of facial reactions was very time consuming and it was often only possible for parts of the video sequences where the manual synchronisation worked properly. At the time of the research design, in theory this difficulty could already have been overcome by using an automatic synchronisation system developed by the Fraunhofer Institute for Integrated Circuits and the enterprise for market research GfK (https://www.iis.fraunhofer.de/en/pr/2012/0718_gfk_emo_scan.html), but unfortunately this innovative system was not available for research purposes. For future research, it is recommended to work with this enhanced version of the SHORE™, because it would speed up the process of analysis, ensure more precise results and a larger amount of data processing.

6.6.2 Research Participants, Travel Companions and the Researcher

An additional reflection is worth mentioning with regard to participation in video ethnographic research. As already noted previously (see Sect. 3.4.2), this dissertation unfortunately appears as a male-only research piece. This is partly due to the small population of female motorcyclists and cyclists, partly to the fact that women tend to be new riders and are, therefore, less frequently riding in the steep and challenging Dolomites' pass roads and, even if doing so, they seem to be less-self-confident than their accompanying men and less willing to participate in video-based research. Indeed, there was only one case of a velo-formation with a woman—the wife of participant 2B Gabriel-, but she was not willing to wear the camera and participate in the research. Even in the recorded videos, the women riding a bike met along the journey are very few, confirming that the female community of cyclists and riders is rather small. Nevertheless, the video collected some information about Gabriel's wife's journey, showing different travel rhythms in the climb but similar behaviour on the pass area. Future research in male-dominated sport and recreational activities on the move should better address the gender issue at the moment of selecting the recruitment strategy, to increase the involvement of women as much as possible. Research addressing women-only cycling or motorcycling communities might also be interesting in the future, but methods should be carefully selected in order to maximise females' participation in research. One possible way of overcoming this limitation might be to work based on autoethnography (Adams et al. 2015), i.e. using the personal experience of the researcher as a source for self-reflection. This method was considered, but not used in this dissertation because, as mentioned in Sect. 3.2.1, the researcher could have only practiced autoethnography on motorcycling experiences, and not on road cycling experiences, due to the lack of specific athletic preparation. Nevertheless, it should be acknowledged that the fact of practicing motorcycling and cycling on the road and the experience of having covered the Sella Pass journey many times on the personal motorcycle during the data collection phase—although not in a velo-formation with the participants—might have enhanced the understanding of the route. As stated in Sect. 3.2.1, this active participation might have partly exercised some kind of control or influence on the knowledge produced. This means that the female perspective of the researcher is somehow included in the multiple understandings and realities of the journey experience on Sella Pass, and that the understanding of the motorcycling experience might be enriched or somehow influenced by the personal experience of the researcher (Fig. 6.4). This personal interpretation layer is perceived as additional and not distortive of the critical realist way of producing knowledge and is thereby to be taken into account as part of the research design.

Fig. 6.4 The researcher (own elaboration)

6.6.3 Methodological Limitations and Future Challenges in Mobile Video Ethnography

A final reflection might include the methodological limitations of video material used in ethnographic research, i.e. the partial understanding it offers on the relationship between infrastructures, interactions and individuals on the road. It was noted in the analytical process that cognitive aspects of the journey experiences, e.g. motivations to take actions or to interact with other road users or local infrastructure, are not directly derivable from the audio-visual material. A typical example to understand this limitation might be the stop that almost all cyclists made on the pass summit area. The stop was combined with some picture taking by the sign of the pass, but the reason to stop was more than picture taking. Only through the self-report questionnaires was it possible to understand that some cyclists stopped to regain the concentration needed to focus on the descent. Such information is not derivable from the video, because videos show actions and interactions, but they do not explain meanings. The researcher must use (self-)reflection to interpret actions and reconstruct meanings. To facilitate this interpretation process and minimise bias, the collaboration of participants is crucial and thereby the integration of the self-report questionnaire in the research design was very important. In fact, self-report questionnaires offered additional layers to interpret actions from a cognitive perspective, especially because they deliberately asked for a description of moments when sensory perceptions or emotional arousal happened. Such qualitative material was very precious in understanding dynamics of space negotiation, interaction and mobility along the journey. Probably a qualitative interview after the data collection and video elicitation phase might have been even more effective in helping self-reflection, interpretation and knowledge creation. Therefore, for future research it is recommended to find effective methods to involve research participants in the knowledge creation phase after data is collected (Pink 2007), although their limited time budget in the destination might make this operation difficult.

6.7 Chapter Summary

This chapter provided an overview of the key findings of the dissertation, its theoretical as well as methodological and managerial contributions. Moreover, it has discussed the limitations of the work, using those limitations as opportunities and leverages to improve future research using visual ethnographic methods in tourism and mobility.

Key findings helped to design the mobility space as a stage of unique *interactions* among *infrastructures* and *individuals*. These interactions are described through rhythmical and emotional patterns. Speed variations (more than speed itself) and human-vehicle hybrids play a key role in shaping the emotional perception of the journey. In the case of active riders, speed also affects the perceived broadness/narrowness and richness/poorness of the mobility space, because the higher the speed, the more the traveller is staring at the road and orienting his/her sensory attention to the driving tasks. Findings also highlight the importance of contextual conditions—infrastructure shape, weather, seasonality, and encounters—in shaping the rhythm of the journey, which is in turn influenced by the contextual rhythm or shaped by the vehicle, according to the mode used. Finally, individual attitudes are rewarded as unique and subjective mediators of spatial interactions and perceptions, so that the same event can produce contrasting emotions even in two travel companions on the road.

The theoretical contribution of the dissertation thereby refers to the interpretation of the transport system as a stage for (inter)actions and perceptions that occur among human-vehicle hybrids (more than among vehicles or people alone). The paradigm shift from mode-based descriptions of experience towards user based descriptions is crucial to understand not only the physical displacement (flows), but also the experiential value (emotions) of tourist mobility. *Infrastructures*, *interactions* and *individuals* in their unique and context-specific features can, therefore, work as the crucial elements in the mobility space, whose spatial dimension, individual perception and emotional power is related to speed, its variations, and to travel rhythms.

The methodological contribution of the thesis relates to the innovative use of mobile mixed methods in a real-life environmental setting, integrating mobile video ethnography with traditional surveys for self-reporting of emotional arousal and innovative techniques for facial action coding. This mix of methods enabled a thick description of journey experiences—illustrated through network graphs and individual coding schemes—and a deeper interpretation of the mobility space—based on visual, sensory and emotional data. It further enabled the novel creation of user-based personas for future transport planning.

The *new knowledge* produced about the mobility space and through innovative methodologies highlighted many potentials for mobilities research to contribute to managerial issues related to tourism, transport, and transport as an integral part of tourism. Firstly, the understanding of the key features, actions, interactions and meanings of travel journeys can support the creation of tailored niche products for cycling or motorcycling tourists; secondly, sensory data collected all along the road can support policy-making in the field of road safety, e.g. to control speed or adjust dangerous sections of the road; thirdly, market knowledge on cycling and motorcycling can help encourage and guide sustainable behaviour, changing unsustainable practices, using the leverages of traffic management measures, niche marketing or nudging strategies.

Several limitations stand out when reviewing the data collection process. Among them, the most relevant refer to the difficulty of remote control by the researcher while measuring travel journeys using the ride-along technique; the challenge of synchronising multiple sources of evidence; the difficulties in enhancing the participation of women and managing the individual perceptions of the researcher as (influencing) inputs for self-reflection along the research; finally the (partial) representation of the lived experience through video material.

References

Adams TA, Jones SH, Ellis C (2015) Autoethnography: understanding qualitative research. Oxford University Press, Oxford

Babakhani N, Ritchie B, Dolnicar S (2017) Improving carbon offsetting appeals in online airplane ticket purchasing: testing new messages, and using new test methods. J Sustain Tour 25:955–969

Buscher M, Urry J (2009) Mobile methods and the empirical. Eur J Soc Theory 12:99–116. https://doi.org/10.1177/1368431008099642

Canzler W, Knie A (2002) "New Mobility"? Mobilität und Verkehr als soziale Praxis. Politik und Zeitgeschichte B

Cullinane S, Cullinane K (1999) Attitudes towards traffic problems and public transport in the Dartmoor and Lake District National Parks. J Transp Geogr 7:79–87. https://doi.org/10.1016/S0966-6923(98)00027-1

Delaney H (2016) Walking and cycling interactions on shared-use paths. Bristol

Dickinson J, Lumsdon L (2010) Slow travel and tourism. Tourism, environment and development. Earthscan, Washington D.C

Drottenborg H (1999) Aesthetics and safety in traffic environments. Unpublished doctoral thesis, School of Architecture, Lund Institute of Technology, Lund

Edwards D, Griffin T (2013) Understanding tourists' spatial behaviour: GPS tracking as an aid to sustainable destination management. J Sustain Tour 21:580–595. https://doi.org/10.1080/09669582.2013.776063

Evans GW, Carrère S (1991) Traffic congestion, perceived control, and psychophysiological stress among urban bus drivers. J Appl Psychol 76:658–663

Geertz C (1973) Thick description: toward an interpretive theory of culture. In: Geertz C (ed) The interpretation of cultures: selected essays. Basic Books, New York, pp 3–30

Germann Molz J (2009) Representing pace in tourism mobilities: staycations, slow travel and the amazing race. J Tour Cult Chang 7:270–286

Hall CM (2013) Framing behavioural approaches to understanding and governing sustainable tourism consumption: beyond neo-liberalism, "nudging" and "green growth"? J Sport Tour 21:1091–1109

Holding DM (2001) The Sanfte Mobilitaet project: achieving reduced car-dependence in European resort areas. Tour Manag 22:411–417. https://doi.org/10.1016/S0261-5177(00)00071-6

Larsen J (2001) Tourism mobilities and the travel glance: experiences of being on the move. Scand J Hosp Tour 1:80–98. https://doi.org/10.1080/150222501317244010

Lew A, McKercher B (2006) Modeling tourist movements. Ann Tour Res 33:403–423. https://doi.org/10.1016/j.annals.2005.12.002

Mills B, Andrey J (2002) Climate change and transportation: potential interactions and impacts. In: The potential impacts of climate change on transportation (summary and discussion papers). https://climate.dot.gov/documents/workshop1002/workshop.pdf. Accessed 5 Jan 2018

Mokhtarian PL, Salomon I (2001) How derived is the demand for travel? Some conceptual and measurement considerations. Transp Res Part A Policy Pract 35:695–719. https://doi.org/10.1016/S0965-8564(00)00013-6

Naujoks F, Befelein D, Wiedemann K, Neukum A (2018) A review of non-driving-related tasks used in studies on automated driving. In: Advances in human aspects of transportation. AHFE 2017. Cham, pp 525–537

Nielsen L (2013a) Personas. In: Soegaard M, Dam RF (eds) The encyclopedia of human-computer interaction, 2nd edn. Aarhus, Denmark

Nielsen L (2013b) Personas-user focussed design. Springer, London

Palacio V (1997) Identifying ecotourists in belize through benefit segmentation: a preliminary analysis. J Sustain Tour 5:234–243. https://doi.org/10.1080/09669589708667288

Pechlaner H, Herntrei M, Kofink L (2009) Growth strategies in mature destinations: linking spatial planning with product development. Tour Int Interdiscip J 57:285–307

Pechlaner H, Pichler S, Herntrei M (2012) From mobility space towards experience space: implications for the competitiveness of destinations. Tour Rev 67:34–44. https://doi.org/10.1108/16605371211236150

Pine BJ, Gilmore JH (1999) The experience economy, Updated edn. Harvard Business Review Press, Boston, Mass

Pink S (2007) Doing visual ethnography. SAGE Publications Ltd, London

Ram Y, Nawijn J, Peeters PM (2013) Happiness and limits to sustainable tourism mobility: a new conceptual model. J Sustain Tour 21:1017–1035. https://doi.org/10.1080/09669582.2013.826233

Rodrigue J-P, Comtois C, Slack B (2006) The geography of transport systems. Routledge/Taylor & Francis Group, London and New York

Scuttari A, Della Lucia M (2015) Managing sustainable mobility in natural areas: the case of south tyrol (Italy). In: Orsi F (ed) Sustainable transportation in natural and protected areas. Routledge/Taylor & Francis Group; Earthscan from Routledge, London, New York, pp 99–114

Scuttari A, Volgger M, Pechlaner H (2016) Transition management towards sustainable mobility in Alpine destinations: realities and realpolitik in Italy's South Tyrol region. J Sustain Tour 24:463–483

Spinney J (2015) Close encounters? Mobile methods, (post)phenomenology and affect. cultural geographies 22:231–246. https://doi.org/10.1177/1474474014558988

Thaler RH, Sunstein CR (2008) Nudge: improving decisions about health, wealth, and happiness. Yale University Press, New Haven, CT

Yin RK (2006) Case study research: design and methods. In: Applied social research methods series, vol 5, 3rd edn. Sage, Thousand Oaks, California (Nachdr.)

Chapter 7
Outlook

> *In this bright future you can't forget your past.*
> Bob Marley(1945–1981, 1974)

Abstract This chapter illustrates some avenues for future research in the mobilities and tourism research fields. Methodological innovation using mobile visual methods and bio-sensing tools is rewarded as a unique chance to improve existing data collection strategies. Collaborative patterns between these (quantitative and qualitative) research methods can represent frontiers for future research in the tourism field, providing enlightening perspectives on tourists' (journey) experiences. Nevertheless, ethical issues related to the use of these methods should be carefully taken into account, to avoid privacy concerns and ensure participants' formal consent. The transformative power of tourism is finally assessed, both in changing reseach approaches and societies, with the aim at enabling a more holistic and sustainable development path.

7.1 Introduction

Reflecting on the research findings in a theoretical and managerial context, and critically thinking about the novel methods implemented for this research (Chap. 6), particular avenues for future research have become apparent. In concluding this dissertation, suggestions for future research are presented. A special focus is set on the potential for integrating quantitative and qualitative research methods, as well as traditional and innovative data collection and processing strategies. Further, a reflection on ethical issues is reported, to encourage a responsible use of data. Finally, the power of tourism in fostering transformative processes in individuals, societies and science is highlighted, with particular attention to issues of (journey) experience design and transdisciplinary research.

7.2 Methodological Prospects for Future Research

This dissertation has explored and tested some of the methodological prospects that are likely to be promising and rewarding for future tourism research, i.e. mobile and psycho-physiological methods for emotion measurement and visual ethnographic methods for experience description. They are driven by the mobilities and experience economy turn (Pine and Gilmore 1998; Sheller and Urry 2006) and offer new tools to grasp aspects of tourism that were hardly explicable before. Their introduction is definitely facilitated by the digitalisation shift, that helps in the design of smart tools and computer-based mechanisms to measure and study intangible features of tourist experiences, such as, in this case, speed, interactions or emotions. It can be argued that the introduction of such novel methods could cause a methodological shift in consumer behaviour research and literature, from aggregate survey-based data to individual micro-data, from quantitative and positivist research towards more qualitative and constructivist research, or in other words from representativeness and objectivity towards deepness and subjectivity. Nevertheless, the introduction of these new methods in the tourism field should not be interpreted as an alternative approach for knowledge production, because tangible and intangible elements are so deeply interrelated and amalgamated in tourism that they cannot be detached one from the other. Therefore, traditional and innovative methods should be seen and employed as complementary (and not contradictory) to traditional research. Their integration around a mixed method strategy should be always considered as an alternative approach to a uniquely quantitative or qualitative research design, particularly when investigating the multi-faceted nature of tourist experiences. Quantitative-qualitative complementarity is also crucial in the case of transformative processes in sustainable tourism research, because it is more inclined to provide insights for the promotion of societal change, the management of social desirability, the triangulation of stakeholders' perceptions and the inter-disciplinary cooperation (Molina-Azorín and Font 2016).

This dissertation, by integrating the qualitative research angle of mobilities geography into the predominantly quantitative-based research field of tourist transport geography represents a concrete example of mixed methods for tourist experience assessment, which at the same time enables bridging disciplinary boundaries *and* provides managerial implications and ideas for transformative processes towards more sustainable forms of tourism. Such an interdisciplinary approach based on mixed methods could be explored also in areas of research other than tourist mobility. For instance, one possible field of further application might be that of hospitality, where the tangible assets of infrastructure are not detachable from the intangible aspects of host-guest relationships (Nordhorn et al. 2018). And, while the present research is on transport planning, a similar application to the hospitality industry might influence destinations' architecture and—at the same time—users' experience and comfort perceptions in buildings. As clearly revealed in this research, interdisciplinarity often requires quantitative-qualitative complementarity; the tourism research of the future now has the chance to design new paths to facilitate this integration.

7.2.1 Mobile and Bio-Sensing Methods to Understand Tourist Transport Systems

Mobile and bio-sensing methods represent one of the promising methodological prospects for future tourism research: They are crucial to the understanding the sensory, emotional and kinaesthetic aspects of people (Law and Urry 2004; Büscher et al. 2011) and they are substantially facilitated by technological innovations such as action cameras and portable sensors, which enable the investigation of phenomena happening *on the move* (Spinney 2015). As highlighted by Büscher et al. (2011), through the mobile ethnographic investigation of journeys it becomes evident that movement—and mobility in general—is not (only) subject to norms, but rather generates spaces—just like single moves generate a game: "by immersing themselves in the fleeting, multi-sensory, distributed, mobile and multiple, yet local, practical and ordered making of social and material realities, researchers gain an understanding of movement not as governed by rules, but as methodically generative" (Buscher and Urry 2009). As explained above, this Lefebvrian perspective of socially constructed space (Lefebvre 1991) offers an additional, but not substituting layer to interpret tourist transport systems. In fact, the traditional elements of transport systems driven from transport geography are enriched by the innovative elements analysed through mobile methods. Mobile methods provide *different* data types to understand tourists' mobility and, therefore, they need to work along with (and not instead of) the more traditional survey-based approaches.

7.2.2 Visual and Psychophysiological Methods to Investigate Tourist Experiences

A second set of promising methodological prospects in tourism research relates to psycho-physiological and visual methods (Rakić and Chambers 2012a; Scuttari and Pechlaner 2017). Similarly to mobile and bio-sensing methods, psycho-physiological and visual methods provide *different* information on tourists and their inner perception of experiences. This kind of qualitative information is not to be interpreted as objective and should be accompanied by participants' cognitive interpretations and researcher's self-reflection, to valorise the power of psycho-physiological and visual research in generating market information.

As argued by Rakić and Chambers (p. 4–5), "much of tourism is about images", therefore images are precious at the moment of understanding tourism-related phenomena and in presenting tourism-related results. Additionally, as explained above, tourism research is often an interdisciplinary research field: images have the power to fit different disciplinary backgrounds, facilitating the bridging of disciplinary approaches. Visual methods in tourism research can refer to the analysis of secondary or primary sources, but they can be used also to create data based on elicitation techniques. This dissertation relies on primary data sources and uses them as elicitation material, in combination with facial action coding systems. It also produces visual outputs, in the form of video stills and video clips that enable a better understanding of results. This multiple use of visuals as sources, stimuli and outputs of tourism research is novel in the tourism field and has a high potential to create new knowledge in future research, as well as to better convey textual knowledge already produced. Similarly to what has been previously said about mobile and bio-sensing methods (see Sect. 7.2.1), visual methods should be seen as complementary methods to uncover unknown aspects, rather than novel methods to substitute the traditional ones. Embodiment, rhythm or sounds are just a few examples of the issues that textual research fails to grasp (Scarles 2010), while visual research succeeds in recording these features. Video-based visual research using mobile video ethnography as a methodological framework enables not only to explore sight as the sensory experience of participants, but also to integrate sound patterns, as well as verbal interactions possibly describing other types of perceptions. Since sight was rewarded in this dissertation as one of the most important senses for tourist experiences on the move, together with hearing and sounds, it can be argued that video-based ethnographic research represents an innovative frontier for future tourism research. Looking back at Carneiro et al.'s (2015) paper on tourists' perceptions of rural landscapes, so much more could now be learned using the modern methods outlined above. Carneiro et al. (2015, p. 1229), noted then that "[l]andscape is not just what can be seen. It is what can be heard (or not heard), it is about the smells and the scent of the countryside." But additional richness, with valuable marketing and landscape conservation detail, could have been added to the traditional interview gathered material acquired on field work undertaken just four years ago.

Moreover, the relationship between what is seen/heard and what is felt is explicable using video-elicitation techniques, that help recall past experiences and facilitated the sensation of embodiment while watching video material. The combination of psycho-physiological methods for emotion measurement with video elicitation techniques increases the power of visual methodologies for tourism research, specifically because—through computer-based analytical tools such as SHORE^{TM}—it might enable the testing of the emotional patterns related to one specific experience not only on research participants, but even on a wider community of tourists or potential tourists—taking into account the related ethical issues. Regarding mobility research, sound was found to be a relevant element of the tourist experience for motorcyclists. Future research could focus on the capacity of sound—detached from visuals—to evoke positive feelings, or to recall a travel experience. To conclude, it is argued that visual, sensory and emotional data can represent together the new prospects of experience research in tourism.

7.2.3 Ethical Issues Related to Bio-Sensing, Psychophysiological and Visual Methods

Notwithstanding their innovativeness and power, bio-sensing, psycho-physiological and visual tools and data raise some ethical concerns, both in the academic field and in the general public. Ethical issues arise mainly in the field of visual research and when using emotional decoding software based on visuals.

As it is argued by Prosser et al. (2008), the ethical behaviour of researchers should be guided by three principles: moral beliefs, the ethical standards of the scientific community and legal regulation frameworks. All these three aspects should guide the decision-making process of data collection, keeping in mind that what is legal is not necessarily (enough to be) ethical. While moral beliefs are individual evaluations of what is right and wrong according to personal values, the general principles for research ethics refer traditionally to "The European Code of Conduct for Research Integrity" and they are: reliability, honesty, respect and accountability (ALLEA - All European Academies 2017). Additionally, the Economic and Social Research Council (ERC)—a major founder of social science research in the UK—suggests six key principles for ethical research (Economic and Social Research Council 2015):

- Research participants should take part voluntarily, free from any coercion or undue influence, and their rights, dignity and (when possible) autonomy should be respected and appropriately protected.
- Research should be worthwhile and provide value that outweighs any risk or harm.
- Researchers should aim to maximise the benefit of the research and minimise potential risk of harm to participants and researchers. All potential risk and harm should be mitigated by robust precautions.
- Research staff and participants should be given appropriate information about the purpose, methods and intended uses of the research, what their participation in the research entails and what risks and benefits, if any, are involved.
- Individual research participant and group preferences regarding anonymity should be respected and participant requirements concerning the confidential nature of information and personal data should be respected.
- Research should be designed, reviewed and undertaken to ensure recognised standards of integrity are met, and quality and transparency are assured.
- The independence of research should be clear, and any conflicts of interest or partiality should be explicit.

In the case of visual research, the main concern is that there is no room to preserve the anonymity of the people depicted (Rakić and Chambers 2012b), who are recognizable on pictures and recordings. Namely, pixeled images, even though they could preserve privacy, would mostly destroy the effectiveness of visual methods (Prosser et al. 2008). To overcome this critical aspect, a formal consent is required from participants to have their data collected, shared among researchers and published in scientific publications or online. Research ethics are also influenced by and necessarily must fulfil the legal regulatory norms, which in the case of the Italian law is related to the EU General Data Protection Regulation (UE Regulation 2016/679)—which also introduces the need for an explicit formal consent to use personal data—and partially admits the freedom from copyright issues when using images for scientific and pedagogical purposes (Art. 70, National Law 633/1941). It should be noted here that regulatory norms often represent the minimum requirements to be fulfilled, but not necessarily ensure ethical behaviour, especially in visual research.

For instance, the use of cameras without the storage of recordings is formally allowed when using facial action coding systems. With regard to this issue, a newspaper article appeared in the German newspaper "Die Zeit" in February 2017 (https://www.zeit.de/2017/08/unternehmen-software-gefuehle-analyse) titled "Sie blicken in dein Herz [They look into your heart]", critically discussed the ethical and privacy issues related to the use of affective computing and emotional decoding, making reference also to the software SHORE^{TM} and its use in the retail industry. It was argued that emotional decoding programmes could potentially become dangerous instruments for consumer manipulation, because of the lack of consumers' formal consent to data processing. This lack of consent is allowed because emotional decoding programmes, when placed in shops or public spaces, do not work with individual-based data—for which a formal consent is necessary. They measure metadata related to aggregate emotions only—without needing formal approval. This trick enables users to get round the system of existing regulatory norms about privacy, and collect precious data on consumers' feelings and emotions without asking permission. For instance, SHORE^{TM} was certified to conform with German General Data Protection Regulation, based on the fact that the image data collected by the camera accessed by SHORE^{TM} is discarded and anonymized as soon as it is turned into figures to be analysed, with no possibility to be traced back to individuals. Notwithstanding the formal fulfilment of the existing regulatory framework for data protection, it should be considered that a software like SHORE^{TM} not only process aggregated data, but they can also instantly turn the collected figures into inputs for the selection of automatic responses e.g. individually-targeted advertisements if a camera with SHORE^{TM} is placed on a screen. This allows the use in open spaces—e.g. shopping malls—of what is already made on the internet: tailor-made advertising and monitoring of the effectiveness of the advertisement. The power of this tool goes so far that it can help to shape empathetic machines—e.g. collaborative robots—that can interact with human beings based on their perception of emotional responses measured through the software.

Acknowledging the delicate issues related to the use of visuals and emotion decoding in this research, a formal consent form was prepared for research participants and an update of it was sent via email at the end of the research, when there were minor changes in the Italian regulatory framework on privacy. The form was signed by research participants and ensures their agreement to use, process, and share and publish their data (see Appendix). Moreover, it was decided to share the video clips with the participants in the form of a thank-you for their participation in the research, so that they were aware of the material used for research purposes. Finally, names were substituted by pseudonyms and facial images were avoided as much as possible, in order to preserve private identities as much as possible. The only exception relates to participant 5B, where multiple angles of video recordings were discussed and video stills of the face of the participant were included with the participant's explicit consent (see Figs. 3.6, 4.11, 4.16, 5.15, 5.16 and 5.30). This ensured not only the fulfilment of regulatory frameworks and norms, but also compliance with the ethical standards of the research community and individual principles for ethical research. A last issue to be considered regards the fieldwork context. As remarked by Pink (2007, p. 60) "part of our research necessarily entails an ethnography of the ethical landscape of any given fieldwork context". This is the reason why, for instance, number plates of vehicles crossing the road and faces of travellers other than those expressing formal consent were pixeled in the video footage.

Based on these aspects, it is recommended that future studies should carefully consider the ethical issues related to the research design from the selection of participants, to the data collection and results publication, and to the dissemination and archiving of data (Rose 2012), in order to carefully plan and implement each step of the research without compromising privacy issues. A project-specific code of conduct might be useful to develop in this regard, learning from research standards applied in other fields where privacy issues are in the foreground of data processing, e.g. the health research sector.

7.3 Tourism's Transformative Power

In previous sections it has been argued that interdisciplinary approaches and collaborative patterns between quantitative and qualitative research can represent frontiers for future research in the tourism field, highlighting the power of tourism in integrating disciplines and research approaches. Additionally to his integrative power, tourism has been recognized to have a transformative power on individuals and societies, as reported in the UNWTO 2016 Affiliate Members Global Report titled "The transformative power of tourism: a paradigm shift towards a more responsible traveller" (World Tourism Organization 2016). Transformational tourism deals with the important issue of how travel and tourism can change human behaviour and have a positive impact on the world (Reisinger 2013), and on tourists (Wolf et al. 2017). It includes all those forms of tourist activities that cause an inner change in human beings and, as a consequence, a change in societies and ultimately in destinations themselves. In the light of the above, it can be argued, based on this dissertation project, that the transformational power of tourism not only affects individuals, societies and destinations, but it also affects science itself, fostering a shift from disciplinary ways of thinking, towards interdisciplinary and trans-disciplinary research, i.e. a problem-solving system based on the mutual learning processes between the sciences and societies (Bachinger and Rhodius 2017). The coming sections will deepen the discussion of these aspects, focussing first on the transformative power of tourism on individuals and societies through experience design and then on its transformative power on science through trans-disciplinary approaches.

7.3.1 Experience Design

According to Reisinger (2013, p. xiii), various forms of tourism "can transform human beings and their world-views, such as educational, volunteer, survival, community based, eco, farm, extreme sports, backpacking, cultural, wellness, religious, spiritual and yoga tourism". If classifying these types of transformational tourism using Pine and Gilmore's classification matrix for experiences (see Sect. 2.3), they seem to belong mostly to educational or escapist experience categories, i.e. those experiences where an active participation of the tourist is required, contextualised respectively in a context of absorption of or immersion in the surrounding environment. The analysis of journey experiences in this dissertation has provided evidence on how visual, aural, olfactory and tactile elements of experiences can direct tourists' affect; further, it has provided interesting market knowledge to further investigate the domain of transformative travel, understanding how eudaimonic journey experiences on particularly challenging roads can work as stimuli to individual (hedonic) engagement with the landscape and surrounding system; ultimately, it has tackled the difficult issues of transition management towards more sustainable forms of mobility, envisaging behavioural changes and changes in the destination system. This kind of analytical work is suitable for enriching the tourism product development process in the future, incorporating elements of experience design (Tussyadiah, 2014), taking into account colours, views, sounds, encounters and all the stimuli that can affect tourist's affect. In this sense, the orchestra model by Pearce and Zare (2017) suggests interesting paths for experience design, following the aforementioned four principles: emic view, sustainability boundaries, space-time tracking of the experience and finally co-creation of the experience with the consumers. Experience design for journey experiences should definitely follow these principles, by also acknowledging the double function of the road as a transit space and a recreational space. Therefore, all elements that might be added to enrich the experience—e.g. signs or tourist information on the road—should not compromise the driving safety, while enhancing the tourist experience. In this sense, augmented reality could help enriching the experience design process in the near future, enlarging the possibilities for a sensory and cognitive engagement, e.g. through augmented reality audio information for cyclists working as automated tour guides (Bederson 1995). On the other hand, emotion coding and big data collection and processing could enable a more comprehensive emic view on single experiences in one destination, allowing for a mass-customisation of experiences based on user data.

7.3.2 Transdisciplinarity

The disciplinary status of tourism has been a critical and controversial issue of discussion for many years (Volgger and Pechlaner 2014; Beckendorff and Zehrer 2013; Darbellay and Stock 2012). There are scholars who deny tourism's disciplinary status

7.3 Tourism's Transformative Power

(e.g., Tribe 1997; Cooper et al. 1998) and those who interpret tourism as a discipline (e.g., Leiper 2000; Goeldner 1988). In between there is a third, more cautious, position that acknowledges the inclination of tourism towards disciplinary combinations, bypassing the binary answer on whether it is a discipline or not, and analysing existing multi-, inter- trans- or post-disciplinary approaches (Volgger and Pechlaner 2014).

If looking at the data collection and analysis process in this dissertation, it can be argued that an interdisciplinary perspective is adopted, but the work performed is closer to the principles of transdisciplinarity, because it fosters a collective learning process between researchers, practitioners and participants with the aim to increase the sustainability of the destination area as a whole. Namely, the involvement of participants in video-ethnographic research was initiating per se a transformative process, where the participants and the researcher started to inquire into the scope of journey experiences, the associated feelings and—ultimately— the consequences for the system as a whole. The "symbiotic relationship" between tourism and transport seems to exercise a transformative power on the tourist transport system, while individuals—through emotionally charged experiences—co-create spaces of dynamic interaction.

These types of synergistic relationships are possible for other types of tourism, too. We now know that heritage conservation can find—despite many years of denial—a symbiotic relationship also between tourism and conservation. Both Eagles (2002) and Sharpley and Pearce (2007) have written about the theoretical need for these synergies and ways in which they could be achieved. Kempiak et al. (2017) have noted the need for market knowledge to achieve those successful relationship. But all have relied on the limited power of conventional research techniques. The growing questions surrounding slow tourism and behavioural change would also benefit from the research ideas emerging from this dissertation. The new methodologies discussed here are not entirely peculiar to this dissertation's author. There are some other forward looking authors, and amongst them Professor Sara Dolinicar stands out. Babakhani et al. (2017) explore new psycho-physiological methods in tourism research, for example. Juvan and Dolnicar (2017) explore trans-disciplinarity.

Bob Marley, cited at the outset of this chapter, seems, remarkably, to have got it right. One cannot forget or abandon the past—in terms of research techniques—but the future is bright in terms of innovatory techniques and their vital findings.

References

ALLEA - All European Academies (2017) The European code of conduct for research integrity: revised edition. ALLEA - All European Academies, Berlin

Babakhani N, Ritchie B, Dolnicar S (2017) Improving carbon offsetting appeals in online airplane ticket purchasing: testing new messages, and using new test methods. J Sustain Tour 25(7):955–969

Bachinger M, Rhodius R (2017) Anforderungen an die Governance von transdisziplinären Lernprozessen in Reallaboren. Das Beispiel des "Wissensdialogs Nordschwarzwald (Wi- No)" [Challenges for the governance of transdisciplinary learning processes in real world laboratories. The example of the "Wissensdialog Nordschwarzwald (Wi - No)"]. Die Berichte, Geographie und Landeskunde (BGL) 91(1):81–96

Beckendorff P, Zehrer A (2013) A network analysis of tourism research. Ann Tour Res 43:121–149

Bederson BB (1995) Audio augmented reality: a prototype automated tour guide. In: CHI'95 Conference Companion on Human Factors in Computing Systems. pp 210–211

Buscher M, Urry J (2009) Mobile methods and the empirical. Eur J Soc Theory 12(1):99–116. https://doi.org/10.1177/1368431008099642

Büscher M, Urry J, Witchger K (2011) Mobile methods. Routledge, London, New York

Carneiro MJ, Lima J, Lavrador Silva A (2015) Landscape and the rural tourism experience: identifying key elements, addressing potential, and implications for the future. J Sustain Tour 23(8–9):1217–1235

Cooper C, Fletcher J, Gilbert D, Shepherd R, Wanhill S (1998) Tourism: principles and practices. Pitman, London

Darbellay F, Stock M (2012) Tourism as complex interdisciplinary research object. Ann Tour Res 39(1):441–458. https://doi.org/10.1016/j.annals.2011.07.002

Eagles P (2002) Trends in park tourism: economics, finance and management. J Sustain Tour 22(4):528–549

Economic and Social Research Council (2015) Framework for research ethics: Updated January 2015

Goeldner CR (1988) The evaluation of tourism as an industry and a discipline. In: Paper presented at the First International Conference for Tourism Educators. Mimeo, Surrey

Juvan E, Dolnicar S (2017) Drivers of pro-environmental tourist behaviours are not universal. J Clean Prod 166(10):879–890

Kempiak J, Hollywood L, Bolan P, McMahon-Beattie U (2017) The heritage tourist: an understanding of the visitor experience at heritage attractions. Int J Herit Stud 23(4):375–392

Law J, Urry J (2004) Enacting the social. Econ Soc 33(3):390–410

Lefebvre H (1991) The production of space. Blackwell, Malden, MA

Leiper N (2000) An emerging discipline. Ann Tour Res 27(3):805–809

Molina-Azorín JF, Font X (2016) Mixed methods in sustainable tourism research: an analysis of prevalence, designs and application in JOST (2005–2014). J Sustain Tour 24(4):549–573

Nordhorn C, Scuttari A, Pechlaner H (2018) Customers' emotions in real time: measuring affective responses to service and relationship quality at the reception desk. Int J Cult Tour Hosp Res 12(2):173–184

Pearce PL, Zare S (2017) The orchestra model as the basis for teaching tourism experience design. J Hosp Tour Manag 30:55–64. https://doi.org/10.1016/j.jhtm.2017.01.004

Pine BJ, Gilmore JH (1998) Welcome to the experience economy. Harvard Bus Rev 76(4):97–105

Pink S (2007) Doing visual ethnography. Sage, London

Prosser J, Clark A, Wiles R (2008) Visual research ethics at the crossroads. Manchester, UK

Rakić T, Chambers D (eds) (2012a) An introduction to visual research methods in tourism. Routledge, Abingdon

Rakić T, Chambers D (2012b) Introducing visual methods to tourism studies. In: Rakić T, Chambers D (eds) An introduction to visual research methods in tourism. Routledge, Abingdon, pp 3–14

Reisinger Y (ed) (2013) Transformational tourism: tourist perspective. CABI, Wallingford

Rose G (2012) Visual methodologies. An introduction to researching with visual materials. SAGE Publications Ltd, London

Scarles C (2010) Where words fail, visuals ignite: opportunities for visual autoethnography in tourism research. Ann Tour Res 37(4):905–926

Scuttari A, Pechlaner H (2017) Emotions in tourism: from consumer behavior to destination management. In: Fesenmaier DR, Xiang Z (eds) Design science in tourism: foundations of destination management. Springer, Cham, CH, pp 41–54

Sharpley R, Pearce T (2007) Tourism, marketing and sustainable development in the English national parks: the role of national park authorities. J Sustain Tour 15(5):557–573

References

Sheller M, Urry J (2006) The new mobilities paradigm. Environ Plann A 38(2):207–226. https://doi.org/10.1068/a37268

Spinney J (2015) Close encounters? Mobile methods, (post)phenomenology and affect. Cult Geogr 22(2):231–246. https://doi.org/10.1177/1474474014558988

Tribe J (1997) The indiscipline of tourism. Ann Tour Res 24(3):638–657

Tussyadiah L (2014) Toward a theoretical foundation for experience design in tourism. J Travel Res 53(5):543–564

Volgger M, Pechlaner H (2014) Interdisciplinarity, transdisciplinarity and postdisciplinarity in tourism and hospitality education. In: Dredge D, Airey D, Gross MJ (eds) The routledge handbook of tourism and hospitality education, 1st edn. Routledge, London, pp 85–102

Wolf ID, Ainsworth GB, Crowley J (2017) Transformative travel as a sustainable market niche for protected areas: a new development, marketing and conservation model. J Sustain Tour 25(11):1650–1673

World Tourism Organization (2016) Affiliate members global reports. The transformative power of tourism: a paradigm shift towards a more responsible traveller, vol 14. UNWTO, Madrid

Appendix

Consent Form

Ph.D. research: Mobility spaces and journey experiences. Analysing the physical, sensory, social and emotional value of cycling and motorcycling in tourism.

Ph.D. candidate: Anna Scuttari—Catholic University of Eichstätt—Ingolstadt.

Dear Madam, Dear Sir,

You are participating to the data collection procedure for the Ph.D. research "Mobility spaces and journey experiences. Analysing the physical, sensory, social and emotional value of cycling and motorcycling in tourism". Please thick the appropriate boxes and then sign the form below. The gathered data is used exclusively for scientific purposes under the terms of the decree lgs 196/2003 for data protection.

• I have been given the opportunity to understand the research project and to ask questions about the project
• I understand that my taking part is voluntary; I can withdraw from the study at any time and I will not be asked any questions about why I no longer want to take part
• I understand that any personal details that I may provide, such as name, email address, phone number or postal address will not be revealed to people outside the project
• I understand that my words and video recordings of my journey may be quoted in publications, reports, web pages, and other research outputs, but my identifying information will not be used
• I understand that other researchers may have access to this data provided they agree to preserve the confidentiality of that data and if they agree to the terms I have specified in this form

For further information and question regarding the treatment of personal data, please contact Anna Scuttari: anna.scuttari@eurac.edu; pattucsi@hotmail.com.

Name of Participant	Signature	Date

Survey Form

Date	
Tour direction	
Email	

Experience

1. Why did you decide to take a tour by bicycle/motorbike on the Sellaronda roads/trails? *(more than one answer is possible)*
   - ○ to admire the landscapes
   - ○ to ride on spectacular roads
   - ○ to work out
   - ○ to get in touch with new places
   - ○ to use my bicycle/motorbike
   - ○ to test a bicycle/motorbike (please specify: _____)
   - ○ to reach a destination (please specify: _____)
   - ○ other (please specify: _____)

Satisfaction

Please evaluate how satisfied you feel with following aspects related to your experience. How important are they for you?

	Satisfaction					Importance				
	Very satisfied			Not at all satisfied		Very important			Not important at all	No answer
Infrastructure (state of the street/trail, signposting, maintenance of the street/trail)	○	○	○	○	○	○	○	○	○	○
Network and services (network of connected streets/trails, maps and tourist information on points of interest, rental services, gas/ebike charging station)	○	○	○	○	○	○	○	○	○	○
Travel experience (riding experience, interaction with other means of transport, interaction with landscape)	○	○	○	○	○	○	○	○	○	○
Overall satisfaction	○	○	○	○	○	○	○	○	○	○

Emotions during the experience

The 5 senses

Which of the 5 senses was mainly stimulated during the experience, when and how intense?

	Degree of involvement						Moments when the feeling was more stimulated
	Intense/high				Scarce/low	No answer	
Sight	○	○	○	○	○	○	
Hearing	○	○	○	○	○	○	
Smell	○	○	○	○	○	○	
Taste	○	○	○	○	○	○	
Touch	○	○	○	○	○	○	

Emotions

Which of these emotions did you feel during the experience, when and how intense?

	Degree of involvement						Moments when the feeling was more stimulated
	Intense/high				Scarce/low	No answer	
Optimism (optimistic, encouraged, hopeful)	○	○	○	○	○	○	
Happyness (happy, fulfilled)	○	○	○	○	○	○	
Peacefulness (calm, peaceful)	○	○	○	○	○	○	

Appendix

Loneliness (lonely, homesick) ☹	o	o	o	o	o	o	
Envy (envious, jealous) ☹	o	o	o	o	o	o	
Shame (embarrassed, ashamed) ☹	o	o	o	o	o	o	
Fear (scared, afraid, panicky) ☹	o	o	o	o	o	o	
Sadness (depressed, sad, miserable) ☹	o	o	o	o	o	o	
Worry (nervous, worried, tense) ☹	o	o	o	o	o	o	
Discontent (unfulfilled) ☹	o	o	o	o	o	o	
Anger (frustrated, angry, irritated) ☹	o	o	o	o	o	o	

Guest information

4.	Place of residence:	o Germany (Federal State: _____) o Italy (region: _____)	o Austria o other: _____ o Switzerland
5.	Check-in:		Check-out:
6.	Brand and type of bike used	Brand: _____ type: _____	
2.	What comes to your mind when you think of riding a mountainbike/roadbike/motorbike?		
7.	Which routes are you planning to cover during your holiday?	Description: _____	
8.	How did you know about the Sellaronda experience?	o catalogue/guide o newspaper/magazine	o word of mouth (friends/family) o internet: - _____ o other: _____
9.	How many times did you do the Sellaronda tour before? (including this holiday)	_____ times	
10.	Age:	o < 30 Years o 46-60 years	o 31-45 years o > 60 years
11.	Gender:	o male	o female